International Operations Management

To My God –
Who helps me survive all these crazy commitments
that I get myself into !!!

191339
UCB

Gerhard J. Plenert

International Operations Management

Copenhagen Business School Press

International Operations Management

Cover designed by Kontrapunkt, Denmark
Printed by Gentofte Tryk
Printed in Denmark
1. edition 2002
ISBN 87-630-0068-7

Distribution:

Scandinavia
DJØF Publishing/DKB, Siljangade 2-8, P.O. Box 1731
DK-2300 Copenhagen S, Denmark
phone: +45 3269 7788, fax: +45 3269 7789

North America
Copenhagen Business School Press
Books International Inc.
P.O. Box 605
Herndon, VA 20172-0605, USA
phone: +1 703 661 1500, fax: +1 703 661 1501

Rest of the World
Marston Book Services, P.O. Box 269
Abingdon, Oxfordshire, OX14 4YN, UK
phone: +44 (0) 1235 465500, fax + 44 (0) 1235 465555
E-mail Direct Customers: direct.order@marston.co.uk
E-mail Booksellers: trade.order@marston.co.uk

Table of Contents

Acknowledgements

In order to give credit where credit is due I would have to go to the earliest days of my work experience when I worked in a variety of small-to-medium sized plants in Oregon. Later I worked for NCR Corporation in their international manufacturing division, and for Clark Equipment Company in plants in Indonesia, Australia, Chile, Germany, U.S.A. and Mexico. I've lived and worked in plants in Latin America, Asia, and Europe. My broad exposure to a variety of manufacturing facilities all over the world has given me the background I needed to write this book. Academically, I have taught and researched in Supply Chain Management and Production / Operations Management at Brigham Young University in Provo, Utah and Laie, Hawaii. Similarly I was also at California State University, Chico. Most recently I have worked for Precision Printers and American Management Systems (see the "About the Author" section for more details). All of these experiences involved dozens of people to each of whom I am forever grateful. I am now an independent consultant working in similar environments all over the world.

I need to recognize my family, my wife, Renee Sangray Plenert, and my children, Heidi Lynette Plenert, Dawn Janelle Plenert, Gregory Johannes Plenert, Gerick Johannes Plenert, Joshua Johannes Plenert, Natasha Ida Plenert, Zackary Johannes Plenert, and Chelsey Jean Plenert, who gave me the time I needed to make this book work.

Preface

If every factory in the world worked in exactly the same way this book would have been very easy to write. Unfortunately, no two factories work alike. Even when the factories are producing the same product and are right next to each other, they often operate differently because of management style and methods or corporate influences. Therefore, it is impossible to come up with one book that can claim that it has the perfect way to run an international facility. This reminds me of Newton's law of manufacturing: For Every Expert with a Perfect Solution There is an Equal and Opposite Expert with a Perfect Solution.

This book contains simplistic ideas that have proven to be effective. Most of them will fit to any specific industrial environment, but they are not all intended to fit perfectly in every environment. Which brings us to the purpose of this book. It is designed to be a starting point in discovering what Production and Operations Management is all about in an international setting. It cannot be the final answer.

The key to any successful international operations management environment is to get the basics working first. Without the basics, advancing on to more sophisticated processes is just a waste of time. For example, MRP (Material Requirements Planning) will not work without an accurate inventory system, and an accurate inventory system cannot exist without a comprehensive and accurate data collection system. This book will mention the basics, but will not discuss them in detail. That is the purpose of an introduction to POM (Production / Operations Management) course book. Rather, this book will expand these basics into an international setting.

Understanding the International Operations management setting is critical to competitive success. Nearly every business is effected internationally either by sourcing, production, or marketing issues. The better we understand these issues, the more competitive we can become. The trick is in identifying what changes are necessary in order to make you competitively better than your competition, and then by implementing these changes quicker than your competition.

Additionally, the business universe is being transformed by Web based eCommerce technologies. We are moving away from the inward looking, self focused enterprise, to a new world of outward focused enterprises. Three eCommerce generated events are shaping this change:

- Enterprises are becoming smaller, focusing on their core competencies
- Enterprises are forming partnerships to manage their non-competencies
- The emergence of eBusiness empowered information exchange.

The result is that enterprises will no longer be competing against enterprises. We now have the emergence of networks of enterprises competing against other networks. This has created a new world of enterprise management, referred to as the Next Generation Enterprise. The Next Generation Enterprise (NGE) is where an integrated supply chain value network of enterprises competes against other networks. And the supply chain with the most efficient integration and information network will win.

Supply Chain Management integrates networks of international companies into a structure that allows them to optimize performance as a collective unit. The integration starts with the vendor's vendor and ends with the customer's customer. There are three key measures which identify the successful performance of the international supply chain:

- Cycle time performance
- Operating cost minimization
- On-time performance and customer satisfaction.

Information exchange within the supply chain is critical for it's successful operation. This requires an openness and trust between all the entities of the supply chain. It also requires a mechanism for the efficient transfer of this information. Traditional methods of information transfer, like fax, phone, or even eMail, are too slow. Internet, intranet, and extranet information accessibility allowing all entities in the supply chain to monitor the performance of every other entity, is critical to international competitive success.

International planning and scheduling tools need to be optimized. As international networks of companies compete with other international networks of companies, the network with the most optimal supply chain will win. As stated by Walid Mougayar in Business 2.0 Magazine; "In the vast tract of online business-to-business eCommerce – projected to speed past $ 1 trillion in annual revenue by 2003 – supply chain management is slowly taking center stage: AMR Research of Boston predicts the online SCM market growing 48 percent annually over the next five years. Revenues in 1999 of $3.9 billion will swell to $ 19 billion in 2003 . . . "

Introduction

The definition of Insanity is
Continuing to do the Same Things and
Expecting Different Results.
Breakthrough Thinking, Nadler and Hibino

Operations management techniques have been with us for as long as man has been on the earth. As long as we have been producing goods, including agricultural and animal production, we have been concerned with how to produce more, at less cost, and at higher quality. It seems surprising then with such a long history, that this book on operations management would be one of the first to discuss the topic of "International Operations Management". Perhaps the problem is that international operations management (IOM) is fluid and dynamic. It is influenced by so many factors that there is no steady-state for IOM, nor is there a perfect answer that will work for everyone. IOM can be nothing more than a collection of ideas that have worked successfully. That is why this book focuses on a discussion of World Class IOM techniques and processes. The purpose of this book is to focus on three key issues:

- Operations Management Techniques
- International Perspective
- World Class Integration.

This book integrates operations management into an international setting. It introduces international topics and operationalizes those topics. It demonstrates the international effects of time and competitiveness on operations management.

This book would primarily be used in a graduate (or advanced undergraduate) POM elective course focused on the international considerations of technology transfer, warehousing and logistics, production management, supply chain management, and service operations management. It could also be used in an international business program as an elective course. Prerequisites to the course should include a basic understanding of operations management and the principles of management. These are courses offered in all business programs. However, since there will be students coming from a variety of directions, a quick overview of the basics has been included. For example, operations students my find themselves lacking in some of the management and economics basics. Additionally, business students may need a refresher in operations terminology. Chapter 1 focuses on a review of these basics.

This book focuses on a limited number of quantitative techniques. Most of the quantitative discussions can be found in the introduction to operations textbooks. Rather, this book focuses on the synergistic management elements of how to operationalize a business in an international setting. It focuses on how to operationalize goals. It focuses on how to develop operational systems around these goals, like a manufacturing strategy, an information system, and a measurement system. It discusses international considerations of these systems and demonstrates how these differences would be handled in a underdeveloped, developing, and developed country setting.

This book will also compare some of the international models for effective management, like the Semco model of total employee empowerment and gainsaying, or the Toyota model of TQM (Total Quality Management). It will discuss national operational success stories like Singapore and Malaysia and will focus on what made their operational climates so different.

This book will focus on World Class Manufacturing Techniques like MRP II (Manufacturing Resources Planning), ERP (Enterprise Resources Planning), Finite Capacity Scheduling (FCS), TQM, Process Reengineering, quality and productivity measurement, ISO 9000 and its successors, Schedule Based Manufacturing, Breakthrough Thinking, Concept Engineering, Supply-Chain-Management (SCM), Value Chain Management (VCM), Time-to-Market effectiveness, etc. As such, this book is extremely valuable on the short term.

This book is broken into five sections. They are:

- **Background** which is a brief overview of some basic POM concepts that the reader encountered during their initial class in Operations Management. This section introduces the book, discusses the need for an international focus, and briefly explains concepts like MRP II which are essential for an expanded discussion of International POM.
- **The International Difference** which focuses on what issues make the international operations environment different from traditional operations. This section deals with strategic goal setting and how it influences operational performance. It discusses how to turn these goals into a strategy. It also discusses how an effective information and measurement system needs to be established to communicate and motivate these goals. It then deals with the globalization and localization of these goals. This section has chapters defining the process of internationalization and some of the considerations that need special attention. There is another chapter on goal setting and how internationalization effects goals. The chapter on goals is further expanded with a chapter on international strategy development. The last chapter of this section discusses information transfer considerations that cause challenges when borders are crossed.
- **Managing the Supply Chain** discusses the role of Supply Chain Management in an international setting where vendors, customers, and even producers can exist all over the world. This section also discusses the importance of time as an international competitive instrument. In this section there are chapters that focus on materials and information sourcing. There is also a chapter that discusses the key measures within a Supply Chain network.
- **POMS Support Systems** discusses the operational support systems that need to be established. These include the transport and storage of goods, the decision process that goes into deciding where products should be produced, the relationships and locations of customers, and how the international transaction differs for the local transaction in these situations. In this section there are chapters that discusses the major systems components of a Supply Chain, like the logistics system, the distribution system, and the production system. This section also has a chapter that focuses upward the supply chain toward the customer. Lastly

there is a chapter that discusses international transactional ethics, since, far too often, the transactional ethics between countries come into conflict with each other.

- **POMS Excellence** discusses what World Class operational excellence entails. This section also reviews the future of operations management and what type of strategy competitive positioning would suggest. This section has chapters that discuss international excellence with a focus on the future.

Cross-reference List

80-20 Rule	ABC Analysis
A	Assets
ABC Analysis	Pareto Principle or 80-20 Rule
ABC Costing	Activity Based Costing
Accounts Payable	AP
Accounts Receivable	AR
Activity Based Costing	ABC Costing
Advanced Planning and Scheduling	APS
Advanced Research Agency Network	ARPANET
AFTA	America Free Trade Agreement
Aggregate Production Schedule	APS
America Free Trade Agreement	AFTA
American Production and Inventory Control Society	APICS
American Productivity and Quality Center	APQC
AP	Accounts Payable
APICS	American Production and Inventory Control Society
APQC	American Productivity and Quality Center
APS	Advanced Planning and Scheduling
APS	Aggregate Production Schedule
AQP	Association for Quality and Participation
AR	Accounts Receivable
ARPANET	Advanced Research Agency Network

Assets	A
Association for Quality and Participation	AQP
ATM	Automated Teller Machine
Automated Teller Machine	ATM
B2B	Business to Business Transaction
B2C	Business to Customer Transaction
B2G	Business to Government Transaction
Balance Sheet	BS
BAM	Bottleneck Allocation Methodology
Bill of Materials	BofM
BofM	Bill of Materials
Bottleneck Allocation Methodology	BAM
BP	Business Plan
Breakthrough Thinking	BT
BS	Balance Sheet
BT	Breakthrough Thinking
Business Plan	BP
Business to Business Transaction	B2B
Business to Customer Transaction	B2C
Business to Government Transaction	B2G
C	Cash
CAD	Computer-Aided Design
CAD/CAM	Computer Aided Design/ Manufacturing
CAE	Computer-Aided Engineering
Capacity Requirements Planning	CRP
Carrying Costs	CC
CASA	Computer and Automated Systems Association
Cash	C

CC	Carrying Costs
Center for International Business Edu. And Research	CIBER
CEO	Chief Executive Officer
Certified in Inventory Resources Management	CIRM
Certified in Production and Inventory Management	CPIM
Certified in Purchasing Management	CPM
Chief Executive Officer	CEO
CIBER	Center for International Business Edu. And Research
CIM	Computer Integrated Manufacturing
CIRM	Certified in Inventory Resources Management
CM	Concept Management
CO	Current Ownership or Customer Order
Computer Aided Design /Manufacturing	CAD/CAM
Computer and Automated Systems Association	CASA
Computer Integrated Manufacturing	CIM
Computer-Aided Design	CAD
Computer-Aided Engineering	CAE
Concept Management	CM
CPIM	Certified in Production and Inventory Management
CPM (project management)	Critical Path Methodology
CPM (purchasing)	Certified in Purchasing Management
Critical Path Methodology	CPM
CRP	Capacity Requirement Planning
Current Ownership of the corporation	CO
Customer Order	CO

DC	Developing Country
Decision Support Systems	DSS
Design for Automated Assembly	DFAA
Design for Manufacturing/ Design for Assembly	DFM/DFA
Design of Experiment	DOE
Developing Country	DC
DFAA	Design for Automated Assembly
DFM/DFA	Design for Manufacturing / Design for Assembly
Distribution Requirements Planning	DRP
DOE	Design of Experiment
DRP	Distribution Requirements Planning
DSS	Decision Support Systems
Economic Order Quantity	EOQ or Q
EDI	Electronic Data Interchange
EL	Electrolumisence
Electrolumisence	EL
Electronic Data Interchange	EDI
Enterprise Resources Management	ERP
EOQ	Economic Order Quantity
ERP	Enterprise Resources Management
EU	European Union
European Union	EU
F	Forecast
FA	Fixed Assets
Failure Mode and Effect Analysis	FEMA
FC	Fixed Costs
FCS	Finite Capacity Scheduling
Federation of Malaysian Manufacturers	FMM
FEM	Finite Element Analysis
FEMA	Failure Mode and Effect Analysis
FGI	Finished Goods Inventory

FIFO	First-In-First-Out Inventory Control
Finished Goods Inventory	FGA
Finite Capacity Scheduling	FCS
Finite Element Analysis	FEM
First-In-First-Out Inventory Control	FIFO
Fixed Assets	FA
Fixed Costs	FC
FMM	Federation of Malaysian Manufacturers
FMS	Ford-Mitsubishi-Sony
Ford-Mitsubishi-Sony	FMS
Forecast	F
Fundacion Mexicana Para La Calidad Total AC	FUNDAMECA
FUNDAMECA	Fundacion Mexicana Para La Calidad Total AC
GD&T	Geometric Dimensioning and Tolerancing
Geometric Dimensioning and Tolerancing	GD&T
Geometric Programming	GP
GP	Geometric Programming
I	Inventory
ILQC	In-Line Quality Control
In-Line Quality Control	ILQC
Integer Programming	IP
International Operations Management	IOM
International Standards Organization	ISO
Inventory	I
IOM	International Operations Management
IP	Integer Programming
ISO	International Standards Organization
JHA	Job Hazard Analysis

JIT	Just-in-Time or Lean Manufacturing
Job Hazard Analysis	JHA
Just-in-Time	JIT
L	Liabilities
LDC	Less Developed Countries
Lean Manufacturing	JIT
Less Developed Countries	LDC
Liabilities	L
Linear Programming	LP
LOG	Logistics Systems
Logistics Systems	LOG
LP	Linear Programming
M	Maquiladora
Malcolm Baldrige	USA National Award for Quality Excellence
Management Information Systems	MIS
Management Science	MS
Manufacturing Resource Planning	MRP II
Maquiladora	M
Master Production Schedule	MPS
Material Requirements Planning	MRP
MFN	Most Favored Nation
MIS	Management Information Systems
Most Favored Nation	MFN
MPS	Master Production Schedule
MRP II	Manufacturing Resource Planning
MRP	Material Requirements Planning
MS	Management Science
MSU	Michigan State University
Michigan State University	MSU
NAFTA	North America Free Trade Agreement
National Productivity Corporation, Malaysia	NPC

Newly Industrialized Economies	NIE
Next Generation Enterprise	NGE
NGE	Next Generation Enterprise
NGT	Nominal Group Technique
NIE	Newly Industrialized Economies
Nominal Group Technique	NGT
North America Free Trade Agreement	NAFTA
NPC	National Productivity Corporation, Malaysia
OA	Other Assets
OC	Ordering Costs
OE	Owners Equity
OL	Other Liabilities
Operations Research	OR
OPT	Optimized Production Technology
Optimized Production Technology	OPT
OR	Operations Research
Ordering Costs	OC
Other Assets	OA
Other Liabilities	OL
Owners Equity	OE
P	Payroll
P&L	Profit and Loss Statement
P/L	Profit or Losses Statement
P/PO	Purchase and Production Order
PAC	Production Activity Control
Pareto Principle	ABC Analysis
Payroll	P
PDCA	Plan-Do-Check-Act
PDPC	Process Decision Program Chart
PERT	Project Planning and Review Technique
Plan-Do-Check-Act	PDCA
PM	Preventive Maintenance
Point of Sale	POS

POM	Production/Operations Management
POS	Point of Sale
PP	Production Plan
PR	Process Reengineering
Preventive Maintenance	PM
Process Decision Program Chart	PDPC
Process Reengineering	PR
PROD	Production Schedule
Production/Operations Management	POM
Production Activity Control	PAC
Production Plan	PP
Production Schedule	PROD
Profit and Loss Statement	P&L or P/L
Project Planning and Review Technique	PERT
PURCH	Purchasing Schedule
Purchase and Production Order	P/PO
Purchasing Schedule	PURCH
Q	Economic Order Quantity
QC	Quality Circles
QFD	Quality Functional Deployment
QIP	Quality Improvement Program
QS	Quality Systems
QSD	Quality Systems Deployment
Quality Circles	QC
Quality Functional Deployment	QFD
Quality Improvement Program	QIP
Quality Systems Deployment	QSD
Quality Systems	QS
R	Routing
R&D	Research and Development
RCC	Rough Cut Capacity
Re-Order Point	ROP
Research and Development	R&D
ROP	Re-Order Point

Rough Cut Capacity	RCC
Routing	R
SBM	Schedule Based Manufacturing
Schedule Based Manufacturing	SBM
SCM	Supply Chain Management
Screenprinting and Graphic Imaging Association	SGIA
SFC	Shop Floor Control
SGIA	Screenprinting and Graphic Imaging Association
Shingo Award	USA National Award for Manufacturing Excellence
Shop Floor Control	SFC
SIC	Standard Industrial Classification
Single Minute Exchange of Die	SMED
SME	Society of Manufacturing Engineers
SMED	Single Minute Exchange of Die
Society of Manufacturing Engineers	SME
SPC	Statistical Process Control
Standard for the exchange of Product model data	STEP
Standard Industrial Classification	SIC
Statistical Process Control	SPC
STEP	Standard for the exchange of Product model data
Strengths-Weaknesses-Opportunities-Threats	SWOT
Supply Chain Management	SCM
SWOT	Strengths-Weaknesses-Opportunities-Threats
TC	Total Cost of Inventory
Technology Transfer	TT
Theory of Constraints	TOC
Theory of Inventive Problem Solving	TRIZ
TOC	Theory of Constraints

Total Cost of Inventory	TC
Total Productive Maintenance	TPM
Total Quality Management	TQM
TPM	Total Productive Maintenance
TQM	Total Quality Management
TRIZ	Theory of Inventive Problem Solving
TT	Technology Transfer
Ultraviolet	UV
Uniform Resource Locator	URL
URL	Uniform Resource Locator
USA National Award for Manufacturing Excellence	Shingo Award
USA National Award for Quality Excellence	Malcolm Baldrige
UV	Ultraviolet
VA/VE	Value Analysis/Value Engineering
Value Analysis/Value Engineering	VA/VE
Value Chain Management	VCM
Variable Costs	VC
VC	Variable Costs
VCM	Value Chain Management
Vibration Signature Analysis	VSA
Vice President	VP
VP	Vice President
VSA	Vibration Signature Analysis
WCM	World Class Management
World Class Management	WCM
World Trade Organization	WTO
World War II	WWII
World Wide Web	WWW
WTO	World Trade Organization
WWII	World War II
WWW	World Wide Web

Background

1. Operations Management

Meeting Z, Inc.

Z, Inc. is a multinational conglomerate which is primarily a producer of heavy-duty construction equipment, like earth movers, graders, and haulers. Their headquarters is in Jackson, Michigan, and one of their manufacturing facilities at this location produces transmissions. Although transmission production is somewhat outside of their core competency, the plant has been successful for Z, Inc. in the past. This production facility was part of their diversification program where they attempted to make sure they had supporting industries outside of their core competency that could protect their cash-flow.

Transmission production is extremely labor intensive, resulting in a value-added labor contribution of about 20 percent. Labor rates in the Jackson, Michigan area were some of the highest in the nation, primarily because of the large union influence in the area. The plant was about 30 years old and a lot of the equipment was out of date. This caused the labor intensity to be even higher than normal. An updated plant would increase automation and therefore, it was believed, would increase quality and reduce lead time. An updated plant could be done in several ways, either by improving the automation in the existing facility, or by completely replacing the facility. Either way, Z, Inc. anticipated resistance from the union because there would be a reduction in the current work force due to the automation. At a board meeting of the Z company, the following conversation took place:

Board Member ZA (comments are being directed at the CEO): "The transmission facility is again showing a half-million dollar loss for the month. The P&L (Profit and Loss) report for the plant shows:

- Sales $ 9,500,000
- Labor Expense $ 2,000,000
- Materials Expense $ 4,000,000
- Equipment Expense $ 1,000,000
- Overhead Expense $ 3,000,000.

We're loosing ground with this plant."

Board Member ZB: "I agree. We need a recommendation on how to handle the transmission business. Are we outside of our expertise? Or, is there a way to turn this facility profitable again?"

The CEO was left with the task of organizing a recommendation.[1] Before we look too closely at the Z, Inc.'s problem, let's review some of the basics of operations management. The purpose of this review is to standardize on terminology, which can often be quite inconsistent throughout the operations management industry.

Some Basic Operations Management Terminology and Concepts

There are three levels of management:

- Strategic Management
- Tactical Management
- Operational Management.

Strategic management focuses on planning and developing the business as a whole. Typical job titles include the Board of Directors

1. As part of the discussion throughout this chapter and the rest of the book, we will take further visits into the CEO's conversations and his analysis process. At the same time, you (the reader) are invited to formulate your own opinions and recommendations on how Z, Inc.'s transmission production should be handled. This case and many others in this book are based on actual experiences that the author went through in his 20+ years of operations management. He has, however, changed the names of the company and the people, and has simplified the numbers, in order to protect the misguided. The actions that are taken in these cases are not to be considered the "right answer" or "correct solution." These actions are one of many options and these options will be considered as alternatives throughout the book.

and the CEO. Tactical management is the middle management of an organization and focuses on the month-to-month company performance. Typical job titles include Vice President and Director. Operations Management is organizationally at the bottom end of the management heap. But this is the most critical management function since it is the performance of the operations management function that will make the organization a success. This book will focus on the performance of the operations management function and how this performance is effected by internationalization. However, a lot of what happens at the operations level is effected by decisions at the strategic and tactical levels. The process of how these decisions interrelate will be included in Chapters 3 and 4.

There are three primary functions of a business:

- Financial
- Marketing
- Operational.

The financial function analyzes the financial viability of the business. The marketing function attempts to identify markets for the goods and services produced by the business. The operational function:

- Identifies material sources
- Identifies internal and external production sources
  Evaluates capacities
- Manages an organizations resources in order to produce products that will satisfy the demands generated by the marketing function
- Juggles the accessibility of resources within the limits of the financial constraints
- Produces, packages, or adopts products using these resources
- Evaluates the quality of the product and how well it satisfies the customer
- Manages the storage and distribution of the products produced.

Traditional management thinking suggests that these three organizations are in conflict with each other and that this conflict creates a synergistic balancing effect within an organization through the use of trade-offs. World Class Management wisdom suggests that there is more positive synergy to be gained by focusing these organizations on a common goal. Therefore, the critical part of the process is to identify what that goal should be. Chapter 3 will focus on a discussion of goal-setting and discusses how critical these goals are to the over-all successful performance of the international organization.

Once again we see that this book focuses on the operations management function and takes a look at how this function is effected when globalization occurs within the business. Globalization can refer to:

- International sourcing of products
- International production of the goods and/or services
- International transportation of the products
- International markets for the products produced.

Within the operations management framework we see that there are numerous types of industries. Each of these industries have differing requirements for successful performance. For example, we see:

- Wholesaling – This process includes an extensive purchasing and inventory management function. Packaging and shipping may also be a large piece of operations management. Examples include the major shippers and resellers throughout the world like Hyundai of Korea.
- Logistics – This process involves routing management and location tracking of products and equipment. For example, Wal Mart considers the logistics function to be their competitive edge in performance by always having what the customer wants available when the customer wants it. The airlines industry, as in the case of British Airways or Lufthansa, schedules not just passengers, but also crews, meals, luggage, equipment maintenance, preventive maintenance, ground support, airport schedules, etc., and is an extremely complex example of the logistics process which will be discussed in more detail in Chapter 9.
- Retailing – This requires a purchasing and inventory management function, but may also include a production management

process as in the example of fast food. Excellent international examples include McDonalds and Toyota.

- Service – The management of projects like the implementation of computer systems or consulting projects requires project management expertise. Examples include the major international consulting firms like AMS (American Management Systems).
- Construction – This requires extensive project management tools.
- Process Manufacturing – Process manufacturing is where units produced are not discrete, such as flour, oil, paper, fabric, etc. These processes tend to be machine intensive and require minute-by-minute scheduling.
- Departmentalized Discrete Manufacturing – This factory builds a discrete product like a car or a TV set. The layout of the factory is by departments, focusing on the specialization of labor in each department. For example, you could have a grinding department, a lathe department, an assembly department, etc. Materials are moved from department to department in their process of being converted to a finished good (see Chart 1.1). Automobile manufacturers like Ford or DaimlerChrysler or hearing aid manufacturers like Siemens are excellent examples.

Chart 1.1. Departmental Discrete Manufacturing

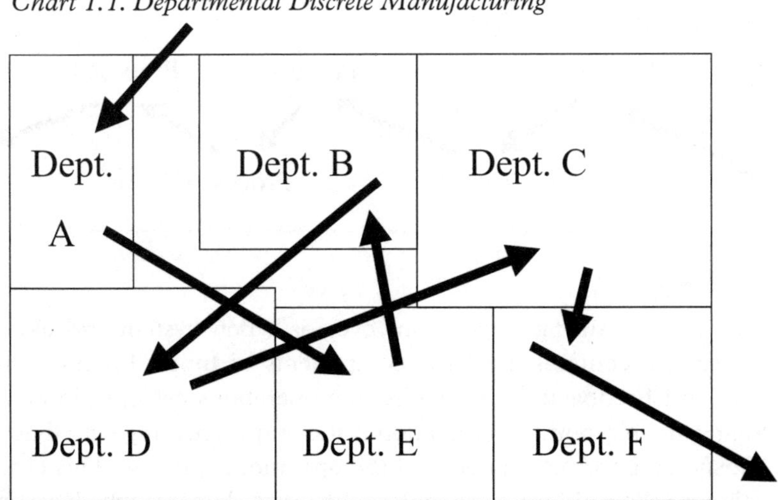

- Job Shop – This is a discrete manufacturing facility that produces customized products. The layout is similar to Chart 1.1, but the flow of product can vary dramatically from one product to the next. Custom product shops like airplane manufacturers Airbus or Boeing, or shipbuilders make excellent examples.
- Flow Discrete Manufacturing – This factory focuses on the continuous movement of materials through the facility. The focus is on the minimization of materials within the organization since materials are considered to be the critical high-cost resource in this repetitive process. The assembly line or the Japanese JIT (Just-in-Time) production process are examples of this type of manufacturing environment (See Chart 1.2). Toyota manufacturing is the master of this process and another excellent example is the Saturn facility in the United States.

Each of these different operations environments requires it's own specific set of tools, as well as some common tools, like inventory management. In Chapter 5 we will be discussing some of the alternative planning and control mechanisms, as well as a variety of information systems. These often vary dramatically in an international environment.

Chart 1.2. Flow Discrete Manufacturing

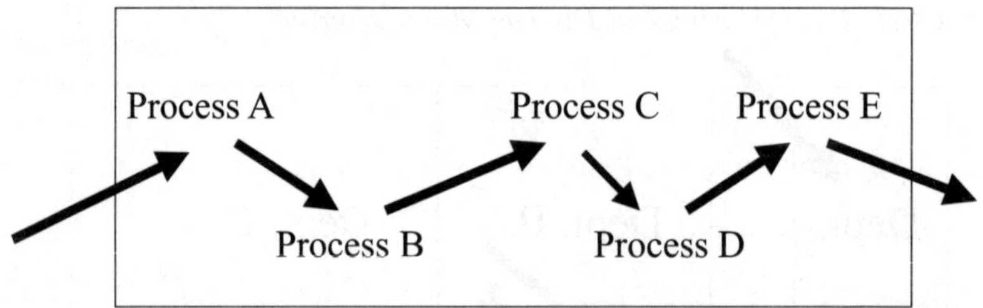

The manufacturing / operations cycle is a flow system and like all systems, it contains the basic components of Input, Process, Output, and Feedback. In evaluating the operations cycle, as in all systems, the key point of evaluation is the output, making sure that we satisfy the information needs of the operational process. This evaluation is followed by a close look at the input elements which assures us that the necessary data / tools are available to create the output. Last of all, we look at the process tool which can take a variety of forms (see Chart 1.3 and Chapter 5). This basic flow systems model will be followed throughout this book when planning options are discussed. The key to selecting and developing a successful operations management system is in making sure the results (output) satisfy the goals. That is why we will spend the next few chapters discussing goal and systems planning options.

Chart 1.3. The Production/Operations Processing Cycle

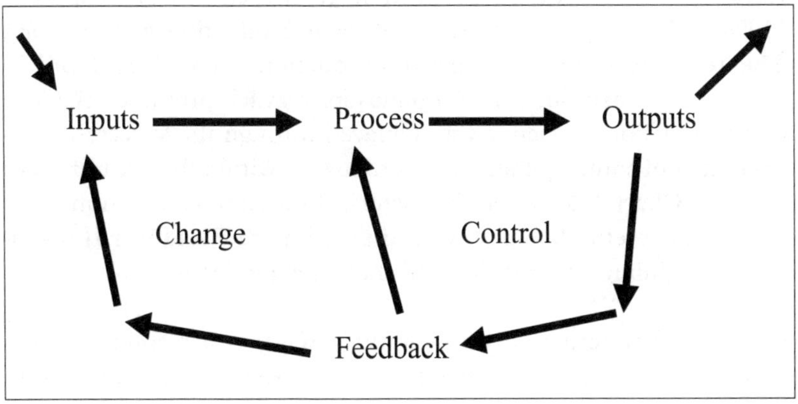

A Little History

As mentioned earlier, operations management goes back to the beginning of man. However, looking into the more recent past, say 50 years, we find that the most dramatic changes have taken place during these few years of history. There are several reasons for these changes. The first seems to be World War II. Prior to WW II the operations methodologies were primarily manual. Tools like EOQ (Economic Order Quantity), LP (Linear Programming), and the 2-Bin system were considered to be "state of the art". Shortly after World War II the computer became available, which created computationally over-burdened systems like MRP and PERT/CPM (Project Evaluation and Review Technique / Critical Path Methodology) feasible. Also, after this war, the Japanese were going through a reconstruction of their industry in a country that had no natural resources, minimal cash flow, and lots of people. In order to grow their industry, they had to bring materials into the country, convert them to end products as quickly as possible, and ship them. They didn't care how many people it took because there was a plentiful work force. This materials efficiency focused strategy became the roots of what is now known throughout the world as Just-in-Time (JIT).

Meanwhile, during the same time as Japan's reconstruction and the introduction of computers, Israel was becoming a new nation and also needed to develop new industries. Rather than copying Europe or the USA they took advantage of their plentiful supply of PhDs and decided to develop their own production methodology. The result was the Optomizied Production Technology (OPT) / Theory of Constraints (TOC) philosophy which promoted the idea that production efficiency was achieved through the successful management of some operational "bottleneck" within the organization.

From Chart 1.4 we see the historical development of numerous operational methodologies. We end up with pre World War II operations scheduling systems that had the following focus:

- EOQ – Economic Order Quantity (EOQ) is a planning system focused on managing inventory levels. EOQ is the most commonly used production planning philosophy because of it's simplicity and minimal data requirements.
- LP – Linear Programming is an optimization process that facilitates optimal routings and loadings and minimizes costs. This can be expanded through the use of Integer Programming (IP) or Geometric Programming (GP) in more complex situations.
- 2-Bin – This system is a simplistic volume based replenishment which requires no sophistication or automation but generally creates a lot of inventory.

These are systems that are still very much in use today, and so their timelines continue through to the year 2000 and beyond. However, after World War II, we had several events that would initiate the reinvention of POM methodologies. These were:

Chart 1.4. Operations Management History After World War II

	World War II		2000
Economic Order Quantity (EOQ)			
Linear Programming (LP)			
2-Bin			
		Material Requirements Planning (MRP)	
		Project Evaluation and Review Technique (PERT) / Critical Path Methodology (CPM)	
		Just-in-Time (JIT)	
		Optimized Production Scheduling (OPT) / Theory of Constraints (TOC)	
		Distribution Requirements Planning (DRP)	
		Manufacturing Resources Planning (MRP II)	
		Bottleneck Allocation Methodology (BAM), Schedule Based Manufacturing (SBM) & Finite Capacity Scheduling (FCS)	
		Enterprise Resources Planning (ERP)	

- The advent of the computer which allowed computationally intense systems like MRP and PERT / CPM to operate.
- The reconstruction of Japan which focused on systems where materials movement was more important than labor efficiency generating systems like JIT.
- The development of the nation of Israel where the efficient use of machinery became a priority generating systems like OPT and TOC.

The result was the creation of three major categories of new POM methodologies, MRP, JIT, and TOC.

- MRP – Material Requirements Planning (MRP) is a production scheduling tool for an environment that has intermittent and/or irregular schedules. The efficiency focus for MRP is to have a perfectly balanced factory, which most often means that all departments are equally balanced in their work-load of labor hours. This system is the most data-intensive and has the toughest data accuracy requirements. The distribution management counterpart to MRP is Distribution Requirements Planning (DRP).
- PERT / CPM – Project Evaluation and Review Technique (PERT) / Critical Path Methodology (CPM) are project planning tools used in industries like construction.
- JIT – Just-in-Time (JIT) focuses on the efficient utilization of the materials resource through the elimination of all inventory waste. JIT is generally used in highly repetitive manufacturing processes.
- OPT / TOC – Optimized Production Technology (OPT) / Theory of Constraints (TOC) focus on the efficient utilization and maximization of the bottleneck which is generally a specific piece of machinery within the facility.

As time went on, inflation would encourage Western interest in some of the Eastern techniques like JIT. This occurred because the MRP labor focused environments generally had high inventory levels, and the carrying costs on these high inventories could quickly make a company non-competitive. Shortly thereafter, Western and international interest was also sparked in the machine efficient scheduling of the OPT / TOC systems. It was found that the inefficient use of the bottleneck was costing companies a small fortune.

However, the materials efficiency of JIT seemed to be very little help in the Job Shop where manufacturing was non-repetitive. The production process in the customized job shop required the sophistication of an MRP scheduler, but also needed the materials efficiencies of JIT. This triggered the introduction of new, leading-edge systems like Schedule Based Manufacturing (SBM) or Bottleneck Allocation Methodology (BAM) which integrate these philosophies. Other systems like Finite Capacity Scheduling (FCS) attempted to deal with the capacity scheduling inadequacies of MRP by integrating some of the optimization of TOC. Advanced integrated systems of this type are often referred to as Advanced Planning and Scheduling (APS) systems.

Business management systems were also searching for a method to integrate the operations management tools with other information management tools like the accounting system, the costing system, and the sales and marketing systems. The first attempt at this integration was Manufacturing Resources Planning (MRP II) (see Chart 1.5). Later this integration was increased to shop floor integration and engineering integration and was labeled Enterprise Resources Management (ERP).

In Chart 1.5 we see the production and operations management functions of an enterprise detailed out along the right side of the chart. Activities begin with a business plan, then they focus on planning functions like forecasting and Rough Cut Capacity Planning. These activities integrate into schedules like the Aggregate Production Schedule and the Master Production Schedule. The execution of the MRP function next creates purchasing and shop floor production requirements.

Down the left side of Chart 1.5 we see all the financial activities of an enterprise including the general ledger and profit and loss functions. In the top center of the chart we see the sales functions. From this chart we can see how the enterprise information integration would function under an MRP II or ERP environment (note: the numbers are connectors, for example the "1" connects to the other "1" in the chart – these connectors are used in order to avoid having lines crossing on the chart, but they have the same meaning as would a connecting line).

Chart 1.5. MRP II Intergration

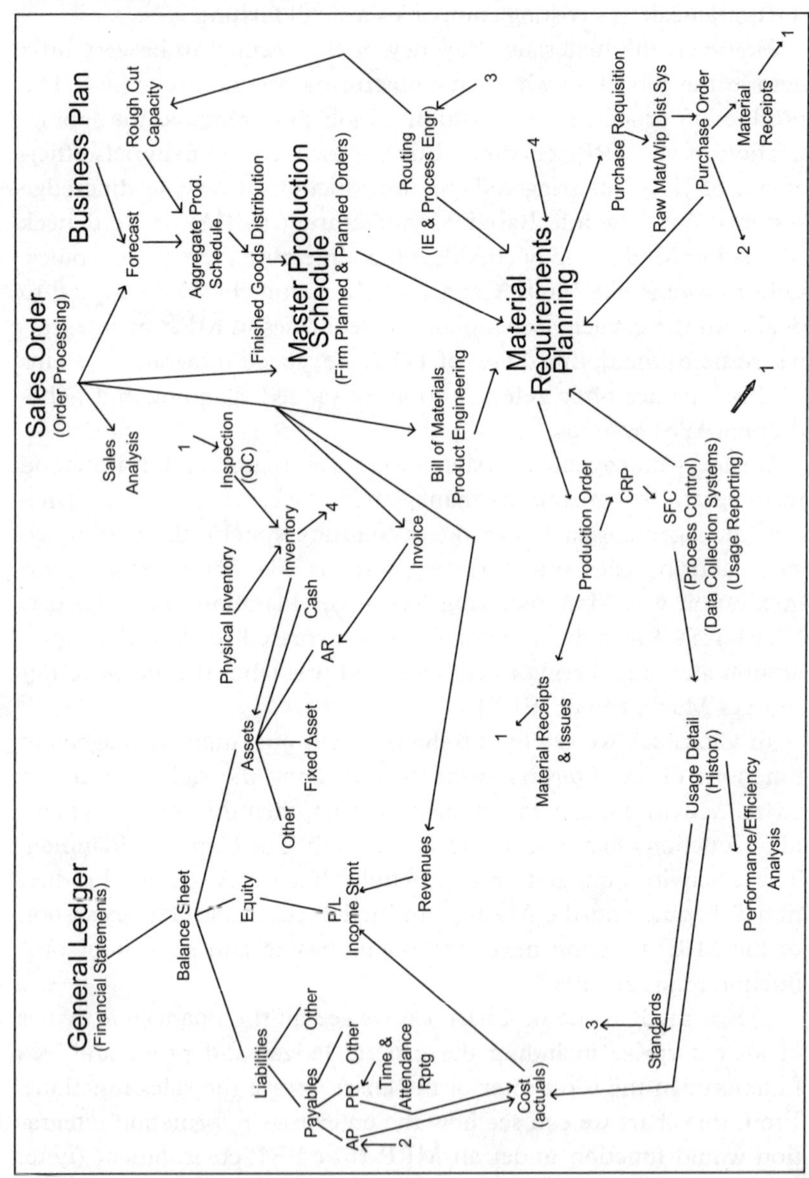

The future of Operations Management methodologies will find the blending of more and more different operations techniques and processes. This offers the flexibility to select a production planning process focused on any resource preference. It also offers optimization in any resource, rather than limiting us to only one critical resource, as the current planning systems tend to do. The future of operations management will also focus more and more on integration, particularly on international integration and on supply chain integration. In this book, the discussion of alternative production methodologies, and how they can vary for one international setting to another, will occur in many chapters, like Chapters 5 and 10.

The Role of Measurement in Operations Management

Referring to Chart 1.3, we discussed the POM processing cycle. Critical to this processing cycle is the creation of a feedback mechanism that reviews and reports on the performance of all resources in the system. There are several measures that are utilized to evaluate performance, and it would be valuable to review a few of them. The process of measurement, and how it is used for data collection and for motivation will be discussed in more detail in Chapter 3.

The key areas of performance measurement in operations management are:

Quality

Quality has always been a confusing term and is difficult to define. It is difficult to get two people to agree on a definition of quality, let alone an entire industry. As a result, there are numerous definitions throughout the world for quality, but let's look at a couple of the common definitions. In the United States, quality is most often used to define "meeting engineering standards." This is the applied definition for quality, not the ones we give lip service to. It means that if a product is built to specification, exactly the way it is designed, it is considered to be a quality product. Unfortunately, this definition does little to focus on the customer. We have formalized this definition of quality through systems like ISO (the European Developed Quality standard that has found international application) or QS (the American automotive quality standard).

In Europe, for example in Germany, the USA definition also holds. The reason why German quality is considered to be higher than American quality is because the engineering specifications are tighter, not because they are any more "customer" oriented. Unfortunately, the "meeting engineering standards" definition of quality is the most commonly applied definition throughout the world.

From Japan we get a more customer oriented definition of quality, which is that a quality product is one that "thrills the customer". The Japanese definition does not focus on durability or flexibility. Rather, it focuses on marketing appeal – give the customer whatever they get excited about. One example would be the "boom box" – the carry around stereo. The Western definition of quality would have the box work, even if it was dropped from 20 feet. The Japanese definition would have the box filled with levers and knobs for the user to move around and effect the sound. For some reason, an increased number of levers makes the boom box seem more valuable to the customer, even if the customer never uses them. Therefore, the perceived quality to the customer would make the customer feel thrilled by the Japanese product and the customer would prefer to buy it over the "durable" product option. This could also be labeled a "marketing" oriented definition of quality.

Quality can be used as a measure of performance by evaluating defect rates, delivery performance, return rates, etc. The issue of quality as a measure of performance will be revisited numerous times through this book since it has variations and complications when viewed from an international perspective (see Chapter 3). Reflect back on Z, Inc. Is lack of quality a reason for their lack of profitability? What should their definition of quality be?

Productivity

Productivity is another measure that permits an unlimited number of variations and is therefore difficult to define. Specifically, productivity is output divided by input. Output is generally accepted to be Net Sales. Output can be the value of production or transfer cost rate if we are interested in factory productivity where product is transferred between factories of the same orgaization. Input can be any number of things. Input can be varied so much so that any company or country can claim excellent productivity, depending on how it's measured. This international inconsistency in the definition of what should be included as input also complicates comparisons of productivity between countries and companies. It has gotten to the point where the only effective comparisons that can be drawn for productivity is to compare a company or country with itself over time to see if it is improving.

$$Productivity = \frac{Output}{Input}$$

In the Western countries, productivity almost always means labor productivity. The Input in the productivity formula is either direct labor hours or direct labor cost. Because of its focus on labor, the United States leads the world in productivity. But there are also disadvantages associated with labor productivity as a measure of national productivity. The primary disadvantage is that labor is less than ten percent of the value-added content of most manufactured products. Therefore, being labor efficient doesn't necessarily mean that the United States is producing product efficiently. Recently it has been discovered that increasing labor productivity, in some cases, can actually result in a loss of profitability, rather than an increase of profitability. For a more detailed discussion of this issue, see Chapter 3.

$$Productivity = \frac{Net\ Sales}{Direct\ Labor\ Hours\ or\ Direct\ Labor\ Dollars}$$

Internationally, we find a multitude of measures of productivity performance. For example, in Japan we find several productivity measures, one of which is value-added productivity. Value-added productivity focuses on getting as much increased value out of the production process as possible. For example, as a Japanese producer we are building a TV, and the TV has a tuner and power supply, each of which costs \$5 to produce. We can sell the tuner for \$10 on the open market. The \$10 includes \$5 of production costs and \$5 of increased value added. We can sell the power supply for only \$7 on the open market (only \$2 of increased value added). We would get more value-added content out of producing the tuner, and have the USA subcontractor produce the power supplies. Both countries would input $5 of productive effort, but for that effort the Japanese would gain $5 of increased value added and the US would only gain $2 of increased value added. It's easy to see why the balance of trade has tended to favor Japan using a value-added productivity calculation.

$$Productivity = \frac{Net\ Sales}{Net\ Sales - Cost\ of\ Goods\ Sold}$$

Another popular productivity measure is Total Factor Productivity. With Total Factor Productivity, the input includes all the resource elements that went into the production process. For example, materials costs, machine costs, and even overhead costs would be included along with the labor costs. Total Factor Productivity is considered to be a more accurate measure of the overall productivity of a particular production environment.

$$Productivity = \frac{Net\ Sales}{Labor + Materials + Energy + Machinery + etc.}$$

More recently, a measure of productivity known as Critical Resource Productivity has become popular because it is easy to measure and focuses an organization on it's most effective area of improvement. For example, in the automobile industry, 7 to 10 percent of the value added cost content of the vehicle is labor while 50 to 60 percent of the value added cost content is in materials. Hence, materials is the critical resource (the dominant value added component) and materials productivity is a lot more meaningful than labor productivity as a measure of operational performance. The input used in this productivity equation is the critical resource in the production process. A more detailed discussion of critical resources is found in Chapters 3 and 4.

$$Productivity = \frac{Net\ Sales}{Critical\ Resource\ Costs}$$

Productivity will be a continuing discussion throughout this book. For example, in Z, Inc. productivity became a critical issue. Loss of profitability could have been blamed on a lack of Total Factor Productivity. How would you focus Z, Inc.'s resources to turn it's P&L statement from red to black?

Efficiency

Efficiency is a minor measure of performance which is primarily used to evaluate internal effectiveness. For example, in the United States, labor efficiency is used to compare labor performance to a standard. This comparison to standard would then be used to measure if and how much of a performance bonus would be paid out to a particular employee. Anything over 100 % would constitute good performance, and anything less than 100% would justify a reprimand.

$$Efficiency = \frac{StandardTime}{Actual\,Time} x100$$

Is efficiency a tool that Z, Inc. could use to improve their loss of profitability? Would efficiency be something that you would suspect is already being used by Z, Inc.?

Financial Measures

Financial measures of performance include profit and loss numbers from the P&L statement as well as performance and liquidity ratios from the Balance Sheet. Appendix A (at the end of the book) includes several of the most common performance ratios that are used for measuring international performance. The applicability and use of many of these numbers is questioned internationally. For example, the Current Ratio is considered to be good the larger the value it has.

$$(Current\ Ratio) = \frac{(Total\ Current\ Assets)}{(Total\ Current\ Debts)}$$

However, Inventory reduction is also considered to be good.

That means, as inventory goes down, the inventory asset ratio would improve but the current ratio would get worse. Which ratio is the better measure of over-all corporate goal achievement?

$$\textit{(Inventory Asset Ratio)} = \frac{\textit{(Total Inventory)}}{\textit{(Total Current Assets)}}$$

There are numerous stories of companies where the president reduced inventories only to get reprimanded by the Board of Directors for a poor Current Ratio performance. The result, in most of these cases, was that the president ended up buying back the inventory, even though it was operationally inefficient to do so. Review the discussion of conflicting goals in Chapter 3.

Are conflicting financial and operational goals a factor in Z, Inc.'s performance?

Benchmarking

Benchmarking is a modern buzzword which refers to comparative measures of performance. There are two types of Benchmarking; Internal and External Benchmarking. Internal Benchmarking is where you use several measures of yourself and retake those same measures over time to see if you are improving. Internal Benchmarking can also measure different facilities within the same company against each other. External Benchmarking is where you measure your performance against that of someone else, like a competitor or like the industry averages that are available for your specific industry, to see how your performance measures up.[2] External Benchmarking can also be used to refer to a comparison of your use of

2. One of the most popular tables of industrial ratios is the Industry Norms and Key Business Ratios put out by Dun and Bradstreet Information Services. This report will give all the average ratios, the average profit and loss statement, and the average balance sheet for one year for each Standard Industrial Classification (SIC) code. It is available in most business libraries but not on the web. Contact the Business Solutions Department at www.dnb.com for information about availability.

methodologies or tools and techniques when compared to your competitors. Appendix A includes a collection of measures of performance and discusses their applicability.

Would Benchmarking be useful for Z, Inc.?

Other Operational Measures

Numerous other measures of operational performance exist, many of which measure the same thing. For example:

Inventory Level

Inventory level has become a measure of performance in many organizations, primarily because it is important in Japanese JIT production. However, it is not always a valuable measure of performance if it is not a critical resource, as it is in the types of products that the Japanese produce. The discussion of critical resources will be expanded on in Chapter 4.

Inventory Turns

Inventory turns measures how often inventory is used up and replaced in one year. A high level of inventory turns is good since it suggests that you don't have a lot of inventory sitting around. Sitting inventory is a resource waste.

Throughput

Throughput is a measure of quality units shipped to the customer. It incorporates a focus on quality and on delivered sales. It leaves out a measure of production since produced goods that are not shipped is operationally inefficient and expensive.

Operating Expense

Operating Expense measures the cost of running the factory floor in aggregate. Often this measure is more meaningful when analyzed along side of Throughput. If Operating Expense goes up and Throughput doesn't, then it's costing us more to do the same amount of business as before. A ratio of the two, called Throughput Performance, gives us a measure of comparative performance. The more the number grows, the better.

$$\textit{(Inventory Asset Ratio)} = \frac{\textit{(Total Inventory)}}{\textit{(Total Current Assets)}}$$

Integration

Integration is a measure of internal performance. It is a measure of how effective the communication channels work within an organization. There are numerous ways of measuring integration which include:

- Number of Cross-Functional Teams
- Level of Integration Within Teams
- Number of Team Implemented Innovations.

Cycle Time

Cycle Time is a measure of the amount of time it takes to process an order, from start to finish. Reduced cycle time means increased responsiveness to customer requirements and reduced in-process inventory levels.[3] This would increase inventory turns. The Japanese use Cycle Time as a measure of performance because responsiveness and reduced inventory are both goals of the JIT process and a cycle time measurement improvement is easily communicable to employees. Cycle Time readily demonstrates an accomplishment of all goals. For example, Toyota has a Cycle Time for automobile

3. Customer responsiveness can be increased by increasing finished goods inventory. However, by reducing the cycle time sufficiently, even carrying finished goods inventory can be a liability because of it's increased carrying cost. Ultimately, if we only had to keep raw materials inventory, and all other levels of inventory are committed to specific customer orders, we would minimize inventory costs.

production of three hours. They produce a car from start to finish in three hours. The Cycle Time for American and European auto manufacturers is measured in weeks and in some plants even in months. Inventory turns every four hours at Toyota so that, over two shifts, the inventory turns numbers are over 1000 turns per year. A good inventory turns number for American or European auto manufacturers would be 10 turns per year.

Another form of cycle time that is "Product Development Cycle Time". Here we focus on the time it takes from the conceptualization of a new product idea, to it's being available to the customer. Responsiveness in this area is critical for the products that require fast responsiveness, for example, the fad fashions in the apparel industry.

A third form of cycle time has gained extensive popularity because of the eCommerce push. This is the cash-to-cash cycle time. This form of cycle time tracks the time from when an order is received, until the product is paid for. When considering internet speed and responsiveness, we also need to take a close look at the financial responsiveness of the internet transaction. For example, in the computer industry, the average cash-to-cash cycle time is 106 days and the best of class cycle time is 21 days. That means that on the average, the cash for sales is tied up for about 3 ½ months. The carrying cost of financing this inventory can be devastating to a computer equipment supplier. That is why the Dell Computer model for purchasing equipment on-line has become so attractive. Dell computers has managed to reduce the cash-to-cash cycle time to a negative 8 days. They have turned the tide to where they are operating on the customers' money. It then comes as no surprise that Dell can sell equipment for significantly less than other computer equipment vendors.

Back to Z, Inc.

Do they need operational measures of performance? Which measures do they need? Should Z's CEO analyze these measures prior to making a recommendation for Z's future? Or should the Z, Inc. decision be primarily a financial one?

This section discussing measurement systems raises more questions than it answers. Which types of measures are valuable and which are not? The answer lies in Chapter 3's discussion of goals. However, at this point, you've had a review of some of the measurement alternatives. The answer to: "Which measurement system is best?" is actually quite simple. It is that "they are all best" depending on what we hope to accomplish.

Structure of the Rest of the Book

The rest of the book is broken into four major sections. They are:

- **The International Difference** which focuses on what issues make the international operations environment different from traditional operations. This section deals with strategic goal setting and how it influences operational performance. It discusses how to turn these goals into a strategy. It also discusses how an effective information and measurement system needs to be established to communicate and motivate these goals. It then deals with the globalization and localization of these goals.
- **Managing the Supply Chain** discusses the role of Supply Chain Management in an international setting where vendors, customers, and even producers can exist all over the world. This section also discusses the importance of time as an international competitive instrument.
- **POMS Support Systems** discusses the operational support systems that need to be established. These include the transport and storage of goods, the decision process that goes into deciding where products should be produced, the relationships and locations of customers, and how the international transaction differs for the local transaction in these situations.
- **POMS Excellence** discusses what World Class operational excellence entails. This section also reviews the future of operations management and what type of strategy competitive positioning would suggest.

Revisiting Z, Inc.

The CEO of Z, Inc. is in a quandary. He realizes that the transmission facility has demonstrated poor performance, but he's unsure whether it is really a deficiency in performance or whether the P&L losses are not just the result of a poor allocation of overhead from the corporate office. It wouldn't take much of a reduction of overhead to turn the red ink to black. His initial approach is to reevaluate the overhead allocation process to see if it validates the poor performance of the transmission facility. Having done that, he proceeded with a review of the measurement process that is used. In a meeting with his Vice Presidents, the discussion proceeds as follows:

CEO: I need the finance department to re-evaluate the overhead allocation process for the transmission facility. I'm not sure they're getting a fair shake. Their allocation of overhead based on square footage of factory floor space, seems to put them at a disadvantage.

VP Finance: This is not an overhead allocation issue. What we need to do is to sell off the transmission facility. It's outside of our core competency and we should sell it before it operationally looks so bad that no one would want it.

VP Operations: The transmission facility hasn't received a fair shake. It's the high labor rates that are destroying performance. If we could relocate the facility to somewhere with lower labor rates, the place would be a viable operation. We may not even need to update the equipment, if we could just get a low enough labor cost. The equipment is old, but it has no salvage value and replacing the equipment to newer technology would be extremely expensive.

VP Marketing: We can't tolerate the defect rate. Our customers are getting tired of all the returns and want to see better performance. If we can't increase quality with the existing equipment, then replacing the equipment is not an option. The customers will force it's replacement by going to someone that is running on newer, more quality effective technology.

CEO: I would like the operations group to come up with an evaluation of why the defect rate is so bad. Is it the result of poor machine performance, poor operator performance, or whatever. We need to control the defect rate before we can make any effective decisions about the need for technology. Additionally, I need an evaluation of the cost of operations to determine if there is any way to reduce labor costs sufficiently to justify maintaining, keeping, or relocating this facility. I need information.

The operations VP wanted to save the transmission facility because he considered losing it as a personal failure. He was convinced that the issue was simply a labor cost issue, and he left the meeting intending to prove it. He wanted to move the plant out of Jackson, Michigan to some lower labor cost location where overhead costs would be lower as well. He intended to prove that he was right.

What would you do if you were CEO? Is this decision process working the way it should? Prepare a presentation or class discussion on the alternatives available. Play the role of the CEO and determine a plan of attack. Believe it or not, this case was not solved by the numbers – it was solved by personalities and hidden agenda issues. Then the correct numbers were created to support this agenda. No one made up the numbers. It was simply a matter of selecting the right numbers that supported their agenda. What would you do? For those of you who need numbers, here's a few to help confuse the issue:

- Current Average Labor Rate in Jackson $25 / hour
- Current Average Labor Rate in Tennessee $12 / hour
- Current Average Labor Rate in Mexico $1.50 / hour
- Current Defect Rate 15%
- Defect Rate of Benchmarked Competitors 2%

Primary reason for defects: Poor vendor performance and inadequate inspection of raw materials – defectives end up being introduced into the final products accounts for 60 % of the defects. Additionally, 15 % is the result of operator error, and 10 % is the result of tooling errors or breakdown.

Overhead allocation is done by square footage and the transmission has about 50 % more floor space per employee and 35 % more floor space per dollar sale than the other facilities of Z, Inc. The total overhead allocation of the transmission facility is 5 % of corporate overhead.

An offer to purchase the transmission facility was recently made by a competitor at a selling price of $ 100,000,000:

- Equipment replacement costs: $ 15,000,000
- Relocation costs: $ 3,000,000 plus a loss of one year of production.

Summary

We have established a foundation for Operations Management terminology, and we are now ready to consider the international management effects of an operations environment.

Classroom Assignment

These are assignments that I use in my classes and have found them extremely beneficial in strengthening the background of the students:

Assignment A

Assign a team to role-play the discussion of Z, Inc. at the front of the classroom. Use a similar process for each of the integrated, in-text cases that are found in each chapter of this book. Include individuals for each of the following roles:

- CEO
- VP Finance
- VP Marketing
- VP Operations
- Chairman of the Board.

The CEO should initiate a discussion, attempting to focus on a solution. After some initial interchange, the class should be encouraged to get involved in the discussion. The objective question should be: "What should we do with the transmission facility?" Utilize numbers and philosophies to justify your positions.

Assignment B

Assign "The Swift Shoe Company" case book – this is an excellent review case that can be used to review basic Production – Operations Management (POM) concepts. It takes some time, but in some classes it becomes very necessary to take this extra time, just to make sure that everyone is on the same wave-length. This case is sold separately as the book: The Swift Shoe Company by Craig G. Harms and Stanley W. Huff, Irwin, Homewood, Illinois, 1991 – 5th edition (BP 21.95).

Other Assignments

Here are some other suggestions for case books and readings books that I have found helpful:

- *Global Operations Perspectives* by Jagdish Sheth and Golpira Eshghi, South-Western, Cincinnati, 1989.
- *Plant and Service Tours in Operations Management* by Riger W. Schmenner, MacMillian, New York, 1997.
- *Cases in Operations Management* by Jeff E. Heyl, Linda A. Stone, and Jon Bushnell, Addison-Wesley Pub Co; ISBN: 0201532891, 1994.

Here are a few organizations that I strongly recommend students to become involved in. They have regional meetings and publications that assist in training and certification. CLM also has logistics focused cases.

- American Production and Inventory Control Society
  (APICS)
  500 West Annandale Road
  Falls Church, VA 22046-4274
  1-800-444-2742
  APICS = www.apics.org

- Council of Logistics Management (CLM)
  2803 Butterfield Road, Suite 380
  Oak Brook, IL 60521-1156
  1-708-574-0985
  CLM = www.clm1.org

- Society of Manufacturing Engineers (SME)
  P O Box 32641
  Detroit, MI 48232-9701
  1-800-733-4763
  SME = www.sme.org

References

Production/Operations Management References

Azadivar, Farhad. 1984. *Design and Engineering of Production Systems*. San Jose: Engineering Press Inc.

Best, Tom and Plenert, Gerhard J., »MRP, JIT, or OPT, What's Best?« *Production and Inventory Management*, Vol. 27, No. 2, 1986.

Brown, R. G. 1971. *Management Decisions for Production Operations*. Hinsdale, III.: Dryden Press.

Hadley, G. and Whitin, T. M. 1963. *Analysis of Inventory Systems*. Englewood Cliffs: Prentice-Hall.

Hanssmann, F. 1962. *Operations Research in Production and Inventory Control*. New York: Wiley.

Hax, Arnoldo C. and Candea, Dan. 1984. *Production and Inventory Management*. Englewood Cliffs: Prentice-Hall.

Holt, C. C.; Modigliani, F.; Muth, J. F.; and Simon, H. A. 1960. *Planning Production, Inventories, and Work Force*. Englewood Cliffs: Prentice-Hall.

Johnson, Alicia, »MRP? MRPII? OPT? CIM? FMS? JIT? Is Any System Letter Perfect?« *Management Review*, Vol. 75, No. 9, 1986.

Magee, J. F., and Boodman, D. M. 1967. *Production Planning and Inventory Control*. New York: McGraw-Hill.

Plenert, *Plant Operations Deskbook*, Homewood, Ill., Business 1 IRWIN, 1993, (501 pages).

Ptak, "MRP II, OPT, JIT, and CIM – Succession, Evolution, or Necessary Combination", *P&IMJ*, 2nd Qrtr, 1991

Sarkis, "Production and Inventory Control Issues in Advanced Manufacturing Systems", *P&IMJ*, 1st Qrtr, 1991

Schroeder, Roger G. 1981. *Operations Management*. New York: McGraw-Hill.

Taylor, Frederick Winslow, *The Principles of Scientific Management*, Norton, 1967, New York.

OPT / TOC References

Cox, III, James F., and Michael S. Spencer, *The Constraints Management Handbook*, St. Lucie Press, Boca Raton, FL, 1998.

Goldratt and Cox, *The Goal*, North River Press, 1986.

Goldratt, Eliyahu M., *The Haystack Syndrome*, North River Press Inc., Croton-on-Hudson, New York, 1990.

Goldratt, Eliyahu M., and Robert E. Fox, *The Race*, North River Press Inc., Croton-on-Hudson, New York, 1986.

McMullen, Jr., Thomas B., *Introduction to the Theory of Constraints (TOC) Management System*, St. Lucie Press, Boca Raton, FL, 1998.

Plenert, Gerhard, and Terry Lee, »Optimizing Theory of Constraints When New Product Alternatives Exist«, *Production and Inventory Management Journal*, 1993, Third Quarter, Pages 51-57. Reprinted in *Selected Readings in Constraints Management* published by APICS, 1996, Pages 23-30.

Plenert, Gerhard, »Optimizing Theory of Constraints When Multiple Constrained Resources Exist« *European Journal of Operations Research*, October 1993, Vol. 70, Pages 126-133.

MRP References

Plossl, *Manufacturing Control, The Last Frontier for Profits*, Reston Publishing, a Prentice Hall Company.

Plossl and Wight, *Production and Inventory Control*, Prentice-Hall.

Wight, *Production and Inventory Management in the Computer Age*, CBI Publishing, Boston.

JIT References

Karatsu, Hajime, *TQC Wisdom of Japan*, Productivity Press, Cambridge, MA, 1988.

Lu, David J., *KANBAN Just in Time at Toyota*, Productivity Press, Cambridge, MA, 1988.

Miller, William B., and Viki L. Schenk, *All I Need to Know About*

Manufacturing I Learned In Joe's Garage, Bayrock Press, (208) 376-2266, 1997.

Pascale, Richard Tanner and Anthony G. Athos, *The Art of Japanese Management*, Warner Books, 1981.

Plenert, Gerhard, »Line Balancing Techniques as Used for Just-in-Time (JIT) Product Line Optimization« *Production Planing and Control*, Vol. 8 No. 7, 1997, Pages 686-693.

Plenert, Gerhard, »An Overview of JIT« *International Journal of Advanced Manufacturing Technology*, 1993, Vol. 8, Pages 91-95.

Plenert, Gerhard »Three Different Concepts for JIT«, *Production and Inventory Management Journal*, Second Quarter, 1990, Vol. 31, No. 2.

Shingo, *Non-Stock Production: The Shingo System for Continuous Improvement*, Productivity Press, Cambridge, Mass.

The International Difference

2. Internationalization

The Return to Z, Inc.

The CEO of Z, Inc. had called a follow-up meeting to discuss the findings of the VP Operations with respect to the transmission facility. The meeting went as follows:

CEO: Today we are going to revisit low profitability issues of the transmission facility. I believe the VP Operations has developed a recommendation for us and I want us to consider his proposal.

VP Operations: The transmission facility is losing money because of an extremely expensive work force that has low quality performance. The $ 2,000,000 labor expense that we are now expending could be reduced to $ 120,000 if we moved the facility to Mexico. Now, I understand that there is a concern about quality in Mexico, but I have worked with F Motor Company, Mexico and they assure me that the quality of trained labor in Mexico is every bit as good as it is in the United States. In fact, they did a study comparing about 20 different countries throughout the world. The study focused on trainability and adaptability, and they found the Mexican work force to be the easiest to train on new processes and to retrain on changed process for any of the countries studied, including the United States and Japan. They beat them all. So I don't think quality is an issue. Productivity has also been mentioned as a concern if we moved the facility to Mexico. However, even if we hire twice as many employees as before, we're still one and three-quarter million dollars better off than we are now. Additionally, we can transfer all the existing equipment to Mexico and we wouldn't have to invest in new equipment. We can just pack this plant up lock-stock-and-barrel and ship it down.

CEO: (addressing the others in the meeting) What are your thoughts?

VP Finance: Have we investigated selling off the facility?

VP Operations: I don't feel right about that option because having the transmission facility minimizes our exposure to fluctuations in the construction industry. People are always buying cars, at least a lot more so than they are building roads and bridges.
VP Marketing: I'm not sure we're doing anything to help the customers with this move. In fact, what we're doing is placing a risk in their lap during the move. If they need products fast, they'll be stuck. Besides, from what I understand, the defect rates are primarily vendor driven. Are we doing anything to assure better vendor performance?

VP Operations (looking a little flustered): I see the move to Mexico as an excellent excuse to renegotiate the vendor contracts. Also, in Mexico we can put more inspectors at the raw materials and the cost of the additional inspectors would be minimal. We can't afford to hire additional inspectors now – it's just too expensive.

VP Marketing: Losing customers is also expensive. We need to solve the quality issues!

CEO: Are we all in a lose mutual consensus agreeing that we want to move this facility to Mexico? – (PAUSE) – I'll assume by your resigned silence that this is going to be our recommendation to the board. Please help me organize the numbers so that I'll be ready for next month's meeting.

In the Z, Inc. case the author is presenting a realistic scenario, not an ideal scenario. This is similar to the way this process occurred. However, it is important for students to reconsider the case at this point. What have the Z, Inc. executives done correctly? What could they have done better? What recommendations would you have presented? How should the CEO proceed at this point?

In this chapter we are now beginning a review of international considerations that effect the Operations Management environment. Since Z, Inc. is considering a move to Mexico, what international considerations should become a part of this decision? As you, the reader, go through this chapter, please consider these issues so that at the end of the chapter you will be able to advise the CEO on what makes sense and what does not make sense in this international relocation.

What's Different?

This chapter focuses on the differences between traditional (keep it all in the United States) manufacturing and the more open operational environments that focus on World Class competitiveness. Some of these topics will be saved for detailed discussions in later chapters. These topics include:

- Thinking Globally and Working Locally (chapters 3, 4, & 5)
- Managing an International Supply Chain (chapters 6, 7, & 8)
- International Logistics and Materials Movement (chapter 9)
- Locating Manufacturing Facilities Internationally (chapter 10)
- Identifying International Vendors and Customers (chapter 2)
- International Customer Expectations (chapter 11)
- International Ethics (chapter 12)
- Economic Issues (chapter 2)
- Political Issues (chapter 2)
- The International Competitive Stance (chapter 13)
- Infrastructure Differences (chapter 2 and chapter 5)
- Cultural Differences (chapter 2 and chapter 12)
- Management Style Differences (chapter 2)
- Organizational / Structural Differences (chapter 2)
- Goal Development Differences (chapter 3).

Let's move forward with these topics to help give us a better sense of what the international operations manager has in store for them.

Why Go International?

The United States is the master in 11 of the world's 13 industrial sectors. The remaining two go to Japan and it's easy to figure out which two they are: automotive production and small electronics components products like TVs and VCRs. So why should a US company go international? Can't it safely exist in its own little world in the United States and ignore the rest of the world, and be perfectly happy? Actually, the answer is: "Yes it could isolate itself." But the bigger question is "How long can it survive ignoring the rest of the world?" Reality is that there are other parts of the world that do things better than the U.S. does them. That being the case, if the US doesn't take advantage of what other's do better, it won't be able to compete with competitors that do look internationally. This principle is know as the "Law of Comparative Advantage" and can be found in any Economics textbook. This principle demonstrates that, for example looking at only two countries like the United States and Mexico, we may see the situation found in Chart 2.1. We could suggest that the United States quit working and quit raising apples and get everything from Mexico. But that wouldn't work simply because of volume. Both countries need to produce output. So which country produces "comparatively" better in which area. We see that in labor, Mexican cost is 6 % of the United States. However, in apples, Mexico is 83 % of the United States. Therefore, using Mexico for factory labor is better than using Mexico to produce apples. The conclusion is that if Mexico supplies the factory labor, and the United States supplies the apples, both countries will be comparatively better off, and both will be busy. This law of "comparative advantage", if spread internationally, would suggest that competitive pressures would bring us to some kind of equilibrium where everything is produced in as comparatively cheaply a method as possible, and the whole world benefits.

Chart 2.1. The Law of Comparative Advantage

	Labor Costs	Apples
United States	$ 25 / hours	$ .30 each
Mexico	$ 1.50 / hour	$ .25 each

The law of comparative advantage is an effective economic strategy. Unfortunately, it also has strategic disadvantages. Following the law of comparative advantage, the United States would ship much of it's production overseas – which is a trend it has been following for the last 20 years. The problem created by this trend is that the United States has also shipped much of it's manufacturing engineering capability overseas as well. This raises an interesting dilemma. The

U.S. is still the world's biggest and best developer of R & D technology. It can come up with anything – just ask NASA. Unfortunately, the U.S. is one of the worst countries in the world at taking this technology and applying it to manufacturable consumer products. For example, in Japan, they are extremely poor at developing pure R & D technologies, but they can take the U. S.'s ideas and turn them into products rapidly and efficiently. For example, the U.S. developed air bags but the Japanese had them in automobiles first. The result is that strict adherence to the law of comparative advantage causes dependencies. For example, the United States had offloaded all of it's oil production to the middle East, Latin America, and the North Sea. Then, when the oil cartel decided to up the price of oil, the United States was left totally dependent on cartel pricing.

Any country needs to balance the requirements of comparative advantage with the requirements caused by dependencies. It needs to follow the law of comparative advantage, taking advantage of pricing structures whenever they benefit all parties. However, everybody needs to avoid dependencies. This balancing act becomes a key piece of what is developed in an international corporate strategic plan of operation. The result is, referring to Chart 2.1, the United States should take advantage of the cheaper Mexican labor, but not lose it's only ability to produce. And the Mexicans should buy U. S. apples, but not lose their ability to produce some apples as well.

Expanding the discussion of comparative advantage a little further, we can look at an area of specialization, like engineering. There are numerous types of engineering, for example, bio engineering, new product engineering, manufacturing engineering, information systems engineering, etc. Each of these areas would have their own relative position in the model of comparative advantage. For example, a research project was conducted where a number of countries were assessed in their ability to adapt new technologies into a manufacturing process. This study included European countries, North American countries, Asian countries like Japan and Taiwan, and Latin American countries like Mexico and Brazil. Much to everyone's surprise, the country that was found to be the most adaptive was Mexico. This gives Mexico a comparative advantage in the area of manufacturing engineering. Similarly, the United States, with its extensive research labs and budget, would take the lead in new product engineering. Because of the extensive high level of education and low labor cost, India has become one of the lead countries in information systems engineering. With the help of the internet, development work can easily be performed in India and used to support development projects all over the world. The result is that even in a specialized area like engineering, the principal of comparative advantage can create a mix of international technology partners.

Other Economic Issues

There are numerous international economic factors that effect the decision of whether or not it is a good idea for a company to be involved internationally. For example inflation is such a factor. The inflation rate in the United States or Europe is generally lower and a lot more stable than the inflation rates in other parts of the world. Inflation rates directly effect interest rates. Therefore, if the international operations transaction requires a financial investment, then attention needs to be paid to the stability of inflation rates. Several countries have inflation rates that exceed 100 %. This means that if you are investing in the local currency at an interest rate of 100 %, it may on the surface sound exciting. Unfortunately, doubling your money each year means very little if the prices of goods and services increases at an even greater rate. That's the reason why a large number of business transactions are conducted in the stable currencies of the world, like the U. S. dollar, the European euro, or the Japanese yen. This is especially true if you are planning for long term. At least you know that when you get paid, your currency has an excellent chance of being worth what you hope to get out of it.

Exchange rates are another valuable economic tool of the international transaction. Exchange rates tend to fluctuate, as can be seen in the graph on Chart 2.2. We can see that transactions with Japan (Yen) from 1996 to 1998 have changed significantly. This is also true for the European euro. Therefore, a transaction made in 1996 in U.S. dollars, has more value in 1998 and conversely, a transaction made in 1996 in yen has lost value. Therefore, if you are receiving funds from Japan, and the transaction was in dollars, you are now worse off, but if you are paying funds to Japan over this same period of time you have made money and will be paying less. Conversely, if the transaction was negotiated in yen, the exact opposite would be true. Therefore, if you are not interested in speculating in currency, it is important that you transact business in the most stable currency possible, which is generally the U. S. dollar, the U. K. pound, or the German mark.

Chart 2.2. Exchange Rates in U.S. Dollars

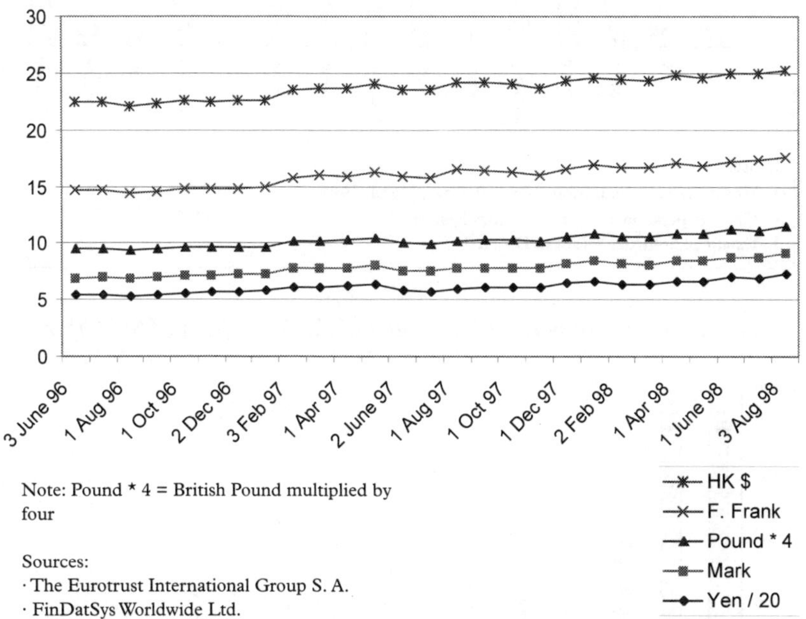

Note: Pound * 4 = British Pound multiplied by four

Sources:
· The Eurotrust International Group S. A.
· FinDatSys Worldwide Ltd.

Another area of economic consideration is the Balance of Trade relationship between countries. This can be seen in Chart 2.3 through Chart 2.7. In Chart 2.3 we see that the major trading economies of the world. The EU, through it's unification and trading pact has taken the number one spot away from the United States. Chart 2.4 shows the top major importing economies and Chart 2.5 shows the major exporting economies. The top six countries always seem to be the same. Chart 2.6 is a ranking table showing the ranking of each of the major trading partners as well as the percentage of change and the per capita effect on the people of each country.

Chart 2.3. Major Trading Economies of the World (1997) from MSU Ciber

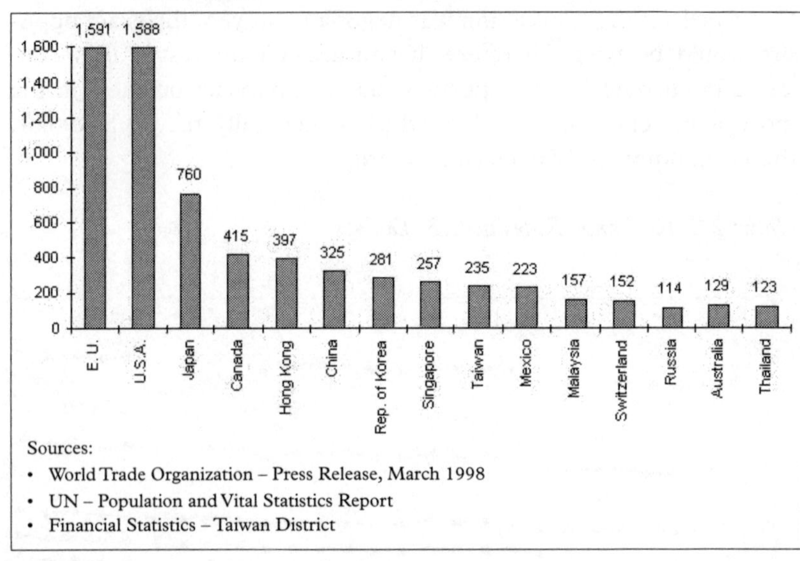

Sources:

- World Trade Organization – Press Release, March 1998
- UN – Population and Vital Statistics Report
- Financial Statistics – Taiwan District

Chart 2.4. Major Importing Economics of the World from MSU Ciber

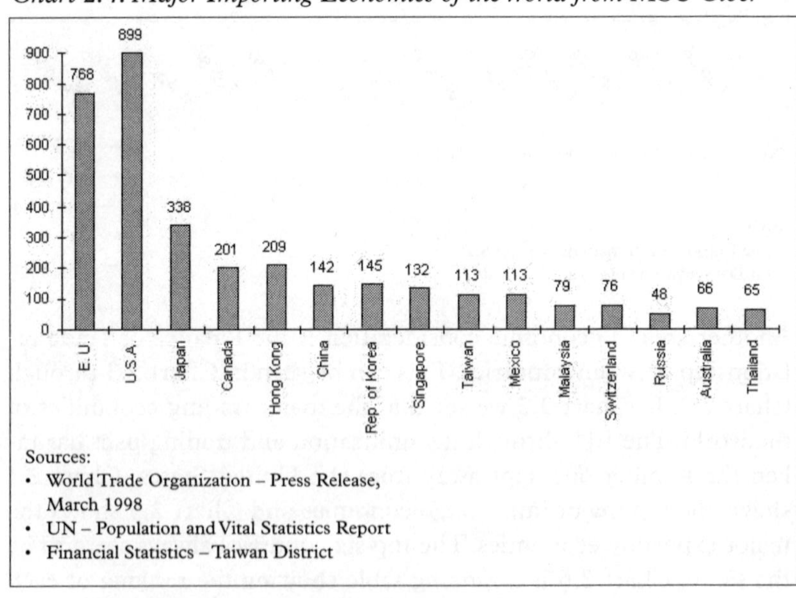

Sources:

- World Trade Organization – Press Release, March 1998
- UN – Population and Vital Statistics Report
- Financial Statistics – Taiwan District

Chart 2.5. Major Exporting Economics of the World (1997) from Ciber

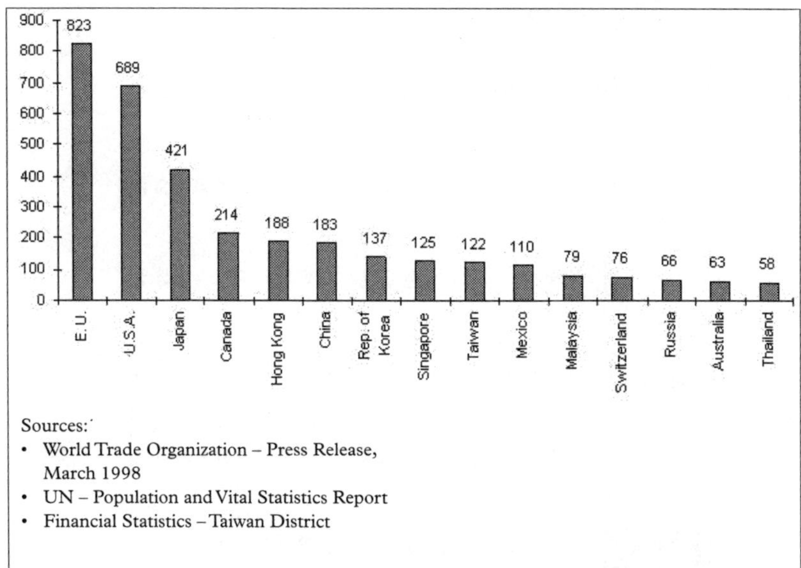

Sources:

- World Trade Organization – Press Release, March 1998
- UN – Population and Vital Statistics Report
- Financial Statistics – Taiwan District

Chart 2.6. Order Volume from MSU CIBER

Countries (Order based on Exports)	Value in 1997 - US$ Bn.			% Change in Value 1997/96			Per Capita – US$ '000		
	Exports	Imports	Total Trade	Exports	Imports	Total Trade	Exports	Imports	Total Trade
World	*4.180*	*4.320*		5	5				
E. U.	823	768	1.591	3	2	4	2,3	2,1	4,4
U.S.A.	689	899	1.588	10	9	10	2,6	3,4	6
Japan	421	338	760	2	-3	*	3,3	2,7	6
Canada	214	201	415	6	15	10	7,1	6,7	13,8
Hong Kong	188	209	397	4	4	4	29,8	33,1	62,9
China	183	142	325	21	3	12	0,1	0,1	0,3
Rep. of Korea	137	145	281	5	-4	*	3	3,2	6,2
Singapore	125	132	257	*	1	*	41,1	43,4	84,4
Taiwan	122	113	235	5	12	7	5,7	5,3	10,9
Mexico	110	113	223	15	23	20	1,1	1,2	2,3
Malaysia	79	79	157	*	*	*	3,8	3,8	7,6
Switzerland	76	76	152	-6	-4	-4	10,7	10,7	21,5
Russia	66	48	114	-5	11	-1	0,4	0,3	0,8
Australia	63	66	129	4	1	3	3,4	3,6	7,1
Thailand	58	65	123	5	-12	-5	1	1,1	2

Note: the * indicates data is unavailable

Sources:

World Trade Organization - Press Release, March 1998
UN - Population and Vital Statistics Report
Financial Statistics - Taiwan District

Chart 2.7. Market Potential Indicators for Emerging Markets from 1999 MSU CIBER

	Market Size		Market Growth Rate		Market Consump-tion Capacity		Commer-cial Infrastruc-ture		Country Risk		Overall Market Potential Index	
Countries	Rank	Index	Rank	Index	Rank	Index	Rank	Index	Rank	Index	Rank	Index
SINGAPORE	23	1	1	100	-	-	3	88	1	100	**1**	**100**
HONGKONG	21	1	16	56	-	-	7	65	3	76	**2**	**76**
PORTUGAL	22	1	5	84	-	-	4	75	2	90	**3**	**62**
ISRAEL	20	1	7	76	5	84	6	66	5	71	**4**	**60**
GREECE	18	2	9	72	-	-	2	90	4	71	**5**	**52**
CHINA	1	100	2	95	7	68	20	8	21	21	**6**	**51**
CZECH REP.	16	3	21	22	3	91	1	100	8	64	**7**	**49**
INDIA	3	48	6	81	4	88	23	1	14	51	**8**	**47**
POLAND	8	9	17	55	1	100	9	52	9	64	**9**	**47**
S. KOREA	7	13	12	68	-	-	10	43	7	66	**10**	**45**
HUNGARY	19	2	19	52	2	91	5	67	11	60	**11**	**43**
PHILIPPINES	12	6	15	62	8	57	13	25	13	54	**12**	**30**
CHILE	17	2	3	91	14	16	16	15	6	70	**13**	**30**
ARGENTINA	11	7	11	70	-	-	11	29	17	43	**14**	**30**
MEXICO	5	19	10	70	13	27	18	14	15	45	**15**	**26**
MALAYSIA	15	4	8	74	11	43	15	22	10	60	**16**	**20**
TURKEY	9	9	4	86	-	-	14	25	18	32	**17**	**20**
THAILAND	14	4	13	66	11	43	21	8	12	55	**18**	**16**
RUSSIA	2	50	23	1	10	50	8	55	23	1	**19**	**16**
VENEZUELA	13	5	20	50	9	53	19	9	19	30	**20**	**14**
BRAZIL	4	23	14	62	15	5	12	25	20	28	**21**	**9**
S. AFRICA	10	8	18	53	16	1	17	14	16	45	**22**	**8**
INDONESIA	6	16	22	14	6	69	22	2	22	19	**23**	**1**

Chart 2.7 shows the market potential for emerging markets, indicating the growth rate, size, infrastructure, and estimated risk associated with each of these markets. These markets may not be large individually, but their potential is enormous and they will become major players in the future balance of trade.

International trade restrictions can vary as significantly as the cultural expectations. Government reaction to trade deficits is often emotional, rather than competitive. For example, the trade deficit that the United States has with Japan causes Americans to demand that Japan open its markets. The general feeling is that it must somehow be Japan's fault that we aren't selling more to them. In a few cases this may be true, for example in the sale of rice to Japan there have been some barriers imposed by the Japanese farm community that limits the amount of rice imports into Japan. However, in general, the U. S.'s ineffectiveness in selling to Japan is their own fault. American producers expect Japanese consumers to have tastes similar to the West. They don't look closely enough at satisfying customers' expectations. The Japanese consumer is not the same as the American consumer. Therefore product "localization" is required. This will be discussed in more detail in Chapter 3.

Governments have devised a number of ways of trying to force the balance of trade to shift to their favor. One of the techniques is taxation or tariffs. Taxing an import increases the price of the import making it less competitive and less likely to be purchased. For example, taxing Japanese automotive imports keeps the American automobile products competitive. The intent of the tariff was to give the American manufacturer more time to establish a competitive stance at which point the tariff could be removed. Unfortunately, the reality is that the tariff keeps the American producers lazy, since the competitive pressures have been artificially removed. Now auto manufacturers live under the hope that the tariff will never be eliminated. This strategy may work within the United States, but it doesn't help if the United States is competing against Japan in the European auto market. Here they will both fall under the same restrictions.

Another attempt at restricting imports is through non-tariff barriers. Artificial limits on the number of imports, or product requirements that are difficult to comply with are considered non-tariff barriers. For example, in order to sell products into Europe, the products have to be produced by a manufacturer that is ISO certified. ISO is a quality certification that was developed for the European market. The cost for this certification process starts at about $ 500,000 U. S. for the average company. Far too many companies cannot afford this option.

Big Emerging Markets

Economic internationalization has similarly gone through the same dramatic transformations. What was formerly a world of super-powers ruled by economic power-house countries, has now become a world of large emerging trading blocks. With the fall of the Soviet Union, the United States was left as the world's dominant economic power-house. In order to exhibit some of their own economic strength, the European Union (EU) was formed so that the collection of smaller European countries could band together and economically compete with the United States. This union is not just a trade agreement but includes an integration of currencies, banking systems, stock exchanges, etc.

The formation of the EU has triggered other regions of the world to consider their own economic plight and similar trading blocks have emerged in the Americas and in Asia. The major trading block groups that have emerged are the North America Free Trade Agreement (NAFTA) which initially included the United States and Canada and later included Mexico and soon Chile. It will become the America Free Trade Agreement (AFTA) with the inclusion of Chile. Other countries are trying to join. The original NAFTA was strongly criticized in the United States. Unions were successful in convincing people that Free Trade with Mexico would cause a surge of plant migrations to Mexico. This hasn't happened. In fact, the United States was the initial big gainer in this free trade agreement, especially in agricultural products, which they were able to produce cheaper than the Mexicans. Some movement to Mexico has occurred, but nothing any more dramatic than was occurring anyway. It is hoped that over time Mexico will in fact regain some of the losses it has incurred against the United States. It is, however, interesting that non-NAFTA countries like Japan have moved factories into Mexico in the hope that they will get within the free trade zone thereby being able to sell products in the U.S. with reduced tariffs. In this way, Mexico has greatly benefited from the NAFTA agreement.

Unlike the EU, NAFTA is strictly a trade agreement, where joining countries agree to reduced tariffs and increased trade. Trade agreements of this type are advantageous to the parties involved because reduced tariffs mean lower prices for consumers. Unfortunately, trade agreements cause international resentment simply because any time you agree to trade more with one country, you are basically agreeing to trade less with everyone else since you have a limited need for goods.

As a result of EU and NAFTA, other trade agreements have sprung up like the APEC or ASEAN agreement between Asian nations. Another agreement is SEATO which incorporates Australia, Japan, South Korea, Chile, and other countries in the Pacific region. Still another is MERCOSUR which integrates South American countries. Like NAFTA, these agreements are between nations in order to trade more with each other and, therefore, less with everyone else.

The ultimate free trade agreement is the WTO (formerly GATT), which, it is hoped, will replace all other free trade agreements by creating an international free trade agreement. The WTO is slowly being developed through joint meetings of many of the nations of the world. International issues are slowly being ironed out through a variety of negotiations and agreements. But this is a slow process. Most favored nation status is also a trading tool which bands nations together. The United States granted a nation such as China Most Favored Nation (MFN) status which gives the trading relationship between the two countries a level of preference through lowered tariffs and possibly reduced purchasing quotas. The hope is that this will help the country develop economic independence.

Political Issues

The world's political environment is continuously restructuring itself in many ways. For example, in the 50's and 60's the world was caught up in a super-power cold war. In the 70's we saw terrorism emerging, but it was primarily for definable organizations that were directly attackable. In the 80's, countries like Libya and Iraq became the focal point for terrorism and war, and these countries were directly identifiable and targetable. Also, during this timeframe, the Cold War ended and the super-power struggle became a struggle of North vs. South or Big vs. Small. And the small saw themselves as needing to attack from a minority position. Therefore, in the 90's we saw a world where individuals were creating their own type of terrorist war through the disguises of freedom struggles or religious movements. An entirely new war has been created and an entirely new plan of attack is needed.

Politics often drives economic environments, as was seen in the previous discussion of tariffs and non-tariff barriers. Some countries have their borders closed to all trade, such as Libya or Iraq, while others have cut off trade in specific product lines, such as in the case of Brazil. Some countries cannot have products shipped to them because economic relationships are strained, as in the case of the United States and Cuba. Therefore, it becomes necessary to ship the products to a neutral country first, such as Canada, and then to resell them to Cuba.

Political pressures can open and shut borders rapidly, and economic trade requires political stability. For example, China has tremendous potential, both as a producer and supplier of goods and services, and as a consumer of imported products. However, the traditional political instability in China, where companies have invested large amounts of money developing industries, only to have their efforts taken away from them through nationalization or newly created barriers, has made investors gun-shy. Many companies keep a small manufacturing presence in China, as a type of wait-and-see game, in the hope that their presence can be grown if a comfortable level of security occurs. But these operations tend to have minimal profitability. The company's presence is primarily politically motivated.

Technological Innovations

Technology is developed in the United States at such a high rate of speed that no one else in the world can come anywhere close to competing. The United States' government is the largest producer of this technology. The U.S. has technology organizations like NASA, and the military organizations, that develop areas of technology that cover all areas of industry. By U. S. law, all this technology is available to anyone, free of charge except for the copying costs. There is a library in Washington, D. C. where any of this technology can be accessed. By law, each technology organization must supply a technology transfer expert. Surprisingly, the largest user of this data-base is Russia, along with other international counterparts.

Technology innovations drive competitiveness. Therefore, international technological considerations drive international competitiveness. There are two types of technology, hard and soft technologies. Up until now we have been discussing the hard technologies, like product or machine technologies. But the soft technologies, like logistics movement or information systems, can be just as critical to competitive success. For example, Computer Aided Design / Computer Aided Manufacturing (CAD/CAM) systems have facilitated tremendous cost reductions in manufacturing. CAD/CAM systems can unfold the wing of an airplane and directly transfer the metal cutting information to the manufacturing processes, thereby facilitating speed and greatly increasing accuracy of traditional trial-and-error wing folding processes. This information can then be transferred internationally to manufacturing equipment anywhere in the world.

Another example of soft technology improvements is in the area of management practices. For example, as we saw in Chapter 1, Japan's competitiveness drove Westerners to consider the materials-cost effective JIT production process for their own facilities. This process incorporates empowered teaming and moves away from a specialization of labor, both of which were somewhat foreign to American manufacturers at the time. Another management technology effect was the development of national and international certification programs, like the APICS (American Production and Inventory Control Society), CIRM (Certified in Inventory Resources Management), or the CPIM (Certified in Production and Inventory Management), or the NAPM's (National Association of Purchasing Managers), CPM (Certified in Purchasing Management) programs. Additionally, reward programs like the U. S. Malcolm Balridge Award or the Japanese Deming Prize have defined what successful companies should look like. Finally, the current management emphasis on continuous improvement programs and change programs like TQM (Total Quality Management) and Concept Management have focused on a more empowered workforce that has ownership in the production processes. See Chapter 13 for a more detailed discussion of these World Class Management and Change Management topics.

Infrastructure Differences

There are numerous infrastructural effects of international involvement. For example, the infostructural (the structure of the information network) processes are different. Various countries have alternative accounting systems, a variety of tax rules, and different rules of contract. For example, in most Asian countries, a persons' "word" has more legal credibility than a written contract. Similarly, the handshake is more binding than a written contract. Or, a developed relationship is more valuable than being the "lowest priced bidder." Just the opposite is true in the West. In the area of accounting, in the United States, inventory is considered an asset, and labor is an expense. This makes labor the first area of focus in cost reduction programs. In other countries we find that labor is an asset and that inventory is the expense, as a cost of carrying the inventory is placed into direct, controllable expenses rather than into overhead. Inventory can change value over time and be costed off as it is carried. This changes the management approach so that materials (inventory) is the cost area that is attacked in cost reduction programs, and labor is kept on the books because of it's accrued value over time. Labor will increase in it's asset value as it becomes increasingly trained and experienced. It should be obvious that these types of differences change the management approach and the management perspective. However, when Western companies come into these countries with their traditional infostructural systems, bringing in local managers can raise difficulties because they need to be culturally adapted to the Western approach and style of management. More will be said about this in Chapter 3 during the discussion of localization vs. globalization.

Another infostructural area of concern is the difference in information gathering / reporting systems. In the Western production process, the collection of data through the process is considered critical, and shop floor data collection equipment can be found throughout the production process. Data accuracy is considered to be critical to effective production planning performance. In contrast, in Toyota, there is no shop floor data collection equipment. Toyota is considered the automotive plant with the most sophisticated production planning processes in the world. In Chart 2.8 we see an example comparing U.S. and Toyota's auto production statistics.

Chart 2.8. Comparing U.S. and Toyota Auto Production Statistics

	US Auto Production	**Toyota**
Cycle Time	4 to 6 weeks	3 hours
Inventory Turns	8 to 10 per year	Every 4 hours or over 1000 per year

Western obsession with computers, data collection, and the information age have made them almost a joke internationally in what is considered to be an information obsession or addiction. The excessive use of information in the West is based on non-trust systems. Systems were developed because individuals don't trust each other. The Japanese consider these systems to be a waste of resources. In fact, it is believed that non-trust systems cost Western companies more than the fraud or mistakes that might have been caused if trust were used. This issue is open for debate, but the difference in perspective is interesting and comes through in the management style differences between the two countries.

Infrastructural differences also include issues like transportation (roads or rail), which can be quite problematic in some underdeveloped countries. Other areas include the accessibility to reliable power supplies, the availability of clean water, the accessibility to telephone services, local materials sourcing through vendors, etc. The quality of the postal service, will vary in each country. For example, I had a "priority package" mailed to me from Boston on July 6 and I finally received it in Sacramento on September 1. Technical training and educational levels may be a consideration, like the ability of the work-force to read, write, and do simple mathematics. Additionally, language ability and the ability of management to communicate with the work-force can be critical to credibility and therefore to effectiveness. Chart 2.9 compares the average education levels of some key countries and demonstrates how vastly the technical abilities can vary. For example, the low level of technical education that is indicated for countries like Turkey and Sweden should be of concern if you are looking for a strong technical base such as engineering expertise. Countries like Canada, the United States, and Australia should be excellent locations for research centers.

2.9. Bachelor Degree Recipients

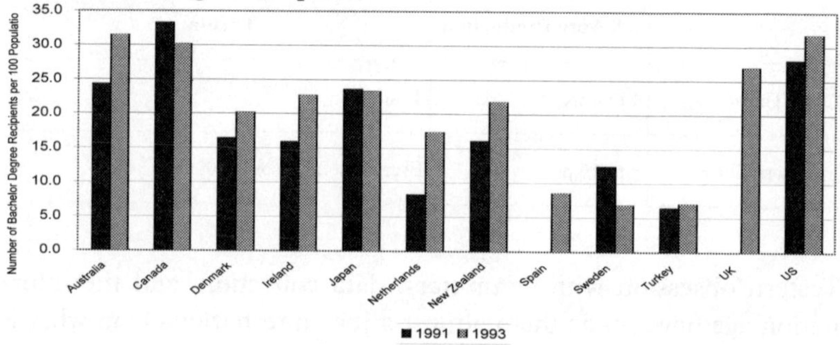

Sources:
- National Education Data Resource enter – September 1998

Cultural Differences

Cultural differences can be both interesting and frustrating. Several of these differences, like the value placed on verbal as opposed to written agreements, can vary dramatically. Religion is a critical cultural sensitivity. Hand gestures that are considered to be acceptable in the West, like pointing at someone or eating with your left hand, or putting a Kleenex in your pocket, can be quite repugnant to other cultures.

Other taboos, like the Latin "machismo" influence, stresses the importance of manliness. For example, it is difficult to get Mexicans to wear protective gear, like dust masks, because that would be considered to be a thing that a real man would never do.

Motivators, also change dramatically from one country to the next. In the United States, you can motivate just about any response if the right amount of money is offered. However, in some countries, increasing pay or offering a bonus would actually encourage employees to work less. The reason is that they need a specific amount of money to live on, and they see no reason to earn more. They would prefer to spend time with the family.

Management Style Differences

Management style differences are often culturally related. For example, Russian managers tend to be extremely authoritarian. Japanese managers, such as in the case of Toyota, prefer empowered participation with a management override whenever appropriate. In Brazil we find Semco where employees have totally empowered participation, even to the point where employees have voted to fire the boss' secretary because they felt she wasn't necessary. The book Maverick, listed in the references, discusses this case. Similarly, FedEx has a program where the employees have the power to fire a manager, via their performance ratings.

In the West, we find that the specialization of labor is critical to productivity. However, as we have seen in the last chapter, labor productivity improvement may actually hurt profitability. However, tradition has taught us that employees should always be busy. Internationally we find that this perspective varies. For example, if we have a factory in which there are ten employees, inventory is stacked to the ceiling on all four walls, and three of the employees are reading a newspaper, we would find significantly different reactions. If a Western manager walked into the room they would rant and rave over the inefficiency of the three employees reading the newspaper. They'd be ready to fire them. But the Western manager would not even notice the inventory. However, if a Japanese manager walked into the same room, their reaction would be that the three employees reading the newspaper must have been very efficient and have done a good job because they have time to read the newspaper. However, they would become extremely upset about the inventory that is lining the walls and they would ask why it isn't moving.

The participative, empowered, team approach to management is considered to be World Class Management (Theory Z), as opposed to the authoritarian, domineering style of management (Theory X). Theory Y falls in between the two. For more detail see the book World Class Manager listed in the references.

Organizational Structure Differences

Management style differences result in organizational structural differences. For example, in Japan, the defined roles of employees are not as pronounced. Employees will change job functions regularly, as much as every two years. The traditional hierarchical structure that we see in the West defines a rigid chain-of-command.

Organizational structures can also be effected by the product / location makeup. Whereas, in the past, it made sense to be a product-based organization, where divisions are delineated by the products sold, it may make more sense internationally to be a location-based organization. Some companies, such as NCR, tried to maintain their product based structure within the United States marketplace, while breaking the international marketplace up into location-based units. This decision is often based on the variability of the product line. If there is too much variability, then the location-based structure would bring inexperience into play.

The structure of the manufacturing process can vary dramatically overseas. As discussed in Chapter 1, the Western focus on the departmentalized specialization of labor is usually structured around an MRP production planning process. Japan has focused on a cell based manufacturing process that utilizes the JIT production process (see Chapter 4). Israel has identified the bottleneck to be the target of productive efficiency in its TOC methodology.

Another structural difference is found in the Supply Chain. The West tends to focus on the producer's core competency, believing that they should do what they do best. For example, Goodyear Tire and Rubber produces tires, but has UPS handle the logistics of shipping the tires. In Japan or Korea we see more of a Supply Chain Management approach (see Chapter 6). In this approach we have a large conglomerate which manages supplier, producers, the distribution process, and even the retail outlets. The key eCommerce and eBusiness success has widely been focused on the optimization of the Supply Chain.

Management Challenges During Globalization

The management challenges of globalization can be extensive. The most difficult part is the need to "jump out of the box" of traditional management. All the rules that are basic, simple, and reliable are rapidly destroyed. The worst error committed by managers who are globalizing is inflexibility. Trying to force everyone to use the same styles, structures, and information systems will cause discord and waste extensive amounts of time and money. There are often better ways to accomplish the same results on a local basis. To find out what the key is for local success, management needs to do only one thing; ASK THE LOCALS!

The bottom line to successful globalization is in people. We need to be able to work with other cultures using their sets of rules. We need to be flexible in our styles and procedures. We need to remove the rigid rules that we have use to run our companies. And we need to understand the cultural, ethical, and religious differences of these countries, and identify how these differences will effect the business transaction. In Asia, the relationship between individuals is so critical, that most Asians would never consider closing a deal based on a phone conversation, a quote, or a piece of paper. Without the human relationship element, no deals would be struck.

Managing in Underdeveloped, Developing, and Developed Countries

The economic structure of a country can be important to the transaction. For example, China, with one-third of the world's population and an extremely low priced work force, is an ineffective producer because of the lack of infrastructure for the transport of goods. It is also an ineffective market for goods and services because the majority of the population can't afford the Western products. The development of the infrastructure would be considered critical prior to effectively entering the country. Other underdeveloped countries suffer the same problems. For example, many countries in Africa are suffering from political and economic turmoil which is keeping them from developing the infrastructure needed to support industries.

The developing countries of the world are an excellent market for both suppliers and customers. These countries, like those of Latin America and Southeast Asia, have political stability and a somewhat stable and growing economy. They are developing their infrastructure so that it can support industries and, although it won't be perfect because of the occasional power outages or traffic congestion, these countries generally have a well educated work force at very low prices. Countries like Malaysia and Mexico are examples.

The developed countries of North America, Europe, and Japan, offer superior infrastructure support, but also higher prices, especially in the labor market. However, in the case of high technology or speed-to-market issues, these countries may be preferable. Generally speaking, the developed countries are the trainers and educators of the world, and they have the sophisticated logistics systems that are necessary for global transactions. The developed countries also have the highest consumption of the world. In the developed countries we find the workers of the world. They generally offer a talented, effective work force. The developing countries are looking for international economic support which would give them the opportunity to make their mark in the world.

Identifying International Vendors and Customers

It is important to understand and visit the country that you plan to deal with. A personal relationship needs to be established. You need to assure that the infrastructure could support what it is you are trying to accomplish. You need to verify the ability of the individual or the location to support what it is that you are trying to accomplish. There are many areas, like Colonia Juarez in Mexico, that are considered to have an excellent, inexpensive work force. This is a prime location since it is just across the bridge from El Paso, Texas.

Unfortunately, this area is so saturated with jobs that companies are openly stealing employees from each other.

This is often true with vendors and customers. Lower labor cost or a large consumer population is not a sufficient reason for entering into a foreign setting. Vendors may offer low prices, but they may also have extremely poor quality. It is important to visit the vendor's location to see what their facility has to offer. Similarly, it is important to look at the marketplace and the competition if you are entering a new international market. Talk to the potential customers and see if they would be interested in your products. Two examples demonstrate this issue. One of the best selling shoes in Mexico was going to be produced in Mexico and sold in the United States. Unfortunately, the product just wouldn't take off in the U.S., and they couldn't figure out why until one day an American told the importer that American's are offended by shoes with the name "Jesus Boots." Similarly, General Motors started to import their compact car into Mexico. They were having extreme difficulty selling the car which had been extremely popular in the United States. It was only later that they realized that "Nova", which in Spanish means "no go", wasn't an appropriate name for a vehicle in the Mexican market.

Information

There are some excellent sources of information with maps and international statistics. One of my personal favorites is the CIA database at: http://www.odci.gov/cia/publications/factbook/country-frame.html

Another is the Organization of Economic Co-Operation and Development at: http://www.oecd.org/

There is a network of Universities that are part of a CIBER (Center for International Business Education and Research) each of which can be very helpful. For example, the MSU (Michigan State University) CIBER (http://www.ciber.bus.msu.edu/) supplied the information on some of the charts in this chapter. If you do a web search on CIBER you will be able to find most of these databases. Start at: http://www.ciber.centers.purdue.edu/

Other excellent contacts are:
International Studies Association
Brigham Young University
316 Herald R. Clark Bldg.
Provo, UT 84602
801-378-5459.

US AID
Development Experience Clearinghouse/Document Distribution Unit
1611 N. Kent Street
Suite 200
Arlington, Virginia 22209-2111
Fax: 703-351-4039
Email: docorder@dec.cdie.org.

Z, Inc. Off To Mexico

The CEO took the proposal to the Board of Directors, and based on the numbers provided by the VP Operations, they approved the relocation of the factory. Plans were made to pack the plant up and relocate it to central Mexico. The location had an excellent and available work force and a facility could be constructed in six months. It was estimated that there would be approximately six months revenue loss, but the production department was gearing up to build an inventory of six months supply. Hopefully, this would service the Michigan customers until the new Mexican plant was in full swing. The plan was as follows:

6 months	build the new facility in Mexico
	double the sifts to build a 6 month inventory supply of finished goods
2 months	transfer all the machines from Michigan to Mexico
1 month	complete the Mexican setup and start production.

Two months into the process, the VP Operations learned that construction on the Mexican plant had not even begun. He became concerned because the shut-down and move had already been scheduled and now the Mexican plant would not be ready on time.

Where does he go from here? What would you do?

Summary

Internationalization involves a change in personalities and culture. It involves jumping out of the box and rethinking all previous assumptions. It involves expecting and attacking challenges. It involves the competitive future and success of your organization. So where do we go from here? The first step is to figure out where your going – to set goals. And that is what the next chapter is all about.

Class Assignments

These are assignments that I use in my classes and have found them extremely beneficial in strengthening the background of the students:

Assignment A [1]

Country Analysis Project – give a five minute class presentation on a country of choice discussing location, population, ethnic makeup, religion, currency, language (including how to say hi), topography, climate, industrial make-up. Country and presentation day must be signed up for so that there aren't any duplications.

The objective of this assignment is to provide you with experience in collecting and analyzing information on a foreign market. You will be expected to examine a country or a regional market, noting among other things:

1. This case was originally the work of Brent Wilson of Brigham Young University but it was later adopted and modified by the author for use in his own classes.

- market demographics – population distribution, literacy, geographic location and size, resource endowment, etc.
- economic and business climate
- political events and developments
- social, cultural, and intellectual trends

This is a market analysis study, not a geography paper. You are expected to analyze the data that you collect and reach conclusions about trade, investment, operations, and other business opportunities. You may select any country or regional market – geographically related group of countries – that may be of interest to you. The only restriction is that you must select a country other than your home country.

Suggested Outline

I. Summary and conclusions
   You should cite specific points and conclusions based on your research and analysis. You could include page references to specific sections of your report.

II. Description of the country or market
   A. Demographic data
      1. Population – age and geographic distribution
      2. Family size
      3. Health and literacy
      4. Religion
   B. Economic environment
      1. Gross national product
      2. Per capita national income and distribution
      3. Sources of employment
      4. Balance of trade and payments
      5. Foreign exchange rates and trends
      6. Government fiscal and monetary policies
      7. Interest rates
   C. Political environment
      1. Political environment and requirements for foreign investment

2. Political stability and risks
3. Security of foreign-owned assets
4. Protection of intellectual property – patents, copyrights, and trademarks
5. Repatriation of earnings
6. Legal system and regulatory environment

D. Social, cultural or intellectual trends that affect foreign trade or investment

1. Racial and/or sexual discrimination
2. Life styles
3. Aesthetics
4. Product preferences

E. Trade, investment, and export opportunities

1. Acquisitions
2. Mergers
3. Joint-ventures
4. Wholly-owned foreign investments
5. Export market

Sources of information

The following references include useful information about many different countries. You should not limit yourself to only these sources. This list is intended to provide you with a starting point for your research. Other references were given throughout the chapter. Using an internet search engine, look for any of the following terms:

- *Balance of Payments Statistics*
- *Business International (several geographic series)*
- *Business Periodical Index*
- *Demographics Yearbook*
- *Demographic Yearbook – Population Census Statistics*
- *Europa Yearbook and World Survey*
- *International Financial Statistics*
- *Lexis/Nexis Data Base*
- *Nikkei Telecom Data Base [Hihon Keizai Shimbun]*
- *OECD Indicators of Industrial Activity*
- *OECD Main Economic Indicators*

- *PC Globe [Electronic Atlas]*
- *Population Index*
- *Statistical Office of the European Community*
- *Statistical Yearbook: Annual Statistics*
- *UNESCO Statistical Yearbook*
- *World Almanac & FactBook*
- *World Economic Outlook*
- *World Statistics in Brief*
- *World Trade Annual*
- *Year-book of Labour Statistics.*

Statistical yearbooks for some specific countries, such as Japan, Germany, and the United States, are available. You should also research general business publications, such as Business Week and The Economist, as well as more regional or country oriented publications, such as Europe, China Business Review, and Korea Business World.

General Comments

It is unlikely that you will find all of the data that you might like. You may also find that the available data is not as current as you might like. Keep in mind that the purpose of the report is for you to analyze the country. Your analysis is more important than the timeliness of the data. If you can't locate the relevant data and need to make some assumptions, clearly identify what your assumptions are.

The important elements of the country analysis report are your analysis and conclusions. You must explain the implications of the information that you are presenting. Merely citing the data is not sufficient.

Provide citations as appropriate. You may use either footnotes or endnotes. Avoid using direct quotations except when citing a recognized authority or when paraphrasing a citation would lessen its impact. You should include a bibliography of the sources of information that you used in preparing your report. The quality of the bibliography will also be considered in grading.

Assignment B

Company visit - This is a team project where you visit a company and study it's international operations, and then report on it through an oral presentation and a paper. You are expected to organize a team (4 to 8 persons). This team will be expected to tour a company in the area. The team is expected to contact, tour, and study the international operations environment of the company. They are to investigate what tools are being used and how they are being used (this should include the highlighting of areas where the tools are successful and where they have failed). The project is to be presented to the class in a 15 minute overview by at least two members of the team. Evaluations will be done by the class members. The project is also to be turned in in written form (maximum 15 pages) by the team.

Visit (in detail):

a) select a company
b) call the international marketing or production/operations department and discuss your project with them to see if they will work with you
c) setup a tour and interview
d) meet with the appropriate managers as a team
e) interview an international representative who can tell you about the financial, marketing and operations systems that exist within the organization (as a team)
f) ask the following questions:

What are the differences between the way you do business domestically and internationally, with respect to:

- marketing
- finance / trade / investment / banking / monetary systems
- operations
- logistics
- government involvement – political forces
- ethical considerations
- unions
- cultural

- human relations
- strategy and goal development
- environmental considerations (or lack of)
- trade barrier / trading block effects
- infrastructure considerations
- education and training
- topography / climate considerations

What countries are you involved with? Why? What are the strategic considerations / advantages?

Offer some successful and unsuccessful examples of international involvement with respect to your company.

How does your company treat ex-patriot employees differently?

g) outline of the team paper – make sure you relate it to the material covered in this class

1. Introduction

- name of company and location (address)
- historical background
- names and titles of key people
- size of facility
- number of employees
- diary of contact activity – be sure you include a recommendation
- indicating if you consider this company good for future visits (name, date, title, phone #)

2. Analysis of Functional Areas
3. Recommendations for Future Improvement

h) comments

- a paper is expected from the team
- all contacts with the company are to be done as a team
- the final papers will not be returned to the students

j) presentation 15 to 20 minutes by at least 2 members of the team. Include a brief overview of the company, the systems they are using, and whether they find them effective or not (do not insert any of your opinions here, that is for the paper – educate the class about your company.

Assignment C

Geography Test - There is a geography test which will be taken from the text, lecture, or country presentations. Anything discussed up to the point of the test is fair game. The test will focus on country location, population, topography, religion, language, currency, business environment, and climate.

Assignment D

Business Simulation – Several simulators exist around which an excellent case and classroom experience can be developed. For example, one that integrates a variety of business functions into an international setting would be Corporation: A Global Business Simulation by Jerald R. Smith and Peggy A. Golden, Prentice Hall.

References

International Production/ Operations Management References

Chase, Richard B., Nicholas J. Aquilano, F. Robert Jacobs: Production and Operations Management: *Manufacturing and Services,* 8th, Richard D. Irwin; ISBN: 007561278X, 1998.

Golovin, Jonathan J., Achieving Stretched Goals: *Best Practices in Manufacturing for the New Millenium,* Prentice Hall; ISBN: 0133769976, 1997.

Gunn, Thomas G., 21st Century Manufacturing: *Creating Winning Business Performance,* John Wiley & Sons; ISBN: 0471132144, 1995.

Plenert, International Management and Production: *Survival Techniques for Corporate America,* Tab Professional and Reference Books, 1991.

Plenert, Gerhard, "Installing Successful Factories into Developing Countries", *The International Executive,* Vol. 32, No. 2, Sept.-Oct. 1990.

Plenert, Gerhard, "International Industrial Management", *Organizational Development Journal,* Vol. 7, No. 1, Spring 1989.

Plenert, Gerhard, "Requirements for Technology Transfer to Third World Countries" *International Journal of Technology Transfer,* Vol. 13, No. 4, 1997, Pages 421-425.

Plenert, Gerhard, "Production Considerations for Developing Countries", *International Journal of Management,* Dec., 1988.

Schumacher, E. F., *Small is Beautiful,* Harper Perennial, 1989.

International Business References

Daniels and Radebaugh, International Business: *Environments and Operations,* Seventh Edition, Addison-Wesley Publishing, 1995.

Dunung, Sanjyot P.: *Doing Business in Asia – The Complete Guide,* Lexington Books, New York, 1995.

Moran, Robert T., and Jeffrey Abbott, NAFTA: *Managing The Cultural Differences,* Gulf Publishing Company, Houston, 1994.

Management References

Plenert, *World Class Manager,* Prima, Rocklin, CA, 1995.

3. Developing International Goals

Y, Inc.[1]

We'll leave Z, Inc. for a while and introduce you to a new company. Y, Inc. is a producer of plastic silk screen laminate products. They are a five million dollar company with about 100 employees. Their facility is located in central California. They produce plastic stickers like the "Intel Inside" label, automobile and truck dashboards, microwave switch panels, exercise equipment control panels, and the like. These products are not POS (Point of Sale) products and are generally used by other manufacturers in their products. Y, Inc. is considered to be one of the best in the industry. They are ISO and QS certified utilizing SPC and TQM to manage their quality processes. However, Y, Inc. has a problem. Their product is extremely competitive and therefore the margins are relatively low. They need to identify areas for larger profitability or run the risk of going out of business. Their high level of quality, although it is appreciated and expected by the customers, is also not able to generate a higher price in this extremely competitive marketplace.

Y, Inc. has several options. They could:

1) reduce the quality level and thereby reduce cost, making them more of a commodity competitor, or
2) find new, higher margin product lines, or
3) find lower cost production and materials sources.

Option 1 is considered to be unacceptable since this has become a trademark of Y, Inc. Therefore, the focus is on options 2 or 3. Y, Inc. decided to focus on both of these options simultaneously. For

1. Once again this a real company in a real environment.

option 2 they decided to develop an R & D department, previously nonexistent, that searched for new product opportunities. In their search for product ideas they experimented with many options, like Crystal Drops, Offset Printing, and Digital Printing. One of the products they experimented with was electrolumisence (EL). This product allows you to print circuitry and phosphors on a piece of plastic, plug it in, and it gives off light. You could basically replace the florescent bulb with a piece of plastic that has relatively no heat output. Numerous competitors had attempted to work with EL, but had been unsuccessful, primarily because of the extreme quality required and most companies could not meet this standard. Additionally, a level of technical know-how outside of the silk screen business was necessary.

Y, Inc. joined partnership with a Bay Area research firm YV, Inc. who was also interested in EL. YV offered the technical, electrical engineering background that became the basis for the theoretical development of the EL process. They developed prototypes and identified the feasibility of the process. Y focused on the repeatability of the process, since, if the process could not be regularly repeated on a quality basis, it would not be manufacturable. Y ran hundreds of experimental runs attempting to identify the characteristics of the process. They needed to identify how the phosphors' thickness, size, and color determined luminescence levels. They needed to identify levels of voltage, current, and power cycles that optimized results. In the end, they created the ability to lay down posters on plastic that could cyclically light up images. They, in effect, created blinking posters that could be powered by a battery and hung anywhere.

It wasn't long before a great deal of interest was generated by industries like the gaming industry (gambling) and the toy industry. Orders for the EL product started to come in. However, the sales for these products would require capacity far in excess of the ability of this small printer to produce. For example, a Sony or Nintendo gaming pad where one would be placed in every Wal Mart or K-Mart in the United States would generate as much revenue as the total produced volume Y currently has, about $5 million. They were confronted with the issues of growth, expansion, and/or outsourcing of their process. They ran the risk of failing to meet on their order commitments and at the same time they ran the fear of giving away too much of their newly developed process ability by teaching others how to do the process. The risks of both sides had to be carefully balanced.

Margins on the EL product range between 40 to 50 percent, whereas the previous products generated margins of at most 5 percent. Therefore the creation of the R&D center has greatly improved the viability of Y, Inc., as long as the manufacturing capacity issues could be resolved.

Lower cost materials and production sources were also researched. The possibility of using international sources was considered, but it became apparent that the only sources with the level of print quality that was required could only be found in the United States or in Europe. Certifying a vendor became very complicated, because ISO and QS certification were required. And going to Mexico or Asia to find compatible producers carried an extremely high cost of certification because a lot of travel and trial production runs would be required. However, the possibility of using international sources for raw materials, like plastics, inks, electronic controllers, or the mounting metals, became a realistic option.

Y, Inc., has a problem. They have been running on the verge of financial disaster for some time. Now they have a product, the EL product line, that has the potential of making them extremely successful and profitable. However, they need cash flow to drive the investment that is necessary for them to expand their production facility. Additionally, the developmental costs of the EL product have not been totally paid, and the creditors are banging on the doors. Add to that the fact that there are still more costs that need to be incurred to finalize the characteristic curves that are being developed. Y, Inc. has waited too long in it's product life cycle, and is now in a mature and declining market for all of it's products except the EL product. It's core business is dealing with extremely low margins causing it's profits to be low. At this point they need additional cash to develop this new EL opportunity. They are between a rock and a hard spot – you're the consultant – what would you recommend?

X, Inc.[2]

We'll leave Y, Inc. and Z, Inc. for a while and introduce you to a new Company. X, Inc., is an international rebuilder of automotive components, like alternators and starters. They have plants in Thailand, Malaysia, England, and at several locations in the United States. They have a major centralized distribution center in the United States where they receive old alternators and starters, ship them to the appropriate production location, rebuild the part, return it to the distribution center, and then ship it to the appropriate car-parts outlets throughout the United States. The facility in Malaysia was struggling. They have a major competitor in the area that has approximately the same number of employees, yet their competitor's production rate is about twice that of X, Inc. Here are the major issues:

1) The defect rate is about 15 %.
2) Employee turnover is large for the industry.
3) On-time customer delivery service rates are poor.
4) Cycle time is several weeks for a product whose run time is less than one hour.
5) Customer complaints are up significantly.
6) Inventory balance is over $ 1 million.
7) Volume throughput is poor compared to competitors.

X, Inc. is confused about it's options. They have decided to bring in an external consultant to help them review their problems. The consult came in and took a tour of their production facility. He had the CEO watch one of the employees and asked the CEO to mentally evaluate the value added contribution of the employees involved in the process. The instructions were:

Watch the employee for a while, without them realizing they are being observed, and evaluate how much of their time is spent adding value. Adding value is defined as doing something that transforms the product and increases it's overall $ value. Non-value-adding includes things like moving or positioning the part, setup

2. Just like in the case of Y, Inc. this is a real company in a real invironment.

processes, and paperwork. The CEO was impressed to learn that about 80 percent of the employee's time was spent on non-value-adding activities. The CEO was so thrilled by this little bit of insight that he asked the consultant to head up a quality improvement program. The consultant decided that in order to improve quality, he would first like to work in the production area in order to see how production was done and how the work flow was accomplished. He spent about two weeks working with the employees on the floor. After this time, he went to the CEO and received approval to run some training programs. The employees were excited about these programs and ended up with a better understanding of what the goals of the organization were, and how these goals should be accomplished.

After the training, the employees were excited about the contribution that a quality improvement program could make, and they wanted to get started. They understood that volume could not be used to drive quality. With the current pressures of a volume measurement system, the best they could do was to measure quality and inspect it after-the-fact. This process is labeled a "quality control" system. They learned that if you focused on quality first, you could learn how to do a process correctly. Then you could learn how to do this correct process faster and faster. The result was that: Volume can never drive Quality, but Quality can be used to drive Volume. The result of this understanding was a cultural shift for the organization, a shift that moved it's focus away from volume and refocused on a "quality management" system.

A one week "quality week" was declared where the plant was basically shut down. The employees were instructed that they could do anything they wanted, change any machine or process in any way desired. The only rule was that they could not produce any bad parts. Only good parts were allowed. The employees were empowered to organize teams and were offered rewards for the implementation of successful changes.

"Quality week" was kicked off with a bang. Managers had to move out of the way because employees were excitedly running around doing things that they had always wanted to try. However, more importantly, this quality week initiated a new culture at X. This was a quality culture focused on a TQM continuous improvement program. The employees were excited.

The CEO of the Malaysia plant was so excited about what was happening that he wanted the entire organization to consider implementing similar programs. He encouraged the corporate officers to bring the consultant to their office and discuss how these quality strategies could be implemented company-wide. He felt that these strategies should be part of the corporate-wide goal structure of X, Inc. However, he was met with resistance. He received an arrogance like; "What does a plant manager from some remote location like Malaysia really know about the needs of the corporate office, let alone the rest of the company." The Malaysian CEO went home to his plant and talked to the consultant.

"What can we do to help them understand?" he asked.

"Perhaps the best thing we can do is to dazzle them with performance results," replied the consultant. "Let's run the program for six months and see what the operational statistics show."

Now you're the consultant. What would you do?

Setting Goals

Goal setting is the basis of any business process. Unfortunately, most goal setting is done in less than ideal ways. For example, often a company will set goals at the top of the management structure and exclude the input of most of the other areas of an organization, especially the international divisions. It is assumed that these areas are too distant and therefore out of touch with the corporate culture. Sometimes goals are created and then not communicated to all levels of the organization because it is felt that this information should be confidential and reserved for top management only.

The one thing that is missing from most goal-setting processes is "ownership." It is not enough to just be involved in the goal development process. Involvement leaves the participants the opportunity to say they don't totally agree with the results. Ownership means that the participants feel an integrated involvement in the goal. Without ownership in the goals, it will be difficult for employees to feel committed to their successful achievement. Without proper goal communication through all levels and areas of an organization, it will be impossible for the divisions to develop measurement systems that are focused on goal achievement. This becomes especially important in the area of Operations Management. It is primarily the operations organization that needs to be focused on goal achievement. The operations area is the most directly involved in the costs of the organization (labor and materials), the assets of the organization (facilities and equipment), the productivity of the organization, and it's quality performance. Therefore, an organization without properly defined and communicated goals is destined to find itself in operational disaster.

One of the first and foremost goals that an organization needs to set is the goal to change. Any organization that is not focused on continuous improvement, thereby constantly focusing on new ways to eliminate waste and increase value-added, will become noncompetitive within a short time. As we saw in the case of Y, Inc., they were not focused on change, which, in their case involved the development of new product ideas. They found themselves trapped with low-margin commodity products that couldn't offer enough cash flow to support the company.

Chart 3.1 shows the Change Function. With this we see that changes have both a short term and long term effect. In the short term, change creates a disturbance to the status-quo, and therefore causes a loss of performance. Some form of negative efficiency occurs. This reduced performance effect decays over a period of time. It is important for us to evaluate both the amount of the negative disturbance (cost), and the term of it (how long it lasts). Can our organization sustain the down-turn in performance over the period of time required. For example, the implementation of a new computer system slows everyone down, causes double data entry for a time, has conversion and new equipment costs, and has a learning curve associated with it. We need to measure the cost of this implementation and determine if the company can sustain the cost of the downturn over the period of time required.

In the long term, the change function offers a gain in performance which offsets the cost of the short term loss. Additionally, the long term increase in performance is designed to make us both more efficient and more competitive. Unfortunately, not all change results in a long term positive effect. In the event that the long term performance generates a level of performance that is lower than before the change, it may be necessary to redo the change to the prior methodology. There is only one guarantee, and that is if you don't continuously look for improvements, you'll lose the competitive battle.

Chart 3.1. Change Function

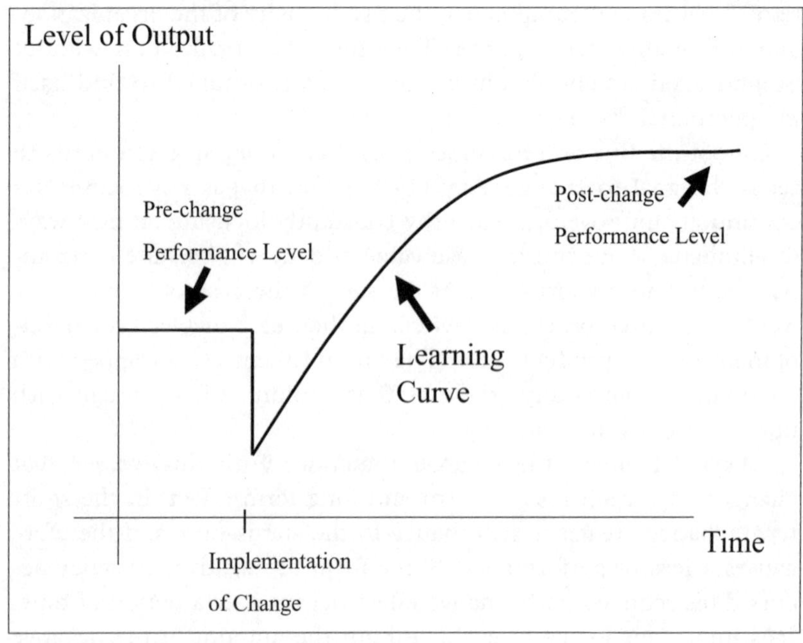

The Goal-Setting Process

Since goals are critical to operations management performance, especially in an international setting, we will quickly review the World Class goal setting process. Then we will show how these goals should be operationalized for effective World Class Manufacturing performance. The goal setting process requires the following fundamental steps:

Values Definition

This first step is where a company defines what it stands for. This is the first critical piece that requires cross-the-board participation. What you hope to create is a "values based company" where all members of the corporate community agree on acceptable levels of conduct, like a process for handling conflict, a way for dealing with customers, etc. These values become the non-compromisable basis for the operation of the organization and for the development of all the rest of the goals of the company.

In the case of Y, Inc., the values that were cooperatively agreed upon are:

Balance	Charity	Confidence
Creativity	Empathy	Family
Friendship	Harmony	Health
Humor	Integrity	Justice
Faithness	Listening	Love, Joy
Happiness	Passion	Patience
Respect	Self-reliance	Spirituality
Teamwork	Trust	Uniqueness

Another example of values are:

Principal Financial Group

• Customer Service Quality Strength Integrity

Pet Incorporated

- Ethics and compliance with all applicable laws
- Consumer and customer driven in the development and delivery of all products and services
- Good citizenship in all the communities where we have operations
- Company-wide continuous improvement activities using team approach
- The development and training of our employees
- An environment which supports the creativity and initiative of all our employees
- Equal opportunities for all employees
- Fulfillment of our commitment – what we say we do, we do do.

These examples demonstrate that there is no one correct format for values, but that values do become the basis of future goal development. As stated by Robert Haas, CEO of Levi Strauss & Co., "A company's values – what it stands for, what it's people believe in – are critical to its competitive success."

Core Competency

In this goal-setting step we are attempting to identify what we are better at than anyone else. What is it that makes us unique? What is our competitive advantage? What is it we should exploit for strategic success? There are two tools that are helpful in the development and definition of the core competency. These tools are used as well in all the later steps of the goal setting process.

The two tools are the SWOT Analysis and the Competitive Position Analysis. In the SWOT Analysis we utilize a cross-functional team of individuals in a brain-storming environment to search out the **S**trengths of the company, it's **W**eaknesses and shortcomings which later become opportunities for improvements, the **O**pportunities of the organization, and last of all the **T**hreats to the success of the company. These are the four SWOT elements and after the SWOT Analysis you would have generated a long list of ideas for strategic development.

The Competitive Position Analysis focuses on the competitive environment under which you operate. It involves taking a look at who your competitors are and what their strengths and weaknesses are. It also focuses on the demands of the market place, looking for areas that have not been serviced and that may offer strategic advantages.

The Core Competency, a statement of what you're good at, is then developed by carefully looking at these two tools. In the case of Y, Inc., the core competency is: Design, marketing, and manufacturing solutions using screen-printing technologies for diverse industries and applications. Some other examples of core competencies are:

- Sony – miniaturization
- Canon – optics, imaging, and microprocessor controls
- Honda – engines and power trains

Vision Statement

The vision statement is a short phrase that expresses the long term objectives of an organization keeping in mind the values and core competencies of the organization. For example, Y, Inc.'s Vision Statement is: We Profit By Thrilling Our Customers! Other excellent examples of vision statements include:

- Walt Disney – To Make People Happy.
- Steve Jobs, Apple Computer – To make a contribution to the world by making tools for the mind that advance mankind
- Pepsi Co. – Beat Coke
- Honda – We will crush, squash, slaughter Yamaha!

"Where there is no vision, the people perish." Proverbs 29:18

Mission Statement

The mission statement brings the time-line in a little closer. It is usually designed to be an achievable, measurable goal with about a five to ten year time-frame. It should be challenging, but reachable, and it should focus on the vision of the company. The best example of a mission statement comes from President John F. Kennedy in 1962 which is: "... achieving the goal, before this decade is out, of landing a man on the moon and returning him safely to earth". This statement had all the characteristics necessary of an excellent mission statement around which a strategy could be developed with a specific, measurable, time-line.

The mission statement of Y, Inc. is: Y, Inc. is the premier source of custom and proprietary products and services in the screen printing industry. We meet and exceed our customers' standards for quality and service. We deliver on time and defect free.

Strategic Initiatives

With the mission in place, it is now necessary to put some meat behind the big, glowing words. It is now necessary to detail a step-by-step process which will lead to the achievement of the mission. The first step in this process is the development of the strategic initiatives. These initiatives are five to ten statements that are focused on the mission, but which will help various parts of the organization focus, in more detail, on goal achievement. For example, the strategic initiatives ofY, Inc. are:

1) Quality and safety defines our culture.
2) Y will profitably generate $ 25,000,000 in revenue in the year 2002.
3) Y will be the premier employer in the county.
4) Y customers recognize us as the defined standard of excellence.
5) R & D is developing technology that produces 20% of our revenue growth yearly.

Each strategic initiative should be a measurable, time stampable identifier of success. It is also important that each step can be detailed by year so that a step-by-step strategy can be developed. In

Strategic Priorities	**Identity**
1) Quality and Safety defines our culture	• Quality – TQM, ISO, QS, Leaderful • Organisation, Delivery, Cycle Time Management • Malcolm Baldrige, Shingo Awards • Safety Award
2) Y will profitably generate $ 25,000 in revenue in the year 2002	• Custom and Proprietary Products • Value Added Processes and Services • Bell Account / Market Leader Focus • International
3) Y will be the premier employer in the County	• Value Based Team Culture • Compensation and Benefits Package that Exceeds Industry Standards • Community Involvement
4) Y customers recognize us as the defined standard of excellence	• Marketing Solutions • Strategic Alliances • Time Sensitive Supply Chain Management • Rapid Prototyping • Customer Relations Systems
5) R&D is developing technology that produces 20% of our revenue growth yearly	• Flexible Circuitry & Electronics • Process, Product and Proprietary • Technology • Development

the development of a strategy, Y, Inc. developed a list of identity areas which became the focus areas for the development of the detailed strategy. These areas had to be covered in order for the strategy to be considered complete.

With the identities defined, we can now proceed with the detailed strategy development.

The Detailed Strategy

Each of the strategic initiatives needs to have a strategic plan developed around it. The detailed strategy looks out year-by-year over the next five to ten years, whatever the time frame of the strategic initiatives is, and looks at all the operational areas determining how they will be effected on a year-by-year basis. The focus is always on the accomplishment of the strategic initiative. In a World Class model for strategic development we have the traditional focus areas for strategic development:

- Marketing Strategy
- Production Strategy
- Finance Strategy

Slightly more advanced and sophisticated models would include:

- Quality Strategy
- Productivity Strategy

A World Class Strategy would incorporate issues like:[3]

People:

- First Employees
    - Education and Training
    - Empowerment
    - Teamwork
    - Organizational Structure, Staff Functions
- Then Customers
    - Involvement

3. This is taken from Chapter 4 of *World Class Manager* by Gerhard Plenert.

- Then Vendors
  - Integration

Integration:
- Elimination of barriers
  - Information
- Globalization

Measurement:
- Internal Performance
  - Quality, Productivity, Efficiency
- External Performance
  - Are you adding value to society?
  - Customer perceived quality
  - Market Share
- Internal Factors
  - Capacity
  - Equipment
  - Operational Performance
- External Factors
  - Competition
  - Economic Conditions
  - Government Regulation
- Focused
- Motivational

Continuous Change Process focused on Adding Value:
- Elimination of Waste
  - Identifying Strengths and Weaknesses
- Identifying Opportunities and Threats
- Time-Based Competition: Time to Market Strategy

Technology:
- Funding
- Facilities and Equipment

World Class strategies focus on World Class competitiveness. Some of the competitive trends that need to be considered for the next decade include:

1. Rapid Change in Technology and Markets
2. More Competitors Globally
3. An Increased Emphasis on Globalization
4. An Invironmental Consciousness
5. Decentralization
6. Shrinking Company Sizes (Strategic Alliances)
7. Closer Links to Customers and Suppliers
8. A Competitive Emphasis on Cost Reduction
   Customer Oriented Quality Improvement
   A Stronger Priority on Flexibility, and
   Time-to-Market Responsiveness
9. Borderless Companies: Removal of Departmentalization.

Some of the key principles of World Class Competitiveness include:

- Focus on the People (Primary Employees)
- Focus on the Customer
- A Quality and Productivity Stance
- A Global Perspective
- Time-Based Competition
- A Technological Orientation
- Information Management
- An Integrative Stance
- Focused Measurement
- A Value-Added Decision Approach
- Continuous Training and Education.

The development of the detailed strategy is quite time consuming and should involve the efforts of employees throughout the organization. This is critical in developing "ownership" of the goals. Only with full participation can we be assured of this ownership and thereby success. After the development of the initial strategy, we break it down into more detail at the lower levels of the organization. Each of these lower-level strategies is also a detailed plan focused on the strategy developed at the level above it, and it attempts to compliment and successfully implement the higher-level strategy.

Divisional or lower-level Strategy Development

Once the corporate strategy has been developed, the lower-level divisions need to follow this same process for each of their areas. They need to focus on the corporate strategy and identify how they plan to execute their piece of the over-all strategy. This is an important step in getting ownership and buy-in at all levels of the organization. This also helps the various divisions think out their piece of the overall strategy.

Plan of Operation

The current year of the strategy is operationalized and placed into a budgeting process. Everyone knows their own piece of the over-all process. Now they bring in the next year of the over-all strategic plan and put this information into budgets. From this they develop measures of performance. These goals can be scrutinized carefully to make sure they are feasible for the current year of operation.

The Measurement Processes

Two axioms are important in operations management. They are:

1) The function of a measurement system is to motivate a particular response, not to collect data for the information or accounting systems!
2) You motivate what you measure.

In Western manufacturing processes we often find an extensive amount of lip service being given to quality. However, when we look at the measurement system of an organization, we see no element of quality. For example, Signetics Corporation invited me into their Provo, Utah plant for a visit. They had been slated for closure and the reason cited was a lack of quality. However, this plant had some of the most sophisticated quality systems in existence. They had ISO, SPC, 6-Sigma, TQM, and on and on. Management felt frustrated that none of these systems were working. I was asked to figure out what went wrong.

The Signetics situation was typical of so many Western facilities.

On the production floor they measured volume throughput. Employees were paid a bonus on the number of parts produced. They were trained in quality, had lots of meetings on quality, had posters all over the facility that discussed quality, but were measured on volume. So they produced volume. If they wanted quality, they needed to measure quality performance. Similarly, if you want to accomplish your strategic initiative, don't measure the number of stars in the sky (or any other unrelated issue).

Developing an effective and appropriate measurement system can take an extensive amount of careful effort. You'll quickly learn that the wrong measurement system will definitely generate the wrong results. The measurement / motivation relationship will be discussed again later in this chapter after a discussion of the critical resource.

Forecasting and Developing a Rough Cut Capacity

With the Plan of Operation in place, we have the details necessary for defining a Forecast and a Rough Cut Capacity. The forecast defines the sales demand that is anticipated. From this we can define the demands that will be placed on the organization's resources. The Rough Cut Capacity is a look at the availability of the organization's resources. This information also comes from the Plan of Operation since resource changes are defined in this plan. With this information about the availability and the demand on resources, we can take the next step which is to balance the two. This process will be detailed in Chapter 5.

Characteristics of Good Goals

All goals are not good goals. For example, if they are impossible to achieve, they will be more discouraging than helpful. On the other hand, if they are set too low and are achieved too easily, then we are not experiencing all the competitive growth that we should be engaged in. A good target should be realistic and attainable. A good set of goals would have as many as possible of the following characteristics:

1) Participatively created by and matched to the personal goals of the employees – this offers goal ownership
2) Shared with all employees so they can participate in their achievement
3) Nonconflicting goals – as will be seen later in this chapter, a volume goal conflicts with a profit or a quality goal and a balance needs to be developed
4) Allows for and encourages change throughout the organization
5) Simple but not simplistic
6) Precise – short, sweet, and to the point
7) Measurable
8) Uncompromised – we need to be committed to the achievement of the goal
9) Focused on as narrow a target as possible so as to avoid confusion or misinterpretation
10) Achievable yet challenging.

Operationalizing the Goals

The next step in our discussion would have us focus on operationalizing our goals. This will be done in the following steps:

- Discuss how the goal targets a specific critical resource
- Demonstrate how each of the goals focuses can target a different critical resource
- Show how the critical resource influences operational performance
- Show how this effects and defines the measurement system

We need to start this discussion by defining what a critical resource is. There are numerous resources that an industrial operation utilizes. Traditionally, we have strictly focused our resource planning on the three M's:

- Materials
- Manpower
- Machinery

A more complete and expanded list of resources would include:

- Traditional:
  - Materials
  - Labor
  - Machinery
  - Burden / Overhead

- Financial:
  - Capital
  - Debt

- Infrastructure:
  - Energy
  - Communications
  - Roadways
  - Education System

- External:
  - Vendors
  - Customers
  - Governmental
  - Political Environment

- Internal:
  - Facilities
  - Energy
  - Maintenance
  - Unions
  - Level of Automation / Technology
  - Management Style
  - Resource Dependence
  - Design / Engineering

- Other:
  - Plant Location
  - Economic Potential

We need to evaluate the value-added contribution of each of these resources toward goal achievement. Tools like Activity Based Costing (ABC) are excellent in this evaluation, particularly if we are focusing on financial goals. For example, Cadillac, a recent Baldrige Award winner,[4] made a presentation at an awards conference.[5] Chart 3.2 shows a chart that was presented which demonstrates the change of focus that they made as an organization. Down the left side is a list of some of their key resources (summarized). Across the top is their old and new focus. The old focus demonstrates their resource priorities under a financial goal of increased profits. The new focus demonstrates their resource priorities under a goal of customer satisfaction.

Chart 3.2. A Shift in Priorities for Cadillac

	Old	**New**
Design Costs	5%	70%
Material Costs	50%	20%
Labor Costs	15%	5%
Burden Costs	30%	5%
Old Goal – profitability		
New Goal – Customer satisfaction		

Under Cadillac's old goal of profitability, material costs had the strongest resource influence on goal achievement. Under Cadillac's new goal of customer satisfaction, the design and engineering resource had the greatest influence. Cadillac modified their planning and control system, and the corresponding measurement systems to stress engineering issues, with materials issues as secondary, rather than materials issues as primary with burden issues as secondary.

How did Cadillac come up with these percentages? The first column (old), is easy to calculate. These numbers come from the profit

4. The Baldrige Award is the national award for exellence in manufacturing. It looks for improvement in the areas of productivity and quality. To get more information about the Baldrige Award, or other national manufacturing awards, contact the American Productivity and Quality Center (APQC) in Houston, Texas.
5. Partners in Business Conference, Logan, Utah, 1991.

and loss statement and the ratios are calculated based on total costs. A better method would be to use Activity Based Costing to detail the resource contributions. Calculating the second column is a little trickier. It required a survey mechanism. Cadillac went out and asked their customers which of these components was the most important in the way the customer perceived quality. Cadillac was determined to get the customer's feeling for priorities. Here is an example of the questions asked in the survey.

What is the most important in the seat of a Cadillac:

a) comfortably designed seats (engineering)
b) expensive upholstery on the seats (materials)
c) hand sewn seat covers (labor)

A series of questions like this will give you a feel for what is the most important to the customer. From this survey you can then formulate a list similar to the "new" list in Chart 3.2. If you are surveying people, don't survey them with a resource list that covers more than five or six categories. They'll soon get tired of it. Do an initial survey to find out where the customer's preferences lie. Then, a later survey can be used to determine a more detailed breakdown of the most important and influential category.

If you are focusing on employee-based goals, you need to do the same type of survey process that you did with a customer-based goal. But, instead of surveying the customers, you survey the employees and ask them what is important.

You now have a list of resources and you have percentages of contributed importance attached to each. The next step is to ABC (Pareto Principle) classify these resources.[6] The "A" Items are the 80 percent contributors. In the Cadillac financial environment, the "A" contributors are Material Costs and Burden Costs. In the Cadillac Customer Oriented environment, the "A" contributor is

6. We have two processes, each of which is referred to as ABC. This first is Activity Based Costing which is an accounting tool for identifying detailed costs based the activities involved in a process. The second is ABC Analysis which is also referred to as Pareto Principle or the 80-20 Rule. This tool claims that 20 percent of the items generate 80 percent of the activity. Both of these topics are covered in detail in a basic Operations Management Textbook.

Design Costs. These are our critical resources, and we need to operationalize a plan around these critical resources.

At this point we have:

- discussed how the goal targets a specific critical resource
- demonstrated how each of the goal focuses can target a different critical resource.

Now we will:

- show how the critical resource influences operational performance
- show how this effects and defines the measurement system.

Recent research has demonstrated that: *increasing productivity can decrease profitability.* This can be demonstrated if we look at an example model of only two resources, labor and machinery. This can be done by comparing any pair of resources. If, for example, we determine that labor is our critical resource, then we need to make labor as productive and efficient as possible. We want to keep labor busy at all times, and we do this by buffering it with other, non-critical resources like materials and machinery. We would keep machinery readily available, and we would stock plenty of materials, so that employees always have enough to work on. Therefore, we buffer labor efficiency with materials and machine inefficiency.

Similarly, if we identify materials as the critical resource, as in the example of a JIT production environment, we would line up all the workers next to eachother in the sequence in which the production process normally occurs. The objective would be to have materials start at one end and be constantly worked on until it drops off at the other end as a finished product. Similar to the previous environment, we find that not all employees in the production sequence have the same amount of work. Some will be sitting around part of the time, because the speed of the line will be determined by the slowest process in the line. Therefore, we are buffering the materials' critical resource by inefficiencies in the labor and machine resource.

These examples demonstrate that: increases in the productivity of one resource may cause inefficiencies and loss of productivity in other resources. With these realizations, we can now look at an example of how the mismanagement of the critical resource can decrease profitability. Using the Cadillac financial goal focused example of Chart 3.2, we see that the materials resource is a 50% contributor to the value-added content and the labor resource is a 15% contributor. If, in this example, we increase the productivity of labor, by 2%, and this costs us a loss in productivity of materials of 3/4%, we would see the effect in Chart 3.3. Total cost went up and therefore profitability went down, in spite of the fact that we increased productivity. Therefore, increasing productivity decreased profitability, or, more specifically, increasing the productivity of a non-critical resource can damage over-all profitability if the critical resource is effected adversely as a result of this increase.

Chart 3.3. Increasing Labor Productivity

	Before Productivity Increase	**Productivity Change**	**After Productivity Increase**
Design Costs	5%		5%
Material Costs	50%	¾% * 50 = .375	50.375%
Labor Costs	15%	-2% * 15 = -.3	14.7%
Burden Costs	30%		30%
Totals	100%		100.075%

Interestingly, when Cadillac was struggling with a lack of profitability under the financial model, they were using a labor efficiency based productivity program. Since labor is less than 15 % of the value-added cost, and since labor efficiency adversely effects materials efficiency, it is easy to see why they were losing profitability. Another interesting point, in the Cadillac financial model, is the high level of burden at 30 %. About half of this burden cost pays for the financing cost of asset investments. The majority of the asset investment is the financing of inventories. Therefore, the true materials cost when loaded with inventory financing costs, should be closer to 65 %, rather than the stated 50 %.

This problem is not unique to Cadillac. In as recently as the 1950's, labor was about 50 % of the value-added content of a manufactured product with materials and overhead (burden) having about 25 % each. By 1990, material had broken the 50 % mark and averaged about 60 % of the value-added content of most products (and even more if you include the inventory financing costs that are buried in burden). Labor ran at about 10 % to 15 %, and the remainder fell into overhead (burden). Therefore, the critical resource has shifted from labor to materials. Unfortunately, the production measurement and planning processes have not changed accordingly. Most companies are still measuring labor performance, and are not measuring inventory performance. In fact, in our accounting structure, labor is recorded as a cost entry which gives it the connotation of being something evil – a bad thing that needs to be eliminated and reduced. Whereas materials is an asset, which is a good thing and something we want more of. Interestingly enough, there are several countries whose accounting systems have these reversed, where labor is an asset, and inventory carried over time is a cost item on the books. This difference in the accounting / measurement system should motivate an entirely different response and a different focus when a down-turn in business occurs. Materials costs would be attacked, rather than labor costs.

Internationally, we find even more variation in the critical resource selection process. We find that the goal structures are different in every part of the world, which in turn causes the critical resource structures to be different. We also find that variations in the labor rates or the material availabilities can effect the selection of the critical resource.

Realizing the important influence that the critical resource has on over-all performance and profitability, we will now look at how to motivate the proper focus on critical resource improvements. To start with, we need to restate the two previous axioms:

1) The function of a measurement system is to motivate a particular response, not to collect data for the information or accounting systems!
2) You motivate what you measure!

Realizing this, we see that in the Cadillac financial model, having a labor efficiency focus can be hurting profitability. They need to move away from the labor efficiency focus to a materials efficiency focus. They literally need to throw out the labor performance reporting process, and institute a measurement system that would get employees to think about inventory efficiencies. For example, pay the employee bonuses based on cycle time reduction, inventory level reductions, or inventory turns increases. They would start measuring and reporting inventory numbers, and would start paying the bonuses based on these numbers rather than the traditional labor efficiency numbers. This shift would be a struggle for most American managers because it says that it is better for an employee to be standing around and doing nothing, rather than to have them building inventories. American managers want their employees busy, but they don't realize that idle inventory can be more costly than idle employees.

International Motivators

In international transactions, it is often assumed that the same things that motivate American employees will also motivate employees of other countries. For example, the most successful motivator in the United States is still money paid out in some form of incentive pay. Prestige awards of various types, like banners, certificates, or trophies, do have some short-term effect, but the most effective, long-term motivation results are still generated by money. This is not true internationally. For example, in Mexico we experienced high absenteeism. We assumed it was because we weren't paying enough and that the more stable employees were working elsewhere, or were supplementing their incomes with part-time jobs. We were surprised to learn that by increasing the pay to the employees, our absenteeism problem actually increased. So we decided to do something innovative; we decided to ask the locals what the situation was. They explained that the average Mexican in this province needed a certain amount of money to survive, and that, when they had achieved that amount of money, their primary interest was in spending time with their family. Paying them more meant that they needed to work less. In order to properly motivate them to work on regular schedules, the greatest influential tool we had would be to offer them opportunities to be with their families more, such as company picnics or activities.

The motivator that worked in this region of Mexico, may not work anywhere else in the world. It doesn't even necessarily work in other parts of Mexico. In countries where the economy is poor or inflation rates are high, the best motivator may come in the form of appliance awards, like refrigerators or TVs. Money becomes worthless too quickly. In other places, such as the island communities or underdeveloped countries, one of the best motivators is to offer benefits for the children of the employees, such as better schooling, better food accessible through a company store, or better medical treatment programs. In some Latin American countries like Brazil, the best motivator might be to organize a winning company soccer team.

Motivators are a "hot button" that need to be properly identified. With the proper motivators, amazing results can be achieved, especially when they are properly focused on a measurement system that keeps the critical resource as it's target.

Defining the Measurement System

In Chapter 1 we started a discussion about some of the tools available for different measurement systems. In the current chapter we have discussed how strong the linkages exist between what is measured and what is motivated. In this section I want to re-simplify the measurement process by stressing that: *measuring too much is no more valuable than measuring nothing because it confuses the motivational signals.*

So how do we select a measurement system? There are some process simplifications that can be applied. For example, in Chapter 5 we will see that the selection of a production planning system and the way a plant is organized should be directly reflective of the critical resource that we are trying to measure. More directly, if we are trying to motivate labor efficiency, then job sheets that report job starts, stops, and volumes are very appropriate. However, if we are interested in materials efficiency, then we should eliminate the time reporting on the job sheets and instead measure inventory levels, cycle time, and scrap rates. If we are interested in quality, we should measure defect performance rates, on-time delivery performance, employee change recommendations, and employee turnover. An excellent collection for World Class areas of performance measurement is found in the Baldrige criteria. This changes from time-to-time so an updated version should be accessed, search the web for Baldrige Award, but the basic award criteria is built around:

- Quality of Products and Services
- Comparison of Quality Results
- Business Process and Operational and Support-Service Quality Improvement
- Supplier Quality Improvement

Often false measures are introduced that claim to be something that they are not. For example, ISO 9000 certification or QS certification claims to be a measure of quality performance. However, these systems are not quality, they are a structure upon which a quality system can be built. They are not, in themselves, a measure of quality. Statistical Process Control (SPC) claims to be a quality system. However, I received a call from a company who said that a consultant had come in and installed SPC about one year ago and they have been collecting data ever since. They were wondering what they should do with all the data. My answer was that they should "throw it out" because SPC is a tool for identifying areas that need continuous, real time, improvement "during the run" rather than just a data collection system. Other companies have found that SPC is an excellent tool for motivation. They set up an SPC system to measure an area that they are trying to motivate better performance in, and then never really do anything with the data.

The measurement process by itself motivates employee interest in the area and the employees make corrections to the process so that the numbers look good. We need to give employees credit for the fact that they can make any number look good, we just have to find the right numbers that we want to see improved. This brings us back to the discussion that motivating performance in a non-Critical Resource area can actually decrease, rather than increase, profitability.

There are several different measurement types and characteristics.[7] These have been categorized by APICS as:

- Financial vs. Non-financial
- Local vs. Global

7. Some of the ideas in this discussion are taken from the APICS CPIM Certification review course on systems and technologies, Chapter 8, which is on measurement. This is an exellence source for more details on the subject of measurement.

- Performance of Process vs. Performance of Worker
- Information vs. Motivation
- Strategic vs. Tactical
- Coordinated vs. Isolated

We have already discussed, in the section about goals, some of the differences between financial and non-financial goals (see also Chapter 1). We have also focused on the need to participatively develop global goals at the corporate level, and then to localize these goals so that they are meaningful and effective at the local level. This is also similar to the issue of strategic vs. tactical goals. Strategic vision, mission, and strategic initiatives need to be developed. Then a tactical level strategy needs to be developed, and this strategy needs to be filtered down and distributed at the divisional levels of the organization where they in-turn develop their own vision, mission, and strategy which is focused on the level above them. The development of lower level strategies will be discussed even further in the next chapter. This issue also addresses the coordinated vs. isolated measures. Measures should be coordinated and integrated in such a way that they focus on the higher level goals. Measures should not be isolated, nor should they be selected based on tradition. Effective measures integrate throughout the organization.

In the area of Performance of the Worker and Performance of the Process, we have discussed the need to focus on the critical resource for measurement. This also suggests that measuring a process performance indicator like cycle time effects many areas, like customer on-time delivery performance, quality, inventory levels, etc., and is therefore more meaningful than "quality units produced by employee."

The discussion of information vs. motivation has been given significant visibility in this chapter. A measurement system should be used to motivate, not as a data collection device.

Some final principles of measurement, again taken from APICS, are:

1. Measurements should focus on strategies and the operational goals of the firm.
2. All measurements should cause the firm to respond in the same direction (i.e., all measurements must be coordinated).

3. Each measure should have a target value, and all targets should be reassessed annually.
4. Local measures should be free to change periodically.
5. Don't confuse process measures with people measures.
6. People at all levels of the firm do better when they choose their own measures (subject to strategy checks).
7. A few well chosen measures are better than many measures – use Pareto's Law.
8. There is a difference between data and information.

An effective measurement system is the key to successfully operationalizing an international strategy. Now we will consider a few operational success stories.

Some Success Stories

The first success story is taken from the book *Maverick* by Ricardo Semler of Semco in Brazil (search the web for both "Semler" and "Semco"). Here is the story of a Harvard trained manager who, after running the business for a period of time, decided he really didn't know what he was doing. He turned the operation of all his factories over to his employees and stood back. His employees made it a booming success story which is well worth while reading. This story demonstrates how successful empowered ownership can be.

Another success story worth reviewing is that of Motorola (web site at mot.com). They followed the Baldrige criteria and required all their vendors to be Baldrige qualifiable (search the web for Baldrige Award). AT&T (go to the web at ATT.com)[8], one of Motorola's vendors, became so serious about the process that they ended up winning two Baldrige awards and a Deming Prize (search the web under "Deming Prize"). This is an interesting story of how one multi-national influenced another multi-national to become world class in their goals.

A third success story worth reviewing is the Fed Ex story where the employees were so empowered and motivated that they had the ability to evaluate and fire their bosses (go to the web at fedex.com). The company's goals focused first on the employees, second on the customers, and third on profits. They constructed a motivation and measurement system that properly stressed these priorities, through the use of surveys and rewards.

Y, Inc. Continued

Y, Inc. has decided that in order to maintain a tighter control of the marketplace, they need to "sew up" the interests of YV, Inc., the research firm. Y is betting so strongly on the success of the EL product that if the cash flow for EL didn't start coming in soon, they would surely fail. The concern is that YV has the R&D technology and has no exclusive contract to deal only with Y. Therefore, if YV gets cold feet in dealing with Y, they could easily find another producer of their product. But, as we remember from the earlier discussion, Y wasn't sure they could handle the volume that the large EL orders would require. Y desperately needed a cash flow source that would strengthen the position that they were in. They could never get the cash out of the core business because the margins were just too low. What should they do?

X, Inc. Continued

X, Malaysia proceeded with it's experiment of a cultural shift towards quality. They monitored performance and paid bonuses based on quality performance for about a six month period. The results were impressive, as can be seen from the charts. These are the real results and they show that the shift in culture dramatically motivated highly efficient quality performance. For example, Chart 3.7 shows a defect rate that was steadily increasing until about November, then you can see a dramatic drop off, and then a steadily decreasing rate of defects. The cultural shift had dramatically effected defect performance. Let me stress that these are the real charts from a real company – not just an invented case. Similarly, in Chart 3.5 we see the steadily decreasing inventory levels. Chart 3.6 shows the improvement on customer complaints. Chart 3.8 shows the on-time delivery improvements. A lot of these issues were related to the cycle time reductions of Chart 3.4. Cycle time reduction means shorter lead times, which means more customer responsiveness, which means that lower inventories levels are needed.

The CEO of the Malaysian facility took this information to the corporate office, as suggested by the consultant. The corporate officers invited the consultant in for a discussion and a presentation. They acted as though they were interested, but after the consultant left, the politics of the X, Inc. quickly killed the project. No one was willing to admit that the plant in Malaysia had outperformed the rest of the organization.

Chart 3.4. Cycle Time Reduction

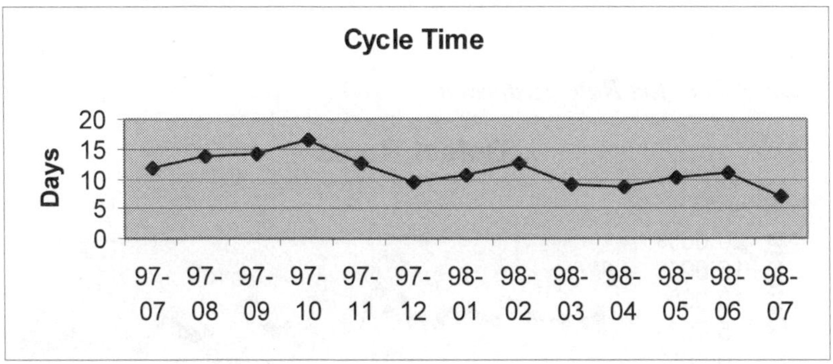

Chart 3.5. Finished Goods Inventory (FGI) Balance Reduction

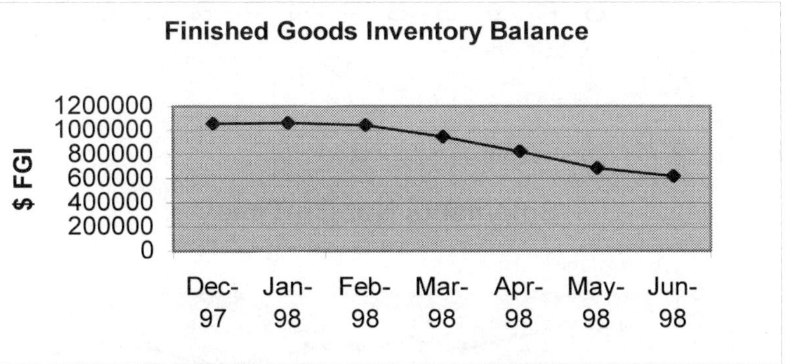

Chart 3.6.Customer Complaints Reduction

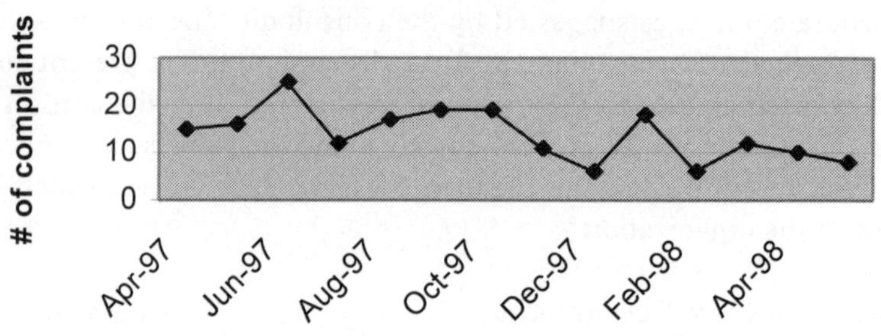

Chart 3.7. Defect Rate Reduction

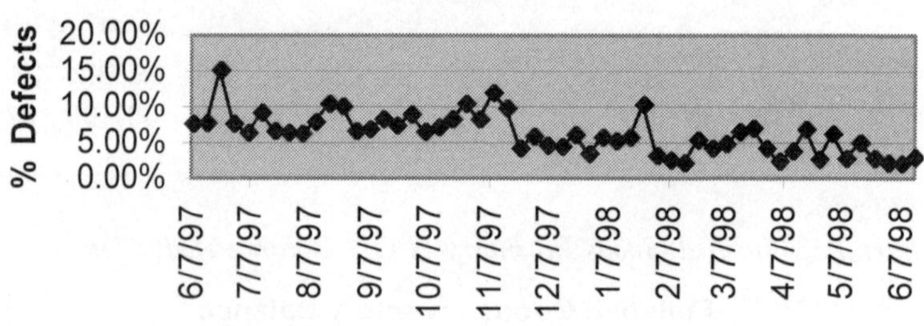

Chart 3.8. On-Time Shipments Improvement

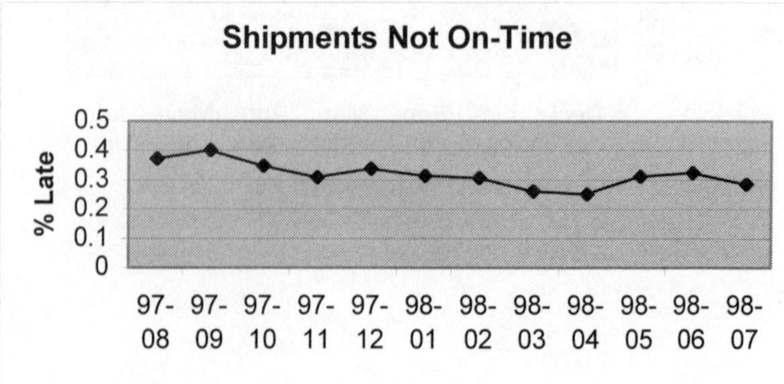

Now you're the CEO of the Malaysian facility. You know what would be best for the company, and you are excited to see this work. What would you do? How would you get around the politics? Formulate your recommendations, and good luck!

Summary

The development of international goals is critical to the successful operational performance of an organization. The steps are:

1) Develop corporate level goals focused on continuous improvement through change processes
2) Values Definition
3) Core Competency
4) Vision Statement
5) Mission Statement
6) Strategic Initiatives
7) The Detailed Strategy
8) Divisional or Lower-Level Strategy Development
9) Plan of Operation (Forecast and Rough Cut Capacity)

The differences in goals internationally are discussed. The four major categories of goal focus are:

- Financial Goals
- Operational Goals
- Employee Based Goals
- Customer Based Goals – Not Quality Based Goals

Next we discussed the operationalization of the goals through the development of a measurement process that focused on motivating a response focused on the critical resource of the organization. This is important if we are to achieve our stated goals. The chapter also discussed many other considerations in the internationalizing of the goals.

In operationalizing the goals, we summarized the process as:

- We identified the international operations' need for goals.
- We discussed how the structure and format of these goals should look.
- We discussed international alternative options for the focus of these goals.
- We discussed how the goal targets a specific critical resource.
- We demonstrated how each of the goal focuses can target a different critical resource.
- We showed how the critical resource influences operational performance.
- We showed how this effects and defines the measurement system.
- We discussed how international motivators vary from location to location.
- We defined the effective measurement system.

Next, in Chapter 4, we will take all this operational wisdom and apply it towards the creation of an international manufacturing strategy.

Class Assignments

This is one of my favorite cases for international operations. It introduces international cultural issues, goal planning issues, and people relationship issues. I like to have this case presented and then evolve a class discussion about all the alternative ways it can be handled. The perspectives become quite interesting.

W Gravel Company[9]

The W Gravel Company (WGC), located in the Caribbean area, is a wholly-owned subsidiary of a large American company. WGC has requested a consulting firm to assist them in a problem. You are a

9. This case was originally developed and used by Gene Woolsey of the Colorado School of Mines. I later adapted it for my own use. It demonstrates many of the "hidden agenda" issues of international management and is therefore excellent for this book.

senior partner, specializing in personnel problems. You have sent a junior member of the firm to W Isle, where their plant is located, to make a brief survey of the situation, define the problem as WGC sees it, and to bring back any information that might be helpful.

It is your practice in such cases to study the information carefully, and then to develop a tentative "Plan of Action," in light of your understanding of the problem and the resources available for dealing with it. Next you will visit the client to put the final touches on the recommendations the firm will make.

You decide to have your Plan focus on three questions:

1) What is the problem, and what are the forces affecting it?
2) In light of the problem and the resources available, what are some alternative actions that might be considered?
   (In this case you might consider actions in such areas as recruitment, employment selection, orientation training, organizational or job restructuring, job training, management training, public and community relations, etc.)
3) After analyzing the facts, what specific objectives would you tentatively establish?

Brief Statement of the Problem

The W Gravel Company began operations on W Isle– one of the Caribbean Islands, five years ago. Within 15 months of their start-up almost 50% of their total work force were natives. But the rapid development of W Isle as a tourist and resort center offering alternate employment, plus a very difficult start-up period, resulted in a high turnover of native personnel. In an attempt to meet the needs workers were recruited intensively from non-native personnel.

In late 1967 a very nationalistic government was elected for the Caribbean Islands, and from their top personnel in H, the capital, to the local government officials on W Isle, they are united in applying pressure to increasingly restrict employment and advancement opportunities to native W employees. They have now passed an "Occupational Tax" on all non-natives employed. It is not onerous now but it is reasonable to assume they will increase it as necessary to force employers to recruit, train and advance native personnel.

The task is clear – to increase the percentage of native personnel in the work force. But money is limited since WGC required heavy capital investment, lost money for the first four years, and barely made money last year. Resources are limited, since there's a small staff for WGC and the local educational resources are limited.

Systems Analysis

The forces which have led Wians to seek employment with WGC can be stated quickly:

1) Steady Work: Assuming a continuing ability to sell the product on a regular basis the work is steady-particularly as contrasted with the irregular pattern of employment available to Wians in the past.
2) Fair Wages: The wages are fair in comparison with the productivity. But there are better short-term opportunities in construction, and in tourist service during the tourist season.
3) Opportunities: The Wian who works steadily for WGC for awhile has a good reference for other employment. Furthermore, the Wian who acquires certain skills while in WGC employment might be able to attain higher paying employment – as in construction work.

As WGC has actually advanced Wians to higher job class work, leader, and management positions, this has also created a better picture of WGC opportunities.

The "dis-satisfiers" which have led Wians not to seek WGC employment, or not to stay in it if they did start, are quite numerous, and some of them have been strong forces. They will be grouped as "Hygiene" forces (roughly categorized as the wages, benefits, hours, working conditions) and "Motivating" forces (opportunities for self-actualization in the employment situation).

Hygiene

1) Conditions of dust, heat, and noise exist in varying degrees.
2) Need to wear full safety clothing – including goggles, hard hat, metatarsal safety shoes in a warm climate.
3) Industrial working conditions are new in the culture. Past work opportunities have been irregular in their daily demands, and ir-

regular on an annual basis. Daily and annually there was work – leisure – work – leisure cycles.

4) Competing jobs are attractive. Construction work offers high wages and cyclical work which is consonant with the past culture. Tourist-related services offer fair wages, opportunities for sociability, tips, and cyclical work.
5) The whole concept of "fringe benefits" which plays such a large role in the American employment system is not particularly relevant at this stage in Wian development.
6) Satisfying interpersonal relationships in the work situation are very strong forces in relative job satisfaction in the U.S., and would be expected to be even stronger in terms of the past "happy-go-lucky" Wian culture. But the international and intercultural tensions and hostilities in the work force, the high turnover of management, the nature of the work in a gravel plant (much of it is "alone"), the varying demands of the work situation (as management and men were alike in learning "how to run the plant"), and the lack of "team" feelings made for dissatisfying interpersonal relationships as perceived by most of the Wians employed.
7) Starting on a new job produces strong feelings of anxiety in *anyone*. Supportive, fear-reducing measures during the initial employment period are particularly important to foster development, productivity and retention of the new employee.[10] The former employment system required practically no employee responsibility or initiative, as industrial employment does. It was anticipated that these anxieties in initial WGC employment for Wians would be so strong that an admittedly extreme 80-hour orientation period for new employees was recommended in 1964.
8) As the employment statistics show out of every 19 Wians hired during the five year period only one was on the payroll at the end of the period. In the relatively small "labor pool" of Wians this obviously creates a poor image of WGC as a place to work. In addition, dust from the plant and occasional sulphurous smells may

10. A scientific study in Texas Instruments revealed that specific fear-reduction measures during initial employment paid for themselves many times over.

bother Bayshore, the principal native housing section of Shipport if there's a strong west wind and Elizabeth Town, the adjoining native town, if there's a strong east wind.

9) During the five year period there has been a very high turnover of management people. In addition, many of these people were not "good" supervisors in the sense of having the ability to be supportive coach-trainer-supervisors as far as the Wians were concerned. This is particularly significant because the demands of industrial employment were so new for the Wians.

When the "Hygiene" factors of a job are relatively satisfactory the individual will tend to stay on that job and not be easily lured to other employment. Obviously they have not been satisfactory for more than 90% of the Wians hired to date.

However, when those factors are reasonably met for an individual so that he stays on the job for some time then the "motivating" factors come into play – the factors that enhance the individual's role in the work situation. These are factors such as formal advancement, increasing recognition, broader responsibilities, opportunities for achievement, and self-fulfillment in the work. In addition there is the role of higher job levels of wages and salaries as they relate to the individuals growing need for "things" and as they relate to earnings as symbols of status, inside and outside the plant. All these things contribute to the individual "putting himself into his job" rather than just "doing it".

In January two of the "highest ranking" Wian employees were thinking of leaving, and it's possible that this may be an "early warning indicator" that "motivating" factors were beginning to have significance in the WGC situation. However, as the "hygiene" factors are improved so that more Wians were in WGC employment, and stay longer in it, then the "motivating" factors will become increasingly significant.

Background

1. The Work Force

When the plant started Shipport had less than 3,000 population – the boom was just getting started – and not many other jobs were available. WGC offered steady employment, fair wages (though suffering by comparison with the scales paid during plant construction, and in construction elsewhere on the island) and, for the more ambitious, the possibility of learning skills which might be useful in potentially better employment later. As a result of these factors the employment of Wians grew in fifteen months to a total of 119 employed – 46% of the payroll at that time.

But then some counter-forces came into being. The Shipport area began to expand at an accelerating pace (it now has over 18,000 people). Jobs were available in construction, which paid better, and in service occupations which were usually easier and which frequently offered the inducement of tips from tourists. Furthermore, the competing jobs were usually much cleaner, usually offered more status and opportunity for sociability, and didn't require safety clothing in a warm climate.

The Wians began to leave at an increasing rate. In an attempt to meet the manpower needs the plant began to employ more Fians, Cians, and people from other locations. This probably accelerated the exodus of the Wians, and fragmented whatever social structure was beginning to develop in the work force.

The average Fian is a refugee from a corrupt and brutal dictatorship and he's possibly on W Isle illegally. He's had little formal education or industrial experience and speaks French as his basic language. Because of the law and administrative procedures of the Immigration and Labor Office officials on W Isle he's usually very reluctant to try to change employers, or to "cause trouble" so he'd be returned to F. There are 66 Fians currently employed, 25% of the payroll.

The Cian comes from a country with some industrial background (sugar mills, bauxite operations, etc.), with a higher stage of economic development than the other countries represented in the work force, and, with a relatively good school system enforcing universal education up to a high school level. Thus the Cian tends to perceive himself as a superior being as contrasted with the others on the work force – and, furthermore, he frequently does have relatively higher entry skills, and does tend to learn more readily because of the extent of his formal education. The Cians have been leaders in the newly-formed labor union. However, he has difficulty transferring to other jobs (though he certainly could get them) for the same reasons as the Fians. There are 76 Cians on the payroll – almost 29% of the work force.

The other members of the work force tend to be somewhere between the Cians and Fians in initial "employability." To add to the difficulties many of the "other" people have Spanish as their basic language.

The Wians tend to resent all of the non-Wians as "interlopers" and the Cians as "wise guys" in addition. The others tend to resent the Wians because they have job mobility, and because the Wians are perceived as being automatically favored in any personnel decisions. Hence the newly-employed Wian is entering into relatively unpleasant working conditions, and gets a relatively hostile reception from most of the other employees, particularly in some departments. This hostility is not only unpleasant to face, but it means the new Wian usually gets little on-the-job help and training from his co-workers.

Throughout the first four years of operation these tensions were further compounded by the fact that the whole plant was still struggling on a learning curve, there were almost constant changes of work routines and practices, and there was a high management turnover as well as work-force turnover.

2. Economic Background

Gravel is a bulk commodity which can be produced in many locations in the United States. The great majority of all gravel produced is used within 150 miles of the plant at which it was made. The 12 gravel plants of A Materials, the American company of which WGC is a wholly-owned subsidiary, are located in an arc from New York to Texas and they are not well located to serve the growing economy of the Southeastern states.

W Isle is 600 square miles of suitable raw material for making gravel. Shipport is a free port – hence bunker oil may be obtained there are relatively low cost. Additional raw materials are available and can be brought to Shipport cheaply by water transportation. The finished gravel can be transported to a number of Southern ports from Delaware to Mississippi. In addition, there is extensive construction underway in the C, and considerable further expansion.

The Shipport area is exempt from ordinary taxes, under the

terms of a comprehensive long-term bill which had the objective of fostering the rapid development of the island as a resort, tourist, and commercial center.

The prevailing wage scale was very low by American standards, and was not expected to rise very rapidly. It was believed that the labor force was adequate in quantity, and, while the level of formal education was expected to be low, the local labor force spoke English. Wians are believed to be trainable for the ordinary work of the plant, under the training direction of skilled management and technical people during the start-up period, expected to be about two years.

The political climate was favorable and expected to remain so. Thus there were valid reasons for A Materials to make an investment in a gravel plant at Shipport.

For a number of reasons the start-up difficulties were much greater than anticipated, and one of the key factors retarding the "plant learning curve" was the very high turnover rate. The start-up period has turned out to be closer to five years, with a substantial portion of the progress being made in the last year so that the operation is finally "in the black." The management group has gained stability and confidence, and now knows how to operate the plant at a reasonable level of cost efficiency.

Thus it is now possible to enlist the aid of a better management group, and to have more resources of money if necessary to increase the Wian ratio.

3. Educational Resources

Shipport is not a city, but a free port zone. Those who do business in the zone pay fees for their license from Shipport Authority to operate. In a certain sense Shipport Authority is the municipal government. It supports municipal services, including schools, from the fees of the licenses.

Thus the Shipport schools are predisposed to cooperate with the licenses such as WGC, but they are not public schools in the American sense. Furthermore they are located on the other side of Shipport, 3-4 miles west of the plant.

A rapidly developing native village, Elizabeth Town, is just east of the plant, and not in the zone. They have two new schools, greatly enlarged and improved over what they had before. These will provide education through the 10th grade, basically in the English system.

Most of the people in the plant work force probably live in and around Elizabeth Town, and these schools are relatively close to the plant. They are under the direction of the central government in H.

None of the schools have developed as yet any significant resources for occupational, vocational, or technical education. Previous attempts to conduct off-hour courses in the plant were unsuccessful.

A current attempt to test and provide basic education for native Wians with the aid of a young instructor from the Shipport High School has had a disappointing initial response.

While some societies have had attitudes that formal education was in itself a good thing, this was certainly never true on W Isle. Under the former colonial system probably only half of the children completed the sixth grade, and only a handful could go higher by attending the limited higher schools – which required going to Hessen. The average level of the typical Wian worker employed by WGC to date has probably been at about the 4th grade level in reading and elementary arithmetic.

As we recently have spent millions of dollars to learn in the United States, the problems of providing basic education for "disadvantaged" adults are exceedingly subtle, complex, and difficult to overcome. So far the results have been very meager when compared with the resources expended.

Conventional school approaches to these adults just have not worked in the United States and probably won't on W Isle.

Since the native government is pressuring all employers to employ, train, and advance Wians there might be some possibilities of joint employer efforts to meet a common problem in basic adult education. However, WGC is the only industrial employer in the area, (except for S which employs only a handful of non-technical employees) – and the personnel, training, and management people do not have formal associations as in the United States. Thus neither the schools, nor the other employers, nor professional societies are "ready" resources for cooperative endeavors.

4. Public and Community Relationships

The "public image" of company at a given moment is partly a result of what the company has done, partly a result of the public's perception of what was done, and partly a result of what people expect the company to do in the future. It's hard to define and hard to measure.

But if WGC is to survive as an effective economic entity it must continue to take positive steps to augment its public image as an effective contributor to the welfare of the Cians.

However, in terms of public understanding and community relationships the plant has operated and is operating under some handicaps.

WGC was the first large-scale manufacturing operation in the area, and there was no base for public understanding of the strength basic industry contributes to the economy. WGC did tear up the landscape, and a gravel plant does not add beauty to the scene. The plant does make dust and sometimes unpleasant smells. A relatively high percentage of the initial local labor force was employed by WGC in its first two years, and the great majority left it quickly – no doubt spreading the word that it wasn't a good place to work. Furthermore, the location of the plant, the unusual institution of the Port Authority as a form of local government, the physical and social distances between the homes of its employees, and the very rapid pace of local development mean that there is no specific "plant community" to which the plant can readily relate.

Shipport and Elizabeth Town are both rapidly developing communities with the social and institutional instability characteristic of such situations. As just one example, there are six churches recently built or now under construction in the relatively small area of Elizabeth Town.

The Caribbean Islands are newly "independent" and in a political upheaval. The long-time "Wians" were displaced, and the new "Wians" are faced with high expectations from their followers, with low financial resources, and with limited experiences in administration.

The old "Establishment", with its clearly labeled lovers of power and influence, is giving way to a more amorphous situation in both Shipport and H and factional struggles of many kinds develop rapidly in any "interregnum" period. As the bitterness of the partisans increases locally and nationally, it becomes increasingly difficult to avoid the trap of "if you're not for us you're against us!" WGC has to stay clear as "friend to all, follower of none" – and at times that kind of position puts you in an uncomfortably friendless middle ground.

Thus in terms of local community relationships, relationships with the Port Authority, and with the central administration in H, WGC has a tricky course to navigate. It must improve its image, particularly in the local community, and it must be seen by the central administrators in H as clearly furthering their aims and objectives – yet what it does can't reflect credit or discredit on any faction.

W GRAVEL COMPANY

Personnel Summary

	End of the Year Payroll Total	End of the Year Wians On Payroll	% Wians	Wians Terminated During the Year
1964	237	109	46	132
1965	259	45#	17.4	247
1966	259	36	14	66
1967	262	26	10	42
1968	266	29##	11	32
				519

Peak during first quarter of 1965, 119. Low during first quarter of 1968, 21.
During 1968 there were 35 Wians hired.

In the five year period WGC hired 1461 people. 584 Wians were hired, and 29 were on the payroll at the end of the period – almost a 19 to 1 ratio. 913 non-Wians were hired and 247 were on the payroll at the end of the period – almost a 3.7 to 1 ratio. On 1/1/69 there were 29 Wian, 66 Cians, 76 Fians, and 95 "Others" (from 17 different countries) employed.

	W. Gravel Personell Mix as of December 1, 1968	
Personell	1 Management 2 Leaders (Quarry) 4 Non-Management Salaried 22 Wage-earners 29	
By Job Class	**Management**	**Salary Grade**
	7	1
	Non-Management Salaried	**N-M-S- Class**
	2	1
	6	2
		2
	7	1
	Wage-earner	**Job Class**
	2	3 1.25-1.30
	6	2
	7	4
	8	4 2.00-2.24
	9	2
	10	3
	12	1
	14	2
	16 (top)	3 3.12-3.26

Productivity, and Wages, Standard of Living

The Wian wage scale goes from $1.25 to $3.26 per hour. Current A Materials non-incentive Wage Scale starts at $6.645 and has a top of $9.125. At approximate average job class, 8, A pay is $7.125 per hour, while Wian pay is $2.00 to 2.24 for that grade.

Of course, A productivity is significantly higher. Original WGC estimates called for 104 wage earners at normal volume-estimates based on A Experience. WGC has almost 200 wage-earners on payroll – though it is doing some packaging not originally contemplated.

Cost of living is high in the Shipport area. Rent for a small company house is $85 per month – and that's low for the area. Food, automobiles and manufactured articles, and clothing usually cost about 30% more than in U.S.A. Gasoline costs $ 1.50 for a U.S. gallon. Only liquor, perfume, fine china, cameras and optical goods are cheap as compared to U.S.A. – and certainly they are not significant factors in family living costs.

An WGC employee, earning about $340 a month for a family of four, would certainly spend most of his earnings for housing, food, and clothing. His "discretionary income" would be quite a small percentage of his earnings.

To make matters worse he has been exposed in recent years to American tourists spending money on a lavish scale, and now is beginning to see TV – with its distorted picture of American life. Thus he is continually reminded of the disparity between what he has, and what "they" seem to have. This has strong economic and political repercussions.

Native Personnel – WGC

The "WCG Handbook" states the education is "compulsory from ages 5 to 14", but this is not so. The native elementary schools provided by the government are small, scattered, and could cover only a part of the age group.

The Shipport School, almost all for whites, had two teachers three years ago, has nine this year for nine grades, and will have fourteen next year for twelve grades.

This is supported by the Port licenses, and its role is primarily to prepare for further education. It will be the only Wian secondary school outside of H.

The parochial school, operated by an order of nuns from the States, suffers from the same problems as some parochial schools in the States, overcrowding and with lay teachers not well qualified.

I asked the principal of the Shipport School to describe the "average" level of educational attainment for a typical graduate of the native school. A graduate would be roughly equivalent in level to the 6th grade in the States but arrived at by rote learning and constant drill. This graduate would read well but with a limited vocabulary. His handwriting and written material would be surprisingly good, but his spoken English might be ungrammatical. In mathematics he probably would be well drilled on the basic arithmetic operations. He might solve simple linear equations but not if they were presented in verbal form. Beyond some limited class discussion on health and nature, he would have had no form of training in Science, and little in Geography or History beyond a very elementary level. They can learn as well as anyone else, but there'll have to be considerable attention to selection, and motivation, and work responsibility.

The principal assured us that all his school resources would be readily available to us – such as, "released time" classes in the day, or evening courses. While he did not say so directly, he is trained in Science and might be prevailed upon to help in any evening classes.

I asked a foreman, who'd worked with native labor, for his comments. He backed up the principal on the education, and said that it was not difficult to find good clerks on an elementary level of keeping time, recording, posting, etc., but it was extremely difficult to train for any technical skill. Some are very anxious to learn, but most have had little reason for aspiration in the past. They have not been expected to think in terms of abstract concepts, to take any economic initiative, nor to keep rigidly to set schedules of time or performance – though they are neat and clean. They need to be continually encouraged and reinforced. They are extremely vulnerable to criticism, direct or implied.

Swearing is not part of their culture, and they must not be sworn at. They tend to react against people who do swear at all.

The natives are very black-descended from tribes from West Coast of Africa, North of Congo River. The range of stature approximates American-average adult male about 5'9", seldom over 6'.

This report was prepared by a member of the A personnel staff after a brief visit early in the year of initial start-up. It now seems that the principal and the foreman quoted were optimistic.

This brief overview suggests:

1) The use of selection tests that are largely non-verbal and appropriate to the culture. A did some work in this area a number of years ago, and this will be investigated. Catalogues of standardized tests will also be reviewed.
2) Provided the vocabulary was simple enough, programmed instruction should be particularly effective. (Man proceeds at own pace, can't "lose face".)
3) Probably the most difficult area of instruction will be for the 18-20 electrical personnel. Models and visual aids will be necessary to help the trainees "get" the abstract concepts of electricity. Programmed instruction materials and The Rider Texts, heavily illustrated, are being sent to WGC as possible training materials. The Chief Electric at WGC must be provided with a wide range

of test and calibration instruments that can be helpful in training – such as, Heath's "Electronic Kit for Scientists."

4) The guides and manuals presently existing in A would need to be rewritten to use a simple vocabulary and relate as specifically as possible to the WGC jobs.
5) Possibly an especially designed "orientation course" for all native employees might be helpful, with selected parts appropriate for all employees. This could cover common industrial terms, basic vocabulary of gravel, safety rules, standards of employment, rectangular and polar coordinates and graphs, basic concepts of heat and measurement, etc. In other words, things that would be appropriate in all placement in the works. In addition, the trainee's performance in such a course would help in placement.

References

Semler, Ricardo, *Maverick*, Warner Books, New York, 1993.

Goal Setting and Strategic Management References

Plenert, Gerhard, *World Class Manager*, Prima, Rocklin, CA, 1995.

Measurement / Motivation References:

Marsh & Meredith, "Changes in Performance Measures on the Factory Floor," *P&IMJ*, First Quarter, 1998, Pages 36-40.

Lockamy, III, Archie, and James F. Cox, III, *Reengineering Performance Measurement*, Irwin Professional Publishing, Burr Ridge, Illinois, 1994, (293 pages).

Staff, "Finding Your Way Through Performance Measurement," *News for a Change*, July 1998, Pages 1,4,6.

Plenert, Gerhard, "Productivity and Quality in a Developing Country", *Productivity and Quality Management Frontiers – V*, ISPQR, February 1995, Pages 194-202.

Plenert, Gerhard, "Leading Edge Production Planning Philosophies and their Effects on Productivity and Quality", *Productivity and Quality Management Frontiers – V*, ISPQR, February 1995, Pages 476-483.

Plenert, Gerhard, "Installing Successful Factories into Developing Countries", *The International Executive*, Vol. 32, No. 2, Sept.-Oct. 1990, Pages 29-35.

Plenert, Gerhard, *Plant Operations Deskbook*, Homewood, Ill., Business 1 IRWIN, 1993 (501 pages).

Quality References:

Shelton, Ken, *In Search of Quality: 4 Unique Perspectives, 43 Different Voices*, Executive Excellence Publishing, Provo, UT, 1995.

4. The International Strategy

Y, Inc.

Y, Inc. was approached by YV, Inc. with a proposal. YV felt that Y was the best producer of the EL (electrolumisence) product. This product allows you to print circuitry and phosphors on a piece of plastic, plug it in, and it gives off light. YV felt that rather than search out a large number of producers, YV was interested in just having one good producer/supplier. Their hope was that they would have one experienced producer where, even if this producer couldn't supply the entire demand for EL, they could go out, certify and train other EL suppliers validating that they would be of the caliber and quality required. Y, of course, was interested in this proposal because they wanted to be YV's primary producer for their newly supplied research. Y expressed it's concerns about it's financial situation and asked if there was some way YV could assist with a loan of some type. YV, Inc. responded by saying they could supply the loan, but that they would prefer to buy out Y, Inc. and make them a division. The dilemma for Y, Inc. was that they would lose control. YV would, of course, focus on the EL products. What would Y do with it's core sticker and label business? And the owners of Y were concerned about their position and financial future if the buy-out occurred.

In the mean time, one of the owners of Y, Inc. had developed a touch-screen technology, which amounted to high-tolerance screen printing on a glass surface. He felt that the market justified the development of this product, but there were two hurdles:

- Touch screen needed an extremely dust-free manufacturing environment at clean-room levels.
- Y, Inc. wasn't experienced in printing on glass.

Touch screen technology was another alternative that may help Y, Inc. get out of its financial struggles. But, similar to EL, there were some developmental costs that required up-front investment. Additionally, touch screen manufacturing had some major competitors in Asia, primarily in Japan. The only way to justify getting into the touch screen product was to identify a competitive niche, an edge that Y would have in the product that would make them unique enough to draw customers. This would cancel out any cost advantages from international competitors. Y, Inc.'s owner felt that they had developed this edge in screen strength, in low screen failure rates, and in reliability. The concern of the owner was in how a merger with YV would effect the development of the touch-screen technology that was now in process.

YV decided to use Y's financial instability as a wedge to motivate the sale. They knew the desperate situation that Y was in. They also knew that Y had a highly experienced and stable employee base, and they felt that they were buying the talent, not necessarily the productive capacity. However, they felt that Y needed a little more defined structure, so that YV knew what they were purchasing. YV wanted Y to develop a financial, marketing, and production strategy, which would demonstrate the future of the company. This chapter will focus on the development of the production strategy and we will show what Y developed.

What would you do? Is the merger with YV appropriate? Will this foster growth and help Y achieve it's goals, as discussed in the last chapter? Or is the merger a desperate attempt to get out of financial trouble? What about the touch screen market? Should YV, Inc. support this market in spite of it's focus on EL? What would you do?

The Development of a Strategy

As discussed in the last chapter, a strategy needed to be developed based on the strategic initiatives. Y, Inc. had developed this strategic plan with a five year window ending in year 2005. Their strategy had annual stepping stones in each of the categories of the strategic initiatives. They included the detailed strategy issues listed in Chapter 3 under the categories:

- People
- Integration
- Measurement
- Time-Based Competition

These issues are fairly common to most organizations. However, to become World Class, another level of strategy development is needed. Generally, the strategy should also include elements of:

- Service Performance Plan
- Logistics Plan
- Globalization Plan
- Technology Transfer Plan
  Defusion of Innovation and Technology Plan
- Plan for Continuous Improvement
  Total Quality Management (TQM).

We will discuss each of these in more detail.

Service Performance Plan

Service focuses on customer responsiveness and competitiveness. It requires us to evaluate on-time delivery performance to the originally "requested" delivery date. It focuses on surveying the customer and defining what the customer's expectations are. And it focuses on identifying how we stack up against our competitors in "Thrilling the Customer". One of the best tools is a survey. Unfortunately, the word "survey" brings fear into the hearts of anyone involved. Chart 4.1 offers the example of a survey used by Y, Inc.

What the Service Performance Plan should discuss is current levels of performance and then it should define goals focused on the improvement of service performance. Again, the sample offered here focuses on one perspective, and internationally, this may change because the motivational drivers change. For example, this survey would not work in a culture that did not use the "A, B, C, D, F" grading scale. However, this example shows that the survey can be a simple process.

Another level of service performance evaluation includes the preventive maintenance process. What we need here is a project plan that focuses on repetitive contact with a customer. When and what type of contact is what should be defined as part of the plan.

Chart 4.1. Sample Customer Performance Survey

Customer Responsiveness Survey

It is important for Y, Inc. to understand how we can serve you better. Please respond to this survey by answering four quick questions. We also welcome any additional comments and suggestions. Please return your responses to

GJP, Director of Quality
Y, Inc., 999 No-where Drive, No-town, CA 99999
Fax 999-999-9999, E-mail gjp@yinc.com

Again – thank you for your help.

Company Name: ______________________________
Respondent Name (optional): ______________________
Respondent Contact information (optional): ____________

Survey Questions (please supply an A, B, C, D, or F grade for each)

Y Responsiveness ____
Y Quality ____
Y Communication ____
Y Delivery ____
Comments: ______________________________

Logistics Plan

A logistics plan focuses on the transportation and interim storage of materials, either at the raw materials or the finished goods level. This plan requires us to consider the entire supply chain, and the performance of the supply chain, which will be discussed in more detail in Chapters 6 through 8. The sourcing, storage, transport, receipt, and delivery of goods can critically effect competitive performance, especially in an international setting, and that is why three chapters will be dedicated to this subject.

Another important element of the logistics plan is the tie into the marketing plan. In the marketing plan, we define the location and types of markets we are addressing. This information directly impacts the logistics plan. Information that is valuable includes the following.

Individual Consumer / Vendor Behavior

In some parts of the world, certain carriers are considered unacceptable. For example Federal Express changed it's name to FedEx in order to remove the "Federal" from it's name which, internationally, had some negative effects. In other parts of the world, wording may be important. For example, I had a shipment rejected in Germany because "Gift" was written on the package and in German that word means "poison".

Time-Based Performance

If you are dealing in a commodity market, time may be your only strategic performance advantage. Then availability of the product for on-time delivery performance becomes critical. For example, Toyota can receive a call in the morning for a specific model of car, and on the same day the car will go through the production process and be produced. However, it then takes 4 to 6 weeks to get the car from the factory to the dealership. What good is it to have short production cycle time if your logistics cycle time is so long?

Environmental Performance

Environmental concerns are often minimized. Usually, environmental concerns imply pollution control of some form. But this can be extremely misleading. For example, the United States often thinks of Mexico as a pollution dumping ground. Some mistakenly believe that if you want to do a dirty production process and you want to avoid environmental regulations, go to Mexico. However, many of the Maquiladora plants in Mexico immediately across the border from the United States, are required to haul, not only their finished goods, but also all their production waste, back across the border to the United States. Mexicans don't want the U.S.'s garbage, and they have developed legal regulations to enforce the fact.

Environmental concerns also include infrastructurial and stakeholder influences. For example, in many cultures, the industrial complex is expected to supply road improvements, power improvements, schooling for both the young and old, clean water, etc. for the entire working community. They are expected to take care of the lives of the worker at home as well as on the job. In China, the employers are expected to supply their employees with at least one warm, nutritional meal per day in the middle of the day. In some cultures, this goes beyond the employees. Employers are often expected to take care of all the stakeholders, which includes the family of the employee, and the surrounding community. The employer may provide stores, restaurants, and sometimes even sporting facilities.

Globalization Plan

Globalization offers numerous synergies. Resources from one location assist performance in other locations. For example, the reduced labor costs of one region assists in reducing product costs, whereas the lower materials costs of another region assists in still another element of cost reduction. These competitive issues lead to pressures to integrate internationally, either through acquisition or through strategic alliances. Additionally, competitive pricing pressures cause lower margins and motivate companies to sell more units of product than can otherwise be sold in only the domestic marketplace. The synergistic development of international alliances shifts the way in which resources are allocated.

Many ask; "Why go Global?" One of the main reasons is to establish and take advantage of economies of scale. You don't obtain economies of scale simply by going global, but globalization does offer expanded opportunities. For example, if you are one big company, rather than two small companies, you can:

- Avoid the duplication of services such as the accounting and information systems functions

- Force better pricing on your vendors because you can purchase at larger volumes
- Exhibit more market strengt in issues like product pricing
- Centralize the Procurement Process
- Centralize the logistics process and take advantage of more optimal loading and routing patterns
- Web based transactions or even Electronic Data Interchange (EDI) can be more efficient
- Consolidation of the common manufacturing processes
- Open new markets and gain access to new marketing resources that are now shared
- International career rotations with a broader scope for employees.

All these advantages are valid, as long as we don't lose site of the fact that the customer generally thinks on a local level, and that these global strategic advantages cannot replace the localization of the product.

A product sold in the United States is not automatically marketable anywhere else. Numerous examples of international disasters of U.S. products demonstrate this. For example, in the Iran hostage crisis, the United States sent the world's best high-tech helicopters to retrieve the hostages, but they never arrived at their destination because the dust of the desert brought them down long before they even got close. Similarly, in Japan, United States cars were restricted from market access because they did not include a kimono guard, which was a basic requirement for all cars produced in Japan. A kimono guard was the bumper end piece that tied the ends of a bumper into the body of the car, so that the loose end of the bumper could not get caught on the long kimonos that the Japanese women wear. The American auto producers cried and complained about Japanese barriers, but, in reality, they were simply not being sensitive to the needs of the Japanese marketplace.

These examples prove what "localizing in a global marketplace" is all about. Localizing requires the identification of the needs for the local product, and incorporates those needs into the global product. For example, most American cars now include kimono guards as a standard feature in all their cars, even though they don't call it that, and most American's didn't even realize it happened.

This helped give Americans access to the Japanese marketplace while, at the same time, fitting into all the other global marketplaces with a standardized product.

In a global environment, companies need to consider required changes so they can compete in several dimensions; by territory, by market, vertically, and horizontally. The dimensional opportunities that are advantageous in one location, may be ineffective in another. For example, products sold across borders within the NAFTA countries need to be evaluated for local content. That means that a certain level of localized vertical integration needs to exist within the production process so that there is enough local content in the product to make it qualify as a tariff-free product. However, if a company plans to transfer and sell product within one of the NAFTA countries, then local value content is unimportant. Vertical integration may also occur as a marketing strategy. For example, if you sew up the majority of the key local sources for materials, then you exclude some of your competition.

Horizontal competitive strength works better in regions like Europe, where ISO certification is practiced. Then, the entire market is open for a product line that has passed the test of certification. Using market as a strategic dimension works in areas where the market is somewhat customized, for example markets that are focused on a religious preference can be targeted by such products. Territorial market dimensioning occurs, for example, in cases where transportation costs are prohibitive, such as a bottling company. In this case, keeping the product focused within a specific region assists in competitive cost minimization.

Globalization opens the door for more marketing opportunities and at the same time offers more competitive pressures. In an international environment, any product that has reached the peak of it's product life cycle in the home market and is ready for decline, can be introduced into a foreign environment and find an entirely new product life. However, global introduction can bring on new obstacles such as patent and copyright infringements, because the U. S. patents and copyrights are not treated and respected in the same way internationally. Therefore, going international may open the door for competition against black marketers where you are in effect competing against your own product, possibly even with your own label on it.

An excellent opportunity that is opened up by globalization is the chance to network. Through networking you may find new sources, markets, and integration opportunities such as strategic alliances, that never existed before. For example, Intel was so impressed with the research knowledge of the Malaysian employee base, that they set up a major research center in Penang, Malaysia. They found that the synergy of an employee base that was 60 % Malay Muslim, 30 % Chinese Buddhist, and 10 % Indian Hindu, created a mixture of perspectives that caused employee teams to look at problems for a variety of perspectives. This did not occur in the traditionally Christian Western employee base.

Global materials sourcing issues can be quite different as well. Materials sourcing to remote locations can be nearly impossible. This effects the supply chain because an inefficient source or distributor performance lengthens the supply chain and makes it too lengthy and unreliable to be competitive. More detailed discussion about the supply chain effects will be discussed in the next section of this book.

Perhaps the biggest frustration of globalization comes in the relocation of operational managers. Managers who work at international locations find themselves isolated. They are left out of the over all planning process. Additionally, when they return to their home-country after their assignment, they are shunned as outsiders and often find themselves leaving the company. This causes managers to not want to relocate overseas, even for a short period of time. The other option, which some international managers take, is to never return to the home country. They just accept one international assignment after another and stay overseas forever. Many companies, in realizing these struggles, have chosen to utilize only localized management for permanent positions. They have frequent visits from the corporate office, but the main management effort comes from the local community. However, in spite of this localization of talent, there is still a lack of networking between the management structure. For example, managers in two different countries may be struggling with the same issues, but rarely does a structure exist to facilitate their communication.

In spite of the many struggles, the opportunities of globalization still outweigh the challenges. Therefore, globalization becomes an integral part of an operational strategy.

Technology Transfer Plan

A technology transfer plan is critical to strategic international positioning. Which technology is transferred and when it is transferred can make a big difference to competitive success. In Chapter 1 we discussed Value-Added Productivity as a measure of performance. If this is an important measure, then we need to look at the value-added content of each product we produce and sell. Those products with the highest value-added content, which almost always equates to the highest technology content, should be kept under lock and key. If competitors learn about the technology, they will start to imitate it and it will lose it's competitive strength. The Japanese see the control of technology as critical to success. They will keep the highest value-added content products in-house and will farm out the low value-added content items. This minimizes their risk of losing the technology edge and keeps their profit margins maximized.

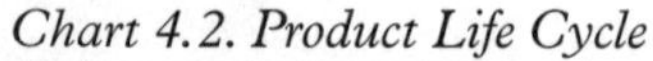

Chart 4.2. Product Life Cycle

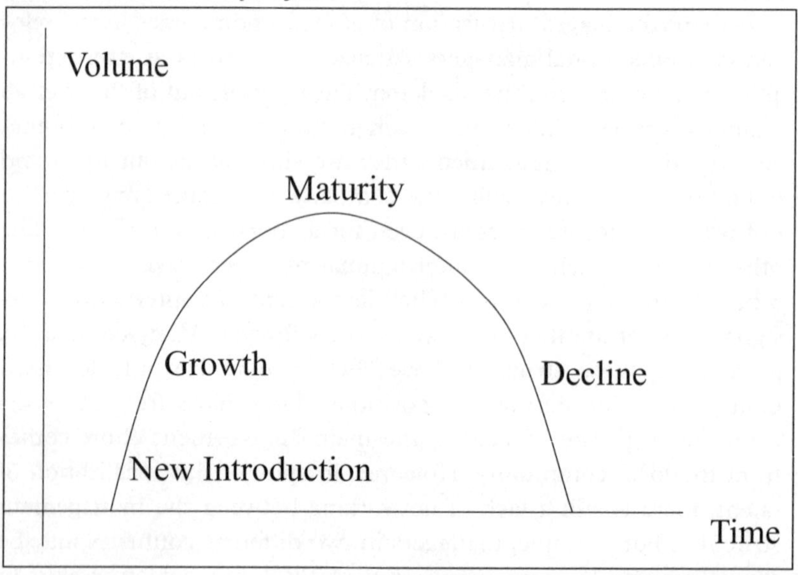

A technology plan also focuses on the product life cycle. What we learn from the product life cycle shown in Chart 4.2 is that when a product is in it's new introduction phase, we have high R&D and developmental costs. Then, during the growth phase we experience high margins because we have a technology edge. In the maturity phase competition increases and margins drop off. Then in the decline phase we drop off into a commodities environment where price becomes the only criteria for competitiveness. The importance of this diagram, as it relates to technology, is that it is during the growth phase where we are cash rich. This is when the company needs to be thinking about the next cycle of innovation. If a company waits until the maturity phase of a product or later, they will find themselves in the situation that Y, Inc. is now experiencing. Y is trying to dig themselves out of low margin products and develop higher margin products during a time when funds are not available for growth. The correct way to manage technology is shown in Chart 4.3 where we see the next product being kicked off during the growth phase of each previous product's life cycle. That way we have a mixture of products in all the phases, some maturing that are supporting our core business, while at the same time others are being introduced.

Chart 4.3. Repetitive Product Life Cycle

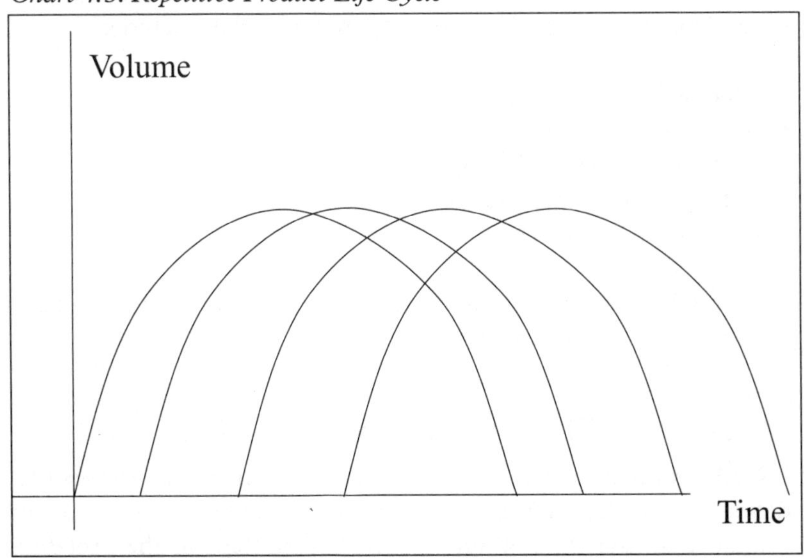

New product life cycles are generated by either the introduction of new products or by the introduction of old products into new markets. Either of these can start a new cycle. That's where the international element comes in. The introduction of U. S. proven products into other parts of the world could supply a company with a cash flow surge that they need for new product development.

Through both of these technology processes:

1) the management of the product life cycle, and
2) the timely control and release of value-adding technologies

we manage the defusion of innovation in our technology plan.

Plan for Continuous Improvement

One of the major reasons for considering internationalization is for competitive improvement. Improvement requires a change process that requires a management process. If this process is not done correctly, if you don't control change, but rather let change control you, you are likely to fail. There are several systems internationally that assist in the planning of the continuous improvement process. It is important to be familiar with each of these because they will all be encountered. Some of the more popular models include:

- Process Re-engineering (PR)
- Root Cause Analysis and TRIZ
- Quality Functional Deployment (QFD)
- Total Quality Management (TQM)
- Concept Management.

Next is a brief discussion of each of these because of their value in international operationalization.

Process Re-engineering (PR)

PR is a tool that focuses on "rapid, radical change". It stresses top-down change that suggests we reinvent the organization, focusing primarily on the elimination of unnecessary steps in the processes and unnecessary layers of management. It is not downsizing, which many companies are using it for. Rather it is work elimination. It is positive, growth-focused change, looking for opportunities to eliminate waste and improve value-added productivity, often through the implementation of technology like image processing.

In 1994, $32 billion was invested in re-engineering of which 2/3 of the re-engineering projects will fail. Why? Because the change process builds up a lot of resistance thereby forcing it's failure. Secondarily, because PR is used as an excuse for downsizing, often the downsizing results in the elimination of critical employees that will be difficult to replace. The downsizing process was not carefully thought through, it is done hastily and the results are disastrous.

However, just like any tool, there are some extremely positive aspects to process re-engineering that make it worthy of our attention. The first is that PR focuses on change implementation at the top of the corporate hierarchy. It generates more of a top-down change culture. It focuses on process oriented changes.

PR's focus on the process emphasizing that the process, not the products, holds the secrets for the most dramatic improvements within an organization. PR focuses on an "all-or-nothing proposition that produces impressive results". PR is defined as "the fundamental rethinking and radical redesign of business processes to achieve dramatic improvements in critical, contemporary measures of performance, such as cost, quality, service, and speed".

The principles of re-engineering include:

- Organize around outcomes, not tasks.
- Have those who use the output of the process perform the process.
- Subsume information processing work into the real work that produces information.
- Treat geographically dispersed resources as though they were centralized.
- Link parallel activities instead of integrating their results.
- Put the decision point where the work is performed, and build control into it.

The three R's of re-engineering are:

- Rethink – Is what you're doing focused on the customer?
- Redesign – What are you doing? Should you be doing it at all?
- Redesign how it can be done

- Re-tool – Reevaluate the use of advanced technologies.

Some characteristics of process re-engineering include:

- Several jobs are combined into one.
- Workers make the decisions – empowerment.
- "Natural Order" Sequencing of job steps.
- Processes with multiple versions depending on the need.
- Work is performed where it makes the most sense.
- Checks and controls are reduced.
- Reconciliation is minimized.
- "Empowered" customer service representative.
- Hybrid centralized/decentralized organizations.

Like TQM, the focus of the re-engineering effort is the team. Departments are replaced by empowered process teams. Executives change their role from scorekeeper to leaders. Organizational structures become flatter. Managers change from supervisors to coaches.

PR has the following steps or phases in the change management process:

- Mobilization
  - develop a vision
  - communicate the vision
  - identify champions and process owners
  - assemble the teams

- Diagnosis
  - identify problems
  - train and educate
  - current process analysis
  - select and scope the process
  - understand the current customer
  - model the process
  - set targets for new designs

- Redesign
  - create breakthrough design concepts
  - redesign the entire system

   - build prototype
   - information technology

- Transition
   - finalize transition design
   - implementation phase
   - measure benefits
   - the role of communication to avoid resistance
   - you cannot over-communicate

PR has many of the procedural characteristics of TQM, however, it is more philosophical than TQM. PR focuses on being competitive via the rapid and the radical, and it stresses the process as the key to successful change. There are numerous books available that discuss the philosophy of PR. The best books are still the original, by the gurus of Process Re-engineering, Hammer and Champy. Many of the comments in this section are taken from these books. SME/CASA has put out an excellent booklet focusing on manufacturing processes that can be re-engineered. *OR/MS Today* also has an excellent article that discusses first and second generation re-engineering programs.[1]

Numerous variations have sprung up in an attempt to correct some of the problems of re-engineering. I will list several of these and offer some brief information about each of them. I will include references for additional information.

1. Hammer, M., and J. Champy, *Re-engineering the Corporation,* Harper Business, New York, NY, 1993.
   Hammer, M., and Champy, "The Promise of Re-engineering", *Fortune*, May 3, 1993, Pages 94-97.
   Hammer, M., "Re-engineering Work: Don't Automate, Obliterate", *Harvard Business Review,* July-August 1990, Pages 104-112.
   Marks, Peter, *Process Reengineeering and the New Manufacturing Enterprise Wheel: 15 Processes for Competitive Advantage,* CASA/SME Technical Forum, Society of Manufacturing Engineers (SME), Dearborn, Michigan, 1994.
   Cypress, Harold L., "Re-engineering", *OR/MS Today,* February 1994, Pages 18-29.
   See a more detailed list of references at the end of this chapter.

John Lipscomb has developed a program that focuses on re-engineering improvements utilizing Quality Systems Deployment (QSD) QSD is a variation of QFD focusing on customer directed systems development. The contradiction is that re-engineering is "rapid and radical" and QSD is systematic and carefully defined. However, blending the two offers a change process that falls somewhere in between the two and attempts to utilize the benefits of each.

Lowenthal stresses that the re-engineering of the organization should focus on the Core Competencies, and that it is the organization itself, and not just the processes within the organization that need re-engineering. The enterprise needs to take advantage of its core competencies when it focuses its organization-wide business process improvements. Organizational Re-engineering is defined as "The rudimentary rethinking and redesign of operating processes and organizational structure, focused on the organization's core competencies, to achieve dramatic improvements such as reduced cost, increased product and service quality, and increased market share and profitability".

Aetna is re-engineering vital business functions across all its business units. The focus of these efforts is on the customer. They are replacing the traditional systems with new, refocused processes. Chairman and CEO Ronald E. Compton of Aetna stresses that there are several commandments inherent to any re-engineering effort. These are:

- You have to give people a mission, a clear understanding of how to achieve that mission, and a road map for choosing the appropriate steps for action.
- Either service the customer superbly, or don't even try.
- Change is not something that happens. It's a way of life. It's not a process, it's a value. It's not something you do, it engulfs you.
- Technology is never really a problem. The problem is how to use it effectively.
- The wrong answer rarely kills you. What it does is wastes time. Further, time is a limited resource – the only absolutely limited one.
- The weak link in re-engineering is will. Re-engineering is a huge job and it is agonizingly, heartbreakingly, tough.

- Once people catch on to re-engineering, you can't hold them down. It's a lifetime venture.

Compton states that Aetna is expecting to save over $120 million annually from streamlining its processes.

Root Cause Analysis and TRIZ

Root Cause Analysis and TRIZ are similar techniques, one from the United States and one from Russia. Root cause analysis focuses on change through analysis. Once a problem or opportunity for change has been identified, we attack the problem through data collection and analysis, trying to identify the root cause of the problem. The focus is on fixing the problem, not the symptom. Root cause is often used in conjunction with TQM in the problem identification phase, or it can be used as an independent system in it's own right.

Theory of Inventive Problem Solving (Russian acronym TRIZ) is a technique for systematically generating innovative solutions to difficult engineering problems. It incorporates an analytical process that draws from the world's patent libraries or other sources of technology. It focuses on searching, identifying, and analyzing the existing base of knowledge thereby increasing technical creativity, reducing time to market, and increasing quality. TRIZ focuses on how to solve technological bottlenecks.

Quality Functional Deployment (QFD)

QFD is the implementation of continuous improvement process focusing on the customer. It was developed at Mitsubishi's Kobe Shipyards and focuses on directing the efforts of all functional areas on a common goal. In Mitsubishi's case the goal was "satisfying the needs of the customer". Several changes were instituted in order to accomplish this, such as increased horizontal communication within the company. One of the most immediate results was a reduced time-to-market lead time for products.

QFD systematizes the product's attributes in a matrix diagram called a house of quality and highlights which of these attributes is the most important to a customer. This helps the teams throughout the organization focus on their goal (customer satisfaction) whenever they are making change decisions, like product development and improvement decisions.

QFD focuses on:

1) the customer
2) systemizing the customer satisfaction process by developing a matrix for
   a) defining customer quality
   b) defining product characteristics
   c) defining process characteristics
   d) defining process control characteristics
3) empowered teaming
4) extensive front-end analysis which involves 14 steps in defining the "house of quality"
   a) create and communicate a project objective
   b) establish the scope of the project
   c) obtain customer requirements
   d) categorize customer requirements
   e) prioritize customer requirements
   f) assess competitive position
   g) develop design requirements
   h) determine relationship between design requirements and customer requirements
   i) assess competitive position in terms of design requirements
   j) calculate importance of design requirements
   k) establish target values for design
   l) determine correlations between design requirements
   m) finalize target values for design
   n) develop the other matrices

QFD has been widely recognized as an effective tool for focusing the product and the process on customer satisfaction. However, as discussed earlier, QFD is a Japanese approach to focused change and therefore focuses on extensive analysis, utilizing the philosophy that we need to: "Make sure we are doing the right things, before we worry about doing things right!"

Total Quality Management (TQM)

TQM is a by far the most popular of all the change models internationally. It is extremely popular in Asia and Europe, primarily because it focuses more on analysis than on speed, as in the case of PR. There are numerous global companies that have focused on the TQM change model. Perhaps the first, and most impressive, United States based global company is Motorola, which has several continuous change programs throughout their plants all over the world. They are using quality councils and empowered teaming, both basic tools of the TQM process, in order to motivate their employees toward change.

Following the Motorola example, more by force than by desire, are many of Motorola's vendors. One of these vendors and probably the most successful implementer of TQM is AT&T, which is another global company with a focus on global efficiency and change. AT&T has systematized their change process to the point where they have corporate wide documentation of how the system works. The result of the AT&T implementation has been that they are only the second U. S. company to win the Deming Award (the Japanese award for quality change). Additionally, they have won three Baldrige Awards (the U. S. award for quality improvement) and the Shingo Award (the U. S. award for excellence in manufacturing).

TQM is not just a tool, it has an entire philosophy about how businesses should be run. The philosophy of TQM is filled with ideas and attitudes. Basic to this philosophy is the idea that the only thing certain in life is change. And we can either wait for the change to happen to us, or we can become an instrumental leader in the changes that will occur anyway. Competitive edge is rampant with changes. Product life cycles are shortening and the lead time to market for new products is becoming increasingly shorter. We may have the best ideas and products in the world, but unless we can get them to the market, in a way that will appeal to the customers, quicker than our competition, what's the use. Following is a list of several of the key elements of TQM philosophy:

- Attitude of desiring and searching out change
- Think culture – move from copying to innovating
- Do the right things before you do things right

- Top to bottom corporate strategy
- Clear definition and implementation of quality
- Education, training, and cross training
- Integration and coordination
- International view point.

As discussed in the last paragraph, change is the universal constant. In TQM, the philosophy behind change is one that suggests that we become excited about changes. We look for opportunity to change, especially because change should mean that we are becoming better. To be a TQM organization is to become an organization that wants to be the best, and realizes that there is always room for improvement.

The idea of a "Think Culture" is that we become a company that moves away from copying to innovating. This type of organization is one that realizes that the best you can ever do by copying someone else is to get caught up with them. A think culture is where we know that in order to be best we need to innovate. We need to create and then implement our new creations. We cannot be afraid of taking the risks that innovations will require us to take. The concept of a think culture also suggests that we need to break free of the fads. MRP II, JIT, OPT (Optimized Production Technology), TOC, CIM (Computer Integrated Manufacturing), BAM (Bottleneck Allocation Methodology), and so many more, are all fads that have been sold to us as world cures. A think culture would be one that looks at each "fad" as having potential benefits, but realizing that nothing fits everyone. These fads have to be looked at in light of the goals that you are trying to achieve. They would be implemented as stepping stones toward improvement, not as stand-alone, complete success packages. Often they will be found to be lacking in the benefits that they were supposed to have.

The idea of a think culture also follows closely with the next concept which I have labeled "Do the Right Things Before You Do Things Right". This means that you need to consider the value of what you are doing (or planning to do) before you do it. There is no value in doing a job perfectly, if the job adds no value to what you are trying to achieve; your corporate goals. All activities in an organization need to be looked at in light of their "value-added" to the organization. This includes rethinking what you are already doing, as well as taking a close analytical look at innovations.

TQM supports a "Top to Bottom Corporate Strategy" which means that the direction for the corporation comes from the top. It means that without top management commitment to change, as well as a commitment to the other philosophies supported by TQM, leaves TQM doomed to failure. This top to bottom strategy also supports integration between the various levels of the organization.

The next TQM philosophy is a clear definition and implementation of quality. There are nearly as many definitions of quality as there are companies. A TQM company needs to define quality for themselves, whether that definition is to meet engineering standards as it is in most U. S. companies, or whether it is the leading edge definition of making a product so exciting to the customer that the customer wouldn't think of buying from anybody else. With a clear definition of quality the company can start to focus on a target for change. It is difficult to focus on implementing changes that will improve quality, if no one agrees on the definition of quality.

Another TQM philosophy is the continual need for education, training, and cross training. Change and innovation look for the implementation of new ideas. In order to search these ideas out and to validate their usefulness requires an open mindedness and a constant look for new technologies. This requires education. Then, when ideas are selected for implementation, the implementers and users of the new technology need to be trained in its application. Additionally, in order to be an effective, integrated organization, cross training (understanding the jobs and functions of coworkers) allows employees to be able to help other employees, as well as to see suggested changes "through their eyes".

Another TQM philosophy states that without integration and coordination of functions, you are ineffective in the exchange and implementation of new ideas. This integration must be both horizontal (between functional areas) and vertical (top to bottom) in the organization. A free exchange of ideas between functional areas without constantly being concerned about the chain-of-command is critical.

The last philosophical point listed is the need to realize that all companies are effected by international transactions, either through the vendor, the customer, or directly. An international view point when it comes to the development of new ideas can mean the difference between a competitive and noncompetitive edge because it opens up a whole world of markets and vendors.

The success stories for TQM can be found in settings all over the world. TQM success are measured in terms of the successful implementation of change. This change can take the form of the implementation of new technology, or the correction and improvement of old technology. Often, a successful TQM project results in the ability of employees to work more effectively together. The result is that measurement of TQM success is an internal success story, and not always externally comparable.

Success in TQM can be found in large organizations like PETRONAS, the national petroleum corporation of Malaysia where, because of it's successes, TQM implementation is moving forward on a company wide basis. TQM, through it's systematic implementation of changes, won the Deming Award, a Japanese quality award, for Florida Power and Light, a United States producer of Electricity. TQM is receiving nationwide attention in Mexico through a sponsoring organization, Fundameca, the Mexican national productivity and quality improvement organization. Many other Latin American countries are also focusing national attention on TQM implementation, like Guatemala's "II Congreso Nacional Y I Cetroamericano De Calidad Total" meeting. Numerous success stories exist about specific individual companies, like the Solectron story, in the publications generated by organizations like:

- AQP – Association for Quality and Participation – http://aqp.org
- APQC – American Productivity and Quality Center – http://apqc.org
- The Shingo Prize – www.shingoprize.com/shingo/busguide.html
- The Deming Award (Japan's International Quality Award)
- The Baldrige Award – www.nist.gov

Now we will discuss what is needed to take the TQM philosophy and make it operational. There are several points that need to be discussed. The first of the operating points, *goal focusing*, emphasizes that the majority of the employees of an organization have no idea what the goals of an organization are. They will offer some guess like profits or sales, but they are guessing. Obviously, if the employees don't know what the goal of the organization is, then how should they know if what they are doing helps to achieve this goal. If we are considering the implementation of a TQM program, then all of the TQM teams need to evaluate the projects being considered for implementation in light of this goal. We need to determine which project contributes the most toward achieving the goal.

The word "focusing" is also very important in the discussion of goal focusing. Here we are stressing the need to isolate a single, specific goal. In goal focusing it is important to realize that there is more than one type of goal available to us. This topic was discussed thoroughly in Chapter 3.

Once we have defined the goal focus, we are ready to look at the *Measurement and Motivation Planning*. Here what we are trying to do is to realize that a measurement system is actually a motivation system. This topic was discussed in Chapter 3. In general, measurement systems need to be revamped. Projects should be selected and measured with a focus on the organizational goal. This was the next point in the operationalization of TQM; keeping an *eye single to the goal.*

TQM implementations start with a *coordinating team*, often referred to as a quality council. This is a team composed of high level corporate leaders from all the functional areas. This team is appointed by the CEO and operates under his/her direction. The CEO takes an active part in directing the activities of the team. This quality council is then responsible for organizing and measuring the performance of the other TQM teams within the organization. It oversees the installation, training, performance, and measurement of the other teams. This team focuses specifically on the corporate goal/vision and definition of quality.

The Quality Council will organize three different types of teams referred to as the cross functional *three "P" teams*. The Three P Teams are process, product, and project teams. The process teams are on going, continuous improvement teams set up at different levels of the organization. They look for improvements in the organization's functioning processes. These teams should be composed of both "insiders" and "outsiders". The insiders know and understand existing functions and operations. The outsiders challenge the status quo.

The second of the Three P Teams are the product teams. These teams are cross functional but focus on a specific product or product line. They are customer and vendor interface teams that are specifically oriented towards the development of new products and the improvement of existing products. Their life span is the same as the life span of the product they represent.

The third of the Three P Teams are the project teams. These teams are limited life teams set up to specifically focus on a specific project, like the construction of a new plant, or a computer installation. These teams may be the result of a specific process or product that is being targeted, or they may be set up to research something that the general management team is interested in developing or improving.

At this point we should know where we are going as an organization (focused goals), how we are performing towards this goal (measurement and motivation systems), and who is going to help us get there (TQM teams). Next we need to discuss the process that a typical TQM team will go through. These are called the TQM *project implementation steps:*

- Identify problems (opportunities)
- Prioritize these problems
- Select the biggest bang-for-the-buck project
- Develop an implementation plan
- Use operations research and MIS tools where appropriate
- Develop guide posts and an appropriate measurement system
- Training
- Implementation
- Feedback – Monitoring – Control – Change
- After successful project implementation and ongoing status, repeat cycle.

The first function of the team is to identify their function and charter. If you are on one of the Three P teams, your team's charter is laid out for you by the quality council. If you are the quality council, this charter is laid out for you by the CEO and is aimed at the focused goals of the organization. Understanding your charter, the team will then search for and identify problems that exist and that prevent the organization from achieving this charter. The word "problems" has a negative connotation. A better wording would be to say that we search of "opportunities for improvements". We are not just trying to correct negative effects, we are looking for techniques or tools that will allow us to become better.

Next we take these problems (opportunities) and prioritize them based on their effect on the charter of the team (which should be focused on the goals of the organization). We do a type of ABC analysis (80-20 Rule or Pareto Principle) to determine which change would have the greatest effect. Then we select the biggest bang-for-the-buck project and develop an implementation plan for this project. This implementation plan needs to contain guide posts that are based on an appropriate measurement systems that points the team towards achieving its charter. The book *Breakthrough Thinking* does an excellent job of discussing opportunity identification techniques.[2]

Training of the implementers and users is critical or else the planned project is doomed to failure. This training makes future users comfortable with the changes. It also offers a bit of ownership since the planned users will now feel comfortable with the changes.

The next step is implementation. The implementation should be trivial, if all the planning and training steps are preformed carefully. Part of the implementation is the installation of feedback, monitoring, and control mechanisms, as laid out in the implementation plan. Careful monitoring allows for corrective changes to occur whenever necessary.

After successful project implementation, and seeing that the ongoing status of the project is functioning correctly, the team repeats the implementation cycle, looking for more new opportunities for change. If this process is performed correctly, the list of change opportunities should become longer with each iterative cycle. This means that your team is now open for newer and broader opportunities for change.

2. Nadler, Gerald and Shozo Hibino, *Breakthrough Thinking,* Prima Publishing and Communications, 1990, Rocklin, CA.

Training programs need to exist before and after project selection. In the before case, the TQM team needs to understand what tools are available to them. This training would involve an understanding of tools and techniques. Initial training could include programs in areas like Operations Research / Management Science tools and techniques, Motivational / Philosophical training, Semi-technical and Technical, the operation of the Systems Approach, etc. It could include workshops like:

- What is TQM?
- TQM task force training.

Initial TQM training would also include general courses like:

- Total Quality Management – An Overview
- Operations Tools in TQM
- Statistics Tools in TQM
- Systems Analysis in TQM
- The Theorists and Applicationists of TQM
- The Measurement Systems of TQM
- Management Approaches to TQM

TQM is the selection and implementation of corrective operations management tools. Many of the tools listed throughout this book would be considered candidates for a TQM implementation.

Concept Management (CM)

CM is the last of change processes that will be discussed. Concept Management (CM) is the innovation process that Toyota utilizes for the implementation of integrated change. It utilizes three major components:

- Breakthrough Thinking as the innovation creator.
- Total Quality Management as the change management driver.
- World Class Management as the management structure incorporating empowered teaming to motivate change.

CM is the culmination of two leading-edge philosophies focused on change management. The first is "Breakthrough Thinking" (from the book of the same name by Nadler and Hibino), which focuses away from the traditional backward looking approach to change toward innovative, creative, forward-looking change. This book focuses on making innovation happen by utilizing the "Breakthrough Thinking" (BT), opportunity-generating paradigm.

The second leading-edge philosophy is "World Class Management" (WCM), which stresses that managers need to make change happen, rather than make changes only because they are forced to. Managers need to be the source of innovation. Both philosophies, BT and WCM, stress the need for change. BT offers the "how to" of identifying innovative change; WCM offers the "where to" change and shows us how to proceed with the change (innovation) implementation process.

CM puts structure into the change process so that everyone, at all levels of the organization, understand:

- What needs changing
- How to identify innovative alternatives for change
- How to select the best change alternative
- How to initiate the change process
- How to monitor and control the change process
- How to measure the performance of the change
- How to establish an ongoing feedback mechanism under which the change operates.

Unlike Root-Cause Analysis and TRIZ, CM focuses on "Why we are working on this problem", before collecting data and analyzing the problem. CM claims that it solves more problems and solves them much faster than traditional methods. Therefore, CM is considered to be the most advanced and leading edge of the change and innovation models and has gained wide acceptance throughout Asia.

Developing the International Operations/ Manufacturing Strategy

With a thorough understanding of the operations change process, we will now go back to a discussion of how to develop the detailed manufacturing strategy. We start with the last chapter where we discussed the corporate strategy. We will take this strategy and detail it out at the lower levels. For example, a manufacturing strategy would focus on the following issues:

- People
  - Employees
    - Selection and Training
    - Involvement / Empowerment
    - Compensation
    - Job Security
    - Team Development
    - Organizational Structure, Staff Functions
  - Customers
    - Involvement
    - Internal to the Organization
    - The final end user
  - Vendors
    - Integration
    - Extent, Number, Relationships

- Integration
  - Vertical Integration – Direction
  - Elimination of barriers
  - Information

- Globalization
  - Alternative sourcing

- Measurement
  - Internal Performance
    - Quality – Definition, Role, Responsibility
    - Productivity, Efficiency
    - Capital Budgeting Process

- External Performance
  - Are you adding value to society?
  - Customer perceived quality
  - Market Share
- Internal Factors
  - Capacity – Amount, Timing, Type
  - Equipment and Process Technologies:
    Scale & Level of Automation
    Flexibility vs. Specialized
  - Facilities – Size & Location: Specialization
  - Operational Performance: Production Control:
    Flow, Inventory Levels
    Scheduling
- External Factors
  - Competition
  - Economic Conditions
  - Government Regulation
- Focused
- Motivational

•

- Continuous Change Process focused on Adding Value
  - Elimination of Waste
  - Identifying Strengthens and Weaknesses
  - Identifying Opportunities and Threats

- Time-Based Competition
  - Time to Market Strategy

- Technology
  - Funding
  - Facilities and Equipment
  - New Product Development:
    - Interface with Engineering, Marketing, and the Customer

A manufacturing strategy should cover all these basic areas. Additionally, some specific areas that need additional focus include:

- Globalization / Localization
- Quality Strategy
- Productivity Strategy
- Technology Strategy
- Critical Resource Strategy

Globalization / Localization

In the development of a manufacturing globalization strategy there are two areas of concern. The first is the Logistics Strategy, and the second is the Location Decision. The logistics strategy focuses on the sourcing of materials, and the transport of the finished products. This is primarily the focus of the Supply Chain Management section of this book (Chapters 6 through 9), however, it is a critical part of the Manufacturing strategy.

The location decision focuses on the decision tree that selects where our plant should be located. It also considers from where outside sourcing should occur. This is primarily the focus of Chapter 10 and will be discussed in detail in that chapter.

Quality strategy

The quality strategy is a critical part of the total strategy, and should filter down as part of the production strategy. The philosophical approach is that there is not a quality strategy or department, rather, quality is the responsibility of everyone in the company and quality should be a part of everyone's strategy. Quality considerations should include:

- Defect Rate Reductions
- On-time delivery performance
- Customer Complaints / Surveys
- Cycle Time Performance
- Supply Chain Performance

Appendix 4.2 is the detailed Quality Strategy of Y, Inc.

Productivity strategy

It is valuable to appropriately define productivity and then set a methodology for measuring the level of productivity. This should be focused on the critical resource, as discussed in previous chapters. Perhaps an example would demonstrate the point. For example, there is a production facility with ten employees, two of which are reading newspapers. Additionally, the walls of the facility are lined with inventory, we often experience different reactions depending on the perspective of management. If, for example, the manager is a traditional American manager who is focused on labor efficiency, the manager would be very upset about the two employees reading the newspaper. If, however, the manager entering the room was a Japanese manager from the "old school" (not Harvard trained), he might be focused on materials efficiency. He would think that the two employees reading the newspapers must have done a good job in order to have the time to read a newspaper. However, the materials focused manager would become very upset about the high level of inventory.

From this example we see that the two managers have entirely different definitions of what constitutes productivity. In the first case it's labor productivity, and in the second example it's materials efficiency that is the focus. What's important for the company is a level of productivity measurement consistency. The company has to be on the same wave-length as to what productivity definition is important, and this becomes a part of the integrated production strategy.

Two buzzwords that have shifted some of the attention of manufacturing efficiencies and productivity are *lean manufacturing* and *agile manufacturing*. Lean manufacturing focuses on running the factory with the minimal use of resources, similar to total factor productivity. The focus is on minimizing the use of non-value-added resource efforts, thereby maximizing the value-added production processes. Agile manufacturing focuses on flexibility. For example, Toyota can run production in any sequence. A top-of-the-line luxury Lexus can be followed by a bottom-of-the-line Corolla, with no effect on the production flow or efficiency. This type of flexibility allows the factory to be more customer responsive, and reduces lead-time for customized products.

Technology strategy

In the production strategy, the level of technology development primarily focuses on the manufacturing and distribution technology, like CAD/CAM capabilities, shop-floor automation, automatic picking and retrieving systems, bar-coded inventory control systems, robotics, etc. The facilities and equipment strategy needs to reflect the technological advances that the organization needs to move through.

Critical Resource Strategy

The critical resource strategy focuses on the elimination of waste and the increase of value added content. Reflecting back on the previous discussion of the critical resource we remember that the increased efficient use of one resource decreases the efficiency performance of other resources. Therefore, it is critical to select the correct resource focus. This then effects the measurement system, which includes the selection of the correct production / operations management system. Appendix 4.3 lists and compares EOQ, MRP, JIT, and TOC for their advantages and disadvantages. It also defines the categories of each classification. The chart in this appendix shows the differences between each of these production planning and control methods and shows their most appropriate application. This Appendix is the type of general comparative analysis between scheduling strategies. However, this type of comparison is also specifically available with many software comparison vendors. For example, the following web site offers a free ERP / MRP software comparison tool – http://webstats.allegronet.net/ss?click&lakeinteractive&3a7ad5f4

Economic Order Quantity (EOQ)

EOQ is by far the most popular production and purchasing scheduling tool because it is the easiest to use. EOQ dates back to the earliest of production systems and was the only thing that was available prior to the advent of the computer. EOQ doesn't have the detailed inter-linkages that the other systems have because of their complexity. Therefore the chain reaction rippling effect of errors is not felt. EOQ focuses on and measures only one resource – inventory. Chart 4.4 shows the inputs and outputs of the EOQ process. There are other systems that are more efficient than EOQ at managing inventory, like JIT.

Chart 4.4. EOQ Input-Outout Plan

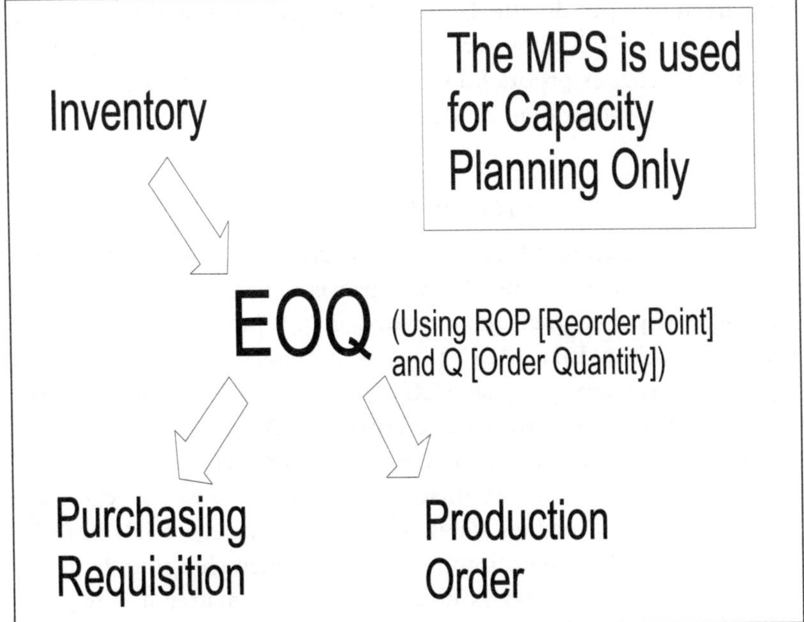

Material Requirements Planning (MRP)

MRP is the second most popular technique for production and purchasing scheduling. It is, however, a lot more complicated than EOQ (compare Chart 4.4 with Chart 4.5). MRP contains a series of inter-linkages between a multitude of resources which made it impossible to use prior to the computer. Therefore, MRP, like its counter-parts of JIT and TOC, is a post-World War II production planning systems. MRP became very popular in the United States and Europe during this era. Prior to the 1960's, the critical resource in the European and American production process was labor. Because of this, MRP was utilized to focus on labor efficiency. It utilized labor-based routings and focused on achieving a balanced factory, which meant that the labor demand equaled the labor capacity. Still today, even in repetitive discrete factories where labor is rarely the critical resource anywhere in the world, labor based routings and labor performance reporting is still a significant part of nearly all MRP environments.

MRP schedules inventory by looking at a collection of resources, usually the three-Ms (materials, machinery, and manpower). These M's are developed in the Bill of Materials and the Routings (see Chart 4.5). MRP is considered to be a push production methodology since it releases production orders on the production floor based on schedules, rather than on demand.

Just-in-time (JIT)

JIT is the Americanized name given to the Toyota production planning process. It was a production process that was learned in an American super-market and imitated in the Japanese manufacturing environment. Like MRP, JIT was developed in the post World War II era. However, unlike MRP, JIT was developed with an emphasis on materials performance efficiency. After World War II, the Japanese were trying to rebuild their industry. However, they had no natural resources, no financial resources, and an excessive amount of labor. So their focus was on bringing materials into the country, converting them into product, and then shipping them out and selling them as soon as possible. It didn't matter if it took an excessive amount of labor to accomplish this – the key was that the materials needed to keep moving. This need for materials efficiency is at the heart of JIT, and the Japanese searched long to find such a system. If you were to ask Toyota how they came up with JIT, they would tell you it took 30 years of work.

JIT is referred to as a pull production system since it releases production orders to the floor based on customer orders pulling these production orders through the process. JIT is based on EOQ principles, but it significantly reduces the EOQ inventory levels to nearly nothing. As can be seen in Chart 4.6, the JIT process retains some of the EOQ simplicity in it's planning process. For example, there are no computers on the production floor that are used for production scheduling, whereas, MRP is overrun with computer power.

Chart 4.5. MRP Input-Output Plan

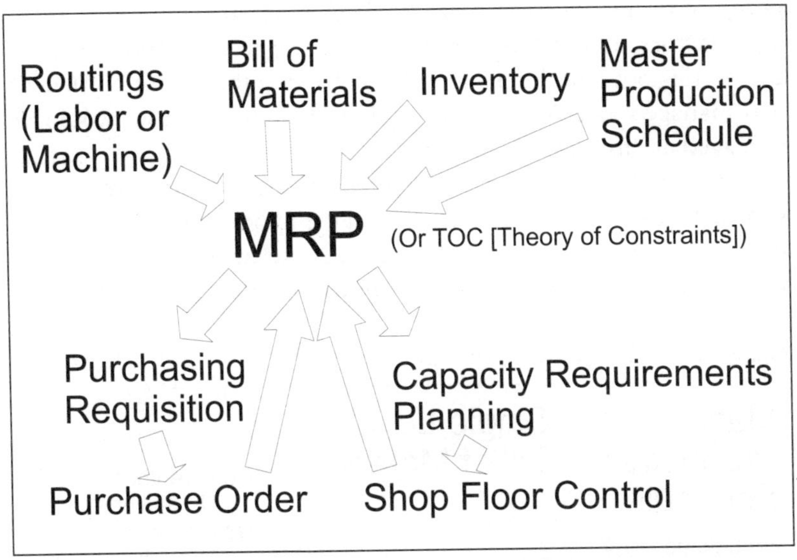

Routings (Labor or Machine)
Bill of Materials
Inventory
Master Production Schedule
MRP (Or TOC [Theory of Constraints])
Purchasing Requisition
Capacity Requirements Planning
Purchase Order
Shop Floor Control

JIT in the United States is very different than the JIT found in Toyota. In the United States version, managers still desperately cling to the labor efficiency focus and are afraid to give up this control. Therefore, they like the MRP base system, and they use a stripped down version of JIT as a shop floor control mechanism (see Chart 4.5). This JIT-Kanban shop floor mechanism gives significant inventory control improvements over the current MRP process. But the U. S. version is not as materials efficient as the full-blow JIT process would offer it's user. However, in spite of this abuse of the JIT process, the second most efficient user of JIT in the world, after Toyota who originally developed the process, is the U. S. Saturn plant.

Theory of Constraints (TOC)

Like MRP and JIT, TOC, formerly known as Optimized Production Technology (OPT), is another multi resource scheduling system that was developed in the post World War II era, this time it was developed in Israel. TOC focuses on identifying and efficiently managing the bottleneck resource in an organization. This resource is most often some critical piece of machinery around which the rest of the plant should be scheduled. In the development of TOC, a group of technocrats were asked to define an efficient way to manage a factory, and they determined that the best way would be to focus on this bottleneck resource. They decided that if this bottleneck was managed as efficiently as possible, the entire factory would be managed as efficiently as possible.

Like MRP, TOC is computer intensive and would have a chart similar to Chart 4.5. However, the mathematics of OPT is focused on resource optimization. TOC became extremely popular in Europe, and has also found a strong following in the United States.

Chart 4.6. JIT Input-Output Plan

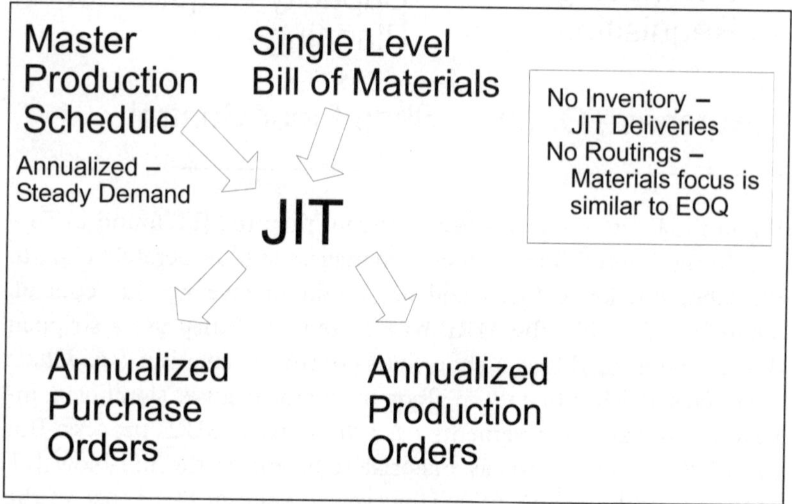

The Different Systems

The three most critical resources, materials, labor, and machinery, each ended up with corresponding systems which became popular after in the post war era. MRP focused on labor, JIT on materials, and TOC on machinery. Appendix 4.3 compares the four production systems discussed in this section. Additionally, Appendix C offers a simulation that compares MRP, JIT, and TOC, and it is extremely helpful in analyzing the perspectives of the three multi-resource scheduling international production and operations management strategies.

Y, Inc. Continued

Let's return for a moment to Y, Inc. and see what they developed as their operations strategy. As the long-term relationship with YV, Inc. drew near, Y developed the necessary operations, marketing, and financial strategies. Included in the operations strategy was a production strategy, a quality strategy, a purchasing department plan, an engineering plan, and a R & D strategy focused on technology development. A detailed example of the production strategy is included in Appendix 4.1. The detailed quality strategy is found in Appendix 4.2.

Y, Inc. decided that in order to maintain a tighter control of the marketplace, they needed to "sew up" the interests of YV, Inc., the research firm. Y is betting so strongly on the success of the EL product that if the cash flow for EL didn't start coming in soon, they would surely fail. The concern is that YV has the R&D technology and has no exclusive contract to deal only with Y. Therefore, if YV gets cold feet in dealing with Y, they could easily find another overseas producer of their product. But, as we remember from the earlier discussion, Y wasn't sure they could handle the volume that the large EL orders would require. Y desperately needed a cash flow source that would strengthen the position that they were in. They could never get the cash out of the core business because the margins were just too low.

Y, Inc. is looking for an international attack on the EL marketplace. They want a plan that will address their production needs from potential customers like Sony, who is looking for a play-station production process that would require the production of 10, 000 units every six months, or the Barbie Doll Collector's Edition Christmas Box which would require 100,000 units of production in the six month period. These would require production and shipment internationally. Can Y, Inc. satisfy this demand, or should they look elsewhere? How should the international demand be handled, with local production and then shipped, or with international production? And what about keeping the EL production process proprietary? How would you handle the Y, Inc. and YV, Inc. relationship?

Summary

The strategy is the tool of operationalizing the goals discussed in the last chapter. An effective operations strategy includes the basic elements of:

- Production Strategy
- Quality Strategy
- Technology Strategy (R&D and Engineering)
- Purchasing / Materials Strategy
- Logistics Strategy

Each of these is considered through the glasses of globalization and localization and reviews not just expenditures, but also identifies appropriate management / measurement / and motivation systems. Now, in the next chapter, we are ready to take a close look at the international flow of information in an organization.

Class Assignments

A) There is a software based case focused on "International Operations Simulation" which presents an excellent opportunity for the development of an international strategy. It needs to be purchased separate from this book and should be used as you proceed through the remaining chapters of this book.
INTOPIA, Executive Guide, by Hans Thorelli, ISBN: 013227034X, Prentice Hall, Englewood Cliffs, NJ, 1994.

B) Assign the students to look up 10 definitions for the items in Appendix A and to write them up. Sometimes I will have them present and discuss one of these items in class.

C) Appendix C is a simulation that compares MRP, JIT, and TOC. It is an excellent comparison that hits home on the operational differences.Present and discuss in class.

D) There is quite a bit of detail offered on Y, Inc. in this chapter. How would you manage the Y, Inc. and YV, Inc. relationship? Don't forget to review Appendix 4.1 and 4.2.

References

Strategic Management References

Garvin, David A., Operations Strategy, Prentice Hall, 1992.

Plenert, Gerhard, *World Class Manager*, Prima, Rocklin, CA, 1995.

Process Re-Engineering References

Boyer, John E., "Re-engineering Office Processes", *APICS 37th Annual International Conference Proceedings*, APICS, October 1994, Pages 522-526.

Cypress, Harold L., "Re-engineering", *OR/MS Today*, February 1994, Pages 18-29.

Hammer, M., and J. Champy, *Re-engineering the Corporation*, Harper Business, New York, NY, 1993.

Hammer, M., and Champy, "The Promise of Re-engineering", *Fortune*, May 3, 1993, Pages 94-97.

Hammer, M., "Re-engineering Work: Don't Automate, Obliterate", *Harvard Business Review*, July-August 1990, Pages 104-112.

Harbour, Jerry L., *The Process Re-engineering Workbook: Practical Steps to Working Faster and Smarter Through Process Improvement*, Quality Resources, White Plains, New York, 1994.

Lowenthal, Jeffrey N., *Re-engineering the Organization: A Step-by-Step Approach to Corporate Revitalization*, ASQC Quality Press, Milwaukee, Wisconsin, 1994.

Marks, Peter, *Process Reengineeering and the New Manufacturing Enterprise Wheel: 15 Processes for Competitive Advantage*, CASA/SME Technical Forum, Society of Manufacturing Engineers (SME), Dearborn, Michigan, 1994.

Plenert, Gerhard, "Process Re-Engineering: The Latest Fad Toward Failure", *APICS – The Performance Advantage*, June 1994, Pages. 22-24.

TRIZ References

Altshuller, G. S., *And Suddenly the Inventor Appeared: The Art of Inventing*, Technical Innovation Center, 1994.

Altshuller, G. S., *Creativity As An Exact Science: The Theory of the Solution of Inventive Problems,* Technical Innovation Center, 1994.

Total Quality Management References

Capezio, Peter, and Debra Morehouse, *Thanking the Mystery out of TQM: A Practical Guide to Total Quality Management*, Career Press, Hawthorne, NJ, 1993.

Nadler, Gerald and Shozo Hibino, *Breakthrough Thinking*, Prima Publishing and Communications, 1990, Rocklin, CA.

Plenert, Gerhard, "The Basics of a Successful System", *Information and Management*, 1988, Pages 251-254.

Concept Management References

Nadler, Gerald and Shozo Hibino, *Breakthrough Thinking*, Prima Publishing and Communications, 1990, Rocklin, CA.

Plenert, Gerhard and Shozo Hibino, *Making Innovation Happen: Concept Management Through Integration*, St. Lucie Press, Boca Raton, 998.

International Production /Operations Management References

Plenert, Gerhard, "Installing Successful Factories into Developing Countries", *The International Executive*, Vol. 32, No. 2, Sept.-Oct. 1990.

Plenert, Gerhard, "International Industrial Management", *Organizational Development Journal*, Vol. 7, No. 1, Spring 1989.

Plenert, Gerhard, *International Management and Production: Survival Techniques for Corporate America*, Tab Professional and Reference Books, 1990, Blue Ridge Summit, PA.

Plenert, Gerhard, "Production Considerations for Developing Countries", *International Journal of Management*, Dec., 1988.

Plenert, Gerhard, "The Development of a Production System in Mexico", *Interfaces*, Vol. 20, No. 3, May-June 1990.

Ramalingam, P. Rama, "Making TQM Pay Off: The Solectron Experience", *APICS 37th International Conference Proceedings*, November, 1994, Pages 472-476.

Production Planning Comparative Articles

Fox, R. E., "Theory of Constraints", *NAA Conference Proceedings*, September, 1987.

Goldratt, Eliyahu M., and Jeff Cox, *The Goal*, North River Press Inc., Croton-on-Hudson, New York, 1986.

Goldratt, Eliyahu M., *The Haystack Syndrome*, North River Press Inc., Croton-on-Hudson, New York, 1990.

Goldratt, Eliyahu M., and Robert E. Fox, *The Race*, North River Press Inc., Croton-on-Hudson, New York, 1986.

Goldratt, Eliyahu M., *What is this Theory called Theory of Constraints?*, North River Press Inc., Croton-on-Hudson, New York, 1990.

Plenert, Gerhard J., "An Overview of JIT", *International Journal of Advanced Manufacturing Technology*, 1993, Vol. 8, Pages 91-95.

Plenert, Gerhard, *World Class Manager*, Rocklin, CA: Prima Publishing, 1995.

Appendix 4.1. The Detailed Y, Inc. Production Plan

Table of Contents

2000 Vision

An enormous amount of effort has gone into this production plan. Virtually every person in production has contributed in some form or another to the reams of data that have been gathered and compiled. The depth at which the data was examined, discussed, reviewed and re-reviewed, I believe, is unprecedented in Y's history. Human and machine capacities, capabilities, ergonomics, inventory levels, safety and quality have been considered, in many cases, to the limits of our educational and experience base. What that means is that the plan is far from perfect but we are confident it is thorough and precise enough to achieve our strategic goals; most specifically $10,000,000 in 2000. Within the production plan there are many assumptions, exceptions and references. Hopefully they are explained with enough detail that the reader will understand their origin or necessity. Most of the requirements are based on the sales department reports that our core business will remain fundamentally the same in 2000. There is consideration given to the shrinking number of "non-bell" accounts and the impact on capacity and yield from anticipated quality improvements. The "EL" project has an impact on capacity and is considered fully in the departments significantly affected. Some of the budgetary items (specific machinery & training) are actually funded under other departments such as R&D or Human Resources. In those cases such items are represented as production needs in this plan but annotated with their accountable department.

Some very exciting and challenging changes will be necessary in 2000 to achieve our goals. Quality and production will build a partnership that will focus our efforts on reduced defects and higher yields through process improvements. A monumental paradigm shift will teach us that quality goals will *lead* to volume goals. Total Quality Management (TQM) will not be a slogan; but the way we manage our house. Investment in our people will be paramount to our success. Education and training will be an ongoing process with each of us required to challenge ourselves to learn more, participate more and risk more.

Balance in our personal and professional lives is the spirit of our vision statement: "We Profit by Thrilling our Customers". *"Our Profit"* is *balance*. *"Thrilling our Customers"* will be the result of our strategic plans. Only when we find a measure of *quality* and *productivity* can we "thrill" our customers and count our "profits". Our vision statement is wonderfully simple in its context yet wonderfully encompassing in its spirit. This production plan comes from the spirit of our vision statement and the *requirements* within are the first steps to meeting our mission statement and the first steps to achieving *real* profits.

Document Structure

This document is separated into three sections:

- Macro function summaries
- Department summaries (micro)
- Appendices (Statistical reports, investments and budgets).

The macro function summaries address the "big picture" issues that impact or interact with what we do in production. Functions like Human Resources, Quality and Safety are discussed from the standpoint of production needs as a whole.

The department summaries focus on the specific requirements of each production department including human resource and equipment requirements and summary budget requirements.

The appendices support the Macro and Micro reports with budgetary data and statistical reports detailing productivity and throughput.

The reader will notice that the statistical reports take on many forms and appear to not follow any standardized template. Part of our 2000 plan will be to consolidate our reporting to a "seamless" department to department flow.

Human Resources

Currently we have 50 employees working in the manufacturing processes. This includes 3 managers (1 loop; 2 post loop), 11 department supervisors and 39 team members. Doubling our volume from $5 to $10 million dollars will require an additional 16 team members. The current number of supervisors and managers will be ample to take us to $10 million and beyond. The majority of the 16 new team members will not be needed until end of first quarter or second quarter when the UV print line and EL are ready for production commitments. The disproportionate ratio of employee increase to volume increase is due to economies of scale, quality improvements and increased margin (as opposed to core business) for EL products.

Education and training is of great significance in achieving our goals and *everyone* in production has been given educational goals to pursue in order to "grow" and in some cases to continue to hold positions as department supervisors or managers. The "new" policy on education bonus allows $250.00 per person per year paid for reimbursement of direct educational cost (i.e. registration fees, books, etc.) See the Human Resource plan for specific detail. Also included are allowances for seminars and "in-house" training. The SGIA convention is also budgeted with the intention of sending 6 employees. In all cases of education and training the funding will come from the Human Resource budget.

Summary information:
Total annual salaries: $1,300,000.00
Total Annual Education and Training: $23,000.00
Assumptions: 30 team members will utilize 100% of available education bonus = $7500.00.

Capacity

Capacity is broken down into two areas: Production and Physical space. Currently there is a team addressing the physical space requirements with a project milestone date of Jan 30, 2001. The physical space requirements will be met primarily through reorganizing existing departments, inventory reduction and the addition of a modular unit in the rear parking lot.

Production capacity has been determined through an extensive data collection system that has been in existence for nearly two years. Set-up times, production run times, and down times are documented on a standard template. Data is entered into an Excel spreadsheet from which reports are generated. Capacity information is reported by operator, shift, department, downtime cause, customer, press and a variety of other variables. Algorithms are also used to display data points as tables to predict capacity requirements. Supporting data for budget request are in the form of appendices and are referenced in each specific department later in this document.

The EL project will have significant impacts on certain departments; specifically Stencil, Print, Color Match, and Registered Lamination. The impacts are *negative* from the capacity standpoint but highly *positive* from the throughput standpoint. Within the plans for the impacted departments there are specific action items or assumptions needed to meet the added capacity demands.

Assumptions:

- In 2000 hidden capacity will be found through a fresh approach to process improvements leading to defect reduction. An approximate 50% reduction (3.5% overall defect rate) in *bad parts* is factored in to departmental capacity.
- The UV print line will be at full (two press) capacity by the end of first quarter.
- Electroluminescent Lamps (EL) will return $2,000,000 with approximately 170000 prints (14,000 job sheets) and 75000 die cuts. Production of EL will begin by end first quarter.

Quality

As stated a "monumental paradigm shift" will show us that quality leads to volume. Fundamentally we envision quality being measured and motivated as opposed to the current total focus on volume. With some $700,000 in defective parts lost in 1999 it seems stupid, for lack of a better word, to continue down the same road. If we can use the same energy that produced 180,000 job sheets from three print presses in one month surely we can reduce our parts defects by 50%. The relationship between quality and production should melt into one function with the inspector and the press operators working as a team toward the same goal.

Process improvements will have the largest impact on quality. We have a three year data base (along with our gut) that tells us clearly where we fail. Our failures are typically processes that have been in place for years with only modest changes yet they account for the majority of our defects.

The concepts of Total Quality Management (TQM) *must* be trained and institutionalized if our needed quality goals are to be realized. TQM fails as often as it succeeds because of a lack of buy in from management and a failure to train the process thoroughly to all employees.

Engineering and production will continue to develop our relationship. Physical space for a "floor engineer" will be made in the production area with the goal of bringing our different functions closer together. Engineering's impact on quality is so significant that we would be remiss if we did not build our team to focus on the same quality goals.

QS 9000 certification will be attained in November 2000 allowing us to keep current customers and pursue a broader base of new customers.

Assumptions:

- The quality budget is approved
- The quality plan is implemented
- TQM is trained and successfully institutionalized.

Safety

Since our greatest safety concerns are in the manufacturing areas production will take responsibility for training and institutionalizing our safety program. Individual team members have been assigned responsibility and are currently training their respective departments on safety procedures. Job Hazard Analysis (JHA) and total team member participation will be the cornerstone of preventive safety measures. With the ever increasing demand on physical space, safety will be continually kept on the forefront of all production considerations.

As part of the overall safety program, an incentive program is being developed which will encourage total team member participation towards safety. A plan will be developed to add incentive to safety. The plan will be developed by the team members affected through the TQM process. Without question, safety is an ideal program for the TQM process to flourish.

Assumptions:

- The safety budget is approved
- TQM is trained and successfully institutionalized.

Inventory

The start of 2000 will find us with a Finished Goods Inventory (FGI) in excess of $1,000,000; an unacceptable level by anyone's standard. A plan will be in place by January 30 to reduce FGI by

$500,000 in first quarter 2000. The long range goal will be to reduce FGI to "under 30 days" in 5 years. This is certainly an ambitious project in light of the fact that currently total reported "shipped" volume is approximately 50% FGI.

2000 will see the introduction of the Japanese KANBAN concept of inventory management. Education and training will be required to find exactly how the new (to us) concepts will best meet our needs. There is no doubt, however, that we carry far to much inventory in the wrong places.

Production and Purchasing will have to develop a new relationship to ensure plans are developed as a team and implemented with the "win – win" concept in mind. The first "test" of the KANBAN will be in January/February involving Serra Metals and Registered Lamination. If the test is successful, the plan will be fully implemented and new opportunities sought out.

Purchasing is also negotiating with certain vendors to maintain critical or safety stock items on Y, Inc. property to be "purchased" as used. This will reduce substantially the current problems associated with getting "caught short" and expediting material at premium shipping cost, not to mention the lost commitment to customers.

Production Equipment

The end of 1997 has found us with several new assets that ease the burden on new purchase requirements in 2000. Of significant importance to our 2000 plan is the implementation of an ultraviolet (UV) print process. All major equipment for the UV process is in place and currently being approved by R&D. The print room currently has enough machine capacity to produce $10 million. The impact of $10 million and EL on stencil and color match is significant. Stencil will need a screen dryer and an exposure unit to accommodate the large number of prints required by EL products. A color match computer is sorely needed and is currently being researched by R&D. Roll lamination has a great deal of capacity available, however, there is no redundancy in equipment therefore we will purchase a "spare parts" machine through the used equipment market. Diecut has procured two new clam shell type press in '97 and is in an excellent position for $10 million and beyond. The tedious task of parts preparation is in need of some type of automation and we have found a "deslugger" that does just that. The impact of the deslugger should allow us to move at least two people from parts prep to either registered lamination or touch switch as needed.

Total equipment investment: $135,500.00.

Building and Support Equipment

Building

Although we've been in our new building less than a year we are already finding ourselves rapidly running out of room. Unless we elect to "overcrowd" ourselves and in some cases *compromise* safety, more space will have to be made available. Several departments are growing rapidly along with request from R&D, Purchasing and Engineering for additional space downstairs. Production is also in great need of a conference and training room. Currently we have *no* space to conduct such activities. Die cut is of the most concern with more room needed for an additional die rack and greater safety space around the die presses. Parts Preparation will also need floor and safety space for the new "deslugger". Our solution is the temporary (two year) addition of a modular building of some 1000 sq. feet on the rear parking area.

Support Equipment

Along with the need for more space we need to upgrade our assembly stations. Currently employees are using standard desk or table tops with no lighting and with little concern for ergonomics. Further, an additional die rack is needed along with suitable equipment to store and maintain parts inventory.

Summary of Information:

- Total module rental (1yr.): $13,990.00
- Total Support Equipment: $27,000.00
- Total Building and Support Equipment: $40,900.00

Production Department Summaries

Precut

Of all the production departments precut has the most capacity available. Current workload is approximately 50% with one dedicated supervisor and a "part time" team member. With a 100% increase in workload our single Challenger Cutter should be adequate. Our plan is to cross train as many team members as needed from other departments to handle the increased workload.

The department is in need of "cleaning up" i.e. reducing inventory and replacing wooden shelving with stainless steel. The stainless steel shelving can wait until 2001, however, getting a handle on our inventory will start in first quarter 2000. Receiving shares some common space with precut and they (receiving) are requesting more space in 2000.

Gains/expenses in 2000
New Hires: 0
Education/Training: Expenses for computer and management training for 1 supervisor
Production Equipment: 0.

Stencil

Stencils largest challenge in 2000 will be to meet the changing capacity demands within the limited space of their department. Reducing inventory and the introduction of EL will lead to increased demand on the number of screens, thus increasing equipment demand and human resource requirements.

Equipment purchases for 2000 to handle increased demand will include a stencil dryer and an exposure unit. Money is also budgeted for a new screen cleaner due to ever increasing maintenance problems with the existing unit.

Some support equipment changes will occur in 2000 (cabinetry, shelving, etc.), however, they are detailed and budgeted under R&D as part of the "clean room" upgrade.

Gains/expenses in 2000
New Hires: 1
Education/Training: Expenses for computer and supervisor training for 2 supervisors
Production Equipment: $91,000.00
Support Equipment: 0 (see R&D).

Color Match

Color match is another one of our completely manual processes that is long overdue for an upgrade. Defects related to color match issues clearly justify investment in a Color Match Computer system. Several vendors have demonstrated their systems for us in-house. At the time of this writing a final selection has not been made but is anticipated by the end of January. Budget for the system is based on Data Color Corporation quote.

Some support equipment changes will occur in 2000 (cabinetry, shelving, etc.), however, they are detailed and budgeted under R&D as part of the "clean room" upgrade.

Gains/expenses in 2000
New Hires: 1
Education/Training: Expenses for computer and supervisor training for 2 supervisors
Production Equipment: $35,000.00
Support Equipment: 0 (see R&D).

Print

The Print Room is currently operating under near maximum capacity of two shifts. Initial consideration was given to a "graveyard" shift in 2000 to accommodate the needs of EL, however, that idea has been abandoned in favor of finding hidden or lost capacity in the form of defect reduction, decreased setup time and down time. An enormous amount of data exists to measure the print process performance. Historically the Print Room has been driven by dollar volume goals. In 2000 we will shift our paradigm to focus on quality (see Quality). The reasons for focus on quality are in some cases obvious and in others not so obvious to the "outsider". The obvious reason is some $700,000 (company wide) lost to defects in 1999 and the excessive overruns caused by a process with few effective quality controls. The less obvious reason is somewhat paradoxical for the print team members. They currently are rewarded and measured on dollar volume; something they have little if any control over. Jobs arrive in the print room "worth what they're worth" and so the print room must "jump through a variety of hoops" including overtime and weekend work to squeeze the dollar volume out of the given job profiles. In the end the print room is able to use its remarkable "job sheet per hour" rate to meet volume goals. The unfortunate trade off is quality and an unacceptable Finished Goods Inventory (FGI) balance.

With the introduction of the UV process and UV equipment the Print Room has enough capacity for $10,000,000 given *current* job profile, job sheet value and quality (i.e. our core business). The requirements of EL, however, reduces print capacity to approximately $9,000,000. This *assumes* no changes in *core business*. EL has a high margin but it requires many and frequent set-ups and restrict the use of the conventional dryer to conductive inks only. For the purposes of production planning we make some assumptions (see below). Given those assumptions are realized, the print room will have capacity to accommodate EL and produce $10,000,000. Notice that there is no assumption made for job sheet value increasing for our core business. Capacity vs. Volume is assumed to drop *no lower* than last quarter 1999 average. An increase in job sheet value will improve significantly our ability to produce $10,000,000.

No significant additional equipment is needed in the print process for the 2000 plan. Color match and stencil will need equipment for capacity and quality needs. See specific departments for detail.

Assumptions:

- Quality/Process improvements will result in a 50% decrease in print defects. (3.5% overall defect rate)
- Non-bell accounts will be reduced to 10% of all print jobs
- Core business job sheet value will be no lower than last quarter 1999
- EL will be in full production in the second quarter
- EL orders comply with current lead time criteria.

Gains/expenses in 2000
New Hires: 4; two press operators, two print coordinators
Education/Training: Expenses for basic computer training for 10 team members
Production Equipment: 0
Support Equipment: shelving-$1000.00.

Note: additional print room support equipment is funded under R&D for clean room upgrade and EL.

Roll Lamination

As with precut, roll lamination has a great deal of unused and "hidden" capacity. Under the current process there is an estimated 30% to 40% available capacity. With process improvements a 100% gain should be realized.

Inventory of partially used lamination rolls is a continuing problem however great improvements were made in '99 to manage the balances. In 2000 we expect to see greater control. Physical space is at a minimum with little room for growth considering the current production floor layout. The impact in '98 should be minimal with purchasing controlling any new inventory increases.

Currently we have only one fully qualified, full time machine operator. Some cross training has been done, however, much more is required to ensure we have adequate efficiencies to handle productivity demands. Roll lamination has excellent quality records so emphasis in cross training will identify and maintain the current standards.

Gains/expenses in 2000
New Hires: 1
Education/Training: Expenses for computer training for 2 and management training for 1 supervisor
Production Equipment: Used roll lam machine for spare parts
Support Equipment: 0.

Diecut

Diecut has acquired two new clamshell type presses in 1999. The presses are faster and have proven to extend die life farther than our "old" Accupress. In some cases, however, the Accupress performs better than the clamshell design and when intend to keep it in full use throughout 2000. Because the Accupress is "hard" on dies we would like to see it replaced in 2001.

The largest issue facing diecut is physical space. Die storage takes up nearly one-third of the space of the existing room and yet another storage rack will be needed in 2000. Part of the expansion plan (see building & support equipment) will give diecut approximately 200 additional square feet which should take us through 2001.

With the 1999 gains in equipment and team members diecut has no "major" requirements for 2000. Focus on quality and set-up time will increase capacity well beyond the requirements for $10,000,000.

EL will only improve the throughput projections so the exercise of calculating the effect is not complete at this time.

Gains/expenses in 2000
New Hires: 0
Education/Training: Expenses for computer training for 3 and management training for 1 supervisor
Production Equipment: 0
Support Equipment: $1500; die rack, $2000 room remodel .

Registered Lamination

Registered Lamination is currently under reorganization and relocation. Increasing demands on the department have required a fresh look at the processes. EL will place a significant demand on capacity and throughput. Physical space in the department is at a minimum for the current demand. Work stations are functionally and ergonomically unfit. Inventory levels, control and material handling and storage need complete revamping. Time line for completion of the registered lamination project is January 30, 1999.

Current volume through the department is approximately

$100,000 per month. It is difficult to determine throughput because process times vary substantially from part to part.

Gains/expenses in 2000
New Hires: 3
Education/Training: Expenses for computer training for 2 and management training for 1 supervisor
Production Equipment: 0
Support Equipment – $5000.00 department relocation and workstation upgrade.

Touch Switch

Touch Switch is in a somewhat nebulas state at the moment with a great deal of growth speculation. While one source will tell you that the market is mature with little growth potential, we have found ourselves with numerous prospects that would most certainly challenge our current capabilities.

As with Registered Lamination, Touch Switch is a difficult process to determine throughput rates. Currently we have no confident statistical data to use in 2000 projections, however, our "gut" tells us that three additional team members will be needed to meet the current sales projections of $1 to $1.5 million in touch switch volume.

The two largest areas of impact for 2000 is in dome placement and testing. Currently all domes are placed manually with vacuum pens. While our assemblers can place quality domes at an impressive rate the quantity of domes to be placed, if all the sales expectations are realized, will be overwhelming. The touch switch budget does include funding for touch switch work stations that have an improved dome placement method. The improved work stations should get us through '98, however, we are looking at a contingency plan of purchasing automatic dome pick and place machine that will handle any future touch switch demands. The drawback to the pick and place machine is the price: $90,000.00. It will take substantial orders with high margins to justify the cost of this machine.

To accommodate the demand on touch switch testing a new testing unit will be purchased. The tester is in the '98 budget and funded under R&D due to the need for more test capability in touch switch and potentially touch glass.

Another similarity with Registered Lamination is the inadequate work station that are currently utilized in touch switch. The above mention work stations with improved dome placement will resolve this issue.

Gains/expenses in 2000
New Hires: 3
Education/Training: Expenses for computer training for 2 and management training for 1 supervisor
Production Equipment: Testing unit (funded through R&D), $1000.00 – improved dome placement
Support Equipment: Workstation upgrade $2000.00.

Parts Preparation, Inspection, Packaging

Currently Parts Prep. is a completely manual process with throughput being part specific. There are numerous ergonomic and associate satisfaction issues associated with the process. Tendonitis has already cost us once and carpal tunnel will surface sooner than later. The process itself is far from challenging and leads to boredom and lack of focus on personal and company goals. Beginning to automate the process is a first priority for 2000. A "deslugging" machine has been manufactured by Mathias Die Company that addresses our needs. Mathias has manufactured a tool for us and demonstrated it on our product. The results were impressive and we plan to purchase the machine in the first quarter 98.

The personnel assigned to parts prep and packaging are in a state of flux with several team members being moved to other departments. The 2000 plan calls for an additional 2 people (for a total of 11), however, the introduction of the de-slugger should offset the need to hire 2 new team members. The future of inspection team members is a bit fuzzy. The quality team has a long range goal of eliminating the "final" inspection process all together. At that time the inspection process will have a new face and the inspectors will play different rolls than they do today. (See the Quality department plan for details.) Until changes are implemented the inspection process will remain fundamentally the same.

The physical space for parts prep, ins., and packaging will change completely in the first quarter 2000. All three functions *may* move into a modular in the rear parking lot. (See Building & Support Equipment for details) This move will open up sorely needed space for various other departments that need to expand. (An alternative plan will be to move FGI & on-site vendor stock into the modular.)

Gains/expenses in 2000
New Hires: 2
Education/Training: Expenses for computer training for 5 and management training for 1 supervisor
Production Equipment: Deslugger $7500.00
Support Equipment: Miscellaneous shelving $1000.00.

Shipping

The shipping department is in good shape overall. The need for appropriate work space and work stations is the largest concern for 2000. With the introduction of the "modular" (See Building & Support Equipment for details) space will open up to accommodate their needs.

The 2000 plan calls for the training of 1 additional team member in the shipping department; most likely in the second quarter.

Part of our plans to improve quality and productivity involve reducing "rush" or overnight shipments. While the root cause of this problem is not specifically the shipping process; shipping will be closely involve with "cost reduction". Shipping team member will also be a part of the plan to reduce Finished Goods Inventory (FGI) (See Inventory or details)

Gains/expenses in 2000
New Hires: 1
Education/Training: Expenses for computer training for 2 and management training for 1 supervisor
Production Equipment: 0
Support Equipment: Miscellaneous shelving and a work station $1000.00.

Appendix 4.2
The Detailed Y, Inc. Quality Strategy

The Y, Inc. Quality Strategic Initiative is a moving target of objectives and strategies focused on moving Y, Inc. through its next five years of growth. It was written 26 November 1999. It is built on goals and programs targeted toward the achievement of those goals. Here are the goals.

Vision: We profit by thrilling our customers

The Quality Team Members:

- Customer Service
- Production Planning and Scheduling
- Engineering
- Quality Management
- Research and Development
- Facilities Management.

Mission Statement For The Quality Team

- Increase the "profitable" customer base while achieving the revenue targets of each year as stated in the Y, Inc. strategic objectives
- Internal: Reduce defects to below 2% by 2000 and half again each year for the next five years. Reduce production and pre-production cycle times by 50 % per year
- External: Improve relationships with Customers (50% reduction in returned parts) and Vendors (improved long-term relationships focused on reliability quality).

Specific Targets (initiatives) necessary for the achievement of this mission:

- Developing a Y, Inc. Strategy – Defining a corporate-wide set of goals utilizing the Total Quality Management (TQM) Structure

- Thrilling Customers – Eliminating Customer Returns and Complaints and Compressing Cycle Time
- Supply Chain Management – Improving the process flow from vendor to customer
- Technology Growth – Maintaining a technological leading-edge in the process and products ofY, Inc.
- Eliminating Waste – Changing the focus of Y, Inc. to "Value Adding" processes through accountability and measures that motivate goal-focused responses.

Developing a Y, Inc. Strategy

Defining a corporate-wide set of goals utilizing the Total Quality Management (TQM) Structure

Program

This program is focused on developing a Quality Council that will do the following:

- Develop and detail out the Y, Inc. Strategic Initiatives
- Focus on continually updating and improving the process utilized for the implementation of the initiatives.

Process

Through the quality council we are addressing each initiative one at a time and developing focus areas. Then the team sponsor (a member of the quality council) organizes a TQM team. The team sponsor is then responsible for organizing the team and keeping it focused Ultimately, what we hope to accomplish is to develop a strategic plan for each of the next five years that details out quantifiable, measurable objectives. These numbers will be used in developing the forecasts and budgets for each years Plan of Operation.

Targets

By the end of First Quarter 2000 we hope to have a detailed Y, Inc. Strategic Plan which many of the Y, Inc. employees participated in developing, thereby giving them ownership and Buy-in.

Integration is critical. We want more cross-training between functional areas so that the walls between the areas are broken down.

Specifically we are bringing engineers down to the production floor and bring quality people into engineering.

Thrilling Customers

Eliminating Customer Returns and Complaints

Program

The program is four-fold:

1) Develop a relationship with the customers, especially the users and inspectors of our parts
2) Identify Customer specific and Job specific areas of discrepancies. These will become the targets of close monitoring throughout the inspection process
3) Carefully monitor the development of first issue parts through the development of a checklist that will help eliminate first run mistakes
4) Monitor. delivery-to-promise performance and develop corrective processes.

Process

The process is as follows:

1) We plan to visit the entire primary ("Bell" – top 80/20) customers with a representative from quality, production, and engineering. The purpose of the visit is primarily relationship building and will focus on meeting the receivers/inspectors, and the production supervisors that use our parts. Initially this will focus on the production manager level of management but it should eventually include some of the line-workers that work on the customer's parts.

   We also need to focus on "prime" customers that will give us the best margins and assist us in moving towards a higher technology future
2) We are doing extensive data collection and analysis focused on identifying which parts and which customers have which specific problems. We have started to adjust the final inspection process to focus more on catching areas of customer concerns. We are also developing job specific inspection instructions so that shop

losses will be caught earlier in the process thereby minimizing the waste of materials and capacity

3) Quality will become heavily involved in the new parts development process, which includes:

- Product margin evaluations
- Design for manufacturability meetings
- Clearly identified "acceptance" standards
- Verification that all the development steps are being checked-off and properly managed
- Meeting with the customer when necessary to satisfy acceptability requirements.

4) Working on the premise that nothing irritates the customer more than a broken promise, quality will be monitoring the on-time delivery performance of shipments. The purpose is to identify issues like:

- Inadequate lead-time specified
- Hold-ups in the process
- Improper shipping procedures
- Unrealistic customer expectations.

From this information we hope to take corrective action and improve customer satisfaction. Part of the process is also to maintain our ISO 9000 certification and, on a customer specific basis, implement the QS 9000 standard.

Targets

The targets are as follows:

- Reduce customer returns by 50 %
- Visit all the "Bell" customers at least once per year
- 90+% on-time deliveries to the original delivery target utilizing least-cost shipment methodologies unless authorized otherwise by the customer
- QS 9000 qualification in the first part of 2000
- Benchmarking will be done both externally (competitors and similar manufacturers) and internally (changes over time)

- Grow the customers by developing closer relationships with between them and Y, Inc. – Customer involvement – Customers in our shop

Supply Chain Management

With Supply Chain Management we attempt to improve the process flow from vendor to customer.

Program

There is a high level of waste in the process that needs to be reduced. For example:

- Redline jobs have a lot more failures than non-red-line jobs
- Revised orders have more reruns (24 %) than do new orders (22 %), which have more reruns than do repeat orders (16 %)
- There is no measurement/motivation system that focuses on job bag throughput. Regular throughput delays result in an excessive number of orders that require customer rescheduling or redline shipment
- Productivity improvements based on total-factor-productivity will reduce total cycle time and increase capacity. This is in integral part of the entire quality initiative.

Process

There are many focuses in this process. Some of them include:

1) Identify why jobs become redline and identify ways to eliminate the problem. – A lot of the jobs are being put on materials hold or customer hold and we are focusing on ways to eliminate or minimize these holds.
2) Assist production with advance scheduling information so that they can anticipate and prepare for redline jobs. This has happened by bringing the materials hold job bags down to production for advanced scheduling.
3) We can reclaim over 20 percent of our capacity in production if we eliminate reprint jobs due to excessive shop losses. Part of the process here requires the calculation of meaningful yields for the various processes. With job specific yields we can come up

with better estimates of how many sheets are required to end up with a specific number of end products. Other Waste-Elimination procedures mentioned in other sections of this report would also improve yields and reduce shop waste.

4) The current measurement/motivation system is focused on "potential" revenue printed per month. It should focus on revenue shipped per month and double deductions should be made for returns and late shipments. This would motivate more time and quality conscious revenue performance.
5) An accountability and measurement / motivation system focused on the Y, Inc. goals needs to be rethought and designed. We need to move away from the revenue based goals that are currently driving incorrect responses.

Targets

Supply Chain Management targets are as follows:

- Reclaim 15 + % of capacity by reducing the number of rerun jobs by 75 %
- Bring the "materials on hold" job bags to the production floor
- Reduce the number of red line jobs by 50 %
- Assist the departments in rethinking their measurement/motivation process. These will require finalizing the strategic initiatives of Y, Inc. so that the measurement can be focused on the new set of goals.

Technology Growth

Maintaining a technological leading-edge in the process and products of Y, Inc.

Program

In this area we are working based on the philosophy that the longevity of Y, Inc. is dependent on its ability to be competitive, and that this will require Y, Inc. to generate leading edge products utilizing leading edge technology. We are also working with the product life cycle model which tells us that new technology should be developed during the cash-rich phase of existing technology, not when technology has peaked out or finds itself in competitive decline. This is currently the problem at Y, Inc. The current technology is generally margin poor because of its competitiveness, which means minimum profits, which means no bonuses, which means that there is barely enough funds to develop new technologies. A history of fewer bonuses and more investment in technology might have avoided the current situation.

The area of technology growth focuses on identify new market niches like EL and touch-screen that will have much greater margins than most of our existing product line. It also focuses on new internal technologies like Color Match computers, UV, and clean rooms, which will allow a new, higher level of technology product to be produced.

Process

The primary source of product ideas and for new in-house technologies is with the customer and at trade shows. We need to identify opportunities and then develop project plans that include a cost/benefit analysis, which evaluates the feasibility and profitability of the new technologies. This development process has been initialized with the EL, UV, and Color Match technologies.

The next wave of internal technologies will include looking at first-article prototyping systems which make us more responsive to customer engineering tests.

Targets

Targets for technology growth are as follows:

- Produce EL by the middle of 2000
- Produce touch-screen product by the start of 2001
- Have the UV line and Color Match up and running by the first part of 2000
- Identify 2 new technologies for thorough R&D study by the end of 2000.

Eliminating Waste

Changing the focus of Y, Inc. to "Value Adding" processes through accountability and measures that motivate goal-focused responses.

Program

The focus here is on internal and external waste elimination. Waste is anything that:

1) Does not add value to the product
2) Does not increase customer satisfaction.

Process

The process is to identify all the different categories of waste within the organization. This includes waste due to parts losses, waste due to processing time losses, etc. Since parts losses have the largest identifiable (measured) dollar losses of between $ 500,000 to 600,000 per year we will address this first. We are focusing on the biggest "bang-for-the-buck" items first. What we found is that the most significant categories of parts losses are:

1) Shop losses due to damaged parts
We are getting a lot of parts with creases and marks on them. This translates to operator roughness with the product. This is a training issue and is being analyzed.

2) Foreign materials
Dust from paper, wood products, and clothing is getting on the parts. This is creating a large portion of our shop losses. We have set up a project focused on dust elimination, which will be phased in over the next year. This project has started with the hiring of "cleaners" which come in weekly and give the loop and touch switch a thorough cleaning. It next includes the removal of as much of the wood and paper products as possible by installing new racking and containers. It includes the wearing of low dust over-garments. It includes the resurfacing of the walls and floors. It includes new filtration systems. And it eventually will introduce clean-room tents and ventilation systems.

3) Coloration Errors
Color matching is an art form that requires extensive training and experience. Color errors have occurred through improper inks, incorrect mixes, and from simply picking up the wrong color ink in

the printing process. Two things are being introduced to reduce coloration errors. The first is the printing of colored engineering drawings that will be used to approximate the colors that should be laid down. This will assist the printer in making sure he grabs the correct can of ink. The second thing that is being implemented is the use of automated color matching equipment that will assist in the color blending process. This will reduce errors and save a significant amount of labor costs.

4) Registration errors
Registration errors occur when the operator misfeeds a sheet or when something moves in the process. The misfeeds can only be corrected by being more careful. The movement of tabs requires careful registration checks by the operator at regular intervals. We have found through the use of SPC techniques that if the registration is carefully checked at the start of the run, it generally remains stable throughout the run.

5) Screen Stretch errors
This error can be very costly because it is often not caught until the parts get to die cut, which means they have gone through several stages of production. Carefully checking the first print of the first color against the art work seems to identify most of the errors in this area We are establishing a procedure where we take the first color print and by utilizing the CMM we are validating the measurement against the artwork to make sure there are no screen stretch errors. This seems to help a lot.

6) Information errors
We are getting a lot of errors, like wrong legends or wrong colors, coming to us from engineering or the customer. These errors cause us to waste an unnecessary number of parts. We are initiating a process engineering function that will verify that the job bags for all jobs, especially in the case of new and revised jobs, have been process accurately.

7) Safety
We have had numerous safety issue crop up recently with the UV process and in die cut. These are being addressed with a safety team

focused on documentation and on taking corrective action.

8) Process Flow
Process flow on the production floor and in paperwork need to be seriously rethought to reduce waste steps. We are working on flow improvements for the floor and several stages of the paperwork process are being revisited. Additionally, the inspection processes are being reevaluated.

9) FGI and Stock
These resources are a waste and need to be eliminated rather than a drain on cash flow. We will monitor, control and evaluate these inventories until we get rid of them as much as possible.

Targets

The targets are:

- Reduce shop loss parts by 50 %
- Implement a measurement / motivation process that will focus on reducing job bag errors
- Implement a measurement / motivation process focused on measuring quality (defect free) output shipped to customers, rather than revenue generated by each production area
- A shift in focus to becoming critical resource efficient. This requires a balance of efficiency focused on both labor and materials
- Capacity management / Yield management / Production Scheduling systems need to be planned and organized
- Inspection on all shifts immediately after print
- Eliminate Final Inspection by bringing the inspections into the process.

Appendix 4.3
Comparison of the Four Major Production Planning and Control Technologies

Chart AP 4.3. Comparison of the Major Production Planning and Control Technologies

(1 of 2)

Feature / Function	EOQ	MRP	JIT	OPT
Complexity				
Computer	None	High	None	Medium
Mathematical	Minimal	Minimal	Minimal	High
Usage	Simple	Complex	Medium	Complex
Installation				
Conversion				
from EOQ		Simple	Simple	Simple
from MRP	Simple		Difficult	Medium
Data Prep.	Simple	Complex	Medium	Complex
User Disruption				
from EOQ		Major	Medium	Major
from MRP	Medium		Major	Major
Cost				
Systems	Low	High	Medium	High
Plant Low		Low	High	Low
Flexibility				
Operation	Minimal	Rigid	Rigid	Simulation
Product	High	High	Low	High
Scheduling	High	High	Rigid	Medium
Quality				
Integration	Minimal	Minimal	High	Minimal
Productivity				
Labor	High	High	Low	Low
Materials	Low	Medium	High	Medium
Machinery	Low	Low	Low	High
Resource	Materials	Labor	Materials	Machinery

(2 of 2)

Feature / Function	EOQ	MRP	JIT	OPT
Production				
Batch Sizing	Rigid	Rigid	Rigid	Flexible
Lead Time	Long	Long	Short	Medium
Order Track	None	Detailed	None	Detailed
Shop Layout	Open	Open	None	Open
Inventory	Very High	High	Low	High
Setup Time	High	High	Low	High
Manufacturing				
Discrete	Good	Good	Good	Good
Process	Good	Poor	Good	Good
Mk to Stk	Good	Good	Good	Good
Mk to Ordr	Poor	Excellent	Good	Good
Repetitive	Good	Good	Excellent	Good
Non-Rep.	Poor	Good	Poor	Good
Capacity Loading				
Flexibility	Low	High-Labor	Minimal	High-Machine
Cost				
Control	Minimal	High-Batch	Minimal-Avg.	Medium
Measurement	Materials	Labor/Materials	Over-All	Medium
Purchasing				
Lead Time	Long	Long	Short	Long
Scheduling	Easy	Easy	Annual	Medium

Comparison of the four major production planning and control technologies

Definition of the terms:

Complexity-Computer – What level of computer complexity is involved with the implementation of this product?

Complexity-Mathematical – What level of understanding of the mathematical/conceptual model is required for the user to correctly use the system?

Complexity-Usage – How complicated is the use (inputs and outputs) of the model?

Installation-Conversion – How difficult is it to convert from EOQ or MRP to the new system?

Installation-Data Preparation – How much new data needs to be prepared and how critical is the accuracy of the new data.

Installation-User Disruption – How disruptive is the new implementation (when converting from EOQ or MRP to the new system) to the users?

Installation-Cost-Systems – How expensive is the computer and networking hardware and software?

Installation-Cost-Plant – How expensive or extensive is the reorganization of the plant that is required by this system? For example, the movement of equipment and walls, or the purchase of new equipment.

Flexibility-Operation – How much flexibility is offered by this system? For example, are mistakes easy to correct, or, how great are the repercussions of a schedule adjustment? Does this system easily allow simulation?

Flexibility-Product – How much flexibility is offered in product variation or customization?

Flexibility-Scheduling – How much flexibility is offered in Product scheduling / rescheduling / cancellation / schedule changes?

Quality-Integration – How easily is quality integrated into the production process generated by this system?

Productivity-Labor – How effectively does this system promote labor productivity?

Productivity-Materials – How effectively does this system promote materials productivity?

Productivity-Machinery – How effectively does this system promote machine/equipment productivity?

Production-Batch Sizing – How rigid is this system in adjusting for variable batch sizing?

Production-Lead Time – How long is the production lead time? In all cases but SBM, the lead time is rigid. In SBM it can vary based on capacity.

Production-Order Track – How detailed and easily accessible is the shop floor order tracking process?

Production-Shop Layout – How flexible and unrestricted is the shop floor layout requirements by this system?

Production-Inventory – How high are the inventory levels generated by this system?

Production-Setup Time – How high are the setup times under this system?

Production-Resource – What resource is driven to be efficient as possible under this system?

Manufacturing-Discrete – How effective is this system for Discrete manufacturing?

Manufacturing-Process – How effective is this system for Process manufacturing?

Manufacturing-Mk to Stk – How effective is this system for a Make to Stock operation?

Manufacturing-Mk to Ordr – How effective is this system for a Make to Order operation?

Manufacturing-Repetitive – How effective is this system in Repetitive manufacturing?

Manufacturing-Non Rep. – How effective is this system in Non-Repetitive manufacturing?

Capacity Loading-Flexibility – How flexible is this system in evaluating and adjusting for capacity? The answer to this question also recognizes which resource is the focus of this capacity evaluation.

Cost-Control – How effective is cost control in this system? The answer also indicates if the cost control methodology is by batch or averaged.

Cost-Measurement – How are costs measured? What is the focus of cost measurement?

Purchasing-Lead Time – How long are the purchasing lead times generated by this system?

Purchasing-Scheduling – How easy is the scheduling of purchase orders under this system? In all but JIT the scheduling is done on an as-needed basis. For JIT an annual purchasing plan is developed.

5. The International Flow of Information

The focus of this chapter is to insert a discussion of the international manufacturing information flow based on the MRP II (Manufacturing Resources Planning) model. This is the most complete and comprehensive of the models and has been effective as a basis for designing information management systems all over the world. We will discuss this base system and then focus on the international variations to the model. But first, let's visit a new company on the block, W, Inc.

W, Inc.

W, Inc. is a manufacturer in Portland, Oregon which specializes in the production of high quality kitchen and hunting knives. They are a family owned company that has grown up through generations of family management. They have long been recognized as the standard for excellence in their industry. However, competitive pressures from Japan and Korea have introduced other, high class products into the market and they now find themselves with eroding margins. Their niche market has found other, lower priced entrants. Therefore, they are being forced to become price competitive, and they have suddenly become interested in integrated product costing and margin analysis. However, they soon realized that in order to get accurate costing, they needed data about the costs of each of their resources. And since they did not have a repetitive product, they needed to identify the costs of each specific product produced. They attended some conferences and brought in a local software consultant and it soon became apparent that they needed an information system that would allow them to cost out their current product line. They knew they were profitable over-all, but they weren't convinced that each specific product was profitable. Additionally, they had no way of evaluating alternative sourcing for materials. For example, they had recently received a great deal of interest from alternative suppliers of foreign wood products for their kitchen knife boxes and for the hunting knife handles. They needed to know more than just total cost and total revenue numbers.

Obviously, W, Inc. needed some type of integrated information system. However, they didn't want to get caught up in paralysis analysis. The software vendor wanted to install a full-blown MRP II system which included a complete job costing module. This system had obvious benefits in the amount of information that was made available. However, it also required detailed shop floor data collection mechanisms, which meant that everyone would need to be trained in data entry. Additionally, the administration of the system would require the introduction of an entire staff of computer teckies. It seemed ironic to the owners that in order to identify and save operating cost they would need to invest a substantial amount of non-value-added dollars. They were not impressed.

Management knew they needed to open new markets. They felt that if they could find a new niche, they could milk that opportunity. For example, they became interested in a multi-purpose folding tool that contained wrenches, screw-drivers, etc. that would be perfect for the repair technician. This tool could easily fit into a pocket or on a belt and avoid the technician needing to run to the tool box for every different tool. However, they weren't certain about the costing of this item. Additionally, they felt that if they introduced some of the current product line into new international markets, like Europe, they may open up entirely new niche marketplaces.

Before anyone had even completed their discussion of whether a computer was needed or not, political maneuvering had started as to which department should control the new computer structure. Accounting felt that they were the company's data masters, whereas production felt they were the biggest users of the new system, and engineering felt that they already had more computer expertise than anyone else. It wasn't long before management felt that getting into a computerized information system would be more trouble than it was worth. However, they also realized that without the information they could be making destructive and expensive decisions on a daily basis.

Now it's your turn. You're the owner, what would you do? Does it make sense to move ahead without a costing system? Or would it be better to introduce the MRP II environment? Or is there some other alternative?

The Flow of Information

The international information flow process starts with the Business Plan which is designed by the strategic management function. This plan defines the goals and directions of the corporation (see Chapter 3). There is a structured format around which these goals are built, starting with the values and vision (see Chapter 3) and ending with the strategy (see Chapter 4). The goals are also given a specific focus (see Chapter 3) and this focus is then operationalized through the remainder of the information planning process until we end up with a measurement system that motivates the desired responses.

Chart 5.1. Strategic to Tactical Management

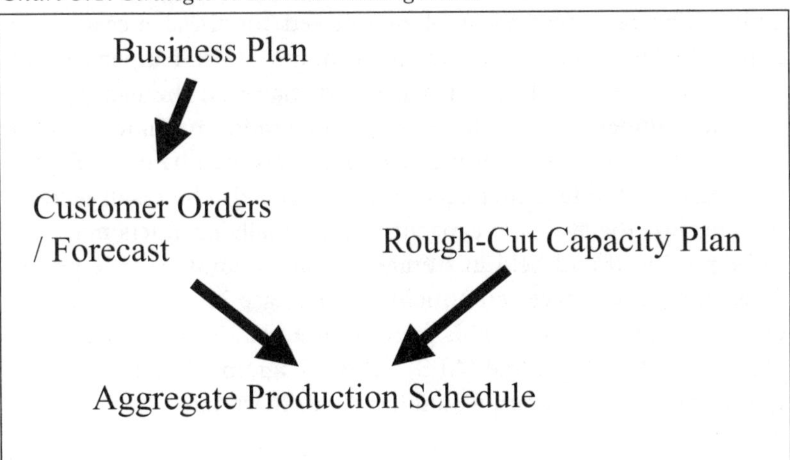

Once the Business Plan (BP) has defined the goals, the rest of the information processing system is built to support these goals. Please see Chart 5.1 for the information flow. For example, the Forecast (F) needs to be pulled out of the Marketing Plan which defines how the sales goals are to be achieved. This forecast is not always a sales volume forecast (although in the United States it usually is). If the goal is market share, then some market share percentage, or some measure of the number of units sold, is used. The Forecast can be relieved (replaced or supplimented) by Customer Orders (CO). The total demand for production on the factory is the combination of the Forecast and the Customer Orders. Operationally, the forecast defines the demand that sales is placing on the organization's resources. For example, the amount of sales generated defines how much labor, materials, and machine resource will be required to satisfy this demand.

The next information processing segment is the Rough Cut Capacity Plan (RCC). This plan highlights the total available resources that the organization has at its disposal. The availability of each resource is calculated here. For example, how much value-added direct labor hours do we have available each working day? A balancing act is now performed between F+CO (Forecast plus Customer Orders) and the RCC (Rough Cut Capacity). The Forecast plus Customer Orders define the demand placed on the plant's resources, and the Rough Cut Capacity Plan defines resource availability. The resources most often selected for these measures are materials, labor hours, and machine hours. What happens is that each product that is forecast places a demand on the factory for a specific number of labor hours by labor grade, machine hours by machine type, and units of material. This can then be multiplied by the number of units anticipated to be produced. The result is measured against the available capacity. Occasionally products may need to be produced and held in storage for sale in another time period. This storage will cover an anticipated increase in demand. A compromise plan will result. This compromise plan is called the Aggregate Production Schedule (APS).[1] If we diagram what has occurred to this point, the diagram would look like Chart 5.1.

1. APS has taken on two entirely seperate and distinct meanings. The first is Aggregate Production Scheduling, the way it is used in this chapter. The second is Advanced Planning and Scheduling, and this will be discussed later in this book. Since both are referred to as APS, it is easy to become confused.

Chart 5.2. Strategic through Operational Management

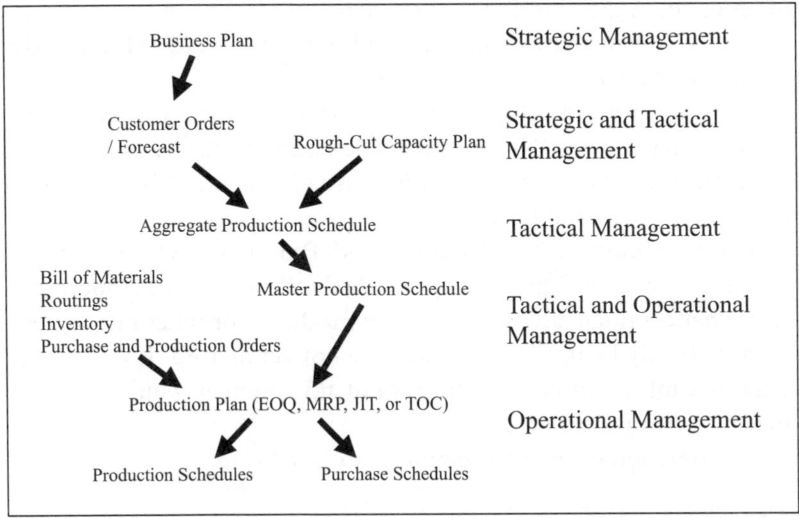

At this point a vision of the total integration process should begin to unfold. We will continue to move down the information flow diagram by looking at the next step, the Master Production Schedule (MPS). The MPS is the detailing out of the APS. What happens in the move to the MPS is that we break the rough numbers of the APS out into specific, definable products that have an identity utilizing a Planning Bill of Materials. Products analyzed in the F, CO, RCC, and APS have been reviewed as families of products up to this point. However, the step moving from the APS to the MPS takes these families and breaks them out into specific identifiable, producible products (see Chart 5.2).

The Master Production Schedule is the first of five inputs that go into the Production Planning (PP) process. The MPS defines the number of end products to be produced specifically by product number. The second input is the Bill of Materials (BofM) which defines the materials makeup of every end product. The third is the Routings (R). The Routings define job functions and time. For example, the routing for a product would specify all the production steps required to combine components together and create the end item. The routing describes what the labor steps are, how much time each labor step takes, and how much machine time and capacity each step takes.

Both the Routing and the Bill of Materials information are used when we defined the capacity demanded by the forecast in the creation of the Aggregate Production Schedule. These give specific information on machine hours, labor hours, and material usage demands for each product to be created.

The fourth input into the Production Plan is the Inventory Status Information (I). This is simply the count of all the inventory in the factory at any point in time. It is usually managed by a perpetual inventory planning process.

The fifth input is the Purchase and Production Orders (P/PO) that are in process. This last input tells the Production Planning system what products are already being produced or what raw materials are already being shipped but have not yet arrived. If we were to draw the information flow diagram at this point it would look like the last part of Chart 5.2.

The function of the Production Plan is to:

(1) take the total number of units to be produced, as defined by the MPS,
(2) calculate the number of units of materials required for each product using the BofM,
(3) define how much labor and machine time will be required for each of these production steps using the Routing,
(4) use the Routing to further define when the materials, labor hours, and machine hours will be needed,
(5) adjust those needs downward by the number of units of inventory we already have on hand, and lastly
(6) further adjust the needs downward based on the items that have already been purchased but have not yet arrived or items that are currently in production but are not yet finished.

In the last chapter we discussed several types of Production Planning models. The first is called Economic Order Quantity (EOQ). This model only plans inventory. It does not consider labor or machinery schedules. It is the most basic form of production planner. EOQ works best in an environment where demand is steady and constant and the parts costs are evenly distributed (there is no part that is exceptionally expensive). This system can be run manually or with a simple computerized inventory control package.

The second type of Production Planning model discussed in this book was Material Requirements Planning (MRP). MRP considers material, labor, and machinery in planning the schedules. It offers advantages for plants with intermittent demand and expensive parts scheduling. However, because of the added control offered by MRP it is much more complex than EOQ and will probably require the use of a computer package with an MRP scheduler. The third type of system that was discussed is JIT (Just-in-Time). This system is a higher degree of sophistication built upon the EOQ model, but is still focused on inventory efficiency just like EOQ. And the last production planning system discussed is TOC (Theory of Constraints). This system focuses on machine bottleneck efficiencies.

Continuing on in our analysis of the information flow diagram we come to the outputs of the production planning process. All of the production planning systems alternatives discussed will give you both of the following outputs:

(1) A production schedule (PROD) is generated that creates shop orders for items that still need to be produced in order to achieve the MPS schedule.
(2) A purchasing schedule (PURCH) is generated that lists purchases of materials that are needed in order to satisfactorily complete the desired production.

The graphic result of all these processes can be seen on the updated information flow diagram of Chart 5.2. The Production Schedule (PROD) starts work on the factory floor. As items are produced, inventory is used up, and new items of inventory are created. This updates the I and the P/PO inputs to the PP. Similarly, the Purchasing Schedule (PURCH) causes items to be purchased and brought into inventory, updating these same two inputs. As products are completed and sold, adjustments need to be made to the MPS which will reduce the number of products still needing to be produced.

When using MRP or TOC as a production scheduler, two more elements enter into the production flow diagram (see Chart 5.3). The first is Capacity Requirements Planning (CRP). This system takes the production schedule generated by the MRP system (PROD) and schedules it out on a department-by-department basis. This is a departmental tool assisting the department in balancing it's work load planning and planning its capacity. Coming out of

CRP is a Shop Floor Control Scheduler (SFC). This is a data collection and shop floor control mechanism that monitors progress on the factory floor. The data it collects feeds the information flow diagram to effect future schedules. In most American environments of JIT, we find JIT used as a shop floor scheduler (SFC), and MRP used as a production planning tool (PP). Often this environment is referred to as MRP III.

The last element that needs to be integrated into this process is the Logistics system (LOG). Logistics applies when products are purchased and special shipping arrangements must be made. It applies when products are sold and shipped. It applies when ware housing occurs at either the shipping or receiving ends. The logistics element is so critical to the international production planning process that the next three chapters of the book are dedicated to this under the heading of Supply Chain Management. The final production information and data flow diagram would look like Chart 5.3.

At this point it is important to reflect back on the concept of integration. Each of the elements of this information flow diagram needs to be integrated. They cannot be treated as isolated entities. What is information to one entity becomes data to the next one up the line. Feedback between the entities is common and important.

The diagramming process used in this chapter has been greatly simplified in order to help us understand how the overall process works. But there are many monkey wrenches that occur in real life and that complicate this diagram significantly, making integration and feedback even more critical. Here are a few examples:

(1) What happens to Rough Cut Capacity (RCC), Aggregate Production Scheduling (APS), Master Production Scheduling (MPS), and the Production Schedule (PROD), if a machine breaks down and it takes several days for it to be repaired?
(2) What happens to the Routings (R), Rough Cut Capacity (RCC), Aggregate Production Scheduling (APS), Master Production Scheduling (MPS), and the Production Schedule (PROD), if a new employee is hired and this new employee only has half the efficiency of the old employee?
(3) What happens to Inventory (I), Purchase and Production Orders (P/PO), and the Production Schedule (PROD) if an error

in production occurs and several hundred units of product need to be scrapped?

(4) What happens to Routings (R), Aggregate Production Scheduling (APS), Master Production Scheduling (MPS), and the Production Schedule (PROD) if a new machine is brought in that increases the total output?

(5) What happens to the Bill of Materials (BofM), the Aggregate Production Schedule (APS), the Master Production Schedule (MPS), the Production Schedule (PROD), and the Purchasing Plan (PURCH) if engineering improves product design and product X is no longer composed of Y and Z, but is now composed of W and Z?

(6) What happens to the Logistics Plan (LOG), the Master Production Schedule (MPS), the Routings (R), and the Purchasing Plan (PURCH) if we shift from a local source to an international source for materials?

Chart 5.3. Operations Planning and Scheduling Information Flow Diagram

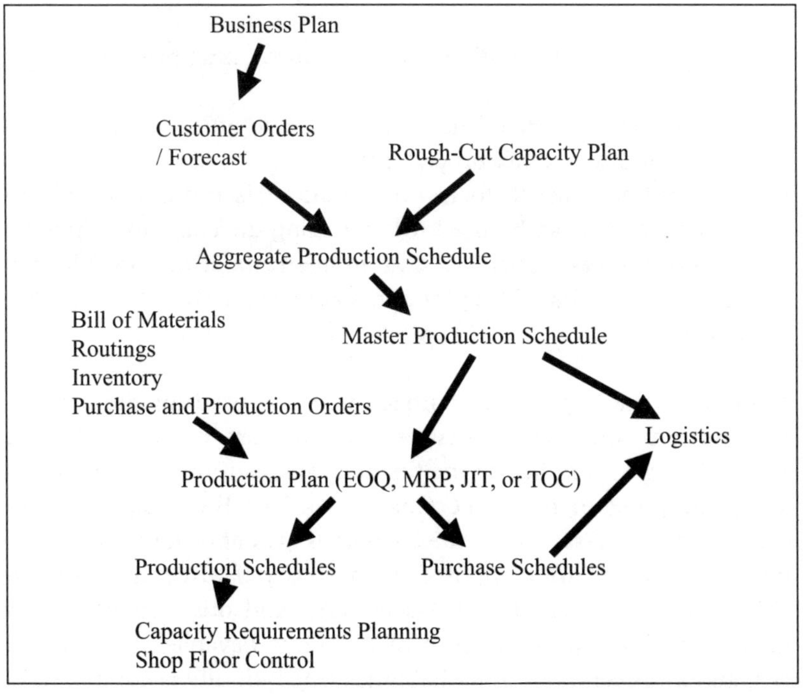

(7) What happens to the Logistics Plan (LOG), the Master Production Schedule (MPS), and the Production Plan (PP) if the customer is an international customer with a long delivery lead time?

The Accounting Information Flow Diagram

The accounting information flow process is an area that most information processors are familiar with. This is primarily because accounting is the first area that is usually automated. It is highly repetitive and lends itself easily to MIS (Management Information Systems) concepts, whereas, the production information flow incorporates primarily DSS (Decision Support Systems) techniques. Next we need to briefly discuss the accounting information flow because it becomes important when we try to integrate it with the production information flow process. Additionally, in international settings, this structure has numerous variations. Many companies end up with several sets of books for an international establishment, like:

(1) a set of books which follow localized accounting procedures and tax laws
(2) a set of books which follow the corporate office's country's set of accounting and tax procedures
(3) a set of books which focus on operationalized measures of performance that can be used for managing the company – this set of books offers a standard that all elements of the organization can utilize so that all departments are playing from the same set of rules.

Using the same top down approach that was used for the production information flow process we would start with the Balance Sheet (BS) which indicates the financial status of the corporation at a specific point in time (see Chart 5.4). The BS is composed of three areas, the Assets (A), the Liabilities (L), and the Owners Equity (OE). Assets are composed of Inventory (I), Accounts Receivable (AR), Cash (C), Fixed Assets (FA), and other similar assets (OA). Liabilities are composed of Accounts Payable (AP), Payroll (P), and a collection of other liabilities (OL). Equity is composed of

Current Ownership of the corporation (CO) which is adjusted by recent Profits or Losses (P/L). A diagram of this process would look like Chart 5.4.

Information is fed into these financial analysis elements from several sources. For example, Accounts Receivable and Cash information comes from Sales. Inventory information comes from (I) in the production flow diagram. Fixed Assets are defined in the Rough Cut Capacity Plan as resources available and are depreciated by their planned usage. Accounts Payable and Cash reductions come from Purchasing. Payroll information comes from the PROD output of the Production Plan which is fed through a costing system. Profit and loss information comes from income (sales) reduced by costs. Adding these elements into the diagram would result in Chart 5.4.

Chart 5.4. The Total Information Flow of Financial Information

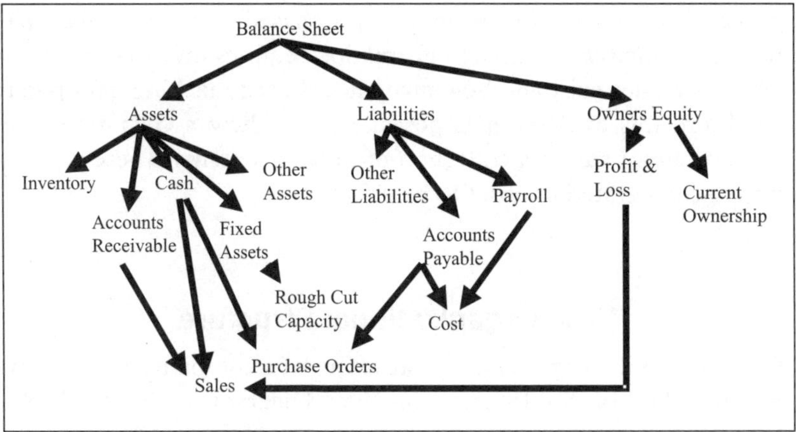

The Integration of the Accounting Information Flow Diagram With The Production Information Flow Diagram

Integration needs to occur between these two information flow systems because of the large number of interfaces that occur. To simplify this integration process we will only take the production inputs that go directly into the accounting system. These also have integration points in the production system. These are:

- Inventory (I)
- Sales
- Costs
- Purchasing (PURCH)
- Fixed Assets (FA)
- Payroll (PR)
- Accounts Payable (AP).

Redrawing the production flow diagram with these added elements of integration would make the chart look like Chart 5.5. Sales is an input into future forecast projections, and sales gets feedback from the MPS on products that have been shipped. Costs receive input from both the purchasing and the production schedule feedback process which indicates what was purchased and what labor has been expended. Fixed Asset information requires information about what machines exist and how many hours each machine has operated. From this analysis, it is possible to see how a corporate wide system cannot run as a collection of isolated systems. These systems must be integrated in order to be effective.

The Organizational Structure

Considering the organizational structure of a company, we can start placing labels on the Information Flow Diagram of Chart 5.5. Referring back to the accounting information flow on Chart 5.4, all functions listed here are performed by the integrative functional areas of Accounting and Management Information Systems.

Chart 5.5. The Production and Accounting Integrated Information Flow Diagram

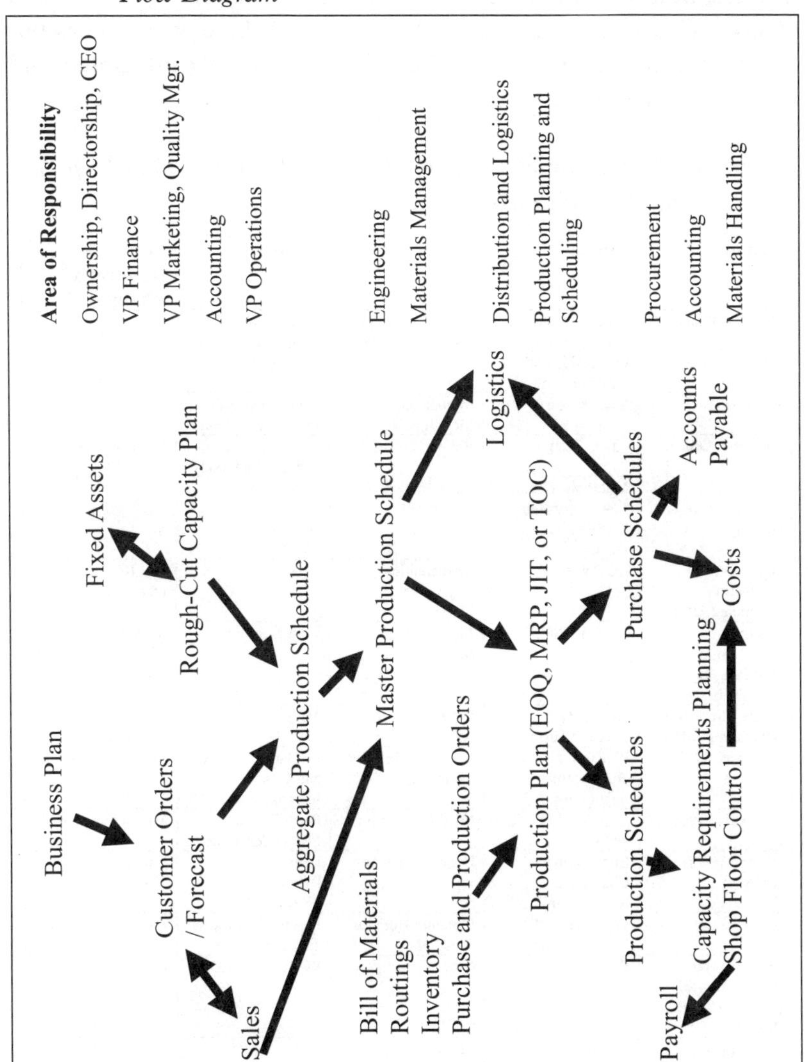

The Manufacturing Cycle

The manufacturing cycle of Chart 1.5 (in Chapter 1) also needs to be integrated with the production information flow diagram of

Chart 5.5. At each stage of the information flow we find inputs, a process, outputs, and a feedback mechanism that offers control and change. Chart 5.6 attempts to show some of the obvious flows but it is important to realize that these flows are highly integrated and can get very complex.

Chart 5.6. The Integration of the Production Information Flow Steps and the Manufacturing Cycle

System	Inputs	Process	Output	Feedback (Control & Change)
Business Plan (BP)	Guidance and Direction from Ownership and Directorship	Written by CEO and Directorship	Goals and Objectives of the Organization	
Forecast (F)	Sales History	Mathematical Modeling	Anticipated Sales for at least 1 Year	
Customer Orders (C/O)	Sales Orders	Relieve Forecast	Shipment and Delivery of Goods	Corrections to F
Rough Cut Capacity Analysis (RCC)	Materials, Labor, Machinery Data, Performance History	Mathematically Calculate the Capacities	Capacity Plan	
Aggregate Production Schedule (APS)	RCC, C/O, F	Mathematical Aggregate Planning	APS	F or RCC adjustments
Logistics / Distribution / Warehousing (LOG)	MPS, PURCH	Mathematical Modeling	Logistics Plan	MPS and PURCH adjustments
Master Production Scheduling (MPS)	APS, C/O, Forecast History	Distribution of APS	MPS	APS and F adjustments
Inventory (I)	PURCH, Issues and Receipts, quality inspections	Inventory Balance Updating	I Balance, Usage, and Cost Information	PURCH, BOM
Production Plan (PP)	I, BOM, P/PO, R, MPS	MRP Generation	PURCH and PROD Schedules	MPS adjustments
Bill of Materials (BOM)	Engineering Change Information	BOM Explosion	Parts Requirements List, PP Input	Engineering Modifications
Routings (R)	Engineering Time Measurements	Planning Horizon Calculation	Production Lead Times, PP Input	Engineering Modifications
Purchase and Production Orders (P/PO, PURCH, PROD)	PP	Order Generation	PURCH & PROD	PP adjustments
Capacity Requirements Planning (CRP)	PP, PROD	Mathematical Capacity Evaluation	CRP	MPS, PROD
Shop Floor Control (SFC)	CRP	Data Collection	Data, Data Base	Corrective Feedback for PP and all its inputs

The final integration of all the functional areas is shown in Chart 5.7. This chart is not as scary as it looks. In Chart 5.8 we see the breakdown of this chart by systems area and we can see how the total integration functions. Understanding the integration of the total information flow of a corporation is critical if effective systems are to be installed. We need to integrate the total flow of information rather than thinking in terms of independent modules. We need to plan these systems so that they have focus and yet simplicity.

Down the left side of Chart 5.7 and 5.8 we see all the financial activities of an enterprise including the general ledger and profit and loss functions. In the top center of the chart we see the sales functions. From this chart we can see how the enterprise information integration would function under an MRP II or ERP environment (note: the numbers are connectors, for example the "1" connects to the other "1" in the chart – these connectors are used in order to avoid having lines crossing on the chart, but they have the same meaning as would a connecting line).

It is interesting to take the information flow diagram of Chart 5.7 and apply the various production planning systems that we considered earlier in this chapter. We find that the effect of the planning system on the integrated information flow can be quite significant. In Chart 5.9 we see the EOQ version of the diagram. Because EOQ only looks at inventory, it's planning process has been greatly simplified. In Chart 5.7, if we replace "Production Planning" with "MRP" we would have the MRP version of this diagram, often referred to as MRP II. This is the full-blown complex version of the integrated process. For MRP III we would also have the "SFC" system replaced by a "JIT-Kanban" job flow system. In Chart 5.10 we see the Japanese JIT version. Since shop floor data collection is too slow, it is skipped and in turn the job costing system has no value. Average costing is utilized. The TOC version uses Chart 5.7 and replaces "Production Planning" with "TOC".

By comparing these diagrams we can see why the Japanese version of JIT does not require the use of computers on the production floor. The data collection process has been greatly simplified. The data collection process has little value if the production process moves quicker than that data collection process can keep up with. Therefore, in true JIT, Shop Floor Data Collection (SFC) has no value.

Chart 5.7. The Total Integrated Information Flow Diagram (see Chart 1.5)

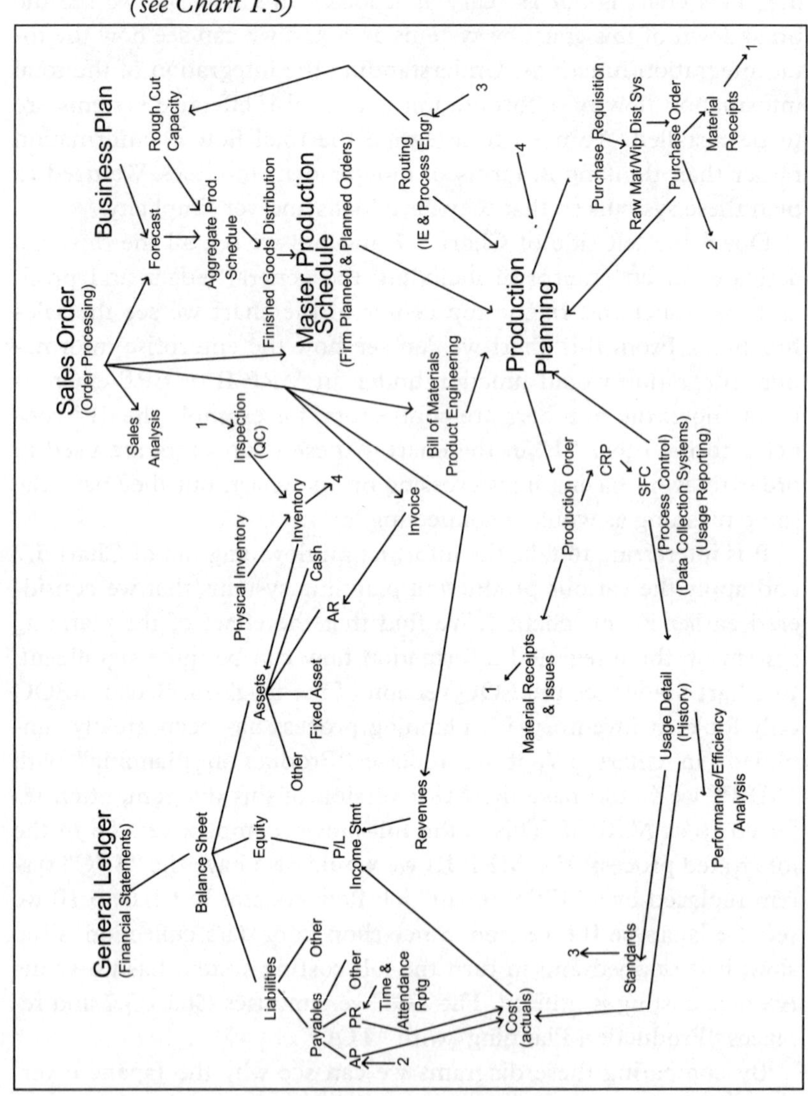

Chart 5.8. The Total Integrated Information Flow Diagram (by System)

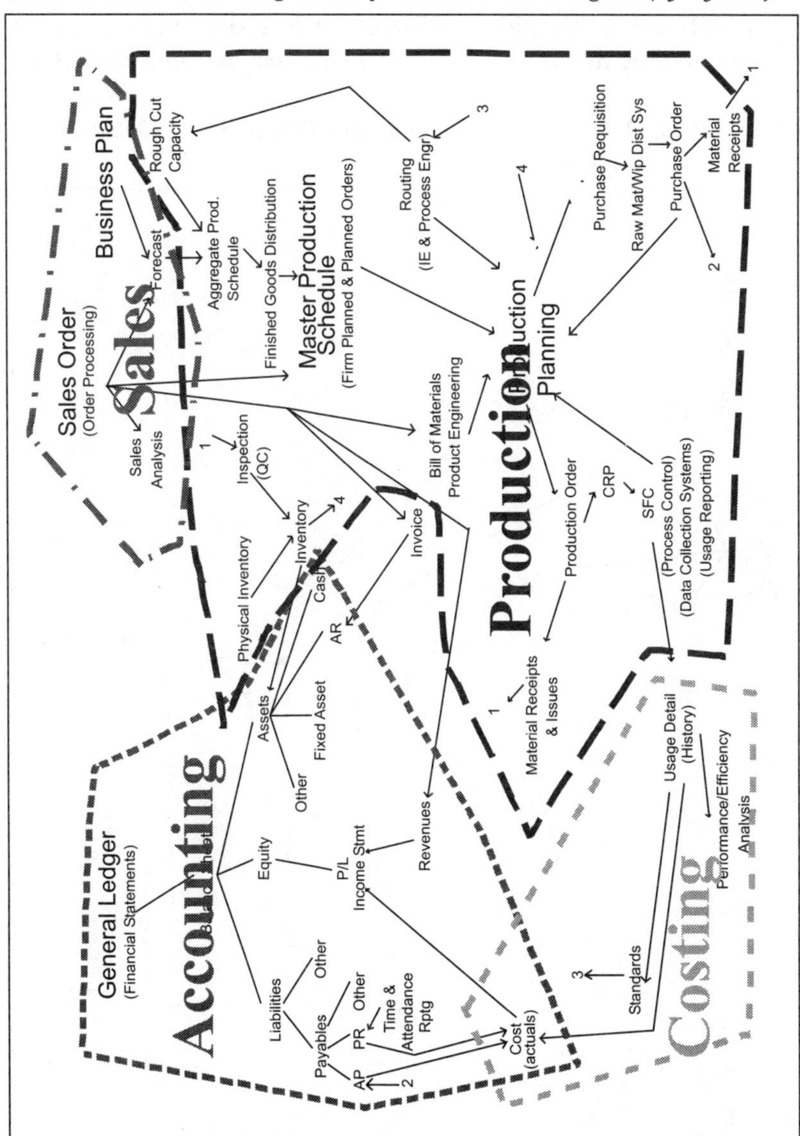

As discussed right at the start of this book, International Operations Management is a selection of choices. These choices need to be based on goals which focus on a specific critical resource. This critical resource varies from location to location, plant to plant, and country to country. Two identical plants, located across the street from each other, but with a different set of goals, could come up with an entirely different set of production management tools. One

Chart 5.9. The Integrated Information Flow Diagram for Economic Order Quantity (EOQ)

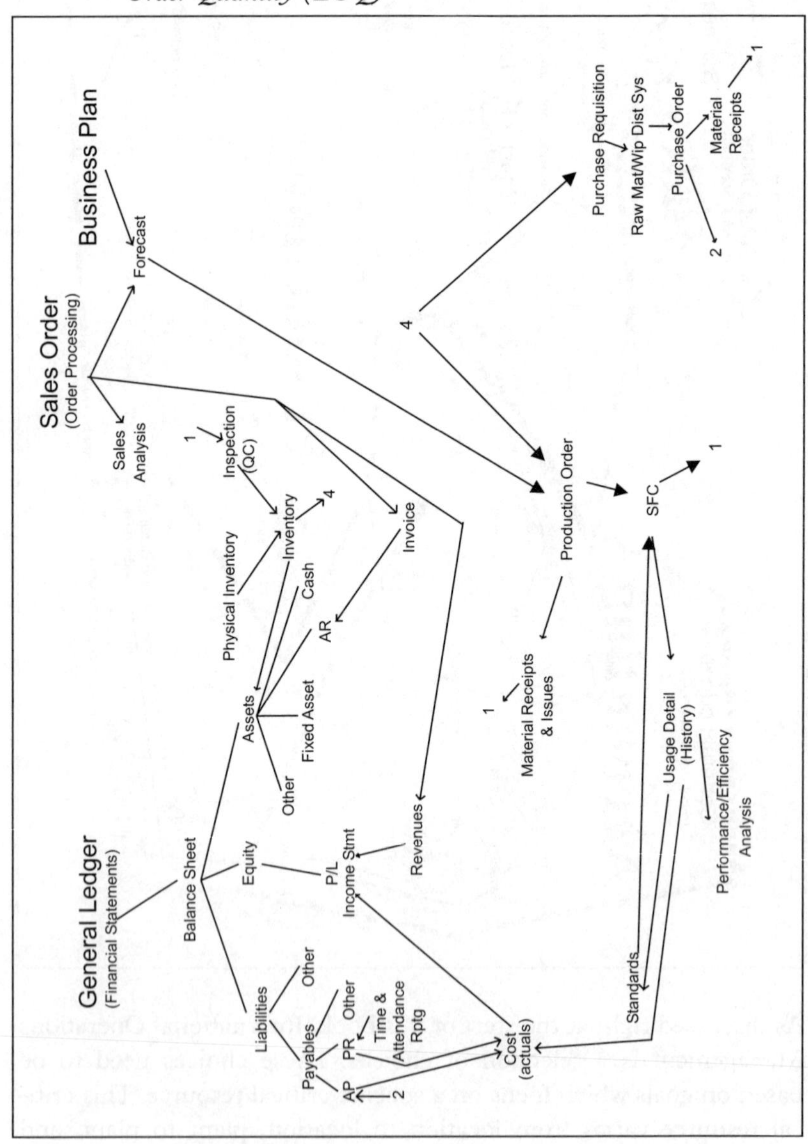

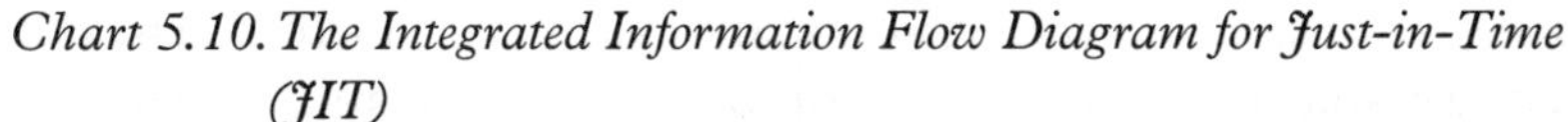

Chart 5.10. The Integrated Information Flow Diagram for Just-in-Time (JIT)

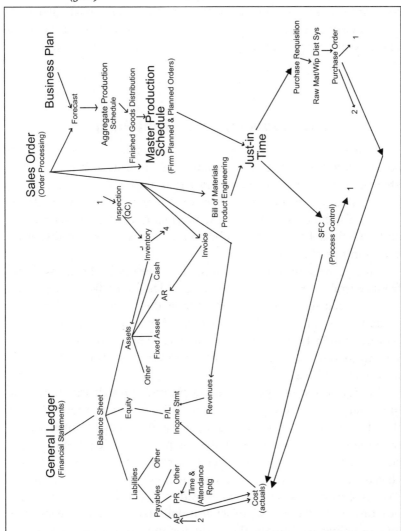

could be labor efficiency based and favor MRP and the other being materials focused could favor JIT. It is important, when taking a global perspective, to realize that MRP is not better than JIT, or vice-versa. They are all excellent tools when used appropriately in the correct environment. The trick for the global operations manager is to select the correct tool for the particular environment, not because someone else in the corporate office favors a particular tool, or because someone down the street is using a particular tool. The appropriate production planning tool is selected because it makes sense based on the critical resource which is focused on the goal.

New Product Development Process

Up to now we have taken a business management perspective when considering the flow of information in an enterprise. It is also valuable to take a product perspective. It is important to look at the flow of a factory from the perspective of a new product being developed. This section will discuss the product development perspective and will tie it back to the information flow perspective discussed earlier in this chapter.

When a new product idea is to be developed, the ideas come from several sources. Many of the best ideas come from customers, and we need to keep a listening ear in their direction. Many also come from the non-marketing personnel of your organization. Employees should be invited to submit ideas and should be rewarded for the good ones. Ideas also come from vendors, especially product improvement ideas.

The ideas that are generated get filtered through the marketing organization. Marketing is responsible for screening these ideas. If the ideas are compatible with the goals and the core competency of the organization, a financial analysis is performed. To do this analysis, marketing will work with engineering, productions, and purchasing to try to estimate the cost of producing the new product. Two cost estimates are needed. The first is a cost to setup. This is a one time cost (fixed cost) of what it will take to acquire machinery and retooling to prepare the plant for the production process required by the new product. The second cost estimate is the cost of production. This is the cost estimate of what it will take to produce each item in a mass production situation (variable cost).

Marketing needs to make some estimates of the sales potential of the suggested product. Two numbers are needed. The first is an estimate of the selling price. The second is an estimate of the annual sales volume. With the four estimates (fixed and variable cost, sales volume, and sales price) an analysis can be performed to see if the product shows enough profitability to be worth producing. This process is called Break Even Analysis.

Chart 5.11 gives us a graphical look at how break-even analysis works. It shows how the Fixed Cost is the starting point for the cost curve (FC+VC). It identifies that the sales curve starts at the zero point (Sales Price * Quantity). Since the selling price is higher than the product cost, the sales curve has a steeper slope. The point at which the two curves intersect is the Break Even Point and that gives us the Break Even Quantity. A typical marketing organization will have several product options to consider. The selection of which product options are the most feasible is done by performing a break even analysis on each of the options. The new product idea showing the best annual profits should be implemented first. Internationally, all these variables can be changed. The FC can be reduced if you utilize outside sourcing and don't have to carry the same level of productive overhead. Additionally, the VC can be lowered if the labor costs or material costs are reduced from an international source. The Sales Price may be lowered to compensate for the lower spending levels often found in other countries however, the sold quantities may be considerably higher.

There are two other considerations that are involved in the selection of a product idea. The first is disruption of the status quo. Although a new product idea may be a good one, it is often avoided because it doesn't fit in well with the other products currently under production. Implementing this new product would be disruptive to the organization. Unless the profitability of this product is dramatic, it may not be worth the trouble. Internationally, this new product idea may be sourced out to organizations that have the missing level of expertise, and, therefore, the product suddenly becomes feasible.

A second consideration in the selection of a new product idea is to estimate the probability of success. This is optional because it may be too much trouble and too hard to estimate. This process is called risk assessment. Once the risk assessments are made, you would compare the profitability of each of the new product ideas and see which is still the most profitable. Then select the option with the most profitability first. Internationally, risk assessments can vary dramatically from country to country. Localization of the product idea is a critical requirement in the evaluation of risk.

Chart 5.11. Annual Break-Even Analysis Graph

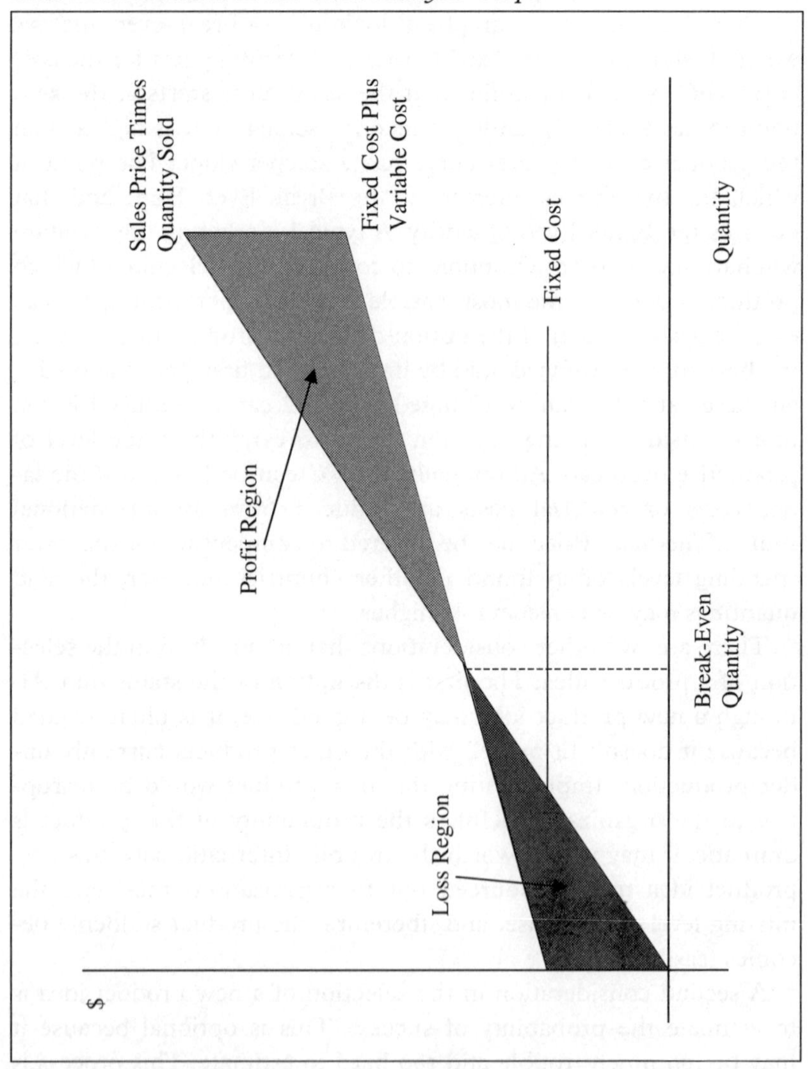

Having selected which products should receive further consideration, marketing now turns to engineering for a prototyping process. Only about fifteen percent of the new product ideas get past this point. This is where a model or example of the product is actually made. This process proves the feasibility of the product and its previous cost estimates. It is possible that a break-even analysis may have to be repeated at this point if any of the previous estimates are changed. Only about five percent of the new product ideas get past this point.

The functions of the engineering organizations are broken out into different groups:

- PRODUCT ENGINEERING – These are the individuals that are responsible for designing the features and functions of the new product. They design how the product will work and how it will look
- MANUFACTURING ENGINEERING – These individuals design how the product will be made. There are two categories of engineers within this category
- PROCESS ENGINEERING – These individuals design the jigs and fixtures that will be used to hold the materials, they design the bits that will drill the materials, and they identify the step by step materials handling process that is necessary to turn the materials into the desired manufactured product
- INDUSTRIAL ENGINEERING – These individuals define the labor and machine steps that are necessary to convert the materials into the desired new form.

It is the analysis performed by these engineers that determines what it will take in materials, labor, and machine time to make this new product. They create the Bill of Materials and the Routings of these products. Then the accountants will add a loaded cost factor to cover overhead. This combination of numbers will then identify the costs associated with the new product to be manufactured. If all goes well and the new product idea is to be implemented into the production cycle, we then move forward with the production planning process.

One area that is nearly as important as the installation of new products, is the elimination of old products. Plants seem to never want to separate themselves from products that have died. They keep inventories of the components and materials that went into these old products, even though these materials are not used anywhere else in the manufacturing process. As much as two-thirds of the inventory items in a factory have been found to be irrelevant. We need to purge our factories of these old components because they are just taking up space and costing us inventory dollars.

This section of the chapter discussed the process required in building a new product. Now we should have a feel for how new product ideas are planned and implemented into the production planning system.

W, Inc. Revisited

The owners of W, Inc. decided that they couldn't survive without more information so they decided to phase in the MRP II environment which included all the functionality, from financial, through accounting, to procurement, resource planning and manufacturing. They started by bringing in the accounting functions and introducing the costing module. They brought in the computer support staff and put them under the direction of the accounting department since they would be working with the accounting process first. Then they started to develop the inputs into the MRP environment, which include the development of a bill of materials and the routings. The bill of materials gave them a materials cost list and the routings incorporated the labor and machine costs. Developing these modules required an extensive amount of data entry effort, since all the drawings for the entire product line had to be translated into a new structure and form, and then they needed to be entered into the computer system. With these two modules, W, Inc. was able to do cost rolls and calculate the total cost of a product. However, these cost rolls were all at a standard cost which is an estimated cost.

The owners wanted to identify and calculate real costs. Therefore, they needed to incorporate a shop floor data collection system that tracked actual costs through the production process. These actual costs could be compared against the system's standard costs as a kind of reality check and for the updating of the standard costs. However, this process turned out to be very time-consuming. It required the data entry training of everyone on the shop floor. It required the development of new shop floor travelers. And it required adjustments to some of the flows and processes of work being done. After about one year of implementation, the shop floor system was ready for use. At this point, the W, Inc. was ready to discuss the implementation of the MRP environment. They had the primary inputs in place, bill of materials, routings, forecasts from sales for the master production schedule, and an inventory management system. They also had the output control mechanisms in place, the purchasing system and the shop floor tracking system. So now they were ready for MRP. However, the owners were getting a little gun shy. They had the costing information they wanted, but they weren't convinced that the scheduling abilities of MRP would gain them a significant advantage, especially if it created the same amount of turmoil that was created by the installation of the shop floor control process.

W, Inc. had also encountered another surprise. They learned that they needed to become ISO 9000 certified in order to enter their products into the European marketplace. They needed to bring in an ISO quality expert who focused and structured the organization for certification. This created nearly as much turmoil in the organization as shop floor data collection caused, because of the extensive amount of documentation that needed to be accomplished. Processes had to be documented and flowcharted into a quality manual, and people had to become trained in the use of the quality standard. However, eventually this was accomplished and W successfully entered the European and Asian marketplace.

The mini-tool idea also turned out to be a great success. The market for this tool exploded and mechanics everywhere started referring to this tool by the name of the company. There was an exceptionally high demand, especially internationally. However, with all good things, there is competition, and it wasn't long before the Japanese and Korean competitors also latched on to the portable tool concept. Fortunately for W, Inc. these copy-cat tools were of sufficiently inferior quality, that they only attracted a hobbyist market and were never considered as a serious alternative for the W, Inc. product.

W, Inc. had learned a lot about it's product pricing and competitive position through the installation of the job costing and through the ISO certification process. But their margins had eroded sufficiently through foreign competition. They were even considering having some of their products produced overseas. Additionally, the installation of the MRP environment was taunted as being good for cost reduction and performance improvement. But management wasn't convinced. All they could see was another enormous non-value-added cost outlay. Now you're the owner. What would you do? Would you do more internationally? Which options would you investigate? And what about the MRP II environment? Does it offer enough benefit to make it worth the headache and cost of installation? What would you do?

C, Inc.

C, Inc. is a brewery outside of Denver, Colorado that also produces high grade ceramics for the microelectronics industry. The clays in the region are perfect for the types of products desired and they have an enormous international demand for their product. But C has long been concerned about their high levels of maintenance inventory. In their maintenance division, they have not been as careful as they have been in other divisions, and they know that maintenance inventory is out of control. They brought in an outside organization to review the status of the maintenance inventory and they found that about 1/3 of the inventory was for maintenance materials for machines that no longer existed. About another third had inventory levels that were way above what was reasonable. For example, they may have 20 units of inventory for a part who's average annual usage was 2 units per year, and the average replacement cycle time was one week. This meant that an excessive number of dollars was unnecessarily tied up in inventory.

The consulting firm recommended two things. First, they recommended that the company collect usage history data so that they could learn the frequency of usage of parts, and so that they could identify parts that had no usage and they could check for obsolescence. The second recommendation was to set up some kind of part's replacement program based on the scheduled preventive maintenance (PM) program. At each PM point in time, a specific collection of parts was required. This set of parts can be identified and scheduled out. Feeling somewhat ignorant of what production tools were available, the general manager of C, Inc. felt that he was wasting an excessive number of dollars in wasted inventory costs and he wanted go get better control of the maintenance inventory situation. If you were the consultant, what would you recommend? If you were the general manager, how would you approach this planning issue?

Summary

This chapter has been a discussion of the flow of information in an operational environment and how it needs to be planned out in order to make an international operation perform effectively. We discussed the components of the over-all flow, and then what some of the differences between an EOQ, MRP, JIT, and TOC environment are. We also discussed the issues involved in new product introductions. Now we are ready to get into some of the details associated with one of the most difficult areas of international operations management, the area of supply-chain-management.

Class Assignments

The W, Inc. case is an excellent example of the struggles many companies are encountering over and over again as technology changes. There is no one correct solution, only a collection of alternatives each with specific advantages and disadvantages. It is important for the student to review the numerous alternatives because they will encounter these when they take on the role of management.

Similarly, C, Inc. has found itself in a struggle that many companies encounter. They have ignored the management of the operations environment in maintenance inventory until it has become uncontrollable. And now they are desperate to do something.

These cases are excellent for class-room chalk-board discussion and should be used as such. They don't require detailed analysis and can be easily read and reviewed for a few minutes at the start of the class.

References

Systems Management References

Kendall, Penny A., *Introduction to Systems Analysis and Design: A Structured Approach,* W. C. Brown Publishers, 1989.

Plenert, Gerhard, "Information Systems Integration for World-Class Manufacturing Management" *International Journal of Flexible Automation and Integrated Manufacturing,* Vol. 5, No. 1&2, 1997, Pages 45-56.

Plenert, Gerhard, "The Basics of a Successful System", *Information and Management,* 1988, Pages 251-254.

Plenert, Gerhard, "The Development of a Production System in Mexico", *Interfaces,* Vol. 20, No. 3, May-June 1990.

Plenert, Gerhard, *The Plant Operations Handbook,* Business 1 IRWIN, 1993, Homewood, Ill.

Suri, R., "A New Perspective on Manufacturing Systems Analysis" *Design and Analysis of Integrated Manufacturing Systems,* W. D. Compton (Ed.), National Academy Press, 1988, Pages 120-121.

Managing
The Supply Chain

6. Suppliers

Probably the single most discussed area of international operations management is the management of the supply chain. The supply chain can best be described by two words:

- Integration
- Time.

Integration refers to the vertical integration of all functions. It refers to managing the suppliers' supplier all the way through to managing the customers' customer. Supply Chain Management refers to the minimization and elimination of all waste as we process through these functions. Supply Chain Management focuses on incorporating only value-added steps in these areas (Chapter 7).

Supply Chain Management also focuses on time (Chapter 8). One of the primary purposes of managing this chain is to attain time efficiency throughout the entire cycle. Only by managing the entire flow can the cycle time be shortened.

In this chapter we will begin our discussion of the management of the supply chain by focusing on supplier sourcing and scheduling. In the next chapter we will look at the integration and waste elimination needs of the supply chain. Then in Chapter 8 we will focus on cycle time efficiencies followed by a discussion in Chapter 9 of logistics and wholesale management. To start this process, let's visit a company, N, Inc.

N, Inc.

N, Inc. is a company that has manufacturing facilities all over the world. Their corporate office is in Dayton, Ohio and the entire company is organized around two major marketing divisions, the Domestic Division and the International Division. Although there is some crossover and interface, the two divisions manage themselves almost totally independently. In the international division, there are regions, like the Austrial-Asia region, the European Region, the Latin American region, etc. The manufacturing division includes plants in Germany, several United States sites, Canada, Mexico, and Asia. Their primary product line is point-of-sale terminals for the retail and banking industries, and small, medium, and large computers. They manufacture many of the computer components that other computer manufacturers utilize and install in their own equipment.

N, Inc. has encountered numerous difficulties in managing it's supply chain. It sources computer components from all over the world. Additionally, it manufactures many of it's own components and brings them into the production process when external resources become too expensive or become hard to access. However, it's divisions are not required to purchase internally produced components.

N has a microelectronics manufacturing division which produces and sells chips to other N divisions as well as to external customers. This division, like all divisions, is encouraged to be internally and externally competitive in all it's processes. This plant is located outside of Dayton, Ohio. One of it's primary customers is a N plant that produces terminals in Augsburg, Germany which does it's own board insertion work. Sales to the Augsburg plant are about $ 1,000,000 per year. Total sales are at $ 10,000,000 per year. However, the Dayton plant is not ISO certified and it would cost about $ 500,000 to get certification. Additionally, the Augsburg plant can get the microelectrocircuitry from a competitive facility in Sweden for slightly more than the Dayton plant costs them. However, if Dayton adds in the certification costs into the parts sold to Augsburg, it would no longer be competitive. The corporate office would prefer to see internal sourcing of components, because of the control this gives to the supply chain, and there are additionally political advantages to maintaining this method of sourcing. But the micro-electronics plant is worried that if they go through certification, Augsburg may not see things in the same light and may pull out on them. Additionally, the Augsburg plant has become concerned about single sourcing the components and is wondering if they shouldn't give the Swedish plant some of their parts demand just to keep a back-up supplier in the loop. What would you do if you were Augsburg management? What would you do if you were Dayton management? What would you do if you were corporate management?

Chart 6.1. N, Inc. Augsburg Plant Detailed Supply Chain with Distribution Links

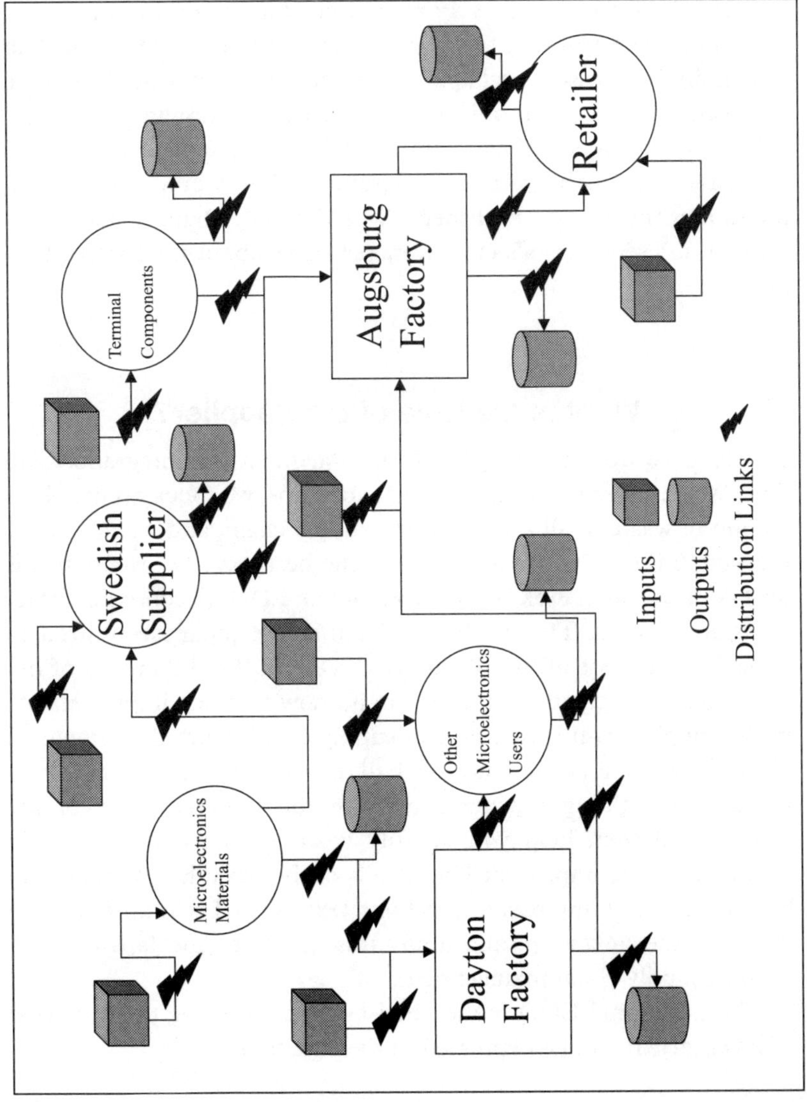

We can see the complexity and therefore the difficulty of managing the supply chain in Chart 6.1 we have the distribution and logistics points of N's supply chain. From this chart we can see that even in a simple, two factory model, the management of the model has become far more complex than can be managed by a simple system. However, this diagram is a beginning in assisting in the understanding of how a supply chain would work. For N, Inc., there is a lack of integrated information flow. For example, if inter and intra-plant information were to exist, the plants could be more efficient in their scheduling processes. Perhaps this communication would assist in the decisions and communication between Augsburg and Dayton.

The management of the supply chain is the second element of this case that needs your consideration. How would you recommend that this be accomplished? Would supply chain management make a difference in N's effectiveness? How about it's competitiveness?

What is the Role of the Supplier?

The focus words in supply chain management are integration and time. When it comes to supplier relationships, we focus on the elimination of waste in all aspects of the supply chain, and we do this by focusing on these two issues. One of the best ways to discuss this is by taking a close look at the traditional EOQ (Economic Order Quantity) model. This is the model that the Japanese utilized in their development of the JIT process. One of the difficulties of describing supply chain management and how to make improvements in the supply chain is that no two supply chains work the same way. What is good for one may be bad for another. I will take you through this thought process because the understanding of the process will then help you identify what elements of the supply chain should be improved. The details of the basic EOQ model can be pulled out of any basic operations text. What I will do now is to take you the next step, and apply this model to the Japanese JIT twist of supply chain management.

The traditional EOQ model focuses on minimizing the total cost of inventory. It can be expressed in the equation:

$$\textit{Total Cost} = \textit{Fixed Costs} + \textit{Variable Costs}$$

Expanding the terms we find that:

$$\textit{Fixed Cost} = \textit{Purchase Costs} + \textit{Safety Stock Costs} + \textit{Quality Costs} + \textit{etc.}$$

$$\textit{Variable Costs} = \textit{Order Costs} + \textit{Carrying Costs}$$

$$\textit{Order Costs} = \{\textit{Cost of Placing One Order}\}\ x\ \{\textit{Number of Orders}\}$$

$$\textit{Carrying Costs} = \{\textit{Average Inventory}\}\ x\ \{\textit{Cost of Carrying One Item of Inventory}\}$$

$$\textit{Number of Orders} = \frac{\textit{Demand}}{\textit{OrderSize}}$$

$$\textit{Cost of Carrying One Item of Inventory} = \{\textit{Value of the Item}\}\ x\ \{\textit{Interest Rate}\}$$

Defining some of the terms further gives us:

- *Demand* is the total number of units of the product that we are analyzing that will be demanded in one year.
- *Value of the Item* is the purchase price, if we are dealing with a purchased item or the manufacturing cost, if we are dealing with a manufactured item. In determining purchase price, do not become overly concerned about price breaks. You know at approximately what quantities you will be purchasing and that is the price you should use for these calculations.
- The remaining two variables, *Cost of Placing One Order* and *Interest Rate*, require a little more analysis. Looking first at Cost of Placing One Order, we have an example of the calculation for both a manufactured and a purchased item.

Ordering Cost Breakdown

(these are examples only and are not to be considered all inclusive)

- Ordering Costs for a purchased order item (these costs include labor, equipment. and materials)
  - preparation of purchase order (includes paperwork and phone calling)
  - transportation costs
  - receiving and inspection
  - preparation of payment documents
  - interplant transportation
  - expediting costs
  - postage costs

- Ordering Costs for a manufactured item
  - preparation of production order
  - materials picking costs
  - inspection costs
  - interplant transportation
  - expediting costs
  - machine set-up and clean-up costs
  - receiving back into inventory.

Next, look at an example of the calculation of the *Interest Rate*. Note that interest values are percentages. Also note that the higher rates should be chosen. For example, if the interest rate at which you are financing your money is 10 percent, but the opportunity cost that you are giving up is 20 percent, use the 20 percent value. An opportunity cost is the interest rate you could be earning by investing this same money in some other way.

Carrying Cost Breakdown

(these are examples only and are not to be considered all inclusive)

- Carrying costs (percent) – loss due to inability to invest funds in profit making ventures (opportunity costs or interest rate – which is higher)

- cost of replacing inventory
- inventory obsolescence
- deterioration of inventory
- handling and distribution
- taxes
- storage
- pilferage
- generel supplies
- insurance.

As we evaluate and calculate the values for *The Cost of Placing One Order* or the *Carrying Cost Interest Rate* we have to be careful and remember that only those components that vary based on the order size should be considered. For example, in the evaluation of *Interest Rate*, we have taxes. A sales tax is the same regardless of how large our order size is or how long we keep the items in inventory before we sell the product. Additionally, some areas have a tax on assets, like an inventory holding tax. An inventory holding tax is effected by our average inventory level, which is effected by our "Q" size. Therefore, the sales tax would be part of the fixed cost (FC) component, whereas the inventory tax would be a part of the carrying cost (CC) component and will be added to the *Carrying Cost Interest Rate*. This type of thinking should go into each of the incremental values used in the development of either *The Cost of Placing One Order* or the *Carrying Cost Interest Rate*.

The graph of all the costs associated with the EOQ model can be seen on Chart 6.2. Here we see how the *Variable Costs* {*Order Costs* (OC) plus *Carrying Costs* (CC)}, and the *Fixed Costs* (FC) accumulate together to make *Total Costs* (TC). Realizing this, we see how the model identifies for us the lowest total cost point. This lowest point on the total cost curve identifies the optimal batch size (Q). Traditional EOQ wisdom would recommend that if we operate at this point we would be minimizing cost and maximizing efficiency. However, from Japan and other parts of Asia we don't stop at this point in the analysis. Instead, we learn that all inventory is bad, especially when it is our critical resource, and we look for ways to reduce inventory within this model. Therefore we would, at this point, attack all the traditional, unchallenged, beliefs.

Chart 6.2. The EOQ Total Cost Model

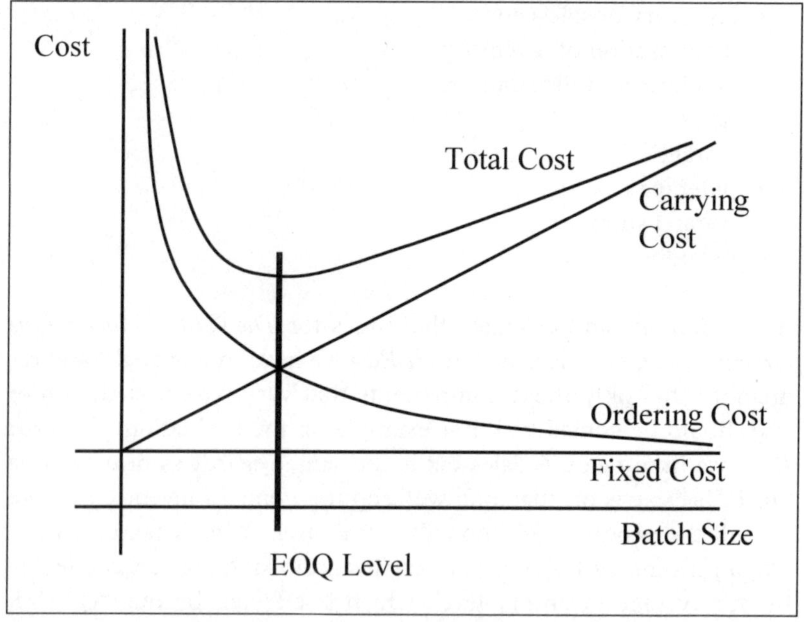

EOQ has not failed. It has in fact taught us a lot about inventory management and it is still the largest production and inventory scheduling tool in use throughout the world. It is continuing to be used primarily because it is so easy to use. And for many companies it has been a very successful tool. However, it doesn't go far enough. The Japanese and others have taught us that inventory costs can be squeezed down even further by focusing on the elimination of all non-value-added processes. This elimination begins with the premise that inventory is extremely expensive for the company to hold on to. Non-value-added is defined as anything that does not directly add more value to the product. And inventory that is not being worked on is non-value-adding. It takes up space, costs us carrying charges, decays, etc. Non-value-adding items are also referred to as "waste" items. An example of an attack on waste would proceed as follows:

Attack on Fixed Costs

Look at all the elements of fixed costs and evaluate them for minimization or possibly elimination. For example:

- Purchase Costs – Minimize these costs by establishing long-term contractual relationships with vendors. This eliminates price bidding and allows you to purchase at quantity discounts. International contractors, especially those in Latin America and Asia, are much more responsive and service oriented to you, the customer, if they are bound under long term relationships.
- Safety Stock Costs – Eliminate safety stock whenever possible. Safety stock is an item that grows but never shrinks. Whenever there is a problem, we tend to add to safety stock, but we never think to reevaluate safety stock to verify that it isn't excessive. Safety Stocks should be evaluated based on Chart 6.3. For example, if there is minimal demand fluctuation and the item is not critical to the production process (is not an "A" item), then there should probably be no safety stock at all. Similarly, if the lead time is effectively zero and the criticalness of the product is minimal, safety stock should be zero. Conversely, if there is high demand fluctuation or long lead time, and the product is critical to the process, then one reorder point (ROP) of inventory should be maintained. Rarely should there ever be more than one reorder point level of inventory. The reasoning is that if you run out, you still have enough safety stock to keep you operational for one order cycle, and by then you should be fully replenished.
- Quality Costs – The elimination of quality costs is simple: eliminate inspections. But that might be easier said than done. To eliminate inspections we need to establish a relationship with our vendors that allows us to certify the quality of the parts coming from the vendor. Similarly, we need to certify the performance of our operations internally to where inspection is no longer necessary. This certification takes time, patience, and a trusting relationship, which is often hard to build.
- Other Fixed Costs Elements – At this point you should have the spirit of how inventory cost reduction works for fixed costs. Apply these principles across the board.

Chart 6.3. Safety Stock Planning Chart

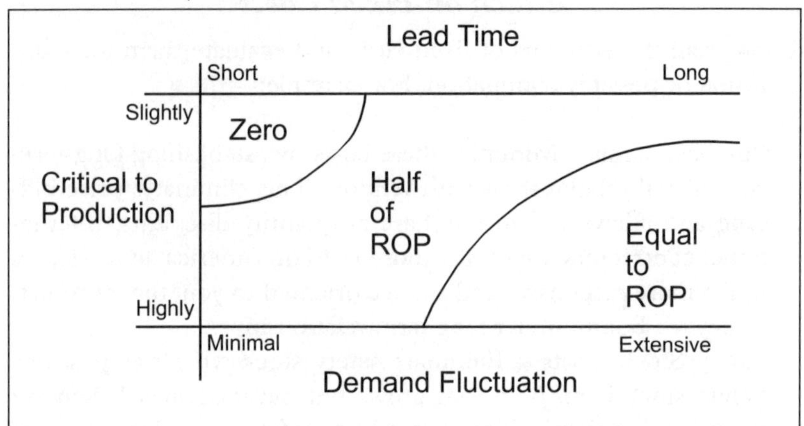

Attack on Carrying Costs

Look at all the elements of carrying costs and evaluate them for minimization or possibly elimination. For example:

- Deterioration of inventory can be minimized by not carrying excess inventories
- Storage can be reduced if inventory levels are reduced

Attack on Ordering Costs

This is the big one! This element is critical and it's importance is rarely recognized. Again we attempt to minimize all related cost elements, like in the case of purchased items:

- Transportation costs – We could move vendors closer to us or we could transport goods in smaller quantities and in pickups rather than in expensive semi-trucks. We could have standardized, recycled containers to reduce the cost of packaging materials.
- Receiving and inspection – Rather than having a receiving area, let's receive product directly into the production process. And let's eliminate inspection by certifying our vendors. Back in the

early days of international business relationships with Japan, Ford Canada had price bid parts out to a large number of vendors, including Toyota. Toyota won the bid. Ford sent their specifications out to Toyota and in the specification was the requirement for a maximum of 3 % bad parts. When the first shipment of parts arrived in Canada, the Ford receiving people opened the box and found within it a small bag of parts with a note. The note read: "We're not sure why you wanted 3 % bad parts, but we separated them out for you so that you wouldn't have any trouble finding them."

- Preparation of payment documents – Through a contractual arrangement, the paperwork can be almost completely eliminated. We don't need to send out orders, billing documents, etc. This greatly reduces the confusion when transacting internationally.

Ordering Costs can similarly be evaluated for a manufactured item, like:

- Preparation of the production order can be accomplished through automated means directly from the sales office.
- Materials picking costs can be reduced through ABC stock-room organization and through automated storage and retrieval systems.
- Inspection costs can be eliminated through quality management tools which would put quality into the hands of the operator, rather than requiring post-operation inspections.
- Receiving WIP goods back into an inventory stockroom can be eliminated if there is no WIP inventory. Rather, the product is moved on to the next production process immediately.
- Machine set-up and clean-up costs is the big one. This is the area where the most improvements can be made since this is the biggest cost in manufacturing order costs. The classic example of set-up time reduction is the fender forming machine that is used in manufacturing facilities all over the world. In the United States, it takes 6 hours to replace the upper and lower dies. It takes a fork lift and lot's of bolts and nuts. The same machine is used in Sweden and the set-up time there is 4 hours. The same machine is also used in Japan. Surprisingly the set-up time in

> Japan is 12 minutes. What is the difference? Are the Americans stupid. Not at all, unless you classify the measurement system as stupid. U. S. costing utilizes the classic EOQ model shown in Chart 6.2. Utilizing this model we calculate the optimal batch size (Q) and run production at this volume. The idea is that at this quantity, the cost allocation of set-up time over the number of products produced is minimized. The fallacy is that this model assumes that set-up time is fixed, constant, and unchangeable, just like all the other variables in the model. Utilizing this assumption we end up with a much larger batch size (Q) than is necessary. The Japanese focused on set-up time reduction whereas the Americans focused on batch size optimization. It's interesting how two different perspectives on exactly the same model lead to two so dramatically different results.

Focusing on order cost reduction, such as set-up time reduction, we end up with Chart 6.4 where we see that the effect of a set-up time reduction is to lower the level of the Total Cost of Inventory (TC), and thereby reduce the size of Q. Therefore, reducing order cost can dramatically reduce inventory levels throughout the facility.

This entire discussion of inventory cost reduction and waste elimination is the basic philosophy behind JIT. In JIT you don't assume anything is fixed and constant; you attack everything that is non-value added, and you end up with lower inventory costs across the board. It should be easy to see how this process effects the international transaction. Because of this process, some concepts make sense to be internationalized while others do not. For example, one of the big differences that occurs internationally is the difference in the evaluation of data collection. The United States believes that it is in an information age, whereas much of the rest of the world sees it as an information obsession. For example, *Activity Based Costing* is a tool for the collection of data at points in the organization. It is assumed that with more cost data you can manage costs better. However, many countries see the measurement of non-critical cost elements as a waste. Rather, they would stress the focus of measuring the critical resource elements as being much more valuable. For example, in the JIT process, there is no shop floor data collection. The recording of who did what and how long it took is not important. Rather, what is important is the efficient movement of the materials resource, which is more than 50 percent of the value-added cost content of the vehicle. Managing inventory's 50+ % will gain you more than managing the less than 10 % value added direct labor content.

Chart 6.4. The EOQ Total Cost Model Demonstrating the Effects of Order Cost Reduction

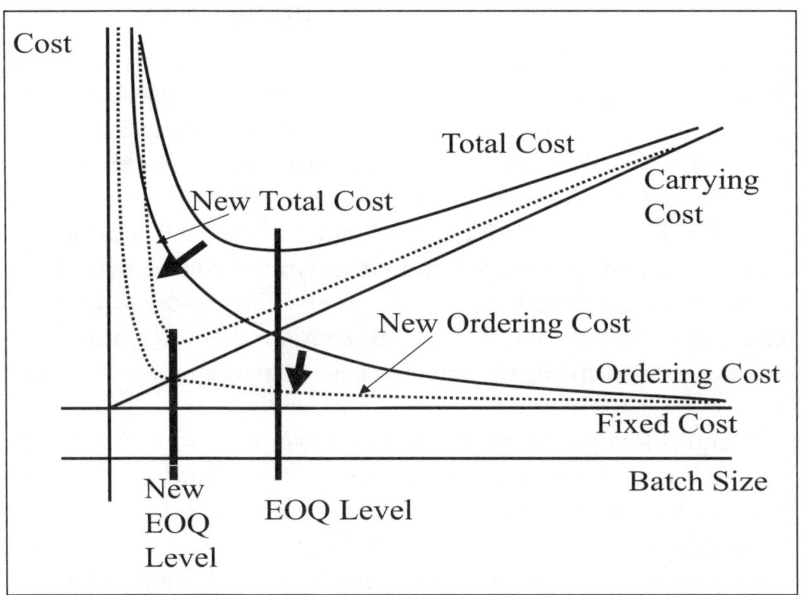

Another example of information waste is found in the non-trust systems that most organizations establish. Every time an undesirable event occurs, a system is created to make sure that it won't happen again. It has been documented in many companies that the non-trust systems, and the cost of the data collection process that they have created, is much more expensive than the problem that they are supposedly solving. It is this type of information obsession and lack of trust that is scoffed at internationally. In Japan, this is labeled as information waste.

At this point we should have a feel for how suppliers are treated differently in a *Supply Chain Management* approach to *Operations Management*. We should also be getting a feel for how some of the international considerations are treated differently through this approach, rather than the more traditional approach of going wherev-

er labor costs are cheapest. More will be discussed about plant relocation decisions in Chapter 10. Next, let's list some of the differences between the traditional management of a facility, and the supply chain approach.

An Example of International Suppliers Linked In A Complex Supply Chain

International supply chains introduce a high level of complexity. Border crossings introduce complexities that are unique, depending on the border being crossed and the direction in which we are crossing it. To demonstrate this complexity, here is an example of a specific case of international supply chain development. We will consider the case of NAFTA, the United States, and the Mexican factories across the border from the United States that supply cheap labor for American manufacturers. This in-depth look will give you a sense of some of the considerations that international operations management, and supply chain management, have to deal with.

Maquiladora plants sprung up in Mexico, right across the border from the United States, in an attempt to take advantage of the low cost work force that was available across the border. These plants were primarily assembly plants where all the technical functions were performed across the border in the United States. However, since the NAFTA agreement was signed, new plants are moving deeper into the heart of Mexico. Additionally, those plants that exist along the border are developing their own technical capabilities. This section discusses these changes through examples and discusses how the new, post-NAFTA Mexican plant, is priming to become a World Class competitor.

What is a Maquiladora Factory?

Maquiladora was originally used to describe a corn grinding process. However, this term has been taken on to identify Mexican assembly plants that are immediately across the border from the United States. A Maquiladora plant is a labor intensive plant where the engineering, marketing, and technical functions are kept in the United States, and the labor assembly work is performed in Mexico.

The Maquiladora plant was established to take advantage of a special, pre-NAFTA, tax arrangement that allows materials to be transferred into, and back out of Mexico in a form of consignment program, without having to pay duties on the materials. Only the value-added labor component was taxed. Now there are approximately 320 of these assembly plants along the U. S. / Mexican border.

There are basically three types of Maquiladora plants. The first type is the *Shelter Program*, where there is a United States based manager who has quality and scheduling responsibility, but the actual production is performed by a Mexican work-force. There is usually one primary customer which justifies the existence of the plant.

The second type of Maquiladora plant is the *Contract Program* where the plant takes responsibility for the *Forecast* and the *Master Production Schedule*. The plant plans *Capacity* and the *Aggregate Plan*. This plant takes in contract jobs of various volumes for a variety of customers. The plant is responsible for customer service and on-time delivery. Purchasing and materials delivery is the responsibility of the customers. The plant just produces the product.

The third type of Maquiladora plant is the *Independent Program* where the plant does its own purchasing, engineering, and marketing. This type of plant is in the minority, but is the new wave for plants in the future growth of Mexico's industrial power.

Cuidad Juarez is the home of the first Maquiladora plants. Approximately 600,000 trucks cross the border between El Paso, Texas, and Cuidad Juarez, Mexico, each year.

What is NAFTA?

The North America Free Trade Agreement (NAFTA) grew out of an agreement between the United States and it's largest trading partner, Canada. NAFTA incorporated Mexico into the initial U.S.-Canada trading alliance, allowing, for the most part, a duty free exchange of goods between the three countries. The goal of a trading partnership of this type is that a reduction of tariffs would benefit the consumers in the three countries by offering them lower priced goods. Mexico hopes that a lot of the industry that was now being moved off shore to Asia or other locations, would instead be relocated to Mexico, thereby taking advantage of both the lower labor costs and the reduced tariff costs. In the long term, Mexico hopes for a transfer of technology into Mexico which will develop Mexico's technological strength.

NAFTA is currently moving toward and even broader trade agreement called AFTA (America Free Trade Agreement). The existing NAFTA alliance is starting negotiations with Chile to include them in a broader, four country free trade agreement since Chile is the most economically and politically stable of the South American countries. However, the hope is that more of the American countries will eventually incorporate themselves into the AFTA.

In theory, a free trade agreement like NAFTA is designed to benefit the consumers of the partnership countries. Primarily, it offers them cheaper goods. It also benefits the businesses of the agreement, by making them more cost competitive, and by reducing the previously complex border crossing process, thereby offering faster turn-around in the time to market process. Unfortunately, free trade agreements also alienate the rest of the world, primarily because an agreement to trade more with a trading partner is also an agreement to trade less with the rest of the world.

Free trade agreements also generate trade barriers against the non-trading partners. For example, in the European Union (EU), ISO 9000 quality certification tends to become a requirement for outsiders who want to do business in the European Block. ISO 9000 certification, for many companies like Motorola and AT&T, is a step backwards, not forwards, since the ISO certification focuses on extensive documentation that proves that the requirements of engineering drawings have been satisfied, and not that customers have been satisfied.

NAFTA, although not as complex and complete as the EU, is becoming the trading block of the Americas, just as EU is for Europe, and APEC is beginning to be for the South-East Asian countries. The hope is that eventually these, and the twenty or so other, smaller agreements, will eventually be integrated together in to one big, international trading alliance.

Pre-NAFTA Maquiladora Plants

Prior to the NAFTA, all businesses in Mexico had to have a primary Mexican ownership. About the time of the implementation of

NAFTA, and in conjunction with it, Mexican law was changed so that businesses could now be dominated by foreign ownership. The 1993 change in the ownership law was intended to encourage foreign plants to locate within the heart of Mexico, and, as we shall see, it has worked well.

Often plants would be located deep into the heart of Mexico, closer to Mexico City where there was a more abundant labor force. Unfortunately, the border crossing process for many of these plants could take days, weeks, and even months. The result was that there was an enormous inventory holding cost associated with these items and often the inventory holding costs would erase much of the benefit of Mexico's reduced labor costs. NAFTA has greatly shortened the border crossing restrictions towards the United States and has change the process to one of having preclassified parts. The border crossings are quicker, but we now have a lot more lawyers employed doing all the paper work.

The Mexican Government and the Maquiladora Plants

The government has become heavily involved in integrating the business, union, community, and government elements. For example, the state Chihuahua, in which lies Cuidad Juarez, the first major Maquiladora city, has developed a 21st Century Plan. This plan includes an integrated vision to make the State of Chihuahua a total quality cell. They want to establish themselves as a *Total Quality Zone* which incorporates continuous improvement processes.

Chihuahua is developing a vision statement for the structure of the state for the next century which focuses on:

- Light manufacturing and automotive components manufacturing. They want to move from the assembly type plants to high tech total manufacturing plants like the new Motorola Pager plant.
- It also focuses on developing its natural resources by establishing a materials technology lab that will assist in developing new materials and their uses. This involves a 40 million peso investment in a *Materials Development Center*. They see materials as a core

competency in spite of its limited competitive value-added stance.

- Lastly, this economic plan focuses on tourism.

The economic strategy focuses on the development of technology support services that will assist in the development of new technologies. They plan to utilize economic development clusters (technology growth centers), infostructure development, and collaborative agreements, to achieve this technology development.

In general, Mexican government programs are focusing on programs that stress:

- Education – attempting to cut the foreign academic dependencies – attempting to establish long term training and technology centers – developing university programs for future leaders.
- Regionally defined value-added development – attempting to define regional core competencies and then to develop visions and missions around these core competencies.
- Initiatives – for example, the North-South roadway connecting Mexico and Canada.
- Society, not government projects – the government develops the structure, but the academics and private industry generate the ideas.

The Mexican government, like most governments, has established a series of incentive programs to lure the targeted industries into Mexico. These include tax incentives, property grants, and loans.

What Changes Were Instituted by NAFTA?

NAFTA has greatly increased the number of products that can now be transferred across the Canada — United States — Mexican borders. Agricultural products are moving down to Mexico at a rapid pace. The speed of the transfers has also improved. And tariffs have been reduced. The result is that the NAFTA consumer has lower prices. The producers have lower costs and they can now be more responsive to the market place.

There have been some big surprises that have occurred because of NAFTA. For example, the United States was expected to be the big loser (Ross Perot's big sucking sound), Canada was expected to be a net loser, and Mexico was expected to be the big gainer. Instead, Mexico has become the big, short term loser. Mexican farmers and small producers are being put out of business at a rapid pace and this has resulted in uprisings, demonstrations, assassinations, and a devalued peso. Mexico is still hoping to be a long term net gainer, but, unfortunately, in the short run, Mexico has not benefited from NAFTA.

The United States, on the other hand, has benefited quite well. There has not been a major migration of plants to Mexico. In fact, some organizations like R & R Donnelly, have decided that for quality and materials sourcing reasons, they are still better off building new plants in the United States, rather than in Mexico.

Employment conditions have always been poor, by United States standards. The average age of the employee is 19 years and continuing education is becoming more and more important. Twelve to fifteen percent turnover has generated a focus on more education because education has been directly linked to employee stability and long term commitment. The employers also offer cafeteria, medical, and education facilities for the employees. Protective equipment is used more often, and waste water treatment has become important. The companies are focusing on protecting their training investment by protecting their employees.

The big winners from NAFTA are the lawyers. I know of one law firm in Juarez that was struggling with five lawyers prior to NAFTA, and now has well over 150 employees. The extensive parts documentation paperwork required by NAFTA has created a field day for legal firms.

Post-NAFTA Maquiladora Plants

Before NAFTA, the Mexican government placed duties on the value-added labor portion of the products produced in Mexico. After the installation of NAFTA and the removal of the duties on Mexican labor the consumer has netted a three to four percent price reduction net gain. However, the operations of the plants in Mexico haven't changed much. What has changed is the amount of time that border crossings now take. Border crossings which used to be measured in terms of days, weeks, and even months, have now been reduced to one-half to four hours. This has enormously reduced the inventory carrying cost effect of border crossings, which often cost more than the labor savings generated by going to Mexico in the first place.

Post-NAFTA plants are moving more and more into the interior of Mexico. However, more importantly, these plants are bringing their design, purchasing, and marketing departments with them, giving Mexico the high value added elements of the production process. The newer, post-NAFTA plants are incorporating EDI (Electronic Data Interchange) in the marketing and purchasing departments, and CAD/CAM (Computer Aided Design / Computer Aided Manufacturing) into their design elements. Companies like General Motors and Motorola are establishing technology centers. Newer plants are focusing on turn-key operations, where the designs are fit directly to the customer's needs.

Mexican plants have changed enormously in their progressiveness, certainly in the plants that I have contact with. They no longer see themselves as labor sweat shops. They are now searching for their own competitive edge, with quality programs, process efficiency improvements, etc. Mexican plants like Vitro, are incorporating world class self directed work teams and *Computer Integrated Manufacturing* (CIM) technology that incorporates SMED (*Single Minute Exchange of Die*) principles to change dies in seconds, rather than minutes. Johnson and Johnson's Juarez plants incorporate JIT (*Just in Time*) focused cellular manufacturing processes with incentive based teaming and employee empowerment. These are examples of processes that already exist, and these companies are looking forward to more improvements in the future.

The training and education process in Mexico has changed as well. For example, there are now six national conferences focusing on productivity and quality improvements. There are productivity and quality centers all over Mexico. And schools like the Monterey Technical University utilize innovative methods in teaching industrial technology. They have one of the most advanced CIM (*Computer Integrated Manufacturing*) labs in all of the Americas (including the United States and Canada).

The Mexicans are developing cooperative arrangements between government, unions, business, and civic groups in an attempt to focus on integrated growth. There are national and state level quality awards where the government is attempting to motivate a new, competitive, integrative strategy.

NAFTA has encouraged an increase in trade and technology transfer. For example, General Motors is putting in a one million square foot warehouse which is totally automated. Similarly, UPS is setting up warehouses. Information and business systems have improved dramatically. Systems like EDI (*Electronic Data Interchange*), JIT, and MRP (*Material Requirements Planning*) are common. This has required an impressive infostructure improvement, starting with changes in the telephone systems.

The Johnson and Johnson's plants in Cuidad Juarez have become leaders in the effective utilization of JIT processes. They utilize cellular manufacturing, teaming and team incentives, and empowerment. They are heavily involved in TQM (*Total Quality Management*) systems throughout all their plants. They employ about 3,700 personnel in Mexico. They have won the Mexican quality award, and the Shingo Prize for manufacturing excellence from the United States.

One Johnson and Johnson Medical Inc. plant in Juarez, a surgical garment production facility, has about 1,800 employees and is ISO and EN 46002 certified (European certification for quality in manufacturing, and quality in medical device production). They are the first Maquiladora plant to win the *National Quality Award*. When I visited them in March, 1995, they had recorded two thousand hours of no labor loss due to injury, and the record was still growing. They use cellular manufacturing with team motivators. The training, for the sewing processes can take as much as twelve weeks.

Elamax, a job shop in Juarez, that builds custom electronic circuit boards utilizes attendance and performance incentives. They have about 800 employees and give about three weeks of training to each. They have water recycling systems to avoid polluted waste water going into the water systems. They return all waste products, like solder particles, to the United States rather than polluting the Mexican environment.

Plants like the Johnson and Johnson or Elamax plants would be considered impressive operations no matter where they are located.

The Future of the Relationship

Recently there are examples of plants being built where the design work is being done in Mexico, and the assembly work is being done in El Paso, Texas with Mexican laborers. This shows that there is a recognition of the technical potential of the Mexican engineer.

With the 1993 new foreign investment law, United States investors can own a Mexican company. They can now incorporate in Mexico. This investment policy has created a surge of Japanese interest and Japanese plants are flooding Mexico, taking advantage of the cheaper labor and then gaining access to the United States and Canadian marketplace.

Today, the Maquiladora plant is the most efficient and productive of all the plants in Mexico. These plants are no longer sweat shops, they are leading edge technology movers. In an over-all measure of customer satisfaction, the Maquiladora plants were rated as being over twice as productive and customer quality conscious as the average, non-Maquiladora Mexican plant. The Maquiladora plants won out in every category in which the ratings occurred, like:

- Customer satisfaction
- Employee satisfaction
- Information systems effectiveness
- Community relations
- Results orientation

The Maquiladora, and their follow up plants that are moving into the heart of Mexico, are becoming World Class international competitors.

The supply chain effects have been substantial. Product delivery cycle times that were previously measured in months because of the slow border crossings are now measured in days. However, infrastructure issues related to moving goods deep within the interior of Mexico have appeared and these have caused a new set of delays. Costs have been reduced. New product development cycle times have been reduced. And delivery schedules are longer unknown, they are now more consistent and therefore planable.

Mexico sees itself as a major international competitor. However, they also feel the pressures of loosing contracts to other locations, like South-East Asia, where labor costs are higher, and transportation costs are higher, but process costs are lower and quality is higher. The net effect that concerns the Mexicans is that the Malaysian or Singaporian product is often selected over the Mexican product.

The future also sees more infostructural support. Phone systems are getting better. Schooling for the youth and for employees (minimum sixth grade education) is becoming more and more available. The future also sees a focus on more comforts, like air conditioning, and employee transportation services.

In the short term, NAFTA has been a blessing for the United States, and a struggle for Mexico. However, the long term effects of NAFTA appear to have positive growth for all the NAFTA countries. NAFTA has triggered a flow of Japanese plants into the labor rich interior of Mexico, offering Mexicans jobs and technology. The new Mexican plant is more technologically based, and incorporates many of the leading edge productivity and quality strategies that we are trying to focus on in the United States. Additionally, the supportive nature of the government and unions, makes a move to Mexico more and more appealing.

International Perspectives on Supply Chain Management

It would be inappropriate to discuss international applications to Supply Chain Management without recognizing that internationally, the term "Supply Chain Management" has many different definitions. For example, the article in Appendix 6.1 offers an Australian and South-East Asian approach to what Supply Chain Management means. The appendix gives an advanced explanation on how a supply chain can be applied in order to increase throughput efficiency. It is included as an appendix in order to emphasize that this is not a generally understood definition. Rather, it is an indicator of where industry standards may be headed in the future. However, the traditional definition of SCM as used in this book is commonly used in the United States and Europe.

N, Inc. Revisited

A new development has occurred since we last visited N, Inc. The Swedish manufacturer is considering putting a plant into Mexico to move it under the NAFTA corridor. They see themselves as a direct competitor of N's Dayton microelectronics plant and they feel that they can under price this facility. If they were to produce in Mexico, they could take advantage of some of the lower operating costs and still get enough product content to be able to move parts into the United States markets, primarily to the half dozen N, Inc. plants that use these components. The Swedish manufacturer also feels that a move of this type will distract the Dayton plant from worrying about ISO certification and thereby give the Swedish plant a lock-in on the Augsburg production facility's need for chips.

Dayton is worried about the Swedish competitor. Not only are they threatened with the loss of 1/10 of their business in Augsburg, but now they may even lose some of their domestic business. N, Inc. is now considering the construction of a plant in Mexico in order to offset costs. Now you're the plant manager in Dayton. What would you do? What analysis could be performed? What would be the basis of your decision to relocate to Mexico? Would you go ahead with the ISO certification and take the Swedish plant on their own turf? What would you do?

Summary

As stated, the single most discussed area of international operations management is the management of the supply chain., which focuses on integration and time. In this chapter we focused on the supplier in the supply chain and saw how to develop appropriate relationships, eliminate waste, and make integration and time savings a reality.

In the next chapter the discussion of *Supply Chain Management* will focus on strategically incorporating value-added steps in the process (Chapter 7). Then, in Chapter 8 *Supply Chain Management* focuses on *time*. Only by managing the entire flow can the cycle time be shortened. It is now time to move forward into these other elements of Supply Chain Management.

Class Assignments

Assignment A

Revisit C, Inc. at the end of Chapter 5 and reconsider how you would manage their maintenance inventories. What would you do about safety stocks?

Assignment B

How would you manage N, Inc.'s relationship between the Dayton and the Augsburg plants? How would you eliminate waste in the N, Inc. supply chain?

References

Supply Chain Management References

Blackburn, Joseph D., *Time-Based Competition; The Next Battle Ground in American Manufacturing*, Business One Irwin, Homewood, Illinois, 1991.

Dornier, Philippe-Pierre, Ricardo Ernst, Michel Fender, and Panos Kouvelis, *Global Operations and Logistics*, John Wilery & Sons, Inc., New York, 1998.

Plenert, Gerhard and Shozo Hibino, *Making Innovation Happen: Concept Management Through Integration*, St. Lucie Press, Boca Raton, 1998.

Smith, Preston G. and Donald G. Reinertsen, *Developing Products in Half the Time*, Van Nostrand Reinhold, New York, 1991.

Thomas, Philip R., *Competitiveness Through Total Cycle Time; An Overview for CEO's*, McGraw-Hill Publishing Company, New York, 1990.

Wheelwright, Steven C. and Kim B. Clark, *Revolutionizing Product Development; Quantum Leaps in Speed, Efficiency, and Quality*, The Free Press, New York, 1992.

NAFTA and International Plant References

Plenert, Gerhard, "Installing Successful Factories into Developing Countries", *The International Executive*, Vol. 32, No. 2, Sept.-Oct. 1990.

Plenert, Gerhard J., "Manufacturing Management – A World Model"

Production Planning and Control, 1992, Vol. 3, No. 1, Pages 93-98.

Plenert, Gerhard J., "Plant Relocation: How Decisions Are Made oday", *Industry Forum*, March 1994, Pages 1-3.

Plenert, Gerhard, "Production Considerations for Developing Countries", *International Journal of Management*, Dec., 1988.

Plenert, Gerhard, "The Development of a Production System in Mexico", *Interfaces*, Vol. 20, No. 3, May-June 1990.

Plenert, Gerhard, *The Plant Operations Handbook*, Business 1 IRWIN, 1993, Homewood, Ill.

Appendix 6.1
Supply Chain Management Seen Through Australian Eyes[1]

Abstract

One of the most crucial components in the manufacturing planning process is to plan for the correct amount of materials to arrive on the shop floor when required by the appropriate activities. If this is not done properly, then either excess material will build up or resources will be idle due to non arrival of required materials. Quite often, it may be a mixture of both; too many materials that are not required and not enough materials that are required.

To help companies try to solve this problem, the main manufacturing philosophies that have been used to date are MRPII (Manufacturing Resource Planning), JIT (Just In Time) and OPT (Optimised Production Technology; a philosophy and an associated computer application package).

Supply Chain Management (SCM) extrapolates the materials supply problem to the entire manufacturing (supply) chain. It is concerned with material supply between companies in the chain, rather than directly addressing the problems *within* an individual company.

This paper investigates the use of SCM with the three main manufacturing philosophies, viz JIT, MRPII and SBM.

1. This article was taken from "Supply Chain Management and Existing Manufacturing Philosophies; Which Ones Work?" by J.R. Barker (Working Paper 1998-3-126/B) dated October 1998. Working papers are a series of manuscripts in their draft form. They are not intended for circulation or distribution except as indicated by the author. For that reason Working Papers may not be quoted, reproduced or distributed without the prior written consent of the author. Contact details: School of Information Technology, Bond University, Gold Coast, Queensland 4229, Australia, Tel: +61 7 5595 3344, Fax: +61 7 5595 3320, E-mail: jbarker@bond.edu.au

Keywords

Supply Chain Management (SCM), Manufacturing Resource Planning (MRPII), Just In Time (JIT), Schedule Based Manufacturing (SBM), material requirements planning (MRP), capacity requirements planning (CRP), master production schedule (MPS).

Forecasting

Let

l be the manufacturing lead time of a product
d be the acceptable delivery time of the same product.

The lead time l is the manufacturing lead time within the factory only. It does *not* include the suppliers' lead times (for any necessary raw materials). The following usually determine the necessity or otherwise of forecasting:

$l <= d$, forecasting is not required (1)
$l > d$, forecasting is required. (2)

As an example; if it takes only 1 week to make the product (l=1) and the delivery time is 2 weeks (d=2), then no forecasting is required. If, however, it takes 6 weeks to make a product (ie l=6) but the market will only accept a delivery time of 3 weeks (d=3), then forecasting is required.

The lead time l can be made smaller by cutting down set-up times, move times, run times and/or clean-down times. This can be done by buying extra machines, improving manufacturing efficiency, buying newer machines, simplifying product design, using different materials, etc.

JIT and Supply Chain Management

If $l <= d$, then JIT can be used instead of MRPII, if desired, in a single factory. The basic JIT philosophy is that nothing is produced until it is needed. In the case of a finished item, the need arises through a customer order. This in turn, creates the need for the components required to make the finished item which creates the need for certain sub-components, etc, all the way down to purchased items (raw material). All of these material 'needs' actually constitute material planning ensuring that raw material items are only purchased when they are required and components (work in process) are only in the factory when they are being processed.

When the purchased items arrive, production commences on the sub-components, then the components all the way up to the finished item. The overall affect of this is that, theoretically, inventories (raw material, WIP – work in process, and finished goods) are minimized.

Now let us turn our attention to the complete manufacturing chain instead of just one factory. According to 'pure' JIT, suppliers of a factory should also use JIT. Consequently, if JIT is implemented according to the theory, all manufacturers in the manufacturing chain should be using JIT.

Note that the manufacturing chain is also the supply chain and hence JIT, in a sense, incorporates supply chain management.

For the purposes of the following analysis, it is assumed that the manufacturing (supply) chain is linear, ie each company in the chain has one supplier and one customer, except of course, for the company at the tail of the chain and the company at the head of the chain.

Assume:

n companies in the chain, where $n >= 2$,
the 'head' company is number 1,
the 'tail' company is number n,
the companies in between (if any) are numbered sequentially from 2 to n-1, for $n>2$.

Then the lead time and delivery time of company i is $l(i)$ and $d(i)$ respectively. Therefore, the *total* lead time for the whole manufacturing chain is:

$$L = l(1) + l(2) + \dots + l(n) \qquad (3)$$

and the *total* delivery time is:

$$D = d(1) + d(2) + \ldots + l(n) \quad (4)$$

Therefore, the lead time to delivery time comparison (*l:d* above) becomes, for the manufacturing chain:

$$L{:}D \quad (5)$$

However, the final customer is only prepared to wait *d(1)* time units. Hence, the comparison L:D is replaced with:

$$L{:}d(1) \quad (6)$$

which is a somewhat different to equation (5). L is, of course, the total lead time of company 4 which is its own manufacturing lead time, *l(4)*, plus the suppliers lead times, *l(3)* + *l(2)* + *l(1)*.

Equation (6) shows that *unless* the *total* lead time of the whole manufacturing chain is less than or equal to the end customer's delivery time, then every company in the chain cannot use JIT.

For some products, it may be possible for the *total* lead time of the whole manufacturing chain to be less than or equal to the end customer's delivery time, but, for the majority, it is not possible. The lead time of a motor car, for example, should include the time taken to dig the required iron ore out of the ground through to the finished product with its glass, plastic, metal, rubber, electrics, electronics, etc.

Thus, the JIT goal that every JIT company has JIT suppliers, is rarely achievable in practice. However, JIT theory is compatible, by definition, with supply chain management. In practice, the non-JIT companies in the chain usually ensure just-in-time supplies to JIT companies. This maintains adequate supply chain management.

As an aside, it is interesting to note that a company can move in and out of JIT. Over a period of time, demand for the company's products may grow to the extent that the lead time for orders (products) becomes greater than the delivery time, ie $l > d$. If this occurs, the company will need to forecast future material requirements and use SBM (or MRPII). At some time in the future, if demand decreases, resources are increased (resulting in shorter lead times) or a mixture of both, the company may again utilise JIT as $l < d$.

To date, I am not aware of this situation being discussed in the literature. I have experienced such a case with at least one company and I intend to describe in a future publication.

MRPII and Supply Chain Management

A simplified schematic of MRPII is given in chart 6.5. As has been stated previously in the literature, MRPII is, at best, an approximating manufacturing philosophy.

Chart 6.5. A simple overview of MRPII

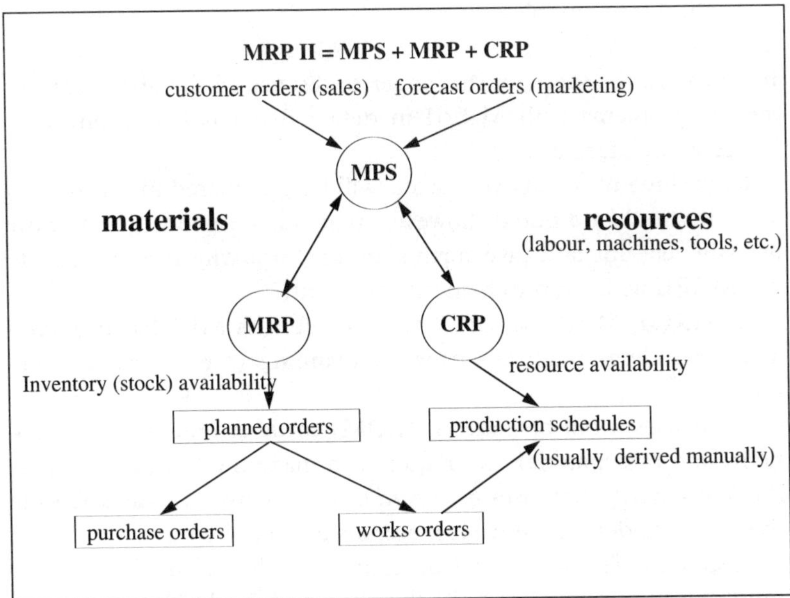

The references given above have documented many problems with MRPII and its implementation. The reasons for these problems are many and include:

- resources, other than machines and labour, were usually not considered
- constant, rather than variable, lot sizes were used
- lead times are static in MRPII but not in reality

- forward scheduling versus backward scheduling
- unrealistic MPS' do not consider actual job sequencing
- lack of accurate data
- sequence dependencies are not considered
- shop floor loadings are not considered in MRP
- difficulty with multiple machines per work centre
- different capacities, speeds and/or capabilities
- dynamic relationships between resources and materials are not considered (horizontal separation)
- interjob dependencies are not considered
- MPS and production schedule are considered independently (vertical separation)

It is beyond the scope of this paper to discuss all the above reasons for the problems with MRPII in detail; that has been done elsewhere in the literature.

Only some of the above reasons will be considered in this discussion. It should be noted, however, that other reasons given above are still relevant and give further insight into why it is difficult to use MRPII with supply chain management.

In MRPII, MRP and CRP are done after an MPS has been created, including rough cut capacity planning (see Charts 6.5 and 6.6).

MRP uses a bill of material (BOM) to determine what components and raw materials are required to make the finished goods in the MPS. MRP then uses *backward scheduling* from the due dates in the MPS, to determine what materials are required and when they are required. The static lead times used in the calculations are almost always wrong and hence, the output of the MRP is almost always incorrect.

Chart 6.6. Typical steps involved in MRPII

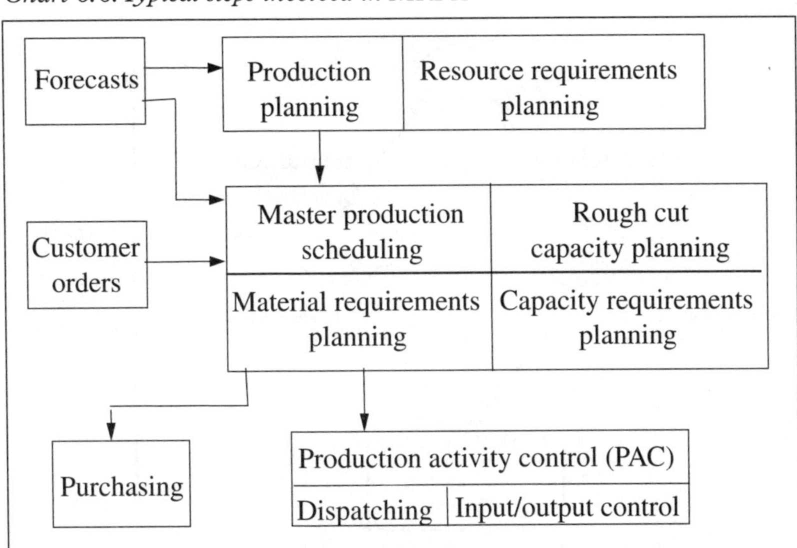

CRP, on the other hand, typically uses *forward scheduling* which will give different answers to backward scheduling. (Note that the usually incorrect static lead times are again used). Therefore, resources and materials are not synchronised.

As can be seen from Charts 6.5, 6.6, and 6.7, the planning functions of materials (MRP) and resources (CRP) are done *separately*. They are treated as if they are *independent* of one another. This is what I have termed *horizontal separation* (see chart 6.7). They should be planned together, not separately.

From a material supply viewpoint, the resulting discrepancies appear as inaccuracies in quantities and/or due dates. These inaccuracies will be propagated through the supply chain and it is not unusual for them to be magnified as they pass down the supply chain. Constant intervention is therefore required to correct the discrepancies throughout the supply chain.

Chart 6.7. A simple overview of MRPII

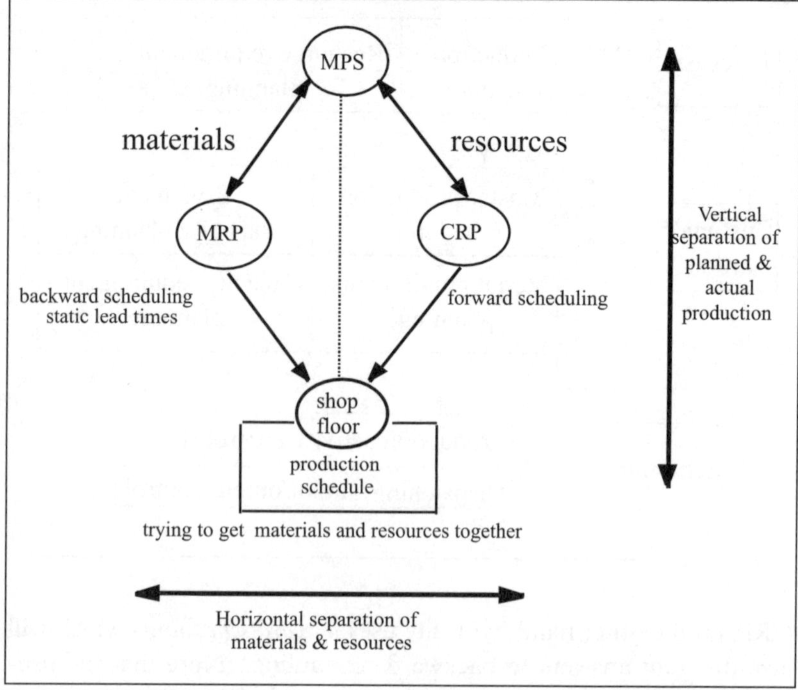

Further, the response rate in MRPII is too slow for SCM which expects timely and accurate data. Consider the case where a machine or work centre fails. The processes required, with manual intervention, to adjust inventory requirements in MRPII are so time consuming that they are often not done. Similarly, it is time consuming to alter resource requirements due to unplanned changes in material supply.

Both of the situations in the previous paragraph occur because there is no direct relationship between materials and resources in MRPII. Such a dynamic relationship would allow automatic adjustment of inventory due to unplanned resource changes and/or automatic adjustment of resource allocation due to unplanned material changes.

SBM and Supply Chain Management

SBM was designed to overcome most, if not all, of the inherent problems of MRPII. There is no horizontal or vertical separation in SBM. MRP and CRP are joined and, consequently, are done together. Further, the MPS and the actual production schedule are also joined; they are not separate entities as they are in MRPII. Therefore, any changes in what is happening on the shop floor automatically affects the MPS. In MRPII, any such changes must be fed back into MPS; hence the term 'closed loop' MRPII. The MRPII 'diamond' as shown in Charts 6.5 and 6.7, collapses into a single entity in SBM, enabling the processes required in Chart 6.6 to be replaced by the simple central procedure shown in Chart 6.8.

The material requirements and their associated due dates in SBM are more accurate than those in MRPII because they are derived from actual schedules which incorporate both material and resources. They are also calculated much faster and use more accurate data.

SBM incorporates a global view of manufacturing based on the assumption that a manufacturer is a part of a manufacturing chain and not a single stand-alone entity. SCM is based on the same assumption whereas MRPII is based on the single entity approach.

To clarify this, refer to the manufacturing chain as depicted earlier and consider the following three situations:

- the raw materials to manufacturer 1 are late
- manufacturer 3 wants material from manufacturer 2 to be delivered later (or earlier)
- manufacturer 4 cancels an order to manufacturer 3 (or changes it's due date)

1) The raw materials to manufacturer 1 are late. Assume that the raw materials to manufacturer 1 are 2 days late. Then it can be shown that, unless extra resources are added somewhere in the manufacturing chain, the delay to a customer at the end of the chain will be at least 2 days. In most cases, it will be greater than 2 days.

All the manufacturers in the chain would have to change their *expected receipt dates* of all affected material.

2) Manufacturer 3 wants material from manufacturer 2 to be delayed. In this situation, the *due dates* of all affected materials on the supply side of manufacturer 3 will need to be altered and the *expected receipt dates* of all affected materials on the customer side of manufacturer 3 will also need to be changed.

3) Manufacturer 4 cancels an order to manufacturer 3. In this situation, all the manufacturers would have to change the *due dates* of all affected materials.

Handling the above situations in MRPII is very difficult because, as has been shown in the previous section, the values used are usually incorrect, the time taken to make the changes is too long and a lot of manual intervention is required.

Recall that the manufacturing chain is a simple linear chain. In practice, the chain is not nearly so simple. Each manufacturer in the chain usually has multiple suppliers and multiple customers. Consequently, the task is much more complicated than that presented in this simple example.

The assumption has also be made that all the manufacturers in the chain are make-to-order. If one or more manufacturers are make-to-stock, then the above example may also involve increased stock holdings in one or more make-to-stock manufacturers in the chain.

Chart 6.8. Production Planning in SBM and resulting Material Requirements

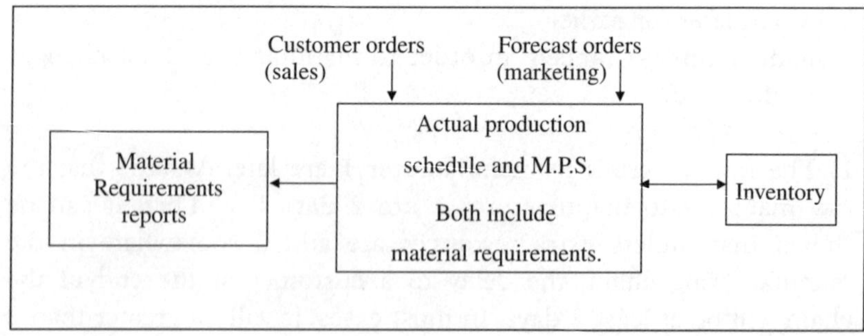

One design criterion of SBM was that its schedules and resulting material requirements could be visible to both a company's suppliers and customers. The increased visibility throughout the supply chain allows all companies in the chain to *synchronise* their material requirements. Any changes in material requirements or supply, by choice or otherwise, of any company in the chain is transmitted quickly to other companies in the chain. Therefore, suppliers are kept up to date with any changes in material requirements from anywhere within the chain and customers are kept up to date with any changes in forthcoming deliveries. This is the very essence of SCM especially with the fast electronic communication that is now available.

Conclusion

SCM is inherent in the use of JIT although forward visibility, ie looking at material requirements in the near to distant future, is rather blurred. Unless the total lead time is less than an acceptable customer delivery time, JIT cannot be used in practice with SCM.

MRPII was not designed to be used with SCM. The material requirements, as generated by MRP, are usually not accurate enough nor responsive enough to be propagated through the supply chain. Inaccuracies in material requirements and/or due dates may be magnified if introduced directly into the supply chain. Constant corrections are usually required to make MRPII work with SCM.

SBM was designed to use the available power of modern computers to solve complex problems beyond the scope of MRPII. It is the only manufacturing philosophy designed after the introduction of SCM hence its ability to facilitate and encourage the use of SCM.

References

Al-Hakim, L. A., Okyar H. and Sohal, A. S., 1992. A Comparative Study of MRP and JIT Production Management Systems (An Australian Case Study), *Unpublished Report*, Monash University, Melbourne.

Barker, J. R., 1993. Schedule Based Manufacturing Philosophy,

School of Information Technology, Bond University, *Working Paper 1993-3-088B.*

Barker, J. R., 1993. SBM – Schedule Based Manufacturing, *1993 Australian Conference on Manufacturing Engineering*, Adelaide, November.

Berger, G., 1987. Ten Ways MRP can Defeat You, *APICS Conference Proceedings* , American Production and Inventory Control Society.

Black, W. and Barker, J. R., 1993, SBM – a Worked Example; a Comparison of SBM and MRPII, School of Information Technology, Bond University, *Working Paper 1993-3-106B.*

Browne, J., Harhen, J. and Shivnan, J., 1988. *Production Management Systems: A CIM Perspective*, Addison-Wesley.

Christopher, Martin, *Logistics and Supply Chain Management: Strategies for Reducing Cost and Improving Service (Financial Times Management)* Financial Times Prentice Hall Publishing, NY, 1999.

Donovan, R.M., 1992. Enhanced Production Scheduling and Capacity Management: Is It Worth It?, *APICS-The Performance Advantage*, pp 42-46, June.

Goldratt, Eliyahu M., *Critical Chain*, North River Press, Croton-on-Hudson, NY, 1997.

Hanfiled, Robert B. and Ernest L. Nichols, Jr., *Introduction to Supply Chain Management*, Prentice Hall, NY, 1998.

LaForge, R. and Craighead, C., 1997. Manufacturing Scheduling and Supply-Chain Integration: A Survey of Current Practice, *APICS E&R Grant 97-13.*

LaForge, R. and Sturr, V., 1986. MRP practices in a random sample of manufacturing firms, *Production and Inventory Management, V28* (3), Pages 129-137.

Plenert, G. and Best, T. D., 1986. MRP, JIT and OPT: What's Best?, *Production and Inventory Management, V27 (2)*, Pages 22-29.

Schroder, R., Anderson, J., Tupy, S. and White, E., 1981. A study of MRP benefits and costs, *Journal of Operations Management, V2 (1)*, Pages 1-9.

Simchi-Levi, David, et al, *Designing and Managing the Supply Chain: Concepts, Strategies, and Cases,* Irwin/McGraw-Hill, NY, 1999.

7. Supply-Chain-Management

This is the second chapter in the discussion of Supply Chain Management. As discussed in the last chapter, Supply Chain Management focuses on time efficiency and integration. In this chapter we will focus on the integration elements and in the next chapter we will discuss time management. But first we need to revisit N, Inc. to see how they are doing.

N, Inc.

N, Inc. went ahead with their plans to build a plant in Mexico. They found the plant to be extremely effective and efficient, but it did not generate the cost savings that had been hoped for. Yields had dropped from 75 % to 60 % but this could be explained by a learning curve. They decided to do a detailed cost comparison between the before and after situations and found that transport costs and inventory carrying costs had jumped significantly. Additionally, the supply chain had become enormously complicated. The materials that originally came from companies like C, Inc. now had to be moved across borders which meant more distribution layers and this was also an increased cost.

In the meantime, the Swedish supplier had strengthened his relationship with the Augsburg plant and was now supplying about 25 % of their demand. The Dayton plant maintained its operations under the assumption that international demand would increase. However, since the capacities have now been balanced between the Dayton and Mexico plants, and since demand has decreased in Augsburg, the corporate office is in a dilemma as to what to do with the excess capacity. They could address a more vigorous marketing effort. To date the marketing for chip production has been weak because the internal demand was strong and very little external marketing was applied. However, the corporate office is concerned about growing a segment of the business that is not really within the core competency of N, Inc.

The distribution of component materials now passes through the Dayton facility. They have kept the quality inspection process centralized and then they containerize all the materials for transport to Mexico. The Mexico facility opens the containers, produces the product, containerizes the product, and sends it back to Dayton where final inspection occurs. Then the product is packaged and shipped to the customers.

The Swedish manufacturer also opened their Mexican facility. However, through extensive marketing efforts they were able to sell nearly all their capacity in Mexico and Canada. They ended up not needing to compete with N's Dayton facility for N's domestic capacity. They are considering an expansion program which will allow them to address even more customers, and ultimately the N, Inc. market in the United States.

Now you are again given the assignment of developing a strategy for N, Inc. Once again it would be valuable to look at each of the perspectives:

- N's Corporate Office
- N's Dayton Plant
- N's Mexico Plant
- N's Augsburg Plant

What would be an appropriate strategy? What would you do?

An Integration Supply Chain Strategy

We have already had a discussion of strategy development in earlier chapters. What we will address now is the development of an Integrated Supply Chain Strategy, which is a component of the over-all international, production, operations, logistics, and distribution strategy. This chapter discusses the international factors that effect successful supply chain management. This chapter focuses on the integration of the supplier, logistics, manufacturing, and customer service of total supply chain management. We will focus on the following key issues:

- The Strategic Framework
- Cycle Time and Response Time as the Key Strategic Issue
- ECommerce and eBusiness effects on the Supply Chain creating a Value Chain
- The Global Supply Chain
- Information Integration
- Risk Management
- Logistics Management

The Strategic Framework

The strategic structure of Supply-Chain Management (SCM) has been recognized as increasingly critical in corporate performance, as is witnessed by the increasing number of CEO's that are coming from the ranks of operations. Running a company strictly by the financial numbers has proven itself to be less than optimal. Operational measures of performance are now used more frequently.

Strategically, managing the supply chain means looking at management from the broader perspective. We have experienced an ever broadening supply chain perspective. Today, SCM requires more detailed levels of management. Whereas traditionally SCM management focussed around the manufacturer and their immediate suppliers, today, SCM focuses on the optimization of all movement, starting with the suppliers' supplier all the way through to the customers' customer. We see that traditionally we were only concerned with the environment immediate around us. Later we broadened that perspective through tools like EDI (Electronic Data Interchange) to included the management of the supply source. We felt that managing the source would allow us to run a leaner production environment with lower inventory levels. More recently we have recognized the need to look even broader, to the management of the entire source supply through the entire customer network. This has been labeled as the management of the entire supply chain. However, this is not management in the traditional sense of the word. We do not take over everyone's responsibility, rather, we integrate the information network so that all elements of the supply chain can interact and extract information from the same supply network. The internet has provided the tool of the future for supply chain management. It moves us away from a traditional point-to-point information exchange to a more connected, interactive information exchange where all elements of the supply chain can continuously interact to monitor the performance of the over-all supply network.

In a simplistic two supplier, two customer, supply chain network there are some many links through so many SCM levels that it would be nearly impossible to manage the exchange of information using traditional point-to-point data transfer methodologies. Not only do the suppliers and customers need to be kept informed, but the distribution and logistics chain which includes transportation and warehousing, needs to be kept in the information loop. This network of information exchanges can now be effective through the use of internet connectivity.

In Chart 7.1 we see the Supply Chain Management approach to the process which requires the sharing of information and a form of integrated independence. Integrated in that they are all connected to the information network, but independent in that a level of trust exists between the organizations which allows them to manage their own piece of the relationship.

The benefits of this type of integration include:

- Greatly reduced inventories since the supply chain manages inventory movement
- Lower safety stock levels
- Greatly reduced cycle times
- Increased customer responsiveness
- A more participative management approach
- Greater information accessibility at all nodes in the supply chain
- Significant cost reductions
- More price and delivery competitiveness which is extremely important when dealing with products that are at the mature stage of the product life cycle
- Fewer middle-men and promotional costs in the sales transaction
- More direct customer problem responsiveness and problem resolution
- Better quantitative indicators for all elements of the supply chain

Chart 7.1. Supply Chain Management Approach

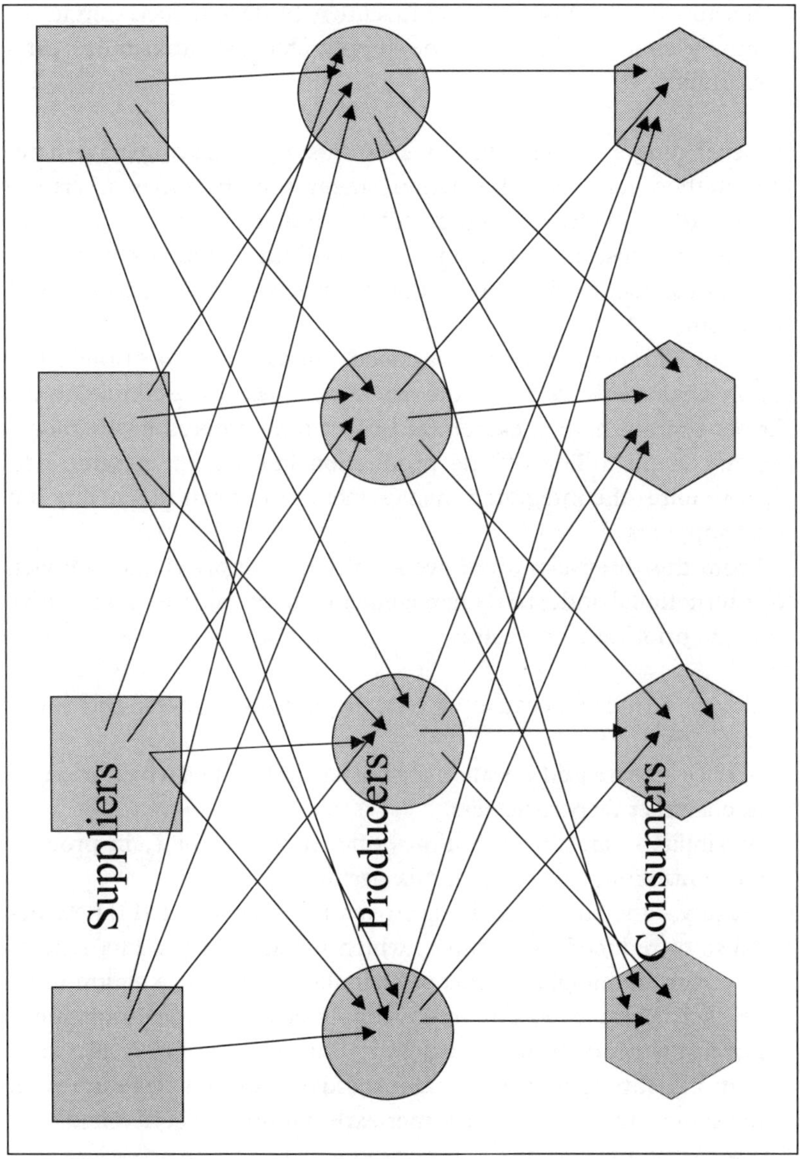

The disadvantages of supply chain management include:

- Loss of direct control of internal information
- Ineffectiveness of the remainder of the supply chain to integrate

- Loss of management control of the over-all process
- Because of the elimination of inventory buffers at each step in the supply chain, a failure in the supply chain is often more catastrophic

In developing a strategy that focuses on supply chain management, the methodology of information integration becomes a critical piece. Additionally, the connectivity and relationships between sources and customers becomes critical. This would not work well in a management environment that focuses on control and authoritarianism.

A third strategic element that needs management is "time". The supply chain network reacts quickly to changes. For example, in the Toyota supply chain, a customized car can be ordered in the morning and come rolling off the production line later that same day. That requires the integrated management of not just the facility but of all suppliers.

From this discussion, we have seen that a supply chain approach to international industrial management effects all the competitive strategic priorities. These are:

- Cost – reduced because of reduced inventory levels and lower sales costs.
- Service – increased because of shorter cycle times which increases customer responsiveness.
- Flexibility – shorter cycle times offer more flexibility in product customization, and product mix performance.
- Quality – the supply chain approach is closer to the JIT flow because of reduced cycle times, which means that product defects or errors are caught quicker, which allows corrective action to be quicker. More importantly, the supply chain approach integrates not just time, quantity, and delivery information, but it also integrates quality specifications and standards so that everyone is on the same page as far as customer expectations are concerned.

In globalizing the supply chain discussion we quickly recognize the integration need becomes international and that point-to-point information transfer under the EDI format becomes both expensive and impractical. The use of the internet for information integration becomes the only reasonable means for integration. However, having recognized that the focus on the internet is critical, we now see that global information integration is no more complicated than in a domestic setting. The key is found in the effective organization of the integrated, trust-based supply chain, and less so in the authoritarian management of the established supply structure.

Cycle Time and Response Time as the key strategic issue

It is important to highlight the importance of time in a global strategic supply chain network. The next chapter is devoted to this topic and the previous discussion has also emphasized this issue. Time is the key to competitive success. Supply chain management reduces several different types of cycle time and therefore increases response time to customer concerns and expectations. An organization that is not integrated in the supply chain will not be an effective competitor.

ECommerce and eBusiness effects on the Supply Chain creating a Value Chain

Supply Chain Management integrates networks of companies into a structure that allows them to optimize performance as a collective unit. The integration starts with the vendor's vendor and ends with the customer's customer. Traditionally a company would focus inward for performance and customer satisfaction. The attitude was that suppliers and shippers were an independent entity of their own, one which the enterprise could not reasonably be held responsible for. The result was that if a customer had a problem in receiving their goods, they had to make independent calls to producers, shippers, warehouses, and sometimes even suppliers, in order to identify the real source of shipment delays.

In Chart 7.2 we see how traditionally the enterprise was internally focused and isolated from the external elements of customer service. In this chart we see how competitive pressures applied on the enterprise made them look outward. They developed relationships with their suppliers and customers. In supply management, the enterprise was starting to take some responsibility for the performance of the supply chain. They were starting to integrate the lead time needs of their suppliers into their own schedules so that they could offer the customer a more realistic estimate of deliveries.

Chart 7.2. The Technology Migration

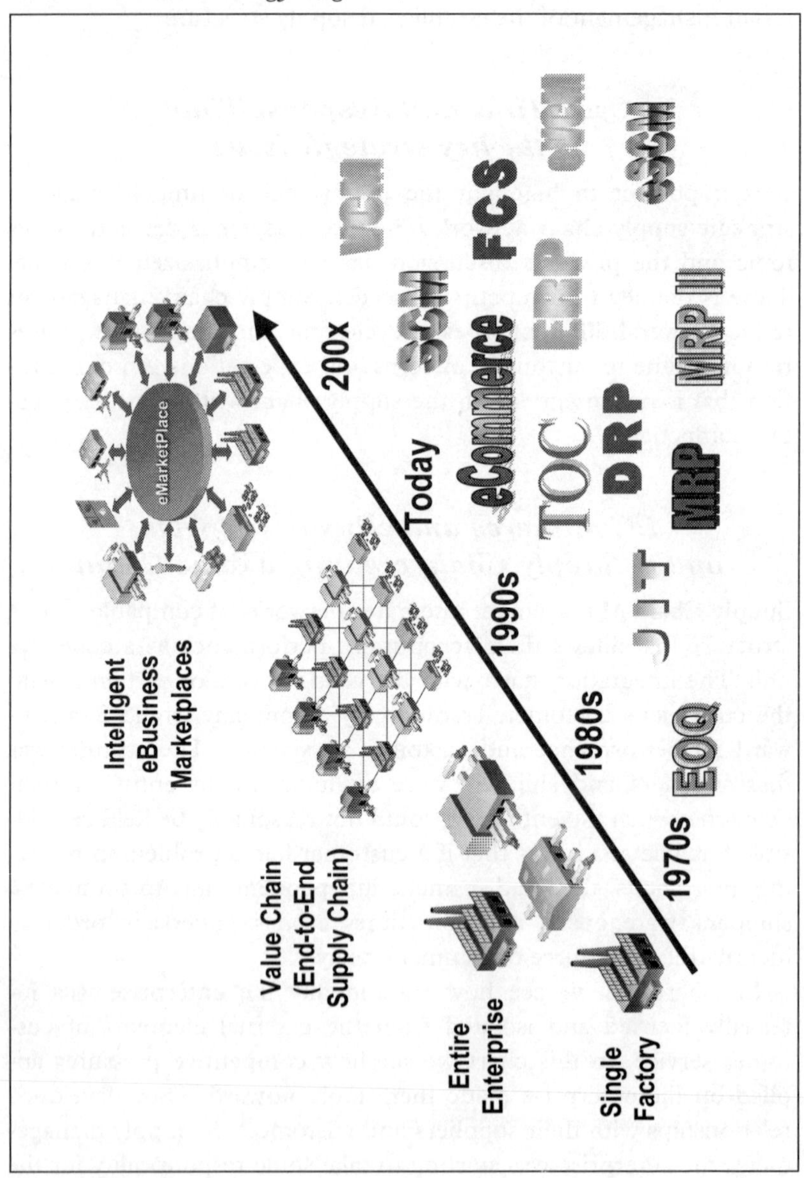

As time went on, an increased competitive strategic opportunity was identified when organizations realized that by centrally controlling all the steps in the customer performance process, an enterprise could do a better job of satisfying the customer. From this realization grew the philosophy of supply chain management. A focal enterprise, generally the one involved in taking the order, would now take control of the interlocking network of activities that would get the customer the promised product on time as committed. Planning was performed which would allow reasonably accurate estimates of the lead times necessary to perform the process. These lead times included supplier, shipper, and warehousing lead times. Supply chain management was born.

Supply chain management is the efficient movement of materials from the vendor's vendor through to the customer's customer. The focus of the supply chain is on the material movement relationships that exist between each of these links in the chain. The planning process was seen in Chart 7.3, where each of the producers had taken responsibility for the product from the supplier through to the customer.

Competitive pressures internationally caused organizations to realize that they weren't good at everything. For example, manufacturers were not necessarily good at warehousing or shipping. Organizations started to focus on what they did best, they focused on their core competencies. This shift away from vertical integration encouraged organizations to look outside of themselves for services. For example, a manufacturer would have a shipping company do all their packaging and shipping. This introduced more steps in the vendor to customer linkage, making the management of the supply chain more complex.

The trend toward operational diversification focused organizations on developing a supply chain where an organization would establish a relationship with shippers, vendors, and customers, so that all the linkages in the supply chain could be effectively integrated. These interrelationships became extremely complex to manage. Initially, the management of these relationships and linkages was primarily performance based. Having too many linkages in the supply chain would often cause poor responsiveness to customer demands. Time-to-market became the buzzword of successful competitive position. The organization that managed its supply chain the most effectively tended to have the competitive advantage.

Chart 7.3. Enterprise Centric Supply Chains

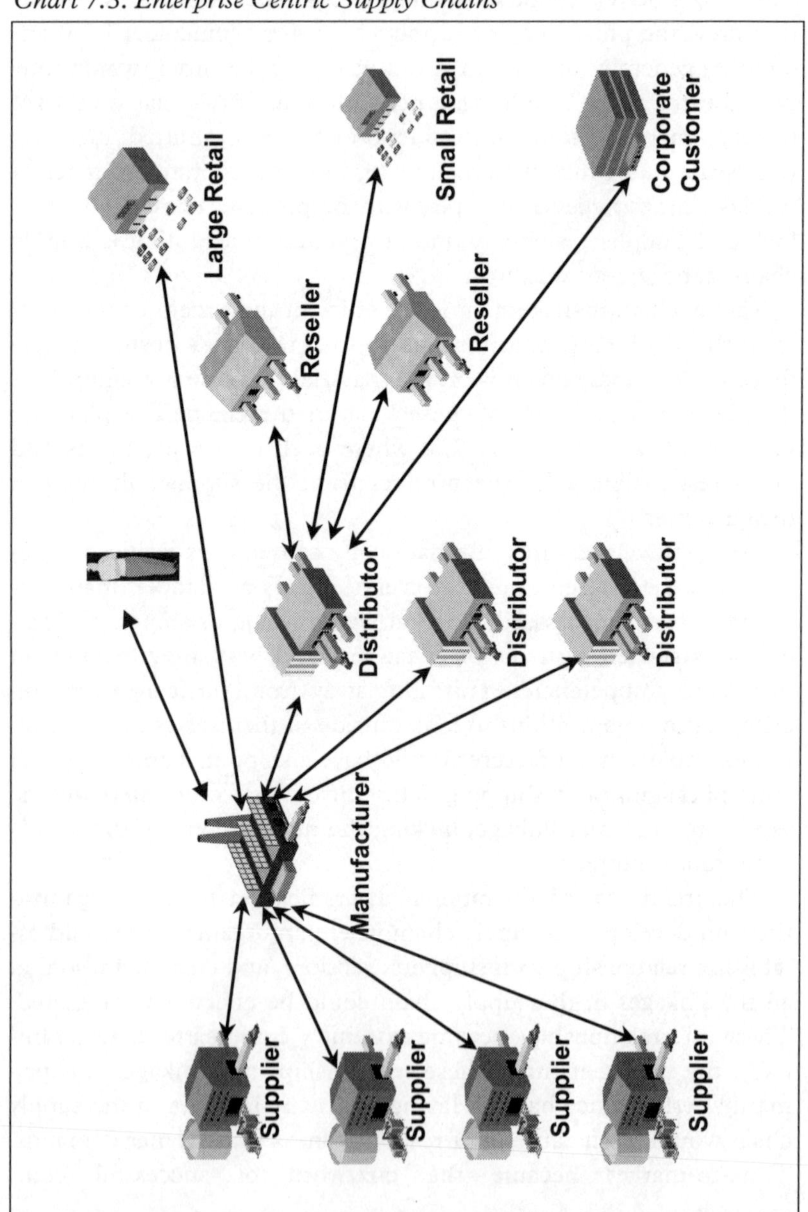

Soon management realized that time responsiveness was not the only important element in customer satisfaction. The supply chain linkages also had a cost element and resource efficiency element associated with them. This realization generated a need for Value Chain Management, which is the management of all the linkages of the supply chain in the most resource efficient way. Sometimes this encouraged the elimination of elements of the supply chain. For example, web marketing has eliminated the need for retail outlets.

ECommerce or eBusiness appeared just in time to ease the burden of information exchange. However, conventional wisdom, up until very recently, claimed that eCommerce will change everything; that the big corporate dinosaurs will face extinction; that life as we know it will not survive. To understand this concept better, let's take a look at what eCommerce really is.

In 1969 the United States Department of Defense established ARPANET (Advanced Research Agency Network) in response to a need to have an open line of communications between all nodes of a communications network. They didn't want the network to be dependent on a single physical line of communication. They wanted the communication system to be free and independent, allowing the network to establish flexible information routes regardless of any disruptions of any type. The result was a network of computers and communications lines that allowed universal access across multiple transmission routes. Originally intended as a military communications system, the network quickly developed into a messaging system that included civilian messages. By 1983, ARPANET had become MILNET and the remains of the original network became known as the Internet. By the mid 1990s the original four ARPANET sites had blossomed into 6.6 million internet computer sites worldwide.

The internet network of computers still required the users to be able to identify which computer node they wanted to address. This frustrated a British physicist Tim Berners-Lee who was trying to search for specific pieces of information without knowing which computer node to address. He established links called hypertext which helped users identify the information they were looking for. By 1990 he linked hypertext to an on-line addressing system called Uniform Resource Locator (URL) and he called the link the World Wide Web (WWW). In 1991 he made the WWW freely available to the public, and the internet age exploded.

By 1996, about 40 million people around the world were connected to an internet with 627,000 domain servers. By the end of 1997, more than 100 million people were connected and the internet had grown to 1.5 million domain servers. World wide internet commerce sales revenue had reached $10.6 billion. Internet traffic doubled approximately every 100 days for the last three years of the 1990s. By 2001, internet revenues are projected to reach $223 billion.[1] What had started as a simple, computer linked, message switching system was rapidly expanded into a system used to perform business transactions.

We have entered a new competitive era of business development – web focused businesses. Not only were traditional business transactions performed through the use of the internet, but new methods of business and new types of business were rapidly developing. New companies have sprouted up in all the traditional avenues of marketing and operations. And the old dinosaur companies have felt the pain of rapidly loosing market share to these new upstarts. In order to hold on to markets that they traditionally dominated, these dinosaurs are now painfully moving into web based enterprises as well, even if it sometimes seems excessively expensive. This new era of business has been labeled eCommerce, or, as the more IBM indoctrinated would refer to it, eBusiness.

Initially, the definition of eCommerce follows the lines of the definition of commerce in general. ECommerce is the exchange of value across enterprises or between enterprises and consumers. But with eCommerce, this exchange is performed electronically. This exchange can include orders, bills, payments, entertainment, or information in many forms, including capacity information. And this is enabled by some simplistic, yet profoundly significant internet-related technologies like internet protocol, web browsers (free tools available to everyone), HTML/XML, and web application servers.

1. Helms, Marilyn M., "Electronic Commerce", *Encyclopedia of Management,* Gale Group Publishers, 1999, Pages 237-241.

Conventional wisdom states that the dinosaurs of today's industry are:

- Too big
- Too cumbersome and therefore too slow to change – difficulty in reacting
- They have tiny little brains compared to their size – not smart enough to realize the changes around them
- ECommerce has made brick and mortar (storefronts, branches, buildings and equipment) became a liability rather than an asset.

The comet called eCommerce had taken on breathtaking pace. The internet was adopted faster than telephones, radios, televisions, video recorders, or CDs. It is exhibiting a growth rate of 100% plus annually. Internet traffic internationally has been doubling every 100 days (first the year 2000). In 1998 there was $300B in U.S. eCommerce which will expand to $970B in U.S. eCommerce by 2002 *(Giga Information Group)*.

What kind of new life forms will emerge that will be adapted and suited to this new eCommerce environment? The ".com" type start-up firms soon became the new players, rapidly assaulting the market share of the traditional dinosaurs. The belief was that innovation would lead to many changes in the food chain, that you would have disentermediation in many cases, reintermediation, the rise of infomediaries, the rise of the virtual enterprise – whole new forms of businesses were being created. The characteristics of these new businesses are interesting and defy conventional wisdom. For example, when compared with the dinosaurs:

Dinosaurs	**.coms**
High Earnings	No Earnings (on average)
Low Multiples	Infinite Multiples
Low Market Cap	Stratospheric Market Cap – belief in that what they are doing has some scalability

Investors believe that the .coms are the future; that the .coms will be dominating market share in such a way that in spite of low or even negative profits, they hold the key to future industry domination. This has created a new investment model, one where investors are investing based on market share growth, and future corporate growth potential, rather than on current profitability levels. The dinosaurs are focusing on profitability, but loosing the market share war.

Managing the supply chain was an important strategic competitive step. But it was no longer sufficient to allow an enterprise to differentiate itself from its competitors. There was more to the supply chain than just the movement of materials. There was a whole list of resources which were being ignored in the SCM management process. For example, the planning systems were a collection of estimated lead times which did not compensate for seasonality, or surges in sales. Therefore, these estimates were often inflated to make sure that, even in the worst case, the product would arrive on time. Unfortunately, this averaging process damaged the competitive stance of the company. Sometimes it would be more advantageous to give an inaccurate short lead time, and gain the business, than to give an accurate lead time that was too long to satisfy the customer. It wasn't long before the planning lead times were recognized for what they really were; worthless! The result was a need for a scheduling system that would generate real schedules based on real orders and real capacities. These schedules would need to analyze realistic resource capacities at all steps in the supply chain, including the suppliers, and the shippers, as well as looking at the internal capacity levels. From this need Finite Capacity Scheduling (FCS) was born.

When looking at resources other than just material movement, it soon became apparent that other metrics had to be employed that would motivate the appropriate responses throughout the supply chain. This measurement technology opened up an entirely new world of measurement optimization, bringing into account resources like:

- Labor by labor category
- Materials
- Machinery

- Facilities
- Finances
- Energy
- Maintenance

The new measurement philosophy made it possible for someone to increase productivity in one area and decrease it in another. For example increasing labor productivity, and, because this increase could force the inefficient use of resources in another area. The increase in productivity could actually decrease profitability.

Another metric change was the need for measures of performance that spanned across the entire supply chain, rather than measures that just focused on the focal enterprise. The entire supply chain required performance efficiencies, as well as an equitable sharing of the profit margins. This need for new metrics also created a need for open information sharing. Previous tools like EDI were too one-directional in their information flow. Interactive information exchange where supply chain members were able to see the capacities and schedules of everyone in the chain, had become critical. Intranets became extranets which incorporated information exchanges between chain partners.

The biggest element that was lacking from the SCM systems was the resource efficient scheduling processes. This included resource efficient procurements. Additionally, these schedules had to be real time schedules, not a collection of average lead times. Realizing these needs would take SCM into a new world of Value Chain Management (VCM).

The data transfer technology was in place with tools like eC; and the resource evaluation methodology was in place with tools like FCS and Enterprise Resource Planning (ERP). The only missing piece was trust. This was perhaps the hardest element. The relationships between the Value Network members requires a free, open, and accurate exchange of information, and this would require a new level of trust between the members of the chain.

The supply chain flow of materials in Chart 7.3 now needed to be expanded into a resource information exchange where information flowed in all directions, as seen in Chart 7.4. Here we see that the flow of the VCM Network is bi-directional.

Chart 7.4. Network Centric Value Chains

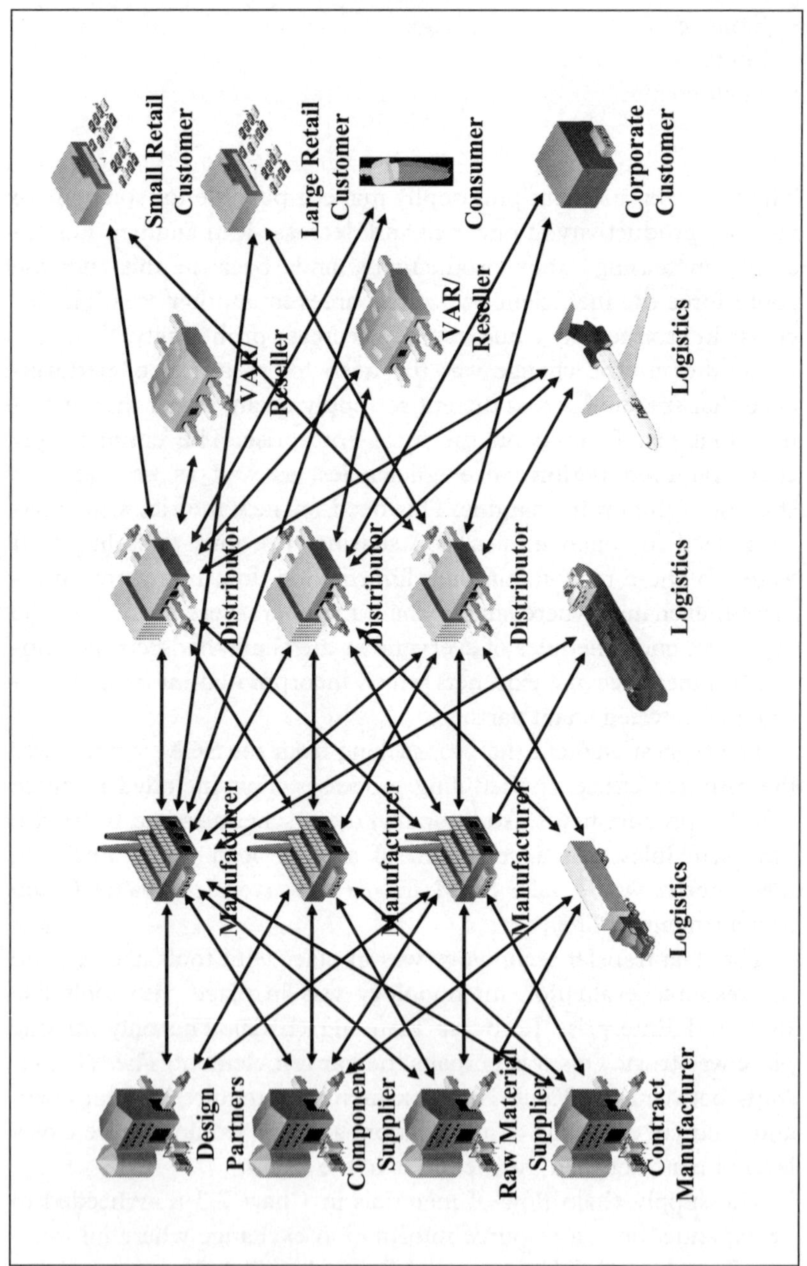

Value Chain Management (VCM) has been defined as the integration of all resources starting with the vendor's vendor. It integrates information, materials, labor, facilities, logistics, etc. into a time responsive, capacity managed solution that maximizes financial resources and minimizes waste i.e. optimizes value for the customers' customer.

Value Chain Management increases the number of steps in the supply chain by focusing on core competencies. VCM attempts to optimize the integrated efficiency of these steps in the management of resources, including the response time and the cost resource.

The key metrics of Value Chain Management will include:

- Integrated Supply Chain Planning and Scheduling Performance
- Cycle Time Responsiveness
- Chain-Wide Resource Optimization
- Information Integration
- Rapidity of Information Exchange

The next generation of enterprises are not individual, isolated entities competing against each other. They are value networks of enterprises competing against each other. These networks will become extremely complex because of the focus on core competency specialization. The performance of the scheduling process will become the competitive driver. Open data exchange in all resource areas will be critical. Companies like Dell computers and Amazon.com have discovered that in spite of the increased complexity created by the core competency focus, the web based marketing approach has allowed them to eliminate links in the value network thereby improving cycle times, reducing costs, and increasing customer satisfaction.

The next generation of enterprises will be found in the value network. Web based networks of enterprises are forming rapidly in an attempt to make a competitive stand, beating out the companies that are still focused on supply chain solutions. Value based performance is no longer a future theory, it is a present necessity.

The Global Supply Chain

Earlier in this chapter we discussed the workings of the supply chain. Additionally, we now can focus on the various forces that effect the performance of the supply chain. Many of these have been stressed in previous chapters. They are:

- Political Forces – government restrictions and expectations that need to be worked with.
- Technology Forces – technological changes both in product technology (which product is competitive and where is the product on the product life cycle) and process technologies (what are the best shipping methods, warehousing methods, or manufacturing methods). The costs of these technologies vary all over the world. Some costs are regional dependent like labor prices and capital equipment costs, and others are not. For example, if we are shipping by container ship, the cost of shipping from Los Angeles to San Francisco is nearly the same as the cost of shipping from Singapore to San Francisco because the majority of the cost comes in handling the containers, not in moving them.
- Market Forces – market interests and demands can vary significantly from region to region. For example, the demand for crosses in Saudi Arabia is somewhat limited, but in Italy the demand would be very strong. Demand will vary significantly as countries change from under-developed, to developing, and then to developed status.

With all these considerations, we can come up with a list of some of the increased complexities of integrating into a global supply chain network. They are:

- Geography – distance tends to slow down the supply chain. Additionally, some areas have infrastructures that are difficult to access.
- Information – not all areas have infostructures that are effective enough to facilitate internet access.
- Training levels including language skills – not all areas have the same standards and expectations from their employees. Additionally, specifications and documentation can be misinterpreted if language skills are lacking. For example, the United States' insistence on using inches has more than once caused products to be produced in meters.

- Demand forecasting becomes more challenging. Demand trends cannot be patterned after the United States in different cultures and environments. Often there is no demand history to base forecast estimates upon.
- Economic factors – exchange rate variations, as discussed earlier, can significantly effect the profitability of a transaction. A minor variation in the exchange rate can destroy the profit margins. Therefore, it becomes important to standardize the supply chain on a common, stable currency. However, the negative effect of this standardization is that the local manufacturer may be driven out of business if the exchange rate variations drive his operating costs up substantially. Therefore there is a level of economic risk associated with the international supply chain transaction that did not exist in a strictly domestic supply chain.
- Technology – levels vary significantly from region to region and from country to country.
- Quality – the expectations on quality can vary significantly.
- Financial resources – The financial ability to gear up for increased production can effect the performance of a supplier.

An example of a global supply chain management process has been included in the discussion of NS, Inc. later in this chapter.

Information Integration

As already discussed earlier in this chapter, EDI, as a supply chain management information integration tool, has been replaced by the internet. Using the internet, individuals can now do much of their demand shopping through a computer terminal. For example, if you need a book, you go into the internet and type "Amazon.com" and you have immediate access to a bookstore that is much more complete than anything you have ever encountered by direct shopping. The prices are competitive because they do not have all the overhead that a normal bookstore requires. Additionally, they can direct ship the book of your choice to you in only a few days. This does not replace the need for someone to occasionally go to a book store to consult a new book on a subject of interest. But the internet does save a tremendous amount of time in the area of demand shopping.

As a consumer you can purchase products from all over the world through the internet process. You can access suppliers that had previously been completely out of your reach. You can evaluate and compare products in ways that had previously been impossible to access. And you can do it without the cost of travel, sales and marketing costs, etc.

The benefits in retailing are just a small part of the benefits of the internet. In the area of supply chain management, we have already discussed how the internet allows integrated information access between suppliers, manufacturers, distributors, retailers, and even the end consumer. This information integration opens up a new world of information sharing between these links of the supply chain, which builds confidence between the various elements.

The internet does not eliminate the need for internal, intra-net systems. Internal production process still need to be managed using the traditional management tools. These need to be carefully evaluated to satisfy the requirements of the local operation. It is the input and outputs of these internal systems that require the access to the internet for information exchange. For example, a customer's placement of an order would trigger all of the following:

1) open a purchase requisition at the customer's site
2) open a sales order at the retailers location
3) open a purchase requisition at the retailer for a purchase from the manufacturer
4) open a sales order at the manufacturer for the retailer's product
5) open a shipment requisition with the shipper for the scheduled due date
6) open a purchase requisition at the manufacturer for the materials needed to build the product – this could be several requisitions for several sets of materials
7) open a work order for the production process to begin when all the materials become available
8) open a sales order with each of the respective vendors
9) open a shipment requisition for each of the materials to be shipped to the manufacturer
10) open a materials requisition at each supplier location for the materials needed at each location

11) etc.

From this example it is easy to see the external interconnectivity that occurs with the placement of an order. This information is then needed to drive the internal information mechanisms.

Risk Management

In the global supply chain transaction there is a great deal of trust. There is trust in the reliability of the information, trust in the logistics mechanisms, trust in the political stability, trust in the financial mechanisms, like the exchange rate fluctuations, etc. This trust is built up over time. It is not automatic, especially internationally where relationships are more important than contractual agreements. Failure in any of these trusts creates transactional risk, and this risk needs to be assessed. There is basically an entire gradient of risk levels that organizations are willing to engage in, going from Risk Averse to Risk Taking. Generally, the reason for taking on an increased level of risk is for the increased level of potential gains that come with the risk. Why take a larger risk if you're not going to gain any more than you would have gained with a smaller risk? In this section I will discuss several areas of risk. However this is not intended to be a comprehensive discussion of all the elements of risk assessment. That would be a text book all by itself.

Political risk is assessed and measured in several international data banks. For example, the CIA evaluates the political stability of a country and assigns a risk value to this assessment. Similarly, the international monetary organizations like the World Bank and the IMF (International Monetary Fund) evaluate and assess the financial risk of all the countries in the world. These risk assessment values are extremely valuable when dealing with international transactions. But these are the easier risks to assess because we have individuals and organizations developing these assessments for us. It is more difficult to assess the risks associated with markets, and their reaction to issues like foreign products, and international trends. For example, there is a defined trend that shows how markets in the United States follow the trends in London, and Japan follows the trends of the United States. The books by Dent and Naisbitt discuss some of these international market trends. This information can be used to initiate some market planning. However, reactions to your product are often extremely difficult to predict. For example, competitive reactions, government reactions, vendor reactions, or customer reactions, have been known to dramatically effect product acceptance.

The objective of managing risk is to minimize the exposure to unforeseen and unplanned risks destroying profitability. If you are a risk averse organization, then you need to minimize all the excessive risk factors. If you are a risk taking organization, then you want to identify and account for as much of the risk as possible so that your financial returns are sufficient to justify the risk taken. This is not the focus of an international operations management text, rather, this is a discussion for an international financial management book where risk assessment becomes part of the project-profit determination. However, the importance of risk and risk assessment strongly effects operational performance and should be carefully considered.

Logistics Management

Logistics management, which includes the transport of goods and the warehousing of them, is an extremely large piece of the supply chain management puzzle. This book has dedicated an entire chapter to this discussion. It is important to note that without the efficient flow of the logistics process, all the gains of manufacturing efficiency are erased. For example, Toyota can manufacture a car in four hours. Then it takes weeks and sometimes months to move the product to the overseas retailer. That is why the flow of this logistics process has become so critical that the supply chain is ineffective without it.

Now lets take a look at some of the struggles of an organization that is developing it's supply chain.

NS, Inc. – A Global Supply Chain Nightmare

NS, Inc. is a health food supplement company located in Provo, Utah. They focus on international research into natural substances that have medicinal properties. They package these substances into pills and sell them over the counter at health food stores. They initially focused their market in the Utah area but quickly spread sales all across the United States and Canada. In these early stages they focused on products that utilized materials available domestically. However, they soon found that in order to complete their product line, they needed to source herbs and plants from all over the world. They searched for international producers throughout Asia and Latin America and in many cases found that they needed to develop their own suppliers. They contracted with growers for their entire crops several years in advance just to lock up the availability of the plants. This made NS not just a producer, but also a manager of the harvest. If the harvest fell short, they would need to find additional sourcing. If the harvest over-produced they would need to purchase product that they didn't need. They found it necessary to make a variety of arrangements with these growers. For example, some growers wanted to get a base value for their crops, plus an extra bonus if they overproduced. Other farmers wanted a fixed price regardless of the output. This concerned NS because they couldn't be assured that the farmer would put as much effort into the crop, if it was already sold. Additionally, NS had to deal with the risks of government regulatory changes, where taxes and tariffs could be changed after the product prices had already been committed to. Risk management became a critical part of the supplier management process. Additionally, exchange rate fluctuations would often increase the cost of the initial arrangement, since most of the farmer contracts were negotiated in local currencies.

NS experienced many of the struggles associated with supply chain management, but found themselves lacking in information integration. Many of the farmers they worked with had never even seen, let alone used a computer. Therefore, it became necessary for someone to visit the various farms to evaluate the anticipated levels of crop output. This required transportation costs and became quite expensive. However, they felt that they couldn't rely on local sources for evaluating the crop outputs. Next came the issue of product movement through the logistics process. The infrastructure was often inadequate. The slowness of the infrastructure would often consume days, weeks, and months, in getting the product to the plant in Utah.

As NS grew, they discovered an extensive international interest in their products. They opened up the European marketplace. Success in Europe caused them to move into Latin America and many Asian countries. This opened an entirely new can of worms in the supply chain process. For example, should they use distributors who would purchase the product from NS and then resell the product? This would eliminate many of the supply chain issues, and greatly simplify NS' involvement. However, this also consumed a large portion of the margin that NS was hoping to earn. Additionally, the capital investment in trucks, etc. forced many of the distributors to go in and out of business fairly quickly. If a truck broke down, they could be out of business for quite some time until they found the capital to make the necessary repairs. As another alternative, NS could also deal directly with the retail outlets. However, to do that they would need to establish their own distribution supply chain within each country. In some countries, like Singapore, this was fairly easy to do. But in other counties, like China, this was much more difficult. Additionally, the international transaction risks became more complicated as NS became more involved in directly managing the vertically integrated process. They couldn't assure that the financial returns would be maintained since they were entering into new, unproven market areas and the risk of failure could be quite high.

Certification of a medicinal product also became an issue in many countries. Their legal requirements forced extensive documentation of the process. Often, localized chemical testing was required to certify the contents of the pills.

What would you do? Would you go for the low margins of distributor relationships, or would you attempt to manage the vertical supply chain yourself? And how about the farmers? Would you trust the locals to evaluate the farm production? What would change in their current operations?

Manufacturing Technology Transfer to Third World Countries

Now we will consider some of the specific issues associated with technology transfer supply chain strategies focused on developing country settings. There are numerous lessons to be learned from these countries. For example, why do Western production planning and control systems including information systems enjoy little or no success in third world countries? Haven't we in the West already learned the best methods of production control? Shouldn't these same control systems be transferable to factories in other countries? We need to discusses the key differences that exist in the installation of production planning systems in developing environments and discusses what these experiences teach Western manufacturers about their plants.

Western countries are failing in their factory implementations in Third World countries. Developing environments can't seem to understand that "profits" are the key to success – or are they? Production control methodologies that seem to be effective in the United States, Japan, or Europe have been frustratingly disappointing. The search for the reasons behind this phenomenon has involved studies in numerous countries and factories. The problems revolve around several key differences:

- Goals
- Data / Information Obsession
- Goal Communication
- Resource Planning

What we learn from our visits to developing countries comes back to haunt us at home. Many of our own inefficiencies are simply magnified when we view them in light of these Third World environments.

Goals

When looking at developing countries, we quickly find that financial goals are primarily a phenomenon of the United States, Canada, and Europe. Even Japan does not aspire to use financial goals. In Japan the primary goal is employee job security. Other countries stress the goal of customer satisfaction. In developing countries the goals often revolve around:

- Full Employment
- Improved Balance of Trade

- Improved Throughput
- Technological Independence

These countries consider these goals much more important than the profitability of one organization. A Western manager will often ask, "How can a company survive if it loses money?" It can't, any more than a company that has profit as its primary goal can survive by beating its employees. The important issue here is "What is the primary goal?" Western countries, in general, still maintain a financial focus. Within the U.S. only a few selected companies, primarily Baldridge, Shingo, or NASA award winners, have moved successfully in new directions.

Data / Information Obsession

The standard answer for academics and consultants who don't know how to approach and deal with a particular production problem is to declare that not enough "data" exists to properly define and solve the problem. If only they had enough "information." The result is that management installs several additional staff functions and adds additional computing systems in an attempt to come up with the magical answer. Unfortunately, what this does is simply build an unnecessary level of complexity into the operation. Additional data is not the answer. Focused data is the answer! Focused data is data collected only from those areas that will help the organization operate better.

The obsession with data collection accompanies another hazard. It sends a false message to the employees of the company. Employees assume that whatever areas data is being collected from must be important to the management of the company. I will discuss more about how to focus data when I deal with resource planning.

For Third World countries, data collection can be difficult if not impossible. The goal of data collection is to collect focused data and to avoid collecting unnecessary "waste" data. This fits well into the focused data approach.

Goal Communication

I asked the managers of the factories I visited how they communicated their goals to employees. They talked about newsletters and memos. Then I asked them what their measurement system on the factory floor contained. They talked about job sheets that recorded labor start and stop times and compared them to labor standards that measured efficiencies. I asked them if they felt that the plant had its goals in harmony at the operational and strategic levels. They looked at me as though I was speaking a foreign language. I reworded the question: "Do you feel that by making your employees more efficient at the expense of stockpiling inventory at each work station you will in fact improve profitability?" They answered, "Of course". Not only was that the wrong answer, they weren't getting the whole message. What I was trying to stress was that the plant should not measure employee efficiency unless that helped it achieve its goals. By measuring employee efficiencies, they were sending a message to their employees about what was important to management: that they should be labor efficient no matter the cost, because that was what they were being evaluated on.

I helped install a production control system in Mexico for a United States manufacturer. At that time the national goal, and the goal of the plant, was full employment. Yet the company wanted me to install a labor-efficiency based production control system. Why would one want to be concerned about labor efficiency when the goal was to hire as many employees as possible, regardless of the labor efficiency level? Fortunately this company is no longer under United States influence and has removed this contradiction. Expecting employees to work toward the goals of the company and then giving them:

- too many and often conflicting goals
- not communicating the goals to them at all
- and improper messages by focusing on unrelated resources

is like expecting them to use one arrow to hit several targets at once, and then blindfolding them for added fun.

Resource Learning

We run our factories as if only two resources were of any importance: labor and materials. Everything else is pigeonholed into something called *overhead.* In reality, labor is often less than ten percent of the value-added cost component of the products we manufacture. Materials are typically between 30 to 60 percent. Overhead is left with from 30 to as much as 80 percent of the value-added cost component. If the goal of our factory is profitability, would it seem more reasonable to strive for a ten percent improvement in labor, or in overhead? Overhead, of course. Then why do United States production control systems still focus on labor efficiency measurements? We are not focusing on the most critical resource.

Another problem with our resource focus is the assumption that we live in a two-resource world. Often other resources, like energy, machinery costs, and maintenance costs, etc., can have a larger value-added cost effect than any other resource. So we return to the issue of focused data collection. If we focus our data collection so that we collect data on only those resources that most affect our goal, then we will send a message to our employees on what is important to us. Then we have a better opportunity to improve the cost effects of that particular resource.

Focusing on Third World countries, we find that they need to prioritize their resources, categorizing them by what effect they have on their primary goal. Then they need to build the appropriate control systems around that goal. For example, if the goal is to improve the balance of trade, the primary focus is to expand exports and a short term control solution may be to focus on reducing imported materials. Everyone knows that, but is that message conveyed to the employees through the monitoring and control system; or are they still monitoring labor efficiency because some United States manufacturer showed them how to do it that way?

Developing environments can't afford to be as trendy as the United States. They can't afford to jump from one three-lettered fad, such as TQC (Total Quality Control), or TQM (Total Quality Management), or JIT (Just in Time), or MRP II (Manufacturing Resource Planning), or ABC (Activity Based Costing), or CIM (Computer Integrated Manufacturing), etc., to another every other year. For this reason, resource and data collection focusing becomes even more important for them.

A multitude of production planning and control systems focus on optimizing on a specific resource. For example, MRP (Material Requirements Planning) is almost always used as a labor efficiency measurement tool through its use of labor-based routings and industrial engineering-generated labor standards. This labor efficiency is achieved at the expense of stockpiled materials in front of each work station and machinery standing idle. JIT (Just in Time) production control methods out of Japan have changed that focus to emphasize on materials efficiency. This is done at the expense of labor or machinery efficiency. OPT (Optimized Production Technology) from Israel focuses on machine efficiency. And the list goes on. However, it is important to realize that specific resource-oriented production planning control systems exist and, that modifications to systems like MRP can be made to change the resource focus.

What's the Best Way?

Up to now, this discussion has demonstrated that there is not one "best" way to manage an organization or run a factory. We should realize that the United States labor-oriented method of management is in fact inappropriate in many instances. In developing countries we often have high unemployment problems. Labor efficiency is near the bottom of the priority list. A lack of jobs is a prevalent situation, and this encourages make-work environments throughout the country.

Realizing this, why do United States managers insist on applying United States methods in plants installed in developing countries? Is it because they don't know any better? Is it because they don't understand anything but a labor-oriented management style?

Most production systems outside the U.S. do not fall into the "United States" or "Japanese" models. Most developing countries have specific problems that they must resolve, such as warehousing or productive space restrictions, infrastructure restrictions, untrained work forces, or distribution restrictions. Often, simply obtaining electricity or installing a telephone system may require years.

To enable us to better understand some of the difficulties that exist in developing countries, I will review two specific examples, one in Mexico and one in Indonesia. These will highlight a few of the problems that developing countries have in their factories, such as differences in system installations, technology transfer, production methodologies, production objectives, logistics problems, and communications.

T in Q, Mexico

The city Q is the home of T and is a major industrial city north of Mexico City. T is a division of a major United States manufacturer. It employs approximately 6,000 people. T is a discrete manufacturer (both fabrication and assembly) of transmissions for automobiles, buses, and small trucks. It also has a small satellite facility a few blocks away that produces forklifts and front-end loaders.

The top levels of management at T are primarily United States citizens. The second and third levels of management are, for the most part, Mexicans trained in the United States or who are heavily indoctrinated in the U.S. way of doing things. Additionally, there always seems to be a sufficient number of U.S. "advisors" sent by either the home office or one of the U.S. automobile manufacturers. These advisors work on the factory floor and try to keep production running smoothly.

The work force on the factory floor is largely unskilled. The average employee has difficulty in filling out time sheets. Most of the production that is scheduled is done by the "expediting" method, which means it isn't scheduled at all. Management has tried to implement educational programs and even has a staff of full-time instructors and classrooms, but the need for a more complete education of the work force far exceeds the capacity of these facilities.

An adversarial relationship has developed between the average worker and the rich Mexican boss. The average worker resents the non-Mexican who has to communicate with him through an interpreter and who makes him feel inadequate. Mexican middle management resents the feeling that North Americans think Mexicans aren't good enough to run the plant.

Production scheduling is a blend of computer-generated MRP schedules wherein production plans are changed by expeditors trying to feed assembly. This schedule is then corrected by non-Mexican advisors who try to push through their pet production jobs. This schedule is in turn overridden by top management trying to please U.S. customers.

The goals of the average factory floor worker are quite different than those of his counterpart in the United States. The worker does not see himself as a part of the company, trying to make it a success. He rarely searches for opportunities to work overtime in order to make more money; rather, he looks for an opportunity to spend as much time as possible with his family. One of the biggest problems that T experiences is that after an employee receives a paycheck, he may not show up for work for several days. Once he again feels the financial necessity to work, he returns.

The selection of foremen or shop supervisors is very difficult. There is no predefined system for evaluating an individual's potential, such as a level of education or grades in school. For the poorer citizens, there is very little opportunity to determine the jobs for which they are best-suited. As a result, promotions often occur through relatives or friends. Occasionally, bribes influence a promotion, and so not necessarily the most qualified individuals are moved up in the organization.

Strikes occur regularly in Mexico, and this forces a total shutdown of not only the production facility, but also of all business once they can create enormous management problems. For example, at T – both plants transmission and forklift – do all their data processing work, including production scheduling, at the larger facility. A strike at this facility severely handicaps the second facility which may not be on strike.

The scheduling of raw material receipts is complex and sporadic. Border crossings require customs, bribes, and time delays. In order to keep production flowing, raw materials are stockpiled, even more so than in the United States.

Equipment maintenance is dependent upon scavenging; it has become easier to replace a broken part in a machine by finding the same part in a similar machine. This brings the needed machine on line quicker with less chance of a repair error. As a result of this practice, several machines throughout the facility are basically worthless except for their value as spare parts.

The number of scrapped parts due to obsolescence, operational error, or overproduction is enormous. Forged gears, several years old and red with rust, are piled high in the yards. Work-in-process inventory is unreasonably high, and the majority of the factory floor is used for inventory storage. Bins of parts that haven't been moved for months can be found throughout the plant.

Quality is poor because of the lack of training and the lack of any organized system to improve quality. On one occasion, the quality of producing a particular part was so bad that it was cheaper to ship the forged part to Japan, have it ground and cut, and then ship the finished part back to Mexico for assembly in a transmission. This was actually a cost saving over T's high scrap rate in spite of shipment costs and higher labor costs.

The infrastructure also presents many problems. The facility has to maintain its own power-enhancement equipment as protection against power surges and brown-outs. It can take as much as one year to install telephones and telex systems. Equipment purchases are accorded the same lengthy delays.

These are just some of the problems that are not handled by "modern" American production methodologies. Many of these problems also exist in factories in the United States, such as the problem with excessive work-in-process inventory. It is important to realize, though, that many of these problems in Mexico are very different from those of a counterpart factory in the United States, and therefore their solutions do not fit into the U.S. mold.

A detailed analysis of how to resolve many of T's problems could fill volumes. Our analysis here will be brief in order to highlight possible solutions. As there are three areas of control – labor, materials, and machinery – taking these one at a time, we can review what is happening at T and apply some techniques for improvement based on what we have stated so far.

In analyzing the *labor* at T, we find job standards and an efficiency reporting system that keeps track of the performance of each employee. The United States philosophy of controlling each individual has been incorporated here, but is labor efficiency a goal of T?

The Mexican government gives T incentives to employ as many people as possible, and this makes it advantageous to overstaff. This brings to light the fact that the goal of the Mexican government is full employment, and two of T's goals are:

- To keep the government happy and
- To promote the government goal of full employment

With these goals in mind, is the goal of employee efficiency, which suggests that each employee do as much work as possible, realistic?

No! Factory floor automation is also inconsistent with these goals. Hiring more workers to do the jobs that automation can do is more in line with the goals of the Mexican society – and of T.

Also in line with the goals of T and Mexico would be a better training program as is found in many developing countries. For example, spending as much as two months per year in education – teaching the employee reading, writing, math, and gardening, or any other subjects of interest – would give the employer a better employee. It would also give T a basis of evaluating who would make the better supervisor when future promotions are considered.

In the case of *materials*, T has a high raw-materials inventory, which is justified because of the excessive lead time for raw materials caused by the border crossing. As was already stated, raw materials is the cheapest of the three types of inventory (followed by work-in-process and then finished goods). If inventory must be stored, it should be stored as cheaply as possible – as raw materials.

In the area of *machinery*, we have already established that T should avoid automation. We also recognize the need for scavenging as a means to keep needed equipment in operable condition. Although this system seems foolish to the typical United States manager, let's consider its advantages:

- The employee knows where to find the part without a lengthy catalog search.
- The employee can see how it is supposed to look and how it should fit into the machine.
- The equipment used is generally old and was most likely purchased second-hand from the United States. Keeping an extra machine strictly for spare parts may not be too costly.
- Very few individuals are needed with the ability to order spare parts. These individuals would spend their time rebuilding the "spare parts" machines after pieces have been taken out. Ordering parts is much easier since you now have a machine to look at. The pressure to get the machine operational is off since it is only a spare parts machine.

Reviewing the three areas of emphasis (labor, materials, and machinery), which is the most critical to manage in the T environment? Not labor, since to have excess is advantageous and fits the goals of the company and the country. Not machinery, since having extra "spare parts" machines is also advantageous. However, inventory is costly because of high interest rates, and currently, inventory levels are out-of-hand. Several inventory-oriented management systems have been highlighted in this book, and any one of them would offer better production management than what T is now experiencing.

N in B, Indonesia

B is a city on the island of Java in Indonesia. This city is the home of N, a military aircraft manufacturing facility. It is a discrete manufacturer primarily involved in assembly, with plans to expand the level of vertical integration to include the fabrication of all necessary components.

The top levels of management are primarily foreign-trained, with many of them holding Ph.D. degrees from major universities in the United States. The work force is largely unskilled and uneducated, but the relationship between the employer and employee is much closer than that in the Mexican facility. The labor force is easier to manage and is more related than that of T.

Problems similar to those of T are found in the source and quality of raw materials. The infrastructure problems are even worse than those of T because good roads are practically nonexistent. Those that do exist are shared by tanks as well as cars and trucks.

The market for N's products – small planes and helicopters – is entirely within Indonesia. N hopes to produce parts for foreign companies in the future, such as Boeing or Airbus.

Now, an interesting conflict in technology and labor force utilization has arisen. N wants to do sophisticated design work, yet the majority of their labor force has a limited ability to read and write. The primary national goal in Indonesia, as in Mexico, is full employment, and automation would defeat this objective. Indonesia has a very limited, highly trained technical work force, but the abilities of these technicians need to be increased with advanced technology. The solution to this appears to require the introduction of high-tech disciplines such as CAD (computer-aided design) along with as *little* automation as possible in the production area.

With regard to the management of labor, materials, and machinery, many of the same conclusions can be reached as with T. However, the spread between the educational levels of the employees and management is much broader. So, an educational program for the employees must be more extensive.

A management system installed here would also have to consider the infrastructure problems more so than at T. These will have a significant effect on lead times.

Both T and N are examples of the types of management problems encountered in industry in a developing country. They provide examples of how the international manager involved with such situations needs to resolve management problems differently than in an industrially developed environment.

Comparing N and T to a Developed Environment

Are all the needs, goals, and problems that exist in Mexican or Indonesian manufacturing facilities similar to those of counterpart manufacturers in a developed country? Of course not! So, why do the United States or European managers install systems that emphasize labor costing, labor efficiency, and production standards within environments that are trying to keep citizens employed?

In developing countries, manufacturing facilities such as T and N need to establish company goals and objectives before a management or production control system is selected. For example, the U.S. assumes that its "get rich" philosophy appeals to everyone, whereas in the case of T, family time is more important than money. Consideration needs to be given to (this is only a partial list):

- Location of plant
- Resource differences
  - Energy
  - Land availability
  - Infrastructure
- Market differences
  - Traveling distances
  - Tariffs and quotas

- Management expertise
- Economic potential
  - Country
  - Company
- Work force
  - Education
  - Motivation
  - Goals
- Availability of machinery
  - Levels of automation
- Inventory
  - Problems with inventory sources
  - Lead times
  - Financing costs
- National goals and guidelines.

For example, in reference to N, the problem of blending high-tech engineering, no factory-floor automation, and an excess work force that is idle much of the time frustrates traditional production management philosophies. However, this is necessary when trying to satisfy the goals of the nation as well as those of the company.

Once we have evaluated the climate of a particular production or management environment, how do we develop an appropriate system? A unique system can be developed for each new environment, but this isn't always practical. However, if we realize that every country of the world was a developing country at some time, then we realize that it is appropriate to look at countries that have already developed production systems under conditions similar to the country under study. (This should be one of the primary applications of this book.)

Referring again to N or T, we see the need for a system that will work for T under conditions of:

- No factory-floor automation
- Limited paperwork
- High worker-manager interface
- Over-employment
- A restrictive union

For N:

- Poor infrastructure
- High technology in engineering
- No factory-floor automation
- Limited paperwork
- High worker-manager interface

By looking for a management system that satisfies these and other needs, a smoother-operating, more effective plant will be the result.

When planning for an appropriate production system, some industries require industry-specific production control systems. Process manufacturing plants are not run the same as discrete manufacturing plants. The critical resource for these types of plants differs from the traditional labor or machine efficiencies of discrete manufacturing plants. For example, process plants like steel mills or paper mills tend to be focused on bottleneck efficiencies rather than on labor or machine efficiencies. Aluminum plants focus on energy efficiencies. Bottling plants focus on logistics efficiencies. Food and drug producers require systems that monitor and schedule based on shelf life and genealogical tracking. Therefore, an industry-specific system often needs to be implemented.

For developing countries, a few additional considerations should be mentioned. Some were evident in the T and N examples.

Infrastructure systems will most likely need improvement. Roadways, schools, electricity, water systems, and housing should not only be looked at from the company's perspective, but also from the community's perspective. This is the best – and many times the only – way to "sell" the company to the people. Don't expect the people to automatically like the plant. They aren't just sitting around waiting for you to give them a chance to work, and they often consider companies as intruders that are trying to take advantage of them. However, if a company is their friend rather than their exploiter, working with the people is much easier, and many extra costs involved will turn out to be minimal when compared to the benefits of improved relations with employees. Additionally, the government will love the company because it has created jobs for people who are working on the infrastructure systems.

Governmental relations are critical. Investigate the structure and procedures within the "system." It is important to work with the systems and not fight with the individuals in power. They should be given the respect that is due. If you treat them as bureaucratic nuisances, they'll recognize your attitude and treat you accordingly.

Border-crossing considerations are important in materials sourcing and product shipments. The distribution process is often critical to the product's effectiveness. Additionally, acquiring spare parts will be important in keeping machinery operational.

Search for local trends and attitudes and maintain harmony with them. One good way of doing this is by utilizing as few "foreigners" as possible in the factory. Foreigners are often considered intruders. When they are brought in, they should always have a local "advisor" on hand to make sure that consistency with local thought and traditions are maintained. The Japanese follow this policy when they install a factory in the United States, an environment with which they are quite familiar.

Find technology that is "appropriate" for the local environment, not technology that is "familiar" to the manager. This includes management methods, production methods, and the types of machines that are selected. Work within the limitations of the assumptions that have been established.

Develop appropriate measures of performance. Measure those areas that will motivate the labor force using their own goals and standards.

Individual performance standards are degrading and humiliating to many cultures, and only help to alienate workers. Team or company-wide performance standards may be much more effective. Additionally, the front-office, authoritarian-management style tends to alienate. A more participative, involved, walk-around management style develops a relationship between the employer and employee. The visibility of management is important in many cultures, even if it seems like a waste of time to the managers; it builds a binding and lasting relationship and will help to avoid confrontations.

The amount of time the employee of a developing country facility should spend in training will typically be much higher than that of his United States counterpart. Several months per year is not uncommon. This training should include areas that reach far beyond the scope of the company itself, such as personal health, first aid, construction skills, living skills, cooking, sewing, sanitation systems, water purification, and so on. The training process will also help in the evaluation and selection of individuals who are natural leaders and who should be used as foremen and supervisors in the plant.

The installation of a management system or factory in a foreign environment must not be considered a short-term, money-making project. It must be looked at with a long-term perspective since that is the way the host population will view it.

The book *Small is Beautiful* by Schumacher (Perennial Library, 1975) is valuable reading in order to get a clearer perspective of how a developing country perceives the United States. The only image many workers have of the United States comes from television shows such as "Dallas", and Clint Eastwood movies. A better understanding of their view of the U.S. can only help in the development of good relationships.

There is much literature that deals with the transfer of technology to developing countries. The World Bank is doing extensive research in this area. More detailed information is available in a book published by the World Bank. Some of the key lessons for developing countries discussed in the Dahlman, Ross-Larson, and Westphal book cited at the end of this chapter include:

1. Targeting markets through the combined efforts of the government, industry, and the unions is valuable. This may include some protectionism while the industry is still in its infant stages within the country. In the long run, protectionism should be removed since its removal promotes technological development and makes the industry more competitive.
2. The selection of target markets should emphasize industries that have a strong export potential.
3. Technological strength is not that important in the early stages of industrial development, but expertise in the newly learned production process is. As long as the industry is in its early growth stages, becoming the best at what it's doing is the most important goal. Later, in order to become a major international contender, technological development and innovation becomes more important.
4. Short-term relationships with other countries and other companies are the most effective ways to learn about the products and production processes of a targeted industry.

5. Education and training programs are vital to long-run success. These may include enticing nationals who are living and working in developed countries. These individuals can be brought "home" to manage and teach the growing industries of the country.

The World Bank is also a source in many other areas that may be of interest. The articles it publishes can be acquired for a minimal cost.

All countries are not alike. Many of the basic assumptions about management styles and techniques are not transferable, as the article by Partridge emphasizes. He lists several reasons, the key one being that the management personnel sent to foreign operations are not up to par with their United States counterparts. They know what the home office wants and how to run the operations, but they lack familiarity with the details and may not have anyone whom they can telephone to help them out. So, they do the best they can.

Couple the lack of experience cited by Partridge with the fact that the foreign environment isn't really conducive to United States methods, and we have an overabundance of struggling overseas plants, just like T and N. Fortunately, steps are being taken to improve management growth in developing countries, as cited in the article by Wallace.

In summary, the basic assumptions upon which we develop a management or production system for a particular country will rarely fit the United States model. We must look for more flexible methods in order to find solutions that will be more appropriate than those we have at home. We must be receptive to systems that can be adapted to these environments. Only by utilizing more appropriate systems will the host population, management, and the production facility be able to maximize their benefits.

The key to working with third world environments is simplicity – getting back to the basics. We need to set a goal, define the resources that are the most critical to the achievement of that goal, and then build a production planning and control data collection system around that goal. The data collection system will then monitor the success of the company in achieving its goal. It also transmits a message to the employees about the most important area of control for management. Often, as in the case of JIT, this data collection and control process does not require any type of computer at all.

Developing country settings are different than developed countries, and they are different from underdeveloped countries. They will not all be managed in the same way. So let's not try to force them all into the same model.

Summary

The development of an international supply chain management structure is focused on the integration. This can be challenging. There are many elements of an international supply chain that are managed quite differently than a domestic supply chain, and this chapter has demonstrated many of them. Because of these differences, the supply chain becomes even more challenging to construct. Distribution networks are managed differently, facilities are managed differently, and resources are managed differently. However, in spite of these differences, the effective management of an international supply chain can be performance responsive and cost effective.

Class Assignments

A) Reconsider N, Inc. What would you do to develop an efficient supply chain management structure for this organization?
B) Reconsider NS, Inc. How would you manage the supply chain in this organization? What would you change on the supplier side of the equation? How about the market side? Would you address the international marketplace with all it's challenges?

References

International Marketing Trends References

Dent, Harry S., *The Roaring 2000s,* Simon and Schuster, New York, 1998.

Naisbitt, John, *Megatrends,* Warner Books, New York, 1982.

ECommerce / eBusiness and Supply Chain Management References

Bovet, David and Joseph Martha, *Value Nets; Breaking the Supply Chain to Unlock Hidden Profits,* John Wiley & Sons, Inc., NY, 2000.

Helms, Marilyn M., "Electronic Commerce", *Encyclopedia of Management,* Gale Group Publishers, 1999, Pages 237-241.

Hughes, Jon, Mark Ralf, and Bill Michaels, *Transform Your Supply Chain,* Thomson Business Press, London, 1999.

Kalakota, Dr. Ravi, and Marcia Robinson, *eBusiness: Roadmap for Success,* Addison-Wesley, Reading, Massachusetts, 1999, Pages 73-76.

Kosiur, David, "Understanding Electronic Commerce", Microsoft Press, Redmond, WA, 1997.

Plenert, Gerhard, *EManager,* Blackhall Publishing, Ireland, 2000.

Plenert, Gerhard and Bill Kirchmier, *Finite Capacity Scheduling,* John Wiley & Sons, Inc., New York, 2000.

Sheridan, John H., "Managing the Value Chain for Growth", *Industry Week,* Sept. 6, 1999, Pages 50-66.

Developing Country References

Bell, Martin, Bruce Ross-Larson, and Larry E. Westphal. *Assessing the Performance Of Infant Industries,* World Bank Staff Working Papers, No. 666, throughout September 1984.

Dahlman, Carl J., Bruce Ross-Larson, and Larry E. Westphal. *Managing Technological Development Lessons From Newly Industrializing Countries,* World Bank Staff Working Papers, No. 717, January 1985.

Nadler, Gerald and Shozo Hibino, *Breakthrough Thinking*, Prima Publishing & Communications, Rocklin, CA, 1990.

Plenert, Gerhard J., "Expanding the Value-Added Cost Component", *Advanced Manufacturing Technology*, Oct., 1989.

Plenert, Gerhard J., "International Industrial Management", *Organizational Development Journal*, Vol. 7, No. 1, Spring 1989.

Plenert, Gerhard J., *International Management and Production: Survival Techniques for Corporate America*, Blue Ridge Summit, PA, Tap Professional and Reference Books, 1990.

Plenert, Gerhard J., "The Development of a Production System in Mexico", *Interfaces*, Vol. 20, No. 3, May-June 1990.

Plenert, Gerhard, *The Plant Operations Handbook*, Business 1 IRWIN, 1993, Homewood, Ill.

Schuhmacher, E. F., *Small is Beautiful – Economics as if People Mattered*, NY, Perennial Library, 1973.

8. Lead Time/ Cycle Time Management

This is the third chapter in the series on supply chain management. The first chapter focused on suppliers, the second on integration, and this chapter will focus on time. This chapter discusses how internationalization stretches lead time and over all cycle time and what can be done to reduce these effects. This chapter focuses on the engineering elements of internationalization, from theoretical, through applied. To understand the importance of time in the management of the supply chain, let's take a look at V, Inc.

V, Inc.

V, Inc. is the world's premiere manufacturer of valves. V, Inc. has plants all over the world, including Europe and South-East Asia, and their headquarters is located in Utah. Their focus is primarily on the petroleum industry, although their products are used in a large number of fluid areas. Their valves vary in size from the very small, to 30 feet tall. Their valves are composed of the valve and a controller. Several of the parts have to be sourced from a variety of plants, some located in various parts of the world. Their problem is one of responsiveness. The typical lead time for valves is measured in weeks and months. Additionally, they have a large backlog of demand for the larger valves. However, they run into difficulty when there is a valve breakage out in the field. Then the pressure is on to come up with a replacement, because a major fuel line may be down. This is where V struggles with a lack of responsiveness to demand. The parts and materials are available for assembly, but they are spread out all over the world and are often too large to air freight. They considered the option of having a centralized warehouse of spare parts, but, since there are so many different valves with thousands of different components, this option was not economically feasible. V, Inc. had reconciled itself with the idea that their customers would just have to make due with the extensive lead times that V worked with.

A European competitor identified a niche for themselves in the valve business. They decided that they could become a supplier of customized emergency valves and produce them with very short lead times. They determined that they could charge as much as twice the normal price and get away with it because the down-time was more expensive than the cost of the valve. They started to become so successful with this niche that they began to drain some of the core business away from V. V became concerned and decided to revisit the need to shorten cycle time. They decided to focus on the supply chain and started with a search to manage the supply chain better, in a more efficient manner, while at the same time not create more inventory. They focused on the fact that a shorter supply chain meant a shorter time for inventory to be lying around, which allowed for less over-all inventory.

What would you do? How would you refocus on a cycle time reduction when your supply chain sourced parts from all over the world? Is the supply chain problem an internal problem or an external problem? Where would you focus your efforts?

The Importance of Time

Supply chain management offers a long list of benefit opportunities for its users. For example, an international research organization lists the improvement areas shown in Chart 8.1 as the key improvement areas for SCM. Taking a look at this list, consider the following:

- Delivery Performance – time responsiveness in delivery
- Inventory Reduction – reducing production cycle time increases inventory turns, which is the time it takes to use up and replace the total inventory of the facility, which reduces inventory
- Fulfillment Cycle Time – time responsiveness to internal order fulfillment
- Overall Productivity – units produced in a specific period of time
- Lower Supply-Chain Costs – inventory carrying cost is the

largest cost component of discrete manufacturing and inventory reduction is directly related to inventory turns (time inventory is on the floor)

- Fill Rates – speed of order fulfillment
- Improved Capacity Realization – inventory increases directly with the amount of space available to store it – as already discussed, inventory size is directly related to the time effects of inventory turns

Chart 8.1. Supply Chain Benefits

Typical Quantified Benefits from Integrating the Supply Chain	
Delivery Performance	16% – 28% Improvement
Inventory Reduction	25% – 60% Improvement
Fulfillment Cycle Time	30% – 50% Improvement
Forecast Accuracy	25% – 80% Improvement
Overall Productivity	10% – 16% Improvement
Lower Supply-Chain Costs	25% – 50% Improvement
Fill Rates	20% – 30% Improvement
Improved Capacity Realization	10% – 20% Improvement
	Source: 1997 PRTM Study

Seven out of the eight improvement areas listed on Chart 8.1 are directly related to time performance. However, there are numerous issues that need focus in a discussion about time in a supply chain. Nearly every chapter so far has mentioned the importance of time. In the August 31, 1998 “Business Week” we read, “Time to Market is superseding labor costs in determining market success”. What is it about time that is so important?

Ten to fifteen years ago, when we wanted to perform a bank transaction, we were at the mercy of the bank. We had to go to their branch office during their specified working hours. Today, banks have lost their power and the power is in the hands of a non-loyal consumer who will quickly change banks simply because it is more convenient. Today, the communication channels for bank transactions are endless. You can perform transactions using the traditional bank teller, or you can do it by phone, ATM machine, in the grocery store over the counter, using fax, EDI, direct deposit, internet, etc. All these new channels of communication have not simplified the process. They have, in fact, complicated the supply chain enormously. Transactions can come in from any source, and each of these transactions have to have a "common face", which means that it has to be handled in the same manner no matter how it originally entered the system. Therefore, not only the methodology of handling the transaction, but the speed of transaction processing, becomes a competitive weapon. If, for example, I purchase a car over the internet and immediately apply for an automobile loan, several different banks receive the loan application. Statistically, it is generally the bank that responds the quickest that will get the business. Hence, speed is critical if banks are to retain their existing customer base and expand by acquiring new customers.

The buzzword that is used the most often in any discussion of SCM time optimization is Cycle Time Management. But there is often a lot of confusion about what cycle time really is. The answer is that it is many things. Here are some examples of cycle time:

- Delivery Cycle Time – How long it takes from the time an order is place until the product is delivered
- New Product Development Cycle Time – How long it takes from new idea inception until the first sale of the new product
- Paperwork Cycle Time – How long the back-office office takes to process the paperwork
- Cash to Cash Cycle Time – The amount of time it takes from the placement of the order until the enterprise gets paid for the order

Taking a look at some simple examples of SCM improvements, we can see performance results like those in Chart 8.2 which shows some industry averages and industry best of class cash-to-cash cycle times. For example, in the telecommunications industry, the average cycle time is 127 days or slightly over four months. Best of class for Telecom is 43 days or about 1½ months. Moving from average to best of class can improve the cash-to-cash cycle time by 84 days or 2½ months. If you have annual sales of $10 million at a financing rate of 10 percent, this SCM improvement will directly increase profitability by $0.2 million. And that is the result of improving just one area of cycle time.

Chart 8.2. Estimated Cash-to-cycle Times

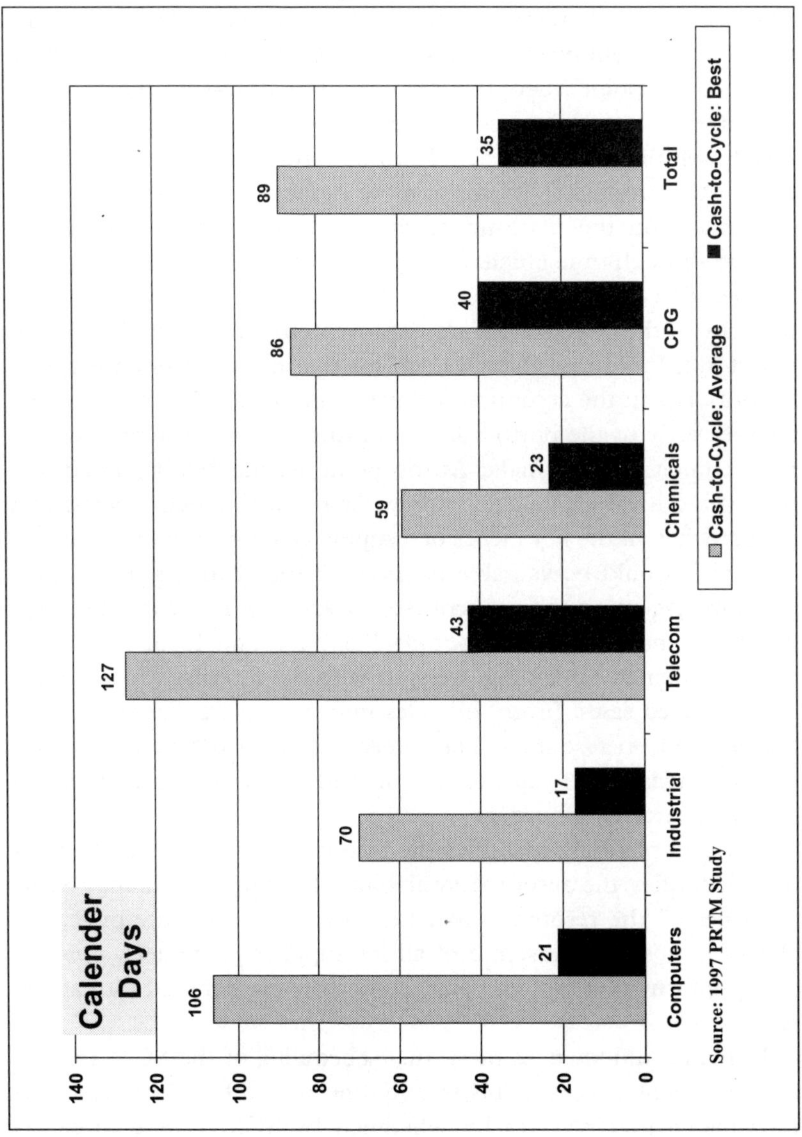

In Chart 8.2, best-of-class for the computer industry averages at 21 days. However, exceptional companies, like Dell Computers, have managed to get the cash-to-cash cycle time down to a negative 8 days. They get paid, on the average, 8 days before they deliver the product. Similarly, retailing organizations like Wal Mart have mastered the time optimization process of their supply chain. They have achieved the point where they have vendors drop-ship the products to their warehouse, or possibly even their stores, where they immediately sell the product. Then 30 to 60 days later they pay the vendor for the product. They make more money on the cash float than they make on the mark-up of the products. And this is accomplished through time efficient supply chain optimization.

Over-all cost reductions of SCM improvements, of which the majority of the effects are time improvement effects, can be seen in Chart 8.3. From this chart we can see that moving from average to best-of-class in the computer industry can move 7.5 percent of revenue directly to the bottom line, and this is more profitability than most companies now make. At this point, having demonstrated that time is a critical element of supply chain improvement, let's take a look at what all the key pieces of a supply chain process include.

Here it would be valuable to show all the elements of a supply chain management engagement (see Chart 8.4). There are three key pieces, Demand Planning, Supply Planning, and Demand Fulfillment. In demand planning, we start with the forecast which identifies predicted sales. From this sales information we can extrapolate the demand on resources. The forecast is relieved by customer orders and ideally the year would end with the entire forecast being consumed exactly by orders.

Demand planning identifies the resource needs and supply planning identifies the resource availability. In supply planning, SCM identifies all the resource capacities of not just the enterprise, but also of all it's suppliers, and of all it's supplier's suppliers. This capacity information is then balanced against the demand for capacity.

Demand fulfillment is the actual scheduling of the SCM materials movement process. This is only one of the three key resource movements that need to be scheduled by SCM. These three resources are materials, information, and finances. The process starts with the initial placement of the order. This order information is then transmitted through the SCM to all the suppliers. In return, capacity information is passed throughout the network and returned to the customer in the form of a schedule.

Chart 8.3. Estimated Total Costs as a Percent of Revenue

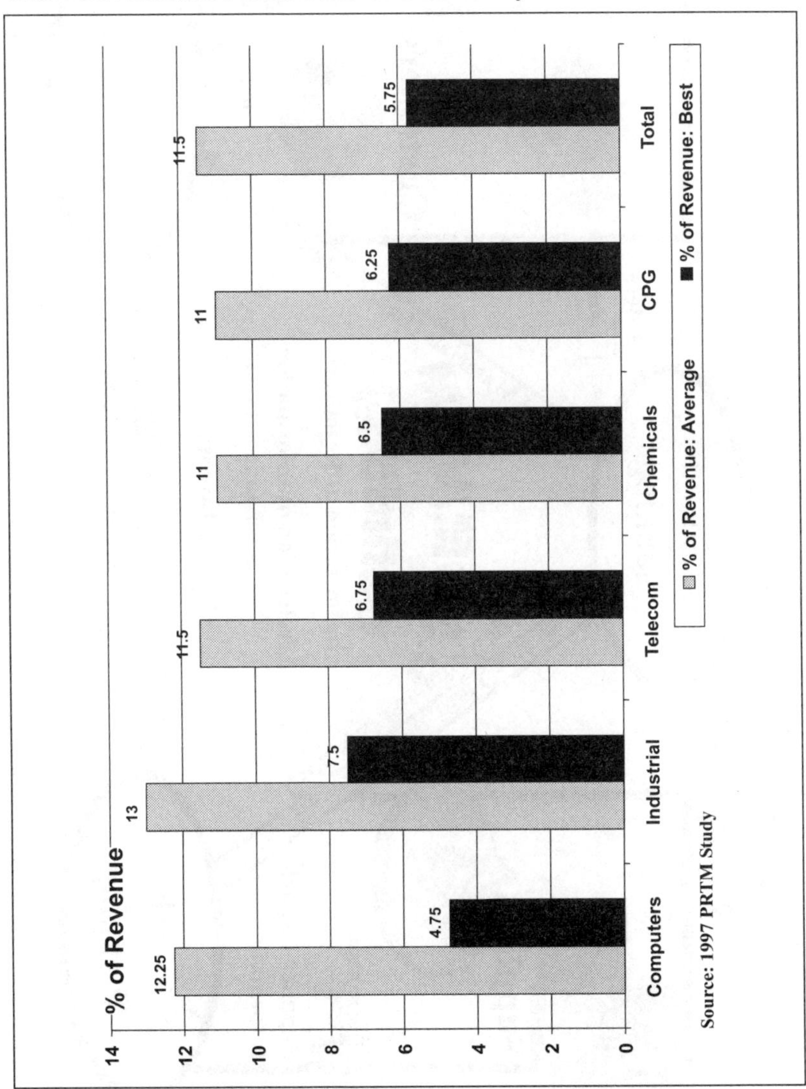

Chart 8.4. Supply Chain Interactions

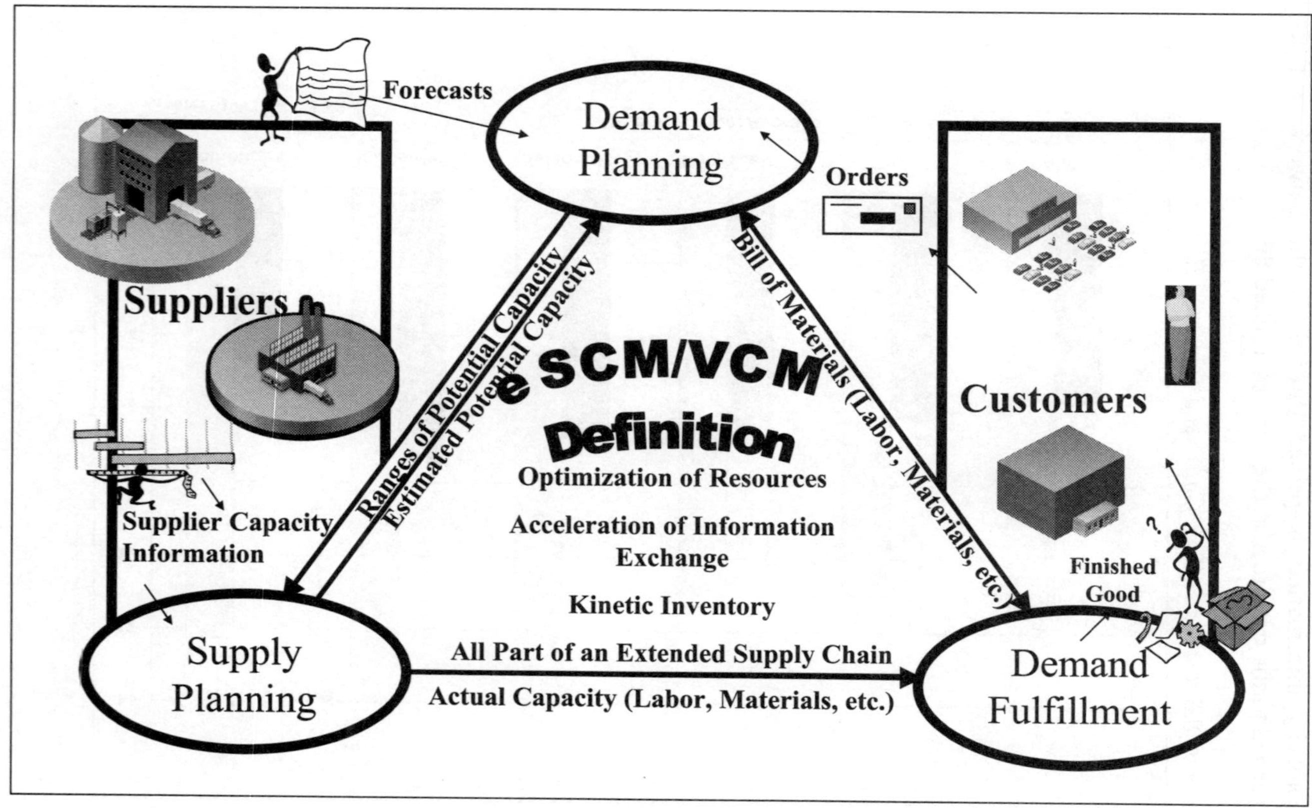

The accuracy of the schedule depends on the demand fulfillment methodology that is being used. The methodologies can be grouped into two major categories; infinite capacity scheduling and finite capacity scheduling. The difference is that in infinite capacity scheduling, no limits on capacity are assumed. The schedules that are generated for the customers are based on average lead times. Unfortunately, that also means that on the average you will miss your schedule.

Finite capacity scheduling means that actual capacities are used in the scheduling process. The actual capacities are allocated (committed) to a specific customer order. As the capacities are used up, the schedules get adjusted. As a result, the schedules that are transmitted back to the customer are actual, not average schedules. Generally, the schedules generated by finite capacity scheduling are shorter, more accurate, and more often achieved than when using the counterpart infinite capacity scheduling.

Successful SCM processing means that the information was transmitted in a timely and accurate fashion to all members in the supply chain, the materials were delivered to the customer as promised, and the financial transfers occurred as expected and in a time frame expected. A model has been created that shows the flow of information from the start to completion of the order (see Chart 8.5). It highlights the B2B (Business-to-Business) and B2C (Business-to-Customer) relationships and shows how the entire supply chain integrates together.

In this chapter we will now concentrate our focus by further developing a few key specific time-based issues. I have selected the following issues for expansion:

- New Product Development
- Time Based Organizations
- Continuous Improvement Systems
- Customer Responsiveness
- Internationalization

Chart 8.5. The Value Chain Life Cycle

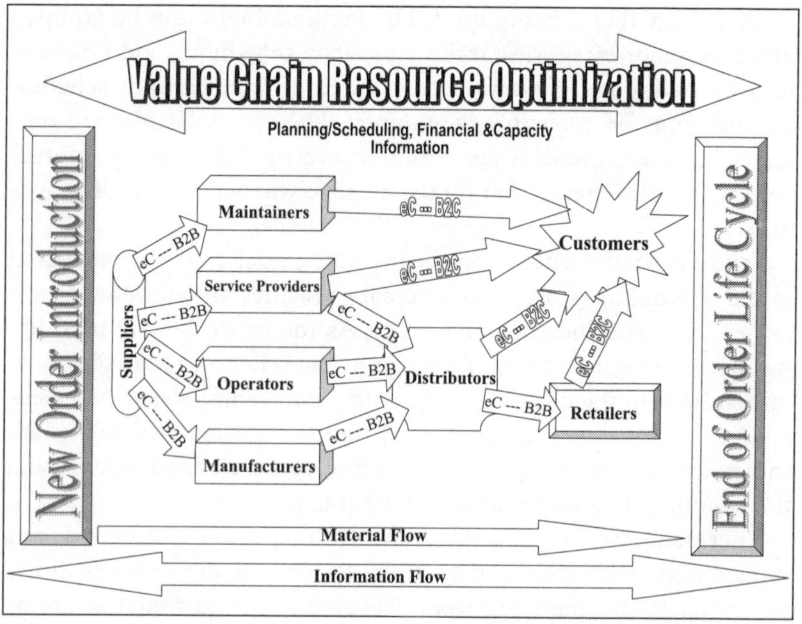

New Product Development

Throughout this book we have focused on being time responsive when it comes to productive cycle time. However, another key element of efficient, time focused, supply chain management is in the area of new product development. Products that are positioned in the early stages of the product life cycle can drag on for years (see Chart 4.2).

The United States is still by far the greatest producer of basic technology in the world. Unfortunately, it is also nearly the worst at implementing this technology. The United States has lost its ability to apply technology to consumer goods. For example, the United States developed the air bags, but Japan had them installed in their cars before the United States. How did this happen? It occurred when companies from the United States were making rapid exits to various parts of the world in search for low cost labor. When you transfer a plant overseas, you also transfer the applied engineering technology along with the facility. As applied technology jobs diminished in the United States, people started looking for other areas of employment and schools stopped teaching the process. The United States lost the ability to focus on applied technology.

Competitive success requires time efficient change, including time efficient product change. Because of this we have recently seen a reversal of the trend to move plants overseas. Companies are returning plants to the United States in order to redevelop the applied technology capability. As a result, the United States will once again be competitive in new product development.

Internationally, countries like Taiwan have already demonstrated and proven themselves as masters in the implementation of applied technology. If a new product idea needs rapid implementation, manufacturers have long known that several Asian countries can convert product ideas into products quicker than anyone else in the world. Therefore, if this element of the supply chain is important, the countries of Taiwan, Singapore, Malaysia, etc. are considered to be prime targets.

In today's competitive world class environment, timing is everything. The development of technology is only one small step for mankind. The second step is to find commercial application for the technology. The third step is to engineer the technology into a commercial product. The fourth step is manufacturing the product so that development occurs rapidly, flexibly, and the product is low cost producible. Then we have to produce the product, and get it out to the customer. Delays in any of these steps will destroy your competitiveness. All areas need innoveering (innovative engineering). Volumes have been written about the importance of an innoveered, especially web-based innoveered, time-to-market effort for United States industry and I can't attempt to reproduce it all here. However, when it takes the United States manufacturers three to four months to build a bicycle, the same bicycle that can be produced in a couple of hours in an Asian plant, we can envision the magnitude of the problem. Other examples of the time differences include the new product introduction time in the automotive industry of as much as four to five years in the United States, and less than a year in most Asian countries. Many Western countries have a long way to go. But they can do it, and there are many examples to prove it. For example, Motorola reduced it's invoice processing from 3.6 days to 30 minutes.

A new tool that has gained international attention is TRIZ which comes from a Russian acronym which means *Theory of Inventive Problem Solving*. The technique focuses on identifying patterns of innovative behavior. By studying these patterns we are able to identify repeated processes that often lead to contradictions. With further investigation of these patterns, the developer of TRIZ, Genrich Altshuler, was able to identify:

1. regularities in the design evolution process
2. the ideal principle
3. the 40 basic principles that are used in most patents

For more information on TRIZ, search the internet and contact Ideation International, Inc. They will explain how engineering processes can be improved by utilizing principles like searching existing data bases for existing technology before redeveloping the technology. One of the best tools for this search is the existing government technology transfer data-base that we discussed earlier in this book.

World Class enterprises realize that long-term strategies, and short-term technology implementations and operations are the competitive advantage for the next decade. The opposite, short-term strategies, and long-term technology, is currently an ingrained part of the United States' method of operation. The most difficult part of this shift is a change in attitudes and culture.[1] For example, IBM, with its development of the IBM Proprinter, was being hammered by its Japanese competitors. They recognized that they had to "find another way of doing things". They redesigned with a "Fast to Market" philosophy. This included changes like a Design for Automated Assembly (DFAA) philosophy which included a new set of rules like their "no-fasteners" rule which was needed in order to satisfy robotics limitations. They incorporated concurrent development knocking 18 months off the product development time. They adjusted the testing process so that it starts sooner and ends sooner.

1. Bodinson, Glenn, "Time-based Competition is the Competitive Advantage of the 1990s", *APICS – The Performance Advantage,* December 1991, Pages 27-31.

The bid and quote purchasing practices of tooling were suspended because they delayed tooling availability. The changes went on and on effecting all areas of technology deployment. In the end, the Proprinter cut 40 percent off normal development time.[2]

Time Based Organizations

You can pull almost any management book off the self off today and it will stress the fact that the competitive stance of any organization in the future is based on time competitiveness. Things change! Change changes! Even the best way to manage change, changes! This is evident by the series of management philosophies that have inundated our management styles. Each philosophical stage was the key to competitiveness during a particular era. For example, there were:

- Guilds – still active in Europe and many developing parts of the world
- Industrial Revolution – Henry Ford and assembly lines
- Scientific Management – Frederick Taylor, the father of time studies
- Humanistic (Human Relations) Management
- Hawthorne Studies on human behavior
- Japanese Management – Edward Deming and inventory efficiency
- Productive Technology – automation replacing workers
- Information Technology – computers
- Change Management – change and time efficiency[3]

As discussed earlier in Chapter 1 (see Chart 1.4), one of the most interesting ways to show this change in management processes is through the migration that has occurred in production systems. In

2. March, Artemis, "Meeting Time and Cost Targets: The IBM Proprinter", *Target, Special 1991,* Pages 18-24.
3. Roth, William, *The Evolution of Management Theory,* Roth And Associates, Orefield, Pennsylvania, 1993.

Chart 1.4 we saw how production control philosophies have migrated through a series of stages to where we now have an innumerable number of "right" ways to run a factory. Of course there is no "one" right way that will work for all factories. The correct way for any one factory needs to be matched to the needs of the factory.

In Chart 1.4 we saw the 2-bin inventory control system is the earliest control system. Today it is still the most common system among small to mid-sized manufacturers. Next we have Economic Order Quantity (EOQ) and Linear Programming (LP) used for production control. After World War II (WW II) we had an explosion of production system technologies. Computers made Material Requirements Planning (MRP) feasible and Integer Programming (IP) possible. Japan developed Just-in-Time (JIT) out of the EOQ model. And Israel created Optimized Production Technology (OPT). Then, about 10 years ago Theory of Constraints (TOC) came out of OPT, and Manufacturing Resources Planning (MRP II) came out of the integration of MRP and the accounting functions. More recently, Schedule Based Manufacturing (SBM) and Bottleneck Allocation Methodology (BAM) have been developed. These are improvements and refinements on some of the problems that existed in some of the other production planning systems.

As a result, we now have a multitude of management philosophies and a multitude of production planning processes, all of which are still being used. Each is competitive when placed in an appropriate environment. Time has blessed us with an enormous bag of competitive tricks, and there will be more, rather than less, in the future. The only disadvantage of all these alternatives is that we have to understand them in order to use them properly.

There is a well known and often discussed corporate life cycle (see Chart 4.2). This life cycle is similar for nations and for products. The life cycle starts at birth and moves into a growth stage. These are the stages where it is common to find the founder running the company. The company's product line is still in transition and the organization is focused on satisfying the customer. Somewhere at around 100 employees, companies start to enter their maturity stage. This is where the founding fathers step back and professional managers take over. This is also where the company tends to focus on a committed product line. Most of a company's existence is at the maturity level. Unfortunately, many companies next experience a decline. This is where they become too rigid and bureaucratic to adapt to new markets, new technologies, and new methodologies. For example, when NCR Corporation decided that consumers would never want electronic calculators and cash registers because they liked the sound of the machine in operation, two VPs left NCR and founded IBM. Similarly, when IBM decided that there wasn't a sufficient market for small computers, Intel, Apple, and Microsoft were able to spin off. Perhaps the internet will be the next wave of technology that brings these new bureaucratic companies into decline.

The length of the cycle averages 600 years for a nation. For the United States, we are somewhere in the maturity stage, and some would argue, starting down the decline. For companies this cycle averages around 20 years. However, it is getting shorter and shorter all the time. For some companies the cycle is only as long as the life of a specific product that they were established to produce. For the company, birth often revolves around some piece of technology, or some entrepreneur's idea of a profitable business. After birth the cycle shifts to start-up where it is still run primarily by the entrepreneurs. However, at some point the company becomes too large to be run by a sole entrepreneur, and professional managers are brought in. For most businesses this is somewhere around 30 to 50 employees. With a professional management staff, the entrepreneur often phases out of the picture and the company jumps into its growth phase. Unfortunately, with growth and a professional management staff comes the search for stability, which results in bureaucracy. We have now entered the maturing phase of the organization. With maturity often comes complacency and a resistance to change. Without change the company starts to loose it's vigor and drive resulting in decline.

For products, the life cycle can be as short as just a few months, especially in the high-tech industries. Or it can be as long as hundreds of years. A company's life, or even a nation's life, can be tied to the life of a product. In the case of a nation, many nations have grown and died around a natural resource that is extracted, and then when the resource is depleted, prosperity ends, and the nation is overthrown. In the case of a company, it is set up to produce a new piece of technology, and it's entire existence revolves solely around the production of the product.

Fortunately, the time-life cycle does not have to signal the end of the enterprise. The life cycle can become a repetitive process through repeated product life cycles that are utilized to maintain growth (see Chart 4.3). Recently, because of the recession and because of competitive pressures, many companies like IBM have found themselves in decline and have decided to down-size and regroup, searching for new products with new product life cycles on which they can hang their growth maintenance. If they don't successfully find new products, death is inevitable.

From the life cycle we see that time and change will eventually kill an enterprise unless the enterprise is willing to innovate and re-innovate, change, and change again, keeping itself on the top of the time-life cycle near maturity. The life cycles need to overlap, so that when one product is in decline, the next is in growth. To be a growth maintenance company we need to have products in each of the stages of the time-life cycle all the time. We cannot focus our efforts on just one product. Growth maintenance is done with the following teams:

- The new product innovation team needs to focus on identifying new product ideas.
- The new product development team needs to focus on making the product producible in a timely and profitable fashion.
- The marketing team needs to focus on market expansion during the growth phase of the product. Production needs to focus on adequately planning productive capacity.
- During maturity, marketing needs to focus on market maintenance and the innovation team needs to look at product modification searching for new product life cycles in the old products.
- During decline phase-out occurs – the product is generally profitable but loosing its consumer appeal – new innovation needs to take it's place.

The time-life cycle teaches us that enterprise growth maintenance is dependent upon repeated change and repeated innovation. Stability leads to stagnation, which is a sure sign of enterprise death.

The competitive power in the future depends on who you're talking to. For manufacturing, as we have considered in previous chapters, the competitive power of the future is in:

- Rapid product change
- Time-to-market efficiency
- Product cycle time reductions
- A commitment to customer satisfaction
- Employee empowerment and teaming
- Stakeholder integration
- Quality and productivity initiatives

Manufacturing is a critical value-added element, third only in importance to agriculture and pure technology development. Manufacturing controls the product development engineering function, the production function, and is a key to customer satisfaction. Maintaining this value-added status is a critical competitive edge in the future.

Boldrin, is his article, claims that the competitive future of manufacturing lies in:

- The efficiency of material flow
- Cycle time reductions
- Employee empowerment

He cites examples of how Hargrove, a manufacturer of gas fireplace logs, reduced floor space by 80 percent and cut cycle time by 50 percent by reengineering and simplifying the production floor.[4]

Burton sees the future of manufacturing requiring:

- The full emergence of the global corporation
- Virtually instantaneous operations (customer responsiveness combined with very short cycle times)
- Total supply chain integration
- Engineering and Manufacturing Integration

4. Boldrin, Bruce J., "Breaking the Time Barrier to Achieve World-Class Manufacturing", APICS 37th International Conference Proceedings, October 1994, Pages 662-664.

- New age of quality
- More rapid continuous improvement
- A growth in strategic alliances
- Flat, unstructured organizations.[5]

In *retailing* we find that for a long time it was believed that the new competitive power base was the retailer. Customers trust the store more and more, and the manufacturer less and less. We are getting a confidence shift. It is the retail establishment that guarantees the quality of the product. However, the competitive edge in retailing in the 1990's and beyond is not in marketing, rather, it is in logistics. Accessibility and timing are the competitive strategies of the future. Future value-added growth comes in the form of getting the customer what they need, when they need it, and in the form (product type) they want to get it in.

The integration of the logistics function into the other functions of the retailer, often referred to as speed sourcing, has been identified by stores like Target and WalMart as a critical success factor. Technological investment into this ability is a key to the speed sourcing strategy for companies like JC Penney.

In retailing and other forms of service organizations like banking, customer service was forgotten for a long time, because it was considered too costly. Marketing was considered to be more important. However, customer service is becoming fashionable again, being considered a strategic competitive edge. Stores like Target and Nordstrom are refocusing on customer service. They are building service into product returnability, and even into the way the store is structured and laid out. Similarly banks are improving their hours and accessibility.

Daniel J. Sweeney, Vice Chairman, Retail Service Industry Group, Price Waterhouse, a retailing industry consultant and a member of the National Advisory Council of Brigham Young University, identified four future vectors for retailing and the service industries:

5. Burton, Terence T., "Manufacturing in the 21st Century", APICS 34th International Conference Proceedings, October 1991, Pages 454-457.

- Globalization will effect 90 percent of all retailers. Retailing will be changed by the new emerging middle classes in developing countries which tend to have a strong family focus. The model for effective retail globalization is IKEA of Sweden.
- Optimization, like taking advantage of scale economies, is growing. WalMart is the grand master in this area.
- Electronification, like greatly improved home shopping and CD-ROM catalogs, is on the increase.
- Personalization, like anticipation marketing, is making its mark.

In his book *The Evolution of Management Theory* (listed earlier), Roth takes a look at the future of management theory. He proposes the organizational structure which includes six dimensions. This is the "multilevel, multidimensional, modular-organization" of Gharajedaghi and includes:

- Output units – manufacturing and logistics
- Input units – supplier or even competitor sourcing
- Environmental units – government and stakeholder relationships
- Planning / Decision Making unit – the integrative unit where all other units are represented
- Control unit – monitor, feedback, data collection
- Management unit – facilitating decisions.[6]

Roth suggests that the key future issues of the organization are:

- Organization size and design
- Marketplace pressures
- Socio-economic doctrine
- The changing role of stakeholders
- Private sector involvement

The life cycle has shown us the need for constant innovation and change development. Chart 8.6 shows how change occurs. What

6. Gharajedaghi, Jamshid, "Organizational Implications of Systems Thinking: Multidimensional Modular Design", *European Journal of Operations Research,* August 1984.

we need to do is integrated change over time by building transition bridges between the change phases. There are stages of growth where we switch roles between change implementation (Stages B and C in Chart 8.6) to change stabilization (Stages D and E in Chart 8.6).

Chart. 8.6. Change Function

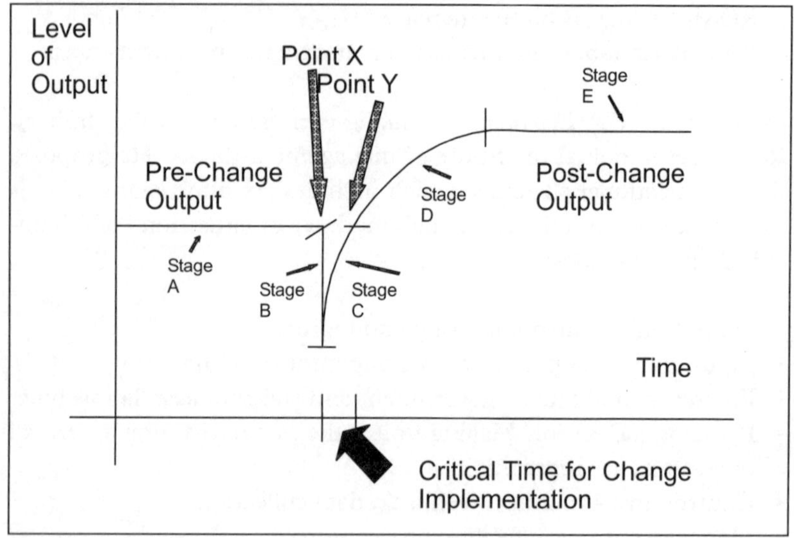

From these charts we learn that change over time is not as easy as stability. In fact, we will often feel like the change wasn't worth it (Stage C of Chart 8.6), but without it we will die as an enterprise.

The tools for change are immeasurable, as we have seen throughout this book. Probably the best tool for world class change implementation is the TQM process. But we cannot forget that we need to change the individual before we can change the enterprise.

A world class global operations manager is a manager who is continually changing over time. A world class manager utilizes time to his or her advantage, understanding that time can both make an enterprise great or kill it. Stability cannot exist. Change will happen. The question is; will you control it, or will it control you, as time goes on.

Continuous Improvement Systems

The business functions of an organization have, for a long time, focused on stability rather than on change. For example, accounting, finance, personnel, the legal department, most upper management, and marketing would love nothing more than to have a steady stable growth. Operations, traditionally, would love a perfectly balanced operation with just the right amount of inventory, just the right work force, and no problems. However, one of the competitive lessons we have learned is that stability breeds failure. If we try to stay where we are, we'll get run over. Just ask the American passenger railroads.

Operations has learned the new competitive lesson of change management, which the remaining functional areas are just waking up to. That is that the only way to competitive success is through change management! The function of the operational organization has changed from one of seeking stability to one of managing change; changes in products and their components, changes in demand, changes in resources and their availability, changes in operational technology, changes in competitive product makeup, changes in competition, etc. And this is a lesson that needs to be shared with the remainder of the organization.

Continuous improvement (change) is critical in a global economy.[7] Changes should include:

- Product innovation
- Process innovation (what the Japanese are good at)
- Technology innovation
- Time-to-market innovation (Taiwan)
- Marketing innovation

But uncontrolled and undirected change can be as disastrous as no change. What we need is to be able to stay ahead of the change

7. Kobu, Bulent, and Frank Greenwood, "Continuous Improvement in a Competitive Global Economy", *Production and Inventory Management,* 4th Quarter, 1991, Pages 58-63.

process. We need to change ourselves faster than external forces have a chance to change us. We need the change to be focused on a target. And we need to maintain our corporate integrity as we institute change.

To manage change we need to incorporate change models into our business which facilitate the change process. Some of these change models, like Total Quality Management and Process Re-engineering, have been discussed previously and will be briefly discussed in this chapter.

Most change models contain some label of quality in them. Quality has become the flag behind which the battle for continuous change is most often fought. But "quality" doesn't fully define everything that is wanted by the change process. Never-the-less, terms like Total Quality Management (TQM) and Quality Functional Deployment (QFD) are change processes that look like they focus on quality, however, in reality, like all change models, they focus on positive, goal direct changes in all the measurement areas including quality, productivity, efficiency, financial improvements, etc. In this chapter we will discuss and compare several of the "trendy" change models (some aren't really change models even though they get credit for being one). Before we discuss some of the change models specifically, let's first discuss some of the psychology behind change.

Psychology Behind Change

Often we take the easy way out when it comes to confronting change. But why do we avoid change? Resistance to change should not be thought of as irrational. Resistance to change is rational behavior. Especially if the change directly effects our job function. Don't just fear resistance, work with it. Remember that all change is not good change. Sometimes the way change is instigated makes the change bad. Sometimes the change fails, no matter how hard we try. But remember also, that without change we are sure to fail because we'll get run over. We need to acknowledge and manage our way around the resistance to change.

In Japan, they use rocks in a river to signify resistance to change. Water flows smoothly down the river until it encounters the rocks.

The water must work it's way around the rocks in order to successfully move on down the river. When change gets implemented in companies, we also encounter rocks. The toughest resistance to change comes from managers who are committed to their way of doing things. They learned to do it that way in school, or they've always done it that way, and they don't understand why they need to change now. The line workers are used to being jerked around. New changes from management are not something new to them. I have seen organizations where over half of the management has quit because of a shift from an authoritarian to a participative management style.

So why does this resistance to change occur? FEAR! Fear of what? The unknown! Why is it unknown? Lack of education and training! Resistance to change should be anticipated and worked with by helping those that fight the change to understand the change and to "buy into" the change. If they feel ownership in the change, the resistance will greatly decrease.

Some Models for Change

Remember the change function shown in Chart 3.1, as expanded on in Chart 8.6. In Stage A we are operating at a steady, stable level of operation. Stage B occurs when change is implemented. The level of efficiency drops and a new learning curve kicks in which is signified by Stage C and D. Stage C is the most critical stage because this is the time when many changes are dropped. If Stage C takes too long (Point X to Point Y) the change may be dropped. This is what occurred with Florida Power and Light and in many JIT, TQM, or Process Re-engineering implementations. Unfortunately, when a change process is dropped during Stage C, a new change function kicks in all over again. Most United States companies don't want Stage C to take more than one year, and with larger changes this short time span is impossible.

Stage D is where we start to see a return on the change process. The final phase of the learning curve is kicking in. Finally, Stage E is where we have once again achieved stability, hopefully at a higher level of output.

The Japanese model for the continuous change process is called Kaizen. It suggests that every process can and should be continually evaluated and continually improved. The primary focus of the improvements is on waste elimination, for example:

- Process time reductions
- Reducing the amount of resources used
- Improving product quality

Kaizen problem solving involves (1) observing the situation, (2) defining the changes that need to take place, and (3) making the changes happen. One example of the implementation of the Kaizen continuous improvement process is at the Repair Division of the Marine Corps Logistics Base in Barstow, California. Utilizing the Kaizen focus on continuous improvement, they ran a pilot project and they received results like:

- 63 % reduction in final assembly lead time
- 50 % reduction in work-in-process inventory
- 83 % reduction in the distance material traveled
- 70 % reduction in shop floor space requirements[8]

The focus of any change model should be on continuous improvement in the broad sense which includes both the Japanese incremental step perspective and the United States breakthrough business process improvement perspective. The need for change is rarely argued. What is different between the various change models is the speed of the change and the depth at which the change occurs. This is where the Japanese and the United States change methods bump heads. In comparison:

The United States

- fast change
- fast return on investment
- radical and dramatic change
- deep and extensive changes feeling the need to redefine the whole process

8. Szendel, Timothy N., and Walter Tighe, "Kaizen American-Style, Continuous Improvement in Action", APICS 37th International Conference Proceedings, *APICS,* October 1994, Pages 496-497.

- on the hunt for the one big change that will fix all the problems
- Process Re-engineering which is characterized by rapid/radical changes and focuses on change implementation and high-tech solutions
- slower to making any change because the change process is viewed as being so extensive, dramatic, and upsetting. The result is that there is more resistance to any change process.
- change ownership belongs to some change "hero" who quite often is the CEO.

The Japanese

- slow change
- long term return on investments
- carefully planned out changes
- think the change through carefully
- plan before you implement
- small step changes
- Total Quality Management which focuses on analysis and planning in the change process and technology-that-fits-the situation solutions.
- the change process is much less painful, because change involves small, undramatic steps. Therefore there is much less resistance and step-wise, small changes, are continuously occurring.
- change ownership is shared.

Some methodologies have attempted, unsuccessfully, to combine the Japanese and United States approaches by suggesting the implementation of "radical changes without being radical". What they are hoping to do is to implement big changes without upsetting the entire organization and developing enormous resistance to the change process. But no one has come up with a good way to accomplish this because no one really understands it. So the conflict between the two change approaches remains. Total Quality Management (TQM) continues to be viewed as "too slow" by the United States, and Process Re-engineering (PR) continues to be viewed as "too destructive" by the Japanese.

Let us now consider the most important models for change and discuss the procedures used in implementing these models. The ones we will consider are:

- Quality Functional Deployment
- Total Quality Management
- Process Re-engineering
- ISO 9000
- Award Processes

Some of these models only supply us with focus areas of improvement. Others have specific procedures for the change process. The models should not be thought of as exclusive in that if you pick one you can't use any of the others. Rather, they should all be considered as stepping stones toward the development of your own successful change program.

Quality Functional Deployment (QFD)

QFD is the implementation of continuous improvement process focusing on the customer. It was developed at Mitsubishi's Kobe Shipyards and focuses on directing the efforts of all functional areas on a common goal. In Mitsubishi's case the goal was "satisfying the needs of the customer". Several changes were instituted in order to accomplish this, such as increased horizontal communication within the company. One of the most immediate results was a reduced time-to-market lead time for products.

QFD systematizes the product's attributes in a matrix diagram called a house of quality and highlights which of these attributes is the most important to a customer. This helps the teams throughout the organization focus on their goal (customer satisfaction) whenever they are making change decisions, like product development and improvement decisions.

QFD focuses on:

- The customer
- Systemizing the customer satisfaction process by developing a matrix for
  - Defining customer quality
  - Defining product characteristics
  - Defining process characteristics
  - Defining process control characteristics
- Empowered teaming

- Extensive front-end analysis which involves 14 steps in defining the "house of quality"
  - Create and communicate a project objective
  - Establish the scope of the project
  - Obtain customer requirements
  - Categorize customer requirements
  - Prioritize customer requirements
  - Assess competitive position
  - Develop design requirements
  - Determine relationship between design requirements and customer requirements
  - Assess competitive position in terms of design requirements
  - Calculate importance of design requirements
  - Establish target values for design
  - Determine correlations between design requirements
  - Finalize target values for design
  - Develop the other matrices.

QFD has been widely recognized as an effective tool for focusing the product and the process on customer satisfaction.

Total Quality Management (TQM)

As mentioned earlier in this book in more detail, Total Quality Management (TQM) focuses on careful, thoughtful analysis. However, the analysis should be creative, innovative, and innoveering oriented. The carefulness comes in when it comes time to implement. We want to make sure that we are implementing positive, goal focused changes before we move a muscle.

TQM is much broader than QFD. TQM is a change model that is enterprise wide. Some people define TQM in general terms as simply making the "entire organization responsible for product or service quality." This is the way TQM is defined in many organizations and it encompasses everything and anything. However, there is also a specific, proceduralistic version of the definition of TQM. Go back to Chapter 4 in this book to review the TQM process.

Process Re-Engineering

Process Re-engineering (PR) is rapid, radical change. It is not downsizing, which many companies are using it for, rather it is work elimination. It is positive, growth-focused change, looking for opportunities to eliminate waste and improve value added productivity, often through the implementation of technology like image processing. Go back to Chapter 4 in this book to review the Process Re-Engineering discussion in detail.

ISO 9000

ISO 9000 is a model that is often advertised as a model for change and improvements. However, the ISO 9000 process tends to focus on stability. The ISO standard was developed by Europe in an attempt to standardize the quality of goods coming into Europe. For many companies it seemed like a trade barrier attempting to keep companies out of Europe. The reason why is because ISO 9000 focuses on quality in the internal process of the organization, assuring that what was designed is what is actually built. It does not focus on the customer. Never-the-less, the ISO standard has become an international standard for quality and systems performance that many companies are utilizing.

ISO has come to define quality, not change. It is a set of standards for quality based on two main foundations:

- Management responsibility and commitment to quality which should be expressed in a formal policy statement and implemented through appropriate measures.
- A set of requirements that deal with each aspect of the company activity and organization that affects quality.

ISO can be used as a standard for improvement, and the ISO quality system requirements can become the focus of change systems. In this way, ISO criteria can be integrated into a change process. However, in-and-of-itself, ISO is not a change model, as frequently believed.

Award Processes

The award programs, like the Baldridge Award, the Deming Prize, and the Shingo Award all have an excellent base of standards from which to build change models. Like the ISO criteria, these award program criteria are an excellent basis for developing a focus for your change program. For example, the Shingo Award organization focuses on continuous improvement processes through total quality systems. The Deming Prize focuses on demonstrated improvements resulting from a continuous improvement process. And the Baldridge Award has the following list of improvement criteria for award evaluation:

- Leadership – Senior management's success in creating and sustaining a quality culture.
- Information and Analysis – The effectiveness of the company's collection and analysis of information for quality improvement and planning.
- Strategic Quality Planning – The effectiveness of the integration of quality requirements into the company's business plans.
- Human Resource Utilization – The success of the company's efforts to utilize the full potential of the work force for quality.
- Quality Assurance of Products and Services – The effectiveness of the company's systems for assuring quality control of all operations.
- Quality Results – The company's results in quality achievement and quality improvement, demonstrated through quantitative measures.
- Customer Satisfaction – The effectiveness of the company's systems to determine customer requirements and demonstrated success in meeting them.

Within these seven categories there are 33 examination items and 133 subitems. As with the ISO process, the award process is not a change process, but it greatly assists an organization in establishing the criteria that should be incorporated into an effective change model. Going through the award process motivates the development of effective change procedures.

Which Change Model Is Best

There is no "best" change model. The best for you is the one you build yourself, fitting your organization, and utilizing your goals and focus. However, some of the model alternatives are better than others. A World Class change model should focus on effective, customer and employee oriented, change management that offers competitive innoveering strategies. World Class change management is Total Quality Management or a modification of the Process Reengineering model which includes an additional focus on the analysis process. TQM offers the most structure and tends to be the least resisted. Therefore, I would tend to prefer it over the PM alternatives. However, I need to stress again, that the best change model for you is the one you customize for yourself.

Customer Responsiveness

Companies have a global mandate to produce cheaper products in less time and for a higher level of quality. To do this we need to eliminate the Re's, like rework, replace, redo, recount, reissue, reinspect, etc. We need to eliminate unnecessary work, and, as Dave Garwood would say, we need to focus on converting as many of our currently necessary activities into unnecessary activities so that they can also be eliminated. The Japanese would say that we need to eliminate as many non-value-added activities as possible so that we are only working on value added activities. An excellent example of this can be found in Dell Computers where 50 percent of their sales occur over the internet. Customers can order a custom designed, customer specific computer directly from the manufacturer. This eliminates retailers and distribution networks. Inventories are lower, cycle time is reduced, and costs for the customer and for Dell Computer are lower. Dell is able to sell more for less cost and still make more money.

In order to accomplish a supply chain network that is customer responsive we need to focus on a supply chain network like the one shown on Chart 7.1. Another way to visualize this model is to consider a collection of gears, each interlinked with the other, going all the way from the customer's customer down to the supplier's supplier. Then we would visualize how the information change at any one point in the collection of interlocking gears would effect change and information transfer to any other point of the interconnected linkages. Information would initiate at the customer point, but after this initiation, all points in the network can effect change to the information. Product would move up the chain, but information could move in any and all directions.

A supply chain network where all elements are tightly linked together offers shorter cycle times, less Re's, and integrated access to information. It is especially significant that the customer also has access to the entire information network. The customer can investigate the status of any order anywhere in the supply chain. The customer can make or change orders and watch how the supply chain reacts to the order.

Network systems have been established to define the integrated information flow that needs to exist from the supplier's supplier to the customer's customer. The Dornier, Ernst, Fender, and Kouvelis book discusses these in more detail. They are the EDI (Electronic Data Interchange), QR (Quick Response), and the ECR (Efficient Customer Response) Systems. These are all point-to-point tools that allow the exchange of information between each element in the supply chain. However, the introduction of the internet has opened up channels of communication that are not as restrictive as traditional point-to-point systems. The internet allows us to access status information for any element in the supply chain, and all these elements can be integrated together into one interlinked inquiry process.

Internationalization

Internationalization stretches lead time and cycle time because the distribution chain has been increased. However, internationalization, or globalization, can also significantly reduce new product introduction lead time, as has already been discussed. Therefore, globalization is a collection of trade-offs where we attempt to minimize the negative effects on the supply chain while at the same time trying to magnify the positive effects.

Globalization is realizing that there's a big world out there, geographically, that reaches far beyond our small little community, and that this world is getting closer to us all the time. Globalization is the realization that, whether we like it or not, this big world is becoming an ever increasing factor in our daily lives. Globalization requires careful strategic planning because it can become very complex depending on where and what you are working with.

A global enterprise is one that is involved in international transactions. These transactions can take many forms:

- Vendors
- Subcontractors
- Customers
- Subsidiaries
- Plants
- Financing (banks and private investors)

Almost every company, no matter how small, is globally influenced in some way, either directly or indirectly. Even if you don't have direct international transactions, it is highly likely that components of what you purchase, or the end user of your output, will be internationally influenced. Often one of your primary competitors will be international.

Globalization does not remove the need for localization. The products and services we provide still need to be culturally distinct. For example, "Jesus boots" or Nova story from Chapter 2 demonstrates a cultural transition error. Also, when United States auto manufacturers were faced with the Kimono regulations of Japan, where bumpers had to be wrapped back into the body of the car so that the long Kimonos would not get caught in them, they cried "trade barrier" and fought it all the way. A global enterprise, and a World Class Global Manager understands the need for product and service localization within a global environment.

The global enterprise is an "insider", not an outsider. It understands how localized markets work from the inside, whether it is in North America, Europe, Japan, Latin America, ... It realizes that there are differences within each region and within each country (compare the United States West, with the North-East, with the South, with Alaska, etc.). A global enterprise focuses on the localization within each of these sub-regions.

The result is that a global enterprise develops a global strategy which builds on localized independence. It develops global visions and missions, but realizes that home office solutions very seldom are workable locally, and that the local organizations need to be empowered to make their own decisions. A global enterprise is one that recognizes that all customers, including those that are rarely or never heard of in the home office, are equally important.

Global management has been the focus of numerous studies. For example, 31 major trends were listed in *The Public Pulse* by the Roper Organization which is shaping the future of American business. Industrial globalization is effected by the majority of these directly, including issues like:

- Time control – time responsiveness
- Home shopping growth
- The environment
- Labor relations changes
- Defense spending shifts
- Government regulations to increase
- Permanent damage to the nuclear industry
- The budget deficit won't go away
- Reversal of tax cuts for wealthy
- etc.[9]

Another study suggests that the first characteristic of 21st Century industry is the emergence of the global corporation. Some of the features of the global corporation are:

- Virtually Instantaneous Operations – A customer will enter in a custom designed order based on something they saw on the home shopping network, and instantaneously, the customized production of that product begins in a plant in Chile. Companies like FedEx handle the shipment of the product, and three days later, the customer has the product in hand.

9. The Roper Organization, Inc., *The Public Pulse*, Vol. 2, No. 1, 1991, Pages 1-8.

- Integrating the Supply Chain
- Flat, Unstructured, Modular Organizations
- Growth of Strategic Alliances
- A Renewed Focus on Quality.[10]

The world class global manager realizes that he/she does not have all the answers. They realize that they do not have a localized perspective for every region in which their enterprise is involved. For example Whirlpool International's management committee is made up of six people from six different nations, and this is typical of most world class global enterprises. Asea Brown Boveri (ABB), the European electrical engineering giant based in Zurich, Switzerland has grouped its entire product line of thousands of products into 50 business categories or Business Areas (BA). The leadership team for each BA is given global responsibility for developing the business unit strategy for its area. This includes the incorporation of global responsibility, selecting product development priorities, and allocating production among countries. None of the BA teams are located in Zurich, rather, they are distributed throughout the world.

Hewlett-Packard moved the headquarters of its personal computer business to Grenoble, France. Siemens A. G., Germany's electronics giant, moved its medical electronics division to Chicago, Illinois. Ford's world class engine factory, where Mexican engineers and technicians produce 1,000 engines per day at world class quality levels is located in Chihuahua, Mexico. Texas Instruments' most complex wafer production facility is in Sendai, Japan. Intel is establishing one of it's prime strategic research centers in Penang, Malaysia. Most consumer electronics products marketed in the United States by American companies such as General Electric, RCA, and Zenith are manufactured abroad. Chrysler has reduced its domestic capacity to 40 percent and now buys the majority of the automobiles it markets under it's brand name from Mitsubishi in Japan. Sears, K-Mart, and J. C. Penney procure a large percentage of their merchandise from foreign manufacturers. Non-U. S.

10. Burton, Terence T., "Manufacturing in the 21st Century", APICS 34th International Conference Proceedings, *APICS*, October 1991, Pages 454-457.

companies like Shell, British Petroleum, Hoechst, Toyota, Nissan, Honda, Sony, and Mitsushita have, through acquisitions and new facilities, introduced production facilities in North America. Other successful global competitors include; IBM, GE, McDonalds, Philips, Toys-R-Us, KFC, NCR, AT&T, Unilever, Procter & Gamble, and the list goes on and on. These companies have all discovered the globalization advantage.

Globalization has been discussed in Chapter 2 and Chapter 4 and will again be discussed in detail in Chapter 13. Globalization is a competitive strategic requirement, and integrating time efficient supply chain management tools into this environment will be the key to successfully managing this tool.

Technology Transfer – A Developing Country Perspective

Let's revisit some of the companies we looked at earlier, and take a look at technology transfer from a developing country perspective. We'll find that developing countries see themselves in quite a different light than what we're used to. This perspective effects the performance of the supply chain, especially in the area of time performance. For example, in the development of timely technology, what do these developing countries consider "appropriate and meaningful technology"? What is useful and acceptable? What is the best method of transferring this technology?

Technology Transfer (TT) means a lot of things, but to the developing country it often means getting the 20 year old, obsolete and replaced technology of a developed country, and trying to make it work for another 20 years. The developed country somehow feels they have done the developing country a favor by giving them more jobs. But what some developing countries feel is really happening is that we are keeping the country behind technologically in order to take advantage of a cheap labor market. In a recent study on TT, labor forces around the world were measured on their ability to adapt to new technology. The number of hours required to adapt to a new technology was measured. For the United States the adaptation took about six hours. For Japan it took five hours. For Mexico it took four and a half hours (source of study results: Fundameca,

Mexico City). The Mexican worker was more effective at TT than the United States worker. Based solely on the results of this study we should transfer new technology to Mexico first, before we try to implement it at home.

T in Q, Mexico

As we were introduced in the last chapter, T is a Mexican factory that was a subsidiary of a Michigan firm. T was established using rejected and left over equipment from plants in Michigan which were being technologically updated. The hope was that T would be able to use Mexico's cheaper labor to produce the required products at competitive prices using the old, labor intensive equipment. However, many important factors were not included in the formula. For example, inventory levels were increased dramatically to compensate for the long border crossing and transportation times. The financing costs of these increased inventory levels far outweighed any advantage gained by the labor savings.

Additionally, some of the parts could not be produced on the older equipment and these were forced to be transferred overseas (in this case Japan) to be produced on more advanced equipment. Then the parts had to be returned to Mexico for installation.

The difficulties in running T also can be seen in the management style. For example, the American managers were Michigan trained and basically had the attitude that "we know best". The same process that works in Michigan should work perfectly well here in Mexico. The goals, culture, government, and aspirations of the Mexican citizen were not even considered.

P in KL, Malaysia

P is a company that was set up as part of a partnership between the Malaysian government and a Japanese counterpart. Malaysia had hopes of learning some of the Japanese manufacturing methodologies through this new partner. However, the Japanese partner refused to install Japanese production techniques, like Just-In-Time (JIT). They claimed that Malaysians could not work effectively in teams, thereby making JIT ineffective. Instead they installed a Material Requirements Planning (MRP) production planning system that is common in the United States and Europe. However, some American manufacturers in Malaysia, like Motorola and Applied Magnetics, are running JIT systems quite effectively. Some people felt that the P example suggests that the Japanese wanted to keep this Malaysian company behind technologically so that they would not eventually become an international competitor. This is supported by the fact that there were no JIT systems installed in any Japanese partnership plant in all of Malaysia.

Another frustration that the Malaysians were feeling with Japanese partnerships was that often Japan would require that certain manufacturing components be purchased from Japan. Japan believed in a value-added philosophy for plant relocation. This means that if you are building a product in a developing country, you let that country produce all those pieces that have minimal value-added content, and you keep all the value-added rich processes for yourself. These value-added rich processes tend to be the most technologically advanced processes. Japan may have found an ingenious way to not only keep advanced technology at home, they also kept a significant portion of the profits at home.

Technology Definitions

Applied Technology is technology that is adapted to a specific situation. In the T example, the technology may not have been wanted in Mexico. It may not have been applied to the needs of the culture and the community. In the P example a technology was adapted that was not the most familiar to the Japanese partner, but the technology transfer process may have been selected so as to restrict competition.

Most developing countries are trying to becoming fully developed. Mexico placed their hopes on the North America Free Trade Agreement (NAFTA). Mexico wanted to be a united partner with the United States and Canada, demonstrating that they had expertise and resources that their North American partners could benefit from. NAFTA focuses on finding appropriate Technology for Mexican industries.

In Malaysia there is a program called “Vision 2020”. The goal of this program is similar to the hope that Mexico has for the NAFTA, which is to transfer technology. In the Malaysian case the goal has a specific target, which is to be fully developed by the year 2020. Toward this end they are trying to attract technology transfer from all parts of the world. For example, INTEL is moving their research facilities to Penang. Malaysia has been very successful in attracting technology transfer from Japan, the United States, and Europe.

Useful and acceptable technology is technology that adds value to the development of a country. It has long been understood that to move from developing to developed what is needed is a technological edge in some niche area in which you can perform better than anyone else. All developing countries are searching for this technological niche. Malaysia seems to have developed a strong attraction for electronics product development and manufacture. Mexico has still not firmly established a niche, but they seem to be searching for it in the manufacturing sector.

Technology Transfer to a Developing Country

What type of technology would be appropriate, applied, useful, and acceptable in a developing country? The first thing we need to change is our attitude that we are dealing with "dumb foreigners that can't even read or write". There are many Malaysian and Mexican workers that could teach many United States producers how to better apply their technology. For example, Mexico has an organization called Fundacion Mexicana Para La Calidad Total AC (FUNDAMECA). Their mission is to communicate knowledge, technology, and experiences in quality and productivity. They tell their story regularly to United States and international audiences all over the Americas.

Similarly, Malaysia has the National Productivity Corporation (NPC) and the Federation of Malaysian Manufacturers (FMM). These organizations have goals similar to those of their Mexican counterpart.

The first step in transferring technology to a developing country is to meet with organizations like FUNDAMECA, NPC, or the FMM. They can tell you what types of technology will transfer well into their country. Additionally, each country has a commercial attaché at the United States embassy. The role of this individual is to interface companies that are considering relocating a plant, with executives that have already gone through the process. For example, in Malaysia they have a monthly breakfast to which interested parties are invited. The potential investor discusses their plans and the group expresses their opinions about the idea. These breakfasts tend to be very informative for the potential transferee.

Assuming that the environment and financial considerations have been found to be acceptable, the transfer should be made with the approach that we are trying to take advantage of the benefits that the country has to offer. For example, both Malaysia and Mexico offer a consistent, reliable, and very trainable work force. These are important considerations when time-to-market considerations are being planned.

Lessons Learned

When attempting to transfer technology to a developing country, we are often confronted by considerations and questions that are very surprising. Even the very goals of our business are often challenged. For example, do we really believe that profit is the primary motivator for business, or is it some ideal like quality or customer satisfaction. And then, if we select one of these goals, we often get into a discussion of how these goals are operationalized. For example, why are factories with differing sets of goals all run the same way. Let me give you an example. Some factories claim their goal is profitability, some claim return on investment, some claim customer satisfaction, etc. However, when you take a close look at the way the factory is run on the shop floor, you quickly learn that they are all run about the same way. In fact, you find that most of the employees do not have any idea what this goal is. The question that is then asked is; "If you don't know the goal of your organization is, how do you know that what you are doing (your job function) is helping the organization to achieve the goal?"

The questions about goals, and the operationalization of the goals, is very eye opening. We have a blindness to these types of considerations in the industrialized countries. We seem to think that because we have always done it this way, it must be correct.

Technology transfer experiences have opened our eyes to many surprising questions. As we attempt to transfer the technology, we need to consider not only the answers to these questions, but also to take a close look at how these questions should be answered differently depending on the country and culture in which we are trying to organize.

The cultural mix of a country needs to be worked with and magnified. For example, teaming, in a Malaysian culture, focuses on never criticizing an individual. Rather, the process, or job function is criticized. Using this strategy, teaming can be very effective. Another example can be seen in a joint venture company in Penang. The company, Ford-Mitsubishi-Sony (FMS), is a joint venture of two Japanese and one American company which was established to manufacture auto stereo systems. It is a struggle to just get the organizing partners to work together culturally, let alone trying to get them to interface with the multi-cultural Malaysian work force. However, through appropriate sensitivity and patience, they are making extremely effective progress.

Technology transfer to developing countries can be very effective if we would stop looking at the developing country as some sort of puppet slave of the big master. Developing countries have a lot to offer, and, if given the opportunity to prove themselves with applied, appropriate, useful, and acceptable technology, the transfer can be a very effective and profitable one.

Summary

This has been the third chapter in the series on supply chain management. From this chapter we have seen how time influences the effectiveness of the supply chain, especially when international influences are brought into play. This chapter discussed the importance of new product development in the supply chain, and it covered some of the developing country considerations that come into play.

Class Assignments

1) How would you manage V, Inc's supply chain and cycle time problems?
2) Revisit some of the earlier cases, particularly N, Inc. and NS, Inc. to see how time elements would effect your previous supply chain decision.

References

Supply Chain References

Handfield, Robert B. and Ernest L. Nichols, Jr., *Introduction to Supply Chain Management*, Prentice Hall, Upper Saddle River, New Jersey, 1999.

Time Based References

Bodinson, Glenn, "Time-based Competition is the Competitive Advantage of the 1990s", *APICS – The Performance Advantage*, December 1991, Pages 27-31.

Boldrin, Bruce J., "Breaking the Time Barrier to Achieve World-Class Manufacturing", *APICS 37th International Conference Proceedings*, October 1994, Pages 662-664.

Burton, Terence T., "Manufacturing in the 21st Century", *APICS 34th International Conference Proceedings*, October 1991, Pages 454-457.

Gharajedaghi, Jamshid, "Organizational Implications of Systems Thinking: Multidimensional Modular Design", *European Journal of Operations Research*, August 1984.

Hamel, Gary, and C. K. Prahalad, "Competing for the Future", *Harvard Business Review*, July-August 1994, Pages 122-128.

March, Artemis, "Meeting Time and Cost Targets: The IBM Proprinter", *Target*, Special 1991, Pages 18-24.

Roth, William, *The Evolution of Management Theory*, Roth And Associates, Orefield, Pennsylvania, 1993.

TRIZ and QFD References

Terninko, John, *Step-by-Step QFD; Customer Driven Product Design*, St. Lucie Press, Boca Raton, Florida, 1997.

Change Model References

Hammer, M., and Champy, "The Promise of Reengineering", *Fortune*, May 3, 1993, Pages 94-97.

Hammer, M., "Reengineering Work: Don't Automate, Obliterate", *Harvard Business Review*, July-August 1990, Pages 104-112.

Jason, R., "How Reengineering Transforms Organizations to Satisfy Customers", *National Productivity Review*, Winter 1992, Pages 45-53.

Marks, Peter, *Process Reengineeering and the New Manufacturing Enterprise Wheel: 15 Processes for Competitive Advantage*, CASA/SME Technical Forum, Society of Manufacturing Engineers (SME), Dearborn, Michigan, 1994.

Harbour, Jerry L., *The Process Reengineering Workbook: Practical Steps to Working Faster and Smarter Through Process Improvement*, Quality Resources, White Plains, New York, 1994.

Cypress, Harold L., "Re-engineering", *OR/MS Today*, February 1994, Pages 18-29.

Ravikumar, Ravi, "Business Process Reengineering – Making the Transition", *APICS 37th Annual International Conference Proceedings*, APICS, October 1994, Pages 17-21.

Miller, George, "Reengineering: 40 U$seful Hints", *APICS 37th Annual International Conference Proceedings*, APICS, October 1994, Pages 22-26.

Melnyk, Steven A., and William R. Wassweiler, "Business Process Reengineering: Understanding the Process, Responding to the Right Needs", *APICS 37th Annual International Conference Proceedings*, APICS, October 1994, Pages 115-120.

Boyer, John E., "Reengineering Office Processes", *APICS 37th Annual International Conference Proceedings*, APICS, October 1994, Pages 522-526.

Stevens, Mark, "Reengineering the Manufacturing Company: 'New Fad or For Real'", *APICS 37th Annual International Conference Proceedings*, APICS, October 1994, Pages 527-530.

John R. Lipscomb, President of Lipscome and Associates of White Lake, Michigan has made presentations with the title "Re-engineering Continuous Improvement Through Quality Systems Deployment".

EDI, ECR, & QR References

Dornier, Philippe-Pierre, Ricardo Ernst, Michel Fender, and Panos Kouvelis, *Global Operations and Logistics*, John Wiley & Sons, Inc., New York, 1998.

International Supply Chain References

Daniels, John D., and Lee H. Radebaugh, *International Business – Environments and Operations*, Addison-Wesley Publishing Company, Reading, Massachusetts, 1994.

Sheth, Jagdish, and Golpira Eshghi, *Global Operations Perspectives*, South-Western Publishing Co., Cincinnati, Ohio, 1989.

Plenert, Gerhard *International Management and Production: Survival Techniques for Corporate America*, TAB Professional and Reference Books, Blue Ridge Summit, PA, 1990.

Reich, Robert B., "Who is Them?" *Harvard Business Review*, March-April 1991, Pages 77-88.

POMS
Support Systems

9. Logistics / Distribution

Logistics and distribution management becomes critical in an international supply chain management program. The logistics and warehousing steps occur so frequently that they become the largest piece of lead time in the entire network. For example, let's take a look at the production and shipment of an automobile. Here is an example of the types of steps that can occur (P = production step and L = logistics or warehousing step):

P Metal comes off the steel mill in Japan
L Metal is placed in finished goods storage
L Metal rolls are loaded on trains
L Metal is rail transported to the harbor
L Metal is loaded on the ships
L Metal is transported by ship to the harbor in Mexico
L Metal is off-loaded into a customs warehouse in Mexico
L Metal is loaded onto trucks at the Mexico customs warehouse
L Metal is transported to the parts assembly production facility in Mexico
L Metal is stored in the parts facility warehouse
P Metal is used in the production process to manufacture components
L Components are stored in finished goods storage
L Components are packaged for shipment to Detroit
L Components are loaded on trucks for shipment to the border
L Components are transported to the border
L Components are off-loaded at the border and placed into temporary storage
L Components are loaded on rail for transport to Detroit
L Components are moved to Detroit
L Components are off-loaded in Detroit and placed in raw materials storage

P Components are used in the production process to create a car
L Car is placed in finished goods inventory
L Car is loaded on rail for transport to the harbor on the way to Europe
L Car is transported to harbor
L Car is off loaded and placed in storage at the harbor
L Car is loaded onto the ship for transport to Europe
L Car is moved to Europe
L Car is off loaded at the harbor in Europe and placed into customs inventory storage
L Car is loaded on trucks to be moved to a warehouse
L Car is off loaded at the warehouse and placed into inventory
L Car is loaded on rail or trucks to be moved to the dealerships
L Car is moved to the dealership
L Car is off loaded at the dealership and placed into dealer inventory.

Does this example demonstrate the point that distribution and logistics plays a critical part in time management of the supply chain? It should. But what should bother you even more is that each of the "L" designated steps are non-value-adding steps in that no "real" value is added to the end product. Each of the "L" steps could have been accomplished in numerous different ways, or possibly even eliminated, without any significant change to the end product's appeal to the customer. And since the "L" steps are non-value adding, we should focus on their elimination, or at least their minimization. In this chapter we will discuss some of these options.

The Flow of Information

In Chapter 5 we discussed the integrated flow of information. In this chapter we also briefly discussed the role of logistics management in this over-all flow. In Chart 5.7 we can take another look at the flow and see where distribution management fits in. It integrates all the materials transport functions external to the production facility, like the receiving of raw materials, and the shipment of finished goods. The over-all management of the flow of these external materials movement functions is often referred to as the *Distri-*

bution Requirements (or Resources) Planning (DRP). In DRP we have three major components:

- Inventory Management
- Routing Management
- Procurement Management

Inventory Management focuses on picking, retrieving, and storage of the goods in warehousing facilities. Much of this process is automated with tools like bar coding and automated storage and retrieval systems. The basics of an inventory management system are found in any introduction to operations management.

Routing Management focuses on optimizing the transport process. It focuses on the movement of the materials to and away from the production facility. An example of routing optimization will be seen later in this chapter. Routing management can be a topic for an entire course and not just for a simplistic example, but this example will demonstrate the difficulty of the process.

Procurement Management is the management of the purchase order process including the packing slips, pick lists, issues and receipts transactions, etc. It is again similar to what is discussed in any operations management text.

An example of a masterpiece in logistics management can be found in American Airlines. They have developed an airline logistics management software package that deals with planning issues like:

- Airplane routing
- On-board crew location and rest time scheduling
- Service support staff scheduling
- Ground crew scheduling
- Equipment preventive maintenance based on take-offs, landings, and air hours
- Equipment emergency service parts availability
- Tooling and supplies availability
- Passenger load planning
- Meal delivery and planning
- Emergency aircraft replacement scheduling
- Luggage tracking
- Parcel tracking

The management of all these elements of the logistics management process can be quite challenging, especially when we realize that many of these elements are inter-linked and are not independently scheduled.

Another logistics management success story is found in Wal Mart. They claim that the secret to their success is found in logistics management. As soon as a product is purchased in a store, an order is placed with the distribution center. This process initiates the replacement of the item the following evening. Wal-Mart credits their commercial success with always having the desired product on the shelf when requested by the customer. They see their edge as offering the customer the convenience of not having to come back to the store several times to get everything that they need. They do this through an integrated DRP supply chain process that tracks sales from the store to the distribution center, and from the distribution center to the supplier. Everyone is kept in the information loop so that customer responsiveness is easily accomplished.

PB, Inc.

PB, Inc. is a re-builder and distributor of automotive components. They have a warehouse and redistribution facility on the Eastern United States seaboard which is their main facility for planning purposes. They have manufacturers all over the world that take their old starters and alternators and rebuild them for reinstallation into cars. The flow is as follows:

- The auto parts retailer receives a "core" of the old part from a customer
- The auto parts retailer sends the "core" to the distribution facility (this could involve international transportation of goods)
- The distribution facility sorts the cores and places them in barrels depending on which re-manufacturing facility they should go to
- The barrels are transported to the re-manufacturing facility where they are rebuilt (this almost always requires international transportation of goods)
- The rebuilt parts are returned to the distribution location (international transport)

- The distribution facility sorts and shelves the rebuilt parts waiting for an order from a auto parts retailer
- The distribution facility ships the part to the retailer.

The challenge for PB is that they never know what parts are coming to them nor what parts are going to be ordered. Often they will receive in cores for alternators or starters that are no longer in high demand and they will not send them out to be rebuilt. Therefore, there is a large inventory of questionable items in the warehouse. Additionally, the rebuilt items will often sit in the distribution facility for long periods of time never to be sold. This is after PB has paid extensive transport and production costs. They are desperate to determine what to do with their ever increasing inventory levels. They would like to do some kind of forecasting that would predict usage, but have never been able to come up with a good method.

Additionally, they have enormous transport costs because far too often they are forced to "rush ship" parts to a customer. These costs can be quite high. PB is wondering if there is any way to reduce the logistics steps in the supply chain process, or to at least make them more efficient. Now it's your turn. What would you do?

Distribution Requirements Planning

I'm not going to pretend that in one short chapter I can possibly cover the entire field of distribution, logistics, and warehousing. So what I will present in this chapter are some of the basics. These basics can be expanded to make them as complex as you desire.

Distribution requirements planning (DRP) is a system that incorporates, not only the sales and shipping functions of an organization, but also the purchasing and receiving functions. It plans the traffic and storing of goods that are coming out of or going into the plant. Inventory planning and control is covered in detail in any introduction to operations management so I will not go into detail about that aspect at this point. However, the added dimension that DRP adds to inventory planning and control is that the same item is stored in a multitude of locations, like plants, warehouses, or in-transit on trucks, rail, or ships.

Product Sales and Shipping

As an example, let's walk through what happens when a product is sold. If the sold item is a finished product sitting in finished goods inventory, it can be shipped from inventory. Then when the product has been completed and turned into finished goods inventory, we follow the same procedure as an item shipped from inventory. These are the steps:

1) The customer order comes in and we generate a picking list. This picking list is a list of what items need to be picked from inventory in order to satisfy the customer order. Often, the order for a particular part also requires the shipment of an instruction manual, and some spare parts. These are not included in the customer order but are included as separate items on the picking list.
2) The picking list goes to the finished goods inventory department and the product is pulled. Shortages are reported for backordering.
3) The product, picking list, and a copy of the customer order used as the shipping order are sent to packaging where they are prepared for shipment. Any special shipping instructions are noted at this time.
4) The product is shipped. If we are using an external carrier, the distribution problem becomes the carrier's problem. If we are using our own trucks, or if we rent a trucking service, we need to plan the routing so that the time spent and miles traveled will be minimized. If we also pick up our own raw materials (backhauls), the shipment scheduling becomes intertwined with the pick up schedule. This scheduling process will be discussed later in this chapter.
5) The shipping document is filled out with date shipped and carrier information. One copy is sent along with the materials. The other copy is returned to the Order Department so that they know that the product was shipped. Then the order and shipping information is forwarded to sales and accounting for sales reporting, carrier reporting, and accounts receivable collections.
6) A performance report is created detailing the results of the

freight / carrier process. In this report we collect data on the timeliness and quality of the shipment process so that it can be improved upon if necessary.

Routing / Transportation Models

The objective of routing and transportation models is to minimize the travel time (cost) of shipments. There are some very complex modeling techniques that calculate shipments from multiple plant locations where the same products are produced. However, for the sake of simplicity we will discuss shipments from a single location to multiple customers with frequent multiple backhauls (pick ups from vendors). That will be the scope of this segment of this chapter. We will cover these types of calculations in the following seven steps:

1) Distribution where each customer shipment requires full load trips
2) Distribution where there are customers and backhauls but each is a full load trip
3) Distribution where multiple customers are serviced during the same trip
4) Distribution with multiple customers and multiple backhauls per trip
5) Mixtures of loads to customers
6) Sectoring
7) Cost or mile optimization.

Now we will consider each of these options in more detail. There is an appendix at the end of this chapter that shows the Linear Programming – Integer Programming (LP-IP) formulations of these problems.

(1) Distribution where each customer shipment requires full load trips

These problems are best demonstrated with examples. Charts 9.1 and 9.2 show the travel distance relationship of our plant to five different customers and three different vendors. For example, the distance from the Plant to Vendor 1 is 13 miles. The distance from Vendor 1 to Customer 3 is 25 miles. Therefore, the distance that a truck travels from the Plant, to Customer 2, to Customer 3, to Vendor 1, and back to the Plant would be 20 miles plus 15 plus 25 plus 13 miles or 73 miles total.

Chart 9.2 is a mileage matrix for each of the locations shown in Chart 9.1. Chart 9.2 is derived from Chart 9.1 and is used to develop computer algorithms. The same distance mileage's can be derived from both charts. For example, both charts show the distance from Vendor 1 to Customer 3 to be 25 miles.

Chart 9.1. Routing Map

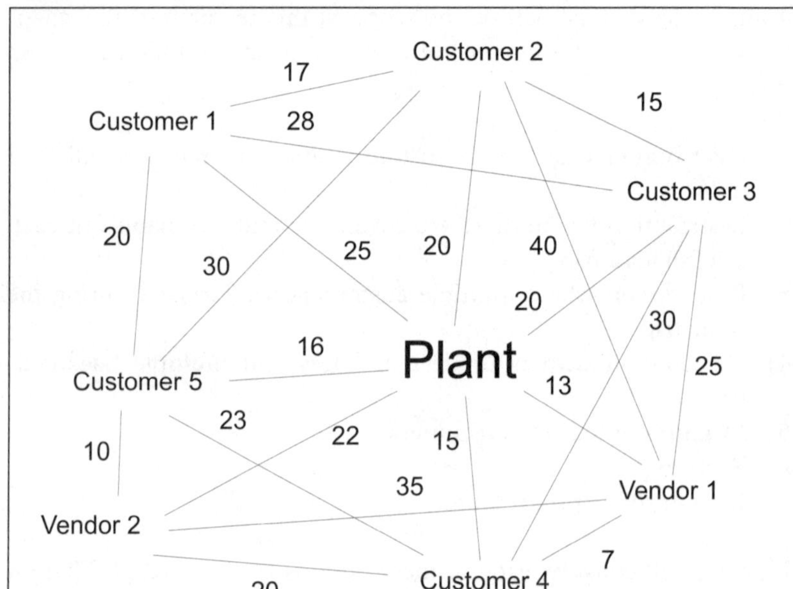

For this initial example, we are assuming that we only service customers and that we have no vendor pickups. Each load taken to each customer is a full load and requires a special trip to do. The scheduling of this situation is fairly simple. If there is no capacity problem and you can handle all deliveries, do it. If there is a capacity problem and some of the shipments will need to be made by other carriers, analyze the pricing method of the carrier. If it is a flat rate carrier, like the post office, have them deliver the furthest shipments. If the carrier rate is by mileage, you deliver the long ones and have the carrier deliver the short trips that are beyond your capacity.

Chart 9.2. Customer / Vendor Milage Matrix

	H	C1	C2	C3	C4	C5	V1	V2
Home (H)	0							
Customer 1 (C1)	25	0						
Customer 2 (C2)	20	17	0					
Customer 3 (C3)	20	28	15	0				
Customer 4 (C4)	15	40	35	30	0			
Customer 5 (C5)	16	20	30	36	23	0		
Vendor 1 (V1)	13	38	40	25	7	29	0	
Vendor 2 (V2)	22	30	40	42	20	10	35	0

(2) Distribution where there are customers and backhauls but each is a full load trip

We will work through a couple of example problems so that you will be able to get a feel for the analysis process. In Chart 9.3 we have a list of customer deliveries and vendor pickups (backhauls) that need to be made over the next couple days. The objective is to minimize the total miles driven.

Chart 9.3. Trips Required for Example (2)

Example 2.1
Customer 1 – 3 trips
Customer 2 – 6 trips
Customer 3 – 1 trips
Customer 4 – 2 trips
Customer 5 – 2 trips
Vendor 1 – 4 trips
Vendor 2 – 6 trips

Example 2.2
Customer 1 – 2 trips
Customer 2 – 0 trips
Customer 3 – 4 trips
Customer 4 – 1 trips
Customer 5 – 1 trips
Vendor 1 – 4 trips
Vendor 2 – 6 trips

In the first example (Example 2.1) each trip is a separate full load. We know that there will need to be 14 trips to customers and 10 trips to vendors. Every time we send a truck out we want that truck to come back loaded with vendor goods, if possible. This should be possible 10 times. What we want to do is minimize the trip miles out to a customer, over to a vendor, and back to the plant. Vendor 1 is closest to Customer 3 and Customer 4. A trip to Customer 3, then Vendor 1, then back to the plant would be 58 miles. Customer 4, then Vendor 1, would be 35 miles, etc. Following is a list of these options:

- Customer 1 – Vendor 1 has us going back by the plant
- Customer 2 – Vendor 1 = 73 miles
- Customer 3 – Vendor 1 = 58 miles
- Customer 4 – Vendor 1 = 35 miles
- Customer 5 – Vendor 1 has us going back by the plant
- Customer 1 – Vendor 2 = 77 miles
- Customer 2 – Vendor 2 = 82 miles
- Customer 3 – Vendor 2 has us going back by the plant
- Customer 4 – Vendor 2 = 57 miles
- Customer 5 – Vendor 2 = 48 miles.

Next, starting with the shortest, let's start allocating out the trips. The procedure would follow:

- Customer 4 – Vendor 1 – 2 trips – that satisfies all of Customer 4 and half of Vendor 1.
- Customer 5 – Vendor 2 – 2 trips – that satisfies Customer 5 and one third of Vendor 2.
- Customer 4 – Vendor 2 is skipped because Customer 4 is already satisfied.
- Customer 3 – Vendor 1 – 1 trip – that satisfies Customer 3 but still leaves us one short on Vendor 1.
- Customer 2 – Vendor 1 – 1 trip – that satisfies Vendor 1 but still leaves Customer 5 short by 5.
- Customer 1 – Vendor 2 – 3 trips – that satisfies Customer 1 but still leaves Vendor 2 one short.
- Customer 2 – Vendor 2 – 1 trip – that finishes off the requirements for Vendor 2 and only leaves.

Customer 2 in need of 4 additional shipments.

- Customer 2 – 4 trips – this satisfies all the deliveries.

Using the same procedure, we will now solve the second example (Example 2.2). In this case we have more vendor pick-ups than we have customer shipments. The process would be to again look at the shortest combined shipment first:

- Customer 4 – Vendor 1 – 1 trip – that satisfies all of Customer 4 and part of Vendor 1.
- Customer 5 – Vendor 2 – 1 trip – that satisfies Customer 5 and part of Vendor 2.
- Customer 4 – Vendor 2 is skipped because Customer 4 is already satisfied.
- Customer 3 – Vendor 1 – 3 trips – that satisfies part of customer 3 and all of Vendor 1.
- Customer 2 – Vendor 1 is skipped because Vendor 1 is satisfied.
- Customer 1 – Vendor 2 – 2 trips – that satisfies Customer 1 but still leaves Vendor 2 three short.
- Customer 2 – Vendor 2 is skipped because there are no shipments to Customer 2.
- Customer 3 – Vendor 2 has us going by the plant so we are left with:
    - Customer 3 – 1 trip
    - Vendor 2 – 3 trips.

Chart. 9.4. Trips Required for Example (3)

Example 3.1
Customer 1 – 3 loads at 30 %, 20 %, and 70 %
Customer 2 – 2 loads at 90 % and 70 %
Customer 3 – 1 load at 40 %
Customer 4 – 3 loads at 50 %, 20 %, and 80 %
Customer 5 – 4 loads at 100 %, 20 %, 40 %, and 50 %

Example 3.2
Customer 1 – 3 loads at 30 %, 20 %, and 70 %
Customer 2 – 2 loads at 90 % and 170 %
Customer 3 – 1 load at 60 %
Customer 4 – 3 loads at 50 %, 20 %, and 30 %
Customer 5 – 4 loads at 100 %, 30 %, 30 %, and 50 %

(3) Distribution where multiple customers are serviced during the same trip

In the remaining examples I will not go into the same level of detail shown previously. I leave it to the reader to work out the results using the same techniques already demonstrated. I will again use two examples to demonstrate the scheduling function. The data for these examples is in Chart 9.4. For Example 3.1 the final trip schedule is:

- Customer 1 – 1 trip
- Customer 2 – 1 trip
- Customer 4 – 1 trip
- Customer 5 – 3 trips
- Customer 1 then Customer 2 – 1 trip
- Customer 3 then Customer 4 – 1 trip.

For Example 3.2 the final trip schedule is:

- Customer 1 – 1 trip
- Customer 2 – 2 trips
- Customer 3 – 1 trip
- Customer 4 – 1 trip
- Customer 5 – 1 trip
- Customer 1 then Customer 5 – 1 trip
- Customer 2 then Customer 5 – 1 trip.

Chart 9.5. Trips Required for Example (4)

Example 4.1
Customer 1 – 3 loads at 30 %, 20 %, and 70 %
Customer 2 – 2 loads at 90 % and 70 %
Customer 3 – 1 load at 40 %
Customer 4 – 3 loads at 50 %, 20 %, and 80 %
Customer 5 – 4 loads at 100 %, 20 %, 40 %, and 50 %
Vendor 1 – 4 loads at 90 %, 20 %, 60 %, and 50 %
Vendor 2 – 5 loads at 30 %, 40 %, 50 %, 60 %, and 70 %

Example 4.2
Customer 1 – 3 loads at 30 %, 20 %, and 70 %
Customer 2 – 2 loads at 90 % and 170 %

Chart 9.5. (continued)

Customer 3 – 1 load at 60 % Customer 4 – 3 loads at 50 %, 20 %, and 30 % Customer 5 – 4 loads at 100 %, 30 %, 30 %, and 50 % Vendor 1 – 4 loads at 90 %, 20 %, 60 %, and 70 % Vendor 2 – 5 loads at 30 %, 40 %, 50 %, 80 %, and 70 %

(4) Distribution with multiple customers and multiple backhauls per trip

Again I will demonstrate this process with two examples. The data can be seen in Chart 9.5.

We start with Example 4.1 where the final shipping loads are:

- C5 + V2 – 3 loads
- C4 + V1 – 1 load
- C2 + V1 – 1 load
- C3 + C4 + V1 – 1 load
- C1 – 1 load
- C1 + C2 – 1 load.

Moving forward with our second example (Example 4.2), the final shipping loads are:

- C5 + V2 – 1 load
- C4 + V1 – 1 load
- C3 + V1 – 1 load
- C2 + V1 – 1 load
- C1 + V2 – 1 load
- C1 + C5 + V2 – 1 load
- C2 – 1 load
- C2 + C5 – 1 load.

This modeling process can get very complex. For example, we may have combinations of shipments to three or more customers and pickups from three or more vendors. The procedure remains the same, but the number of options can become obnoxious.

(5) Mixtures of loads to customers

Sometimes we have different trucks, like a coil truck and a bar stock truck. The bar stock truck cannot haul coils but the coil truck can haul either. The scheduling procedure would be that we would schedule the most restricted materials first, which in this case would be the coils. Then, once we have the coils planned out, we would fill out the coil loads with bar stock and plan the remaining bar stock loads. The procedure is the same as in the process described previously except that we only deal with a limited number of options initially (coils) before we open the scheduling process up to all categories. Then follow the procedure in the previous sections (whichever one fits).

(6) Sectoring

If we have numerous shipments (customers) or many of vendors, calculating the mileage between each becomes unreasonable. Sectoring becomes an important tool. Break your map up into delivery sectors. Everyone within a sector is considered to be at the same delivery point. Deliveries would be scheduled by sector just like if the sector was a customer.

(7) Cost or mile optimization

Sometimes cost is more important than mileage, even though they are usually proportionally the same. Sometimes the type of truck required, or tolls, etc. could make a significant difference in which route we would prefer to use. In that case our mileage chart should be made out as a trip cost chart. All other calculations would work the same as if it were mileage that we were working with.

Freight / Carrier Analysis

Freight and carrier analysis is an attempt to stay on top of the quality of shipments to customers. In this process we track shipping costs, breakages, and timing. We want to make sure the customer gets what they want, when they want it, and in good condition. The process starts with the collection of data. As shipments are made from the shipping dock, information about the date of the shipment and the shipper is recorded on the shipping document (see step 5 at the start of this section of this chapter). One copy of this document goes with the materials being shipped, and a second goes back to the Order Department reporting to them that the shipment has gone out.

A reporting process needs to be set up so that we can track when the product actually arrived at the customer, and if it arrived undamaged. This can be a report filled out by our truckers, if we have our own trucks, or by our carrier, or by the customer. There are many ways to get this information, but the best method for you depends on how many customers you have and what your shipping methods are.

The arrival and condition information is collected with the shipment information. Some companies have a Traffic Department which would handle the data collection and reporting process. Other companies would do this function in the Sales Department as part of the sales reporting process since the completed order information is routed through sales anyway. Other companies may do this reporting process in the Accounting Department. Regardless of where the reporting process occurs, the data needs to be collected and assimilated into a report. On this document we record some information found on the order form:

- Customer Name and Number
- Due Date
- Order Number
- Shipping Costs

Some information is recorded from the shipping document:

- Date Shipped
- Carrier
- Load / Weight Information

Some information comes from the carrier or the customer:

- Arrival Date
- Damage Report

This data collection and analysis process can be done very nicely on some type of computerized data base system. It doesn't need to be a large system and it can be the same system you used for sales analysis.

After the data has been collected over a period of time (usually a month), the data is transferred to the analysis reports. Not all of these reports may be appropriate for you. This is just a suggestion of the types of reports that can be generated. Then a *Freight and Carrier Damage Analysis Report* can be generated which checks on shipment quality. Additionally a *Shipments By Carrier Report* which shows how much we use a particular carrier is generated. This may be important if we are concerned about favoritism or in negotiating a reduced carrier rate. Another report that can be generated is the *Shipments To Customers Made By Different Carriers Report.* This is helpful in analyzing customer complaints about shipments. It also helps us recognize preferences. One last report, which shows the number of days late (the difference between due date and arrival date) for a particular customer / carrier is also useful. This also helps in handling complaints.

With the freight/carrier analysis reports we can get a better control of freight costs, timing, quality, and complaints. This analysis is not necessary on a continuing basis, like the sales analysis is, but it is helpful to do every once in a while to check on potential problem situations.

DRP Summary

Distribution Requirements Planning is a planning tool that either you don't need at all, or you can't live without it. Any company involved in a global supply chain would definitely fall into the second category. If you don't need it now, at least remember it for some future time when you may find it valuable.

Summary

Logistics (routing) and distribution planning are the largest piece of lead time in the entire supply chain system. All of this time is non-value-added. Therefore it is critical to manage this process extremely well, especially since in an international setting the number of steps in a logistics process increases dramatically. Additionally, with customs delays and numerous freight changes throughout the network there are more delays internationally than domestically. As a result, international operations management becomes, in large part, the management of the logistics and distribution supply chain.

Class Assignments

1) PB, Inc. has a logistics and warehousing problem that needs your attention. How would you make this operation more efficient, in light of the international transport of goods that occurs? Would you reorganize the warehousing process in any way?
2) Go to Appendix 9.1 and formulate the routing problems using linear programming. Be prepared for some surprises in the results that I didn't tell you about.

References

Dornier, Philippe-Pierre, Ricardo Ernst, Michel Fender, and Panos Kouvelis, *Global Operations and Logistics*, John Wiley & Sons, Inc., New York, 1998.

Handfield, Robert B. and Ernest L. Nichols, Jr., *Introduction to Supply Chain Management*, Prentice Hall, Upper Saddle River, New Jersey, 1999.

Plenert, Gerhard, *The Plant Operations Handbook*, Business 1 IRWIN, 1993, Homewood, Ill.

Appendix 9.1
Linear Programming Formulations of the Routing Problems

This appendix will give you the linear-integer programming formulations for the examples listed in this chapter. Once in place, these formulations will facilitate rapid calculations of the optimal routings. For an additional discussion of linear programming go to any introductory Operations Management text.

Each of the models in this appendix are calculated using a linear-integer programming package where the variables were specified as continuous, binary, or as integers. A continuous variable will allow any value to be calculated. An integer variable will only allow whole numbers to be calculated. A field specified as a binary number will only allow "0" or "1" to be calculated. Either it is used or it isn't. In our examples, we use binary variables to identify whether or not a trip is made. We also use integer variables to calculate how many trips are made. And we use continuous variables to calculate what percentage of any particular trip is wasted. Specifying each variable is important because you can't make a fraction of a trip to a customer. Either you go there, or you don't go there.

We walked through a manual procedure for each of the calculations that we are going to do using linear programming. The manual procedure is not "optimal", which means it isn't guaranteed to be the perfect answer. However, it does give a fairly good schedule. As we go through the linear-integer programming solutions, we will occasionally find that slightly better solutions exist. However, we do not want to do the same calculation process by hand that the computer goes through if we are going to do the scheduling manually. It would take us all day to work up a schedule. In most cases the manually calculated answer is adequate. But, if you want the "optimal" answer, use liner-integer programming.

I will be referring back to previous headings used earlier in the chapter. I will use the same heading now to identify the same examples recalculated with linear-integer programming.

(2) Distribution where there are customers and backhauls but each is a full load trip

The examples for this analysis are found in Chart 9.3. The linear programming formulation for the first example (Example 2.1) would be:

Objective Function:

Minimize: 50 XC1 + 40 XC2 + 40 XC3 + 30 XC4 + 30 XC5 + 26 XV1 + 44 XV2 + 77 XC1V2 + 73 XC2V1 + 82 XC2V2 + 58 XC3V1 + 35 XC4V1 + 57 XC4V2 + 48 XC5V2

Constraints:

XC1V2 + XC1 = 3
XC2V1 + XC2V2 + XC2 = 6
XC3V1 + XC3 = 1
XC4V1 + XC4V2 + XC4 = 2
XC5V2 + XC5 = 2
XC2V1 + XC3V1 + XC4V1 + XV1 = 4
XC1V2 + XC2V2 + XC4V2 + XC5V2 + XV2 = 6

Where the "X" variables represent how many times each trip is made. For example, XC1 is how many trips we made to Customer 1 only. XC1V2 is how many trips we made to Customer 1, then at the same time did a pick up at Vendor 2.

The 50, 40, 40, 30, . . . values in the objective function are the number of miles each trip takes.

The seven constraints count the number of times we went to each customer or vendor. For example, XC1V2 + XC1 = 3 says that the number of times we did the trip to Customer 1 followed by a pick up at Vendor 2, plus the number of times we just went to Customer 1 and nowhere else, has to add up to 3 trips total.

After processing this model through the linear programming processor where each variable was specified as an integer, we come up with the following solution:

XC1 = 0
XC2 = 5

XC3 = 0
XC4 = 0
XC5 = 0
XV1 = 1
XV2 = 0
XC1V2 = 3
XC2V1 = 0
XC2V2 = 1
XC3V1 = 1
XC4V1 = 2
XC4V2 = 0
XC5V2 = 2

This solution tells us that we need to make the trip from Customer 1 to Vendor 2 three times, etc. When we compare this solution to the one we arrived at earlier we see three differences, which are as follows:

Trip	*Manual*	*LP program*
C2	4 (160 miles)	5 (200 miles)
V1	0	1 (26 miles)
C2V1	1 (73 miles)	0
TOTALS	(233 miles)	(226 miles).

The computer solution was better than the manual system by 7 miles which is relatively insignificant when compared to the 763 total miles traveled (using the computer's values). However, if you want optimality, use the computer.

The second example (Example 2.2) would have the following formulation:

Objective Function:

Minimize: 50 XC1 + 40 XC2 + 40 XC3 + 30 XC4 + 30 XC5 + 26 XV1 + 44 XV2 + 77 XC1V2 + 73 XC2V1 + 82 XC2V2 + 58 XC3V1 + 35 XC4V1 + 57 XC4V2+ 48 XC5V2

Constraints:

XC1V2 + XC1 = 2
XC2V1 + XC2V2 + XC2 = 0
XC3V1 + XC3 = 4
XC4V1 + XC4V2 + XC4 = 1
XC5V2 + XC5 = 1
XC2V1 + XC3V1 + XC4V1 + XV1 = 4
XC1V2 + XC2V2 + XC4V2 + XC5V2 + XV2 = 6

Note that the only difference between this formulation and the previous formulation is in the total number of trips made in the constraints. If you formulate a linear programming model for your situation, this would also be true in your case. You wouldn't need to formulate the model each time. You set it up once, then simply modify the number of trips required and solve the model.

After processing this model through the linear programming processor where each variable was specified as an integer, we come up with the following solution:

XC1 = 0
XC2 = 0
XC3 = 0
XC4 = 0
XC5 = 0
XV1 = 0
XV2 = 2
XC1V2 = 2
XC2V1 = 0
XC2V2 = 0
XC3V1 = 4
XC4V1 = 0
XC4V2 = 1
XC5V2 = 1

When we compare this solution to the one we arrived at earlier using the manual process we see five differences, which are as follows:

Trip	Manual	LP program
C3	1 (40 miles)	0
V2	3 (132 miles)	2 (88 miles)
C3V1	3 (174 miles)	4 (232 miles)
C4V1	1 (35 miles)	0
C4V2	0	1 (57 miles)
TOTALS	(381 miles)	(377 miles).

The computer solution was better than the manual system by 4 miles which is relatively insignificant when compared to the 579 total miles traveled (using the computer's values).

(3) Distribution where multiple customers are serviced during the same trip

I have again taken the data from the previous examples (Chart 9.4) and used it to formulate a linear-integer program. Below is the actual formulation of the problem worked out in detail using a computer package. This formulation, as a linear program, would take about 30 seconds to run. But that would give us fractional results and it is impossible to make a half a trip to a customer. Either you go to the customer or you don't. Therefore, some of these variables are specified as binary and some as integer. Unfortunately, linear-integer programming runs much slower than strict linear programming. The formulation is:

Objective Function:

Minimize: 50C1 + 40C2 +40C3 + 30C4 + 30C5 + 62C12 + 73C13 + 61C15 + 66C25 + 65C34 + 54C45

Constraints:

(1) ab.3C1L1S1 + .2C1L2S1 + .7C1L3S1 – 1C1S1 + 1C1B1 = 0

(2) ab.3C1L1S2 + .2C1L2S2 + .7C1L3S2 – 1C1S2 – 1C1B2 = 0

(3) ab1C1 – 1C1S1 – 1C1S2 = 0

(4) ab.9C2L1S1 + 7C2L2S1 – 1C2S1 + 1CB1 = 0

(5) ab.9C2L1S2 + 7C2L2S2 – 1C2S2 + 1CB2 = 0

(6) ab1C2 – 1C2S1 – 1C2S2 = 0
(7) .4C3L1S1 – 1C3S1 + 1C3B1 = 0
(8) ab1C3 – 1C3S1 = 0
(9) ab.5C4L1S1 + .2C4L2S1 + 8C4L3S1 + 1C4B1 = 0
(10) ab.5C4L1S2 + .2C4L2S2 + 8C4L3S2 + 1C4B2 = 0
(11) ab1C4 – 1C4S1 – 1C4S2 = 0
(12) ab1C5L1S1 + .2C5L2S1 + .4C5L3S1 + 5C5L4S1 – 1C5S1 + 1C5B1 = 0
(13) ab1C5L1S2 + .2C5L2S2 + .4C5L3S2 + 5C5L4S2 – 1C5S2 + 1C5B2 = 0
(14) ab1C5L1S3 + .2C5L2S3 + .4C5L3S3 + 5C5L4S3 – 1C5S3 + 1C5B3 = 0
(15) ab1C5 – 1C5S1 – 1C5S2 – 1C5S3 = 0
(16) ab.3C12L1S1 + .2C12L2S1 + .7C12L3S1 + .9C12L4S1 + .7C12L5S1 – 1C12S1 + 1C12B1 = 0
(17) ab1C12 – 1C12S1 = 0
(18) ab.3C13L1S1 + .2C13L2S1 + .7C13L3S1 + .4C13S1 – 1C13S1 + 1C13B1 = 0
(19) ab1C13 – 1C13S1 = 0
(20) ab.3C15L1S1 + .2C15L2S1 + .7C15L3S1 + 1C15L4S1 + .2C15L5S1 + .4C15L6S1 + .5C15L7S1 – 1C15S1 + 1C15B1 = 0
(21) ab.3C15L1S2 + .2C15L2S2 + .7C15L3S2 + 1C15L4S2 + .2C15L5S2 + .4C15L6S2 + .5C15L7S2 – 1C15S2 + 1C15B2 = 0
(22) ab.3C15L1S3 + .2C15L2S3 + .7C15L3S3 + 1C15L4S3 + .2C15L5S3 + .4C15L6S3 + .5C15L7S2 – 1C15S3 + 1C15B3 = 0
(23) ab1C15 – 1C15S1 – 1C15S2 – 1C15S3 = 0
(24) ab.9C25L1S1 – .7C25L2S1 + 1C25LS31 + .2C25L4S1 + .4C25L5S1 + .5C25L6S1 – 1C25S1 + 1C25B1 = 0
(25) ab1C25 – 1C25S1 = 0
(26) ab.4C34L1S1 + .5C34L2S1 + .2C34L3S1 + .8C34L4S1 – 1C34S1 + 1C34B1 = 0
(27) ab1C34 – 1C34S1 = 0
(28) ab.5C45L1S1 + .2C45L2S1 + .8C45L3S1 + 1C45L4S1 + .2C45L5S1 + .4C45L6S1 + .5C45L7S1 – 1C45S1 + 1C45B1 = 0
(29) ab.5C45L1S2 + .2C45L2S2 + .8C45L3S2 + 1C45L4S2 +

.2C45L5S2 + .4C45L6S2 + .5C45L7S2 – 1C45S2 + 1C45B2 = 0

(30) ab.5C45L1S3 + .2C45L2S3 + .8C45L3S3 + 1C45L4S3 + .2C45L5S3 + .4C45L6S3 + .5C45L7S3 – 1C45S3 + 1C45B3 = 0

(31) ab1C45 – 1C45S1 – 1C45S2 – 1C45S3 = 0

(32) ab1C1L1S1 + 1C1L1S2 + 1C12L1S1 + 1C13L1S1 + 1C15L1S1 + 1C15L1S2 + 1C15L1S3 = 1

(33) ab1C1L2S1 + 1C1L2S2 + 1C12L2S1 + 1C13L2S1 + 1C15L2S1 + 1C15L2S2 + 1C15L2S3 = 1

(34) ab1C1L3S1 + 1C1L3S2 + 1C12L3S1 + 1C13L3S1 + 1C15L3S1 + 1C15L3S2 + 1C15L3S3 = 1

(35) ab1C2L1S1 + 1C2L1S2 + 1C12L4S1 + 1C25L1S1 = 1

(36) ab1C2L2S1 + 1C2L2S2 + 1C12L5S1 + 1C25L2S1 = 1

(37) ab1C3L1S1 + 1C13L4S1 + 1C34L1S1 = 1

(38) ab1C4L1S1 + 1C4L2S2 + 1C34L2S1 + 1C45L1S1 + 1C45L1S2 + 1C45L1S3 = 1

(39) ab1C4L2S1 + 1C4L2S2 + 1C34L3S1 + 1C45L2S1 + 1C45L2S2 + 1C45L2S3 = 1

(40) ab1C4L3S1 + 1C4L3S2 + 1C34L4S1 + 1C45L3S1 + 1C45L3S2 + 1C45L3S3 = 1

(41) ab1C5L1S1 + 1C5L1S2 + 1C5L1S3 + 1C15L4S1 + 1C15L4S2 + 1C15L4S3 + 1C25L3S1 + 1C45L4S1 + 1C45L4S2 + 1C45L4S3 = 1

(42) ab1C5L2S1 + 1C5L2S2 + 1C5L2S3 + 1C15L5S1 + 1C15L5S2 + 1C15L5S3 + 1C25L4S1 + 1C45L5S1 + 1C45L5S2 + 1C45L5S3 = 1

(43) ab1C5L3S1 + 1C5L3S2 + 1C5L3S3 + 1C15L6S1 + 1C15L6S2 + 1C15L6S3 + 1C25L5S1 + 1C45L6S1 + 1C45L6S2 + 1C45L6S3 = 1

(44) ab1C5L4S1 + 1C5L4S2 + 1C5L4S3 + 1C15L7S1 + 1C15L7S2 + 1C15L7S3 + 1C25L6S1 + 1C45L7S1 + 1C45L7S2 + 1C45L7S3 = 1

Integer:
C1, C2, C3, C4, C5, C12, C13, C15, C25, C34, C45

Binary:
C1L1S1, C1L2S1, C1L3S1L C1S1L C1L1S2, C1L2S2, C1L3S3,

C1S2, C2L1S1, C2L2S1, C2S1, C2L1S2, C2L2S2, C2S2, C3L, 1S1, C3S1, C4L1S1, C4L2S1, C4L3S1, C4S1, C4L1S2, C4L2S2, C4L3S2, C4S2, C5L1S1, C5L2S1, C5L3S1, C5L4S1, C5S1, C5L1S2, C5L2S2, C5L3S2, C5L4S2, C5S2, C5L1S3, C5L2S3, C5L3S3, C5L4S3, C5S3, C12L1S1, C12L2S1, C12L3S1, C12L4S1, C12L5S1, C12S1, C13L1S1, C13L1S1, C13L2S1, C13L3S1, C13L4S1, C13S1, C15L1S1, C15L2S1, C15L3S1, C15L4S1, C15L5S1, C15L6S1, C15L7S1, C15L5S3, C15L6S3, C15L7S3, C15S3, C25L1S1, C25L2S1, C25L3S1, C25L4S1, C25L5S1, C25L6S1, C25S1, C34L1S1, C34L2S1, C34L3S1, C34L4S1, C34S1, C45L1S1, C45L2S1, C45L3S1, C45L4S1, C45L5S1, C45L6S1, C45L7S1, C45S1, C45L1S2, C45L2S2, C45L3S2, C45L4S2, C45L5S2, C45L6S2, C45L7S2, C45S2, C45L1S3, C45L2S3, C45L3S3, C45L4S3, C45L5S3, C45L6S3, C45L7S3, C45S3

The variables are defined as follows:

C1 = a round trip to Customer 1 (integer)
C12 = a trip to Customer 1, then to Customer 2, then back (integer)
C1L1S1 = Customer 1, load 1, shipment 1 (binary)
C1B1 = Customer 1, buffer 1 (continuous)
C1S1 = Customer 1, shipment 1 (binary).

The objective function attempts to minimize the total traveled miles. The variables in the objective function are an integer count of how many times each of these trips are made. The constraints come in two groups. The first group is made up of constraints 1 through 31 (see Chart 9.6). Using constraint 1, 2, and 3 as an example, I will explain how these constraints work. These first three constraints are for Customer 1. It is impossible to do all the shipments to Customer 1 in one load, so we set up two shipments (constraints 1 and 2). In constraint 1 we identify each of the loads (.3, .2, and .7). By turning on (setting equal to 1) the value of C1L1S2 we are saying that this load (.3) should be shipped with shipment 1). The C1S1 in this equation turns on (equal to 1) if any one of the loads are shipped in shipment 1. The C1B1 is a buffer that shows how much of the loads are wasted. For example, if we ship the .2 and the .7 loads together, 10 % of the truck will be empty and C1B1 will equal .1. Constraint three counts how many C1 shipments are made by counting C1S1 and C1S2.

Starting with constraint 16 we are dealing with shipments to multiple customers. For example C12L1S1 says that for a customer 1 (C12L1S1) then customer 2 (C12L1S1) shipment we have .3 (see Constraint 16) of a load available for shipment and we are calling this Load 1 (C12L1S1) of Shipment 1 (C12L1S1). All the loads for Customer 1 and Customer 2 are available for shipment on this combined load.

Constraints 31 through 44 make sure that each load is shipped, and that it is shipped only once. In constraint 31, we track every time the .3 load for Customer 1 can be shipped, which occurs in C1L1S1, C1L1S2, or in the combined loads of C12L1S1, C13L1S1, C15L1S1, C15L1S2, or C15L1S3. The "=1" says that it can only be shipped (and must be shipped) once in one of these shipments.

Note that some shipments like C14 do not exist because it would be equivalent to shipping to C1 and then to C4. Also, the number of constraints that exist are dependent on how many possible combination loads can be made.

Now we know how to achieve the perfect computer solution from example 3.1. The final computer solution would be:

Customer 1 – one trip
Customer 2 – one trip
Customer 3 – one trip
Customer 4 – one trip
Customer 5 – two trips
Customer 1 then Customer 2 – one trip
Customer 4 then Customer 5 – one trip.

The differences between these results and those achieved manually are:

Trip	*Manual*	*LP program*
C1	1 (50 miles)	1 (50 miles)
C2	1 (40 miles)	1 (40 miles)
C3	0	1 (40 miles)
C4	1 (30 miles)	1 (30 miles)

C5	3 (96 miles)	2 (64 miles)
C12	1 (62 miles)	1 (62 miles)
C34	1 (65 miles)	0
C45	0	1 (54 miles)
TOTALS	(343 miles)	(340 miles).

The computer solution is an improvement over the manual system by 3 miles which is insignificant.

For Example 3.2 I will not be giving the formulation. It is for you to figure out. The final computer solution would be:

Customer 1 – one trip
Customer 2 – two trips
Customer 3 – one trip
Customer 4 – one trip
Customer 5 – three trips
Customer 1 then Customer 2 – one trip.

The differences between these results and those achieved manually are:

Trip	*Manual*	*LP program*
C1	1 (50 miles)	1 (50 miles)
C2	2 (80 miles)	2 (80 miles)
C3	1 (40 miles)	1 (40 miles)
C4	1 (30 miles)	1 (30 miles)
C5	1 (32 miles)	3 (96 miles)
C12	0	1 (62 miles)
C15	1 (61 miles)	0
C25	1 (66 miles)	0
TOTALS	(359 miles)	(358 miles).

The computer solution was better than the manual system by 1 mile which is relatively insignificant.

(4) Distribution with multiple customers and multiple backhauls per trip

The computer generated solution for the problem 4.1 is the following:

Customer 1 – one trip
Customer 2 – one trip
Customer 3 then Vendor 1 – one trip
Customer 4 then Vendor 1 – one trip
Customer 5 then Vendor 2 – two trips
Customer 1 and 2 then Vendor 2 – one trip
Customer 4 and 5 then Vendor 1 – one trip.

Generate the formulation to come up with these results. Comparing these results with the results we achieved manually we have the following results:

Trip	*Manual*	*LP program*
C1	1 (50 miles)	1 (50 miles)
C2	0	1 (40 miles)
C12	1 (62 miles)	0
C2V1	1 (73 miles)	0
C3V1	0	1 (58 miles)
C4V1	1 (35 miles)	1 (35 miles)
C5V2	3 (144 miles)	2 (96 miles)
C12V1	0	1 (95 miles)
C45V1	0	1 (59 miles)
C34V1	1 (70 miles)	0
TOTALS	(434 miles)	(433 miles).

The computer solution was better than the manual system by one mile.

Moving on to the second example (Example 4.2), the computer generated solution for the problem is the following:

Customer 1 – one trip
Customer 2 – two trips
Vendor 1 – one trip
Customer 3 then Vendor 1 – one trip
Customer 4 then Vendor 1 – one trip
Customer 5 then Vendor 2 – three trips
Customer 1 and 2 – one trip.

Comparing these results with the results we achieved manually we have the following results:

Trip	*Manual*	*LP program*
C1	0	1 (50 miles)
C2	1 (40 miles)	2 (80 miles)
C12	0	1 (62 miles)
C25	1 (66 miles)	0
V1	0	1 (26 miles)
C1V2	1 (77 miles)	0
C2V1	1 (73 miles)	0
C3V1	1 (58 miles)	1 (58 miles)
C4V1	1 (35 miles)	1 (35 miles)
C5V2	1 (48 miles)	3 (144 miles)
C15V2	1 (77 miles)	0
TOTALS	(474 miles)	(455 miles).

The computer solution was better than the manual system by 19 miles.

We now have examples of each of the linear-integer programming models that are needed in order to solve the routing and scheduling problems in this chapter.

10. Production/Location Decisions

This chapter will take a close look at the plant relocation issue. It will discuss the criteria utilized for making the relocation decision and the basis for the decision process. But first let's visit with PT, Inc.

PT, Inc.

PT, Inc. is a tool manufacturer in Portland, Oregon. They are part of a larger conglomerate of international tool manufacturing organizations. They have been extremely effective in their operations and demand has steadily increased. They are now concerned about capacity and they are considering shipping some of their more labor intensive products to be manufactured off-shore. However, they are struggling with the Union's reaction to the fear about loosing jobs. But, to send some of their more automated processes off-shore would require the relocation of large amounts of equipment and would drain value-added content away from the existing facility. The unions have made PT one of the highest labor cost operations in the area, and PT sees the relocation as a chance to reduce some of these costs. However, if they get the Union upset, they may end up with a shutdown, which would be even more costly to the overall process.

Since PT's mother organization already has facilities established in other parts of the world, it would be fairly easy to select a site close to one of these facilities and eliminate a lot of the infrastructure development that would go into a new facility. However, management is not convinced that they need the new capacity. They are hesitant because they don't want to be caught in a down-turn in business which would cost them even more with a second facility. Additionally, there are inherent costs associated with relocating a facility, such as materials movement costs, technical staff development (or movement), and the risks associated with countries that have government instabilities or poor infrastructures.

Now it's your turn. What would you do? Should PT take an optimistic perspective in expand local capacity, or should they go international to develop more capacity? How would you handle the unions? How would you decide where to locate a facility?

The Comparison of Facility Relocation Alternatives[1]

As discussed earlier and in more detail, manufacturing plants are relocated overseas for a number of reasons. In the United States the basis for plant relocations has primarily been labor cost or total cost. In Japan the value-added cost approach is being used. A new approach, the goal / critical resource based approach is gaining wide acceptance. This chapter will review various facility relocation alternatives and compare the advantages and disadvantages of each.

The term "relocation" will be used in the broad sense including both the removal of an existing facility, or the expansion of capacity by adding an additional facility. Internationally the reasons for relocation vary dramatically. Traditional models for relocation exist, however, they are seldom used. In the United States the primary basis for plant relocations is still labor cost or total cost. In Japan the value-added cost approach is being used although the total cost approach has also become very popular. Numerous other alternatives exist, however, a new approach, the goal / critical resource based approach, is gaining wide acceptance. This chapter will review the primary approaches for the facility relocation decision and compare the advantages and disadvantages of each.

1. A lot of the pieces of this segment of the chapter are taken from:
Plenert, Gerhard, "The Basis for Plant Relocations", *Advanced Manufacturing Technology,* March 1995, Pages 1-2.
Plenert, Gerhard, "Plant Relocation: How Decisions Are Made Today", *Industry Forum,* March 1994, Pages 1-3.

Traditional Location-Decision Analysis

Traditional text book location analysis models suggest that the selection of a facility location should be based on a strategy, such as:

- market position – close to the final customer
- production position – close to source of supply for the production facility
- intermediary position – at some midpoint between the customers and the suppliers (Hoover)

Numerous other models exist that focus on the market, the materials sourcing, or some type of midpoint of activity (Schmenner) (Coyle) (Greenhut). The models can get extremely sophisticated in an attempt to make sure all the variables are analyzed prior to a site location, which includes factors like quality, cost, labor rates, tax structure, building codes, etc. Often strategic issues like time-to-market considerations or order cycle-time considerations play an important role in the relocation decision process for these models.

Some relocation models evolve around an organizational behavior approach and get so complex that they incorporate a series of steps which include discussing the site location with various persons and setting up corporate teams for the decision making process. These models are appropriate and valuable in the over-all decision process. This chapter is not attempting to minimize the importance of these models. These models have already been thoroughly discussed in the referenced material and do not need to be redisplayed. This chapter focuses on the computational process that occurs, suggesting that the traditional basis for the calculation should change and should no longer be based on the labor cost or total cost solutions that many of the multi-step processes still incorporate.

The Labor Cost Approach

When utilizing the labor cost approach for the facility location decision, a corporation generally has their cost accounting books organized into three major categories; Materials, Labor, and Burden.[2] Burden is allocated as a component of product cost based on labor cost and often includes things like transportation and storage costs which should be included in the materials cost classification because it is a cost of receiving the materials. Labor is only looked at under the Direct Labor category, and Indirect Labor is included under Burden. Labor cost, when looked at in isolation, is compared to the labor cost of running the exact same plant in a reduced cost area, for example Mexico or Malaysia. The relocation of the plant shows some extremely significant cost advantages, when only direct labor is considered.

The fallacy of the labor cost strategy has been demonstrated in numerous situations. For example, in one situation, a plant was relocated from the United States to Mexico using the labor cost savings strategy.[3] The plant was used to manufacture automobile transmissions. The analysis showed significant labor cost savings even when twice and three times as many employees were used in the production process in Mexico. However, there was one transmission component, a gear that needed to be included in the transmission that had to be cut so precisely that there was an enormous amount of waste generated through errors and trial runs. The result was that it was less costly to ship the stamped product to Japan, have them cut the gear correctly, and ship the cut part back to Mexico where it was assembled into the transmission. Of course the transport to Japan, and the Japanese subcontractor costs, were not included in labor, rather they were broken up into the Materials and Burden category. Therefore, based on the labor costs strategy, the move to Mexico still looked like a good decision.

2. The labor cost approach is still the primary basis for financial/accounting decisions when it comes to plant relocations. (Betz) (Lee) (McClain) (Vonderembse)
3. Although this was an actual plant that is still in existence today (Plenert, 1990(c)) (Plenert, 1990(b)), the exact numbers could not be used because of proprietary reasons. However, the approximations used here are accurate enough to demonstrate the actual situation that occurred.

Chart 10.1. Cost Comparison for Plant Relocation Decision

	United States (amounts in $ 1,000 US)	*Mexico*
Direct Labor Costs	1,000	300
Materials Purchase Costs	3,000	3,000
Burden		
Indirect Labor Costs	1,000	750
Materials Transfer Costs	100	500
Materials Carrying Costs	100	1,500
Other	2,000	2,000
Total Cost	*7,200*	*8,050*

Approximating the numbers offers an example of how the labor cost decision was made. This example also demonstrates some of the shortcomings of the methodology. The amounts in Chart 10.1 are in $ 1,000. From this relocation example, utilizing direct labor cost, the relocation was a good idea because labor cost was reduced by 70 percent. Even when considering total labor cost, it was still a good idea, reducing the cost by about half from $ 2,000,000 to $ 1,050,000. However, when considering some of the other cost elements, like materials transfer costs, the inadequacy of the labor cost approach appears. For example, materials transfer costs went up five times because the transfer of materials from Michigan down to the middle of Mexico and back again was considerably more expensive than a transfer of materials within plants that are all in Michigan. Additionally, the materials carrying costs went up by fifteen times because the transfer, which used to take a few days now took as much as a couple months due to the hold-ups at the border. Some of these border delays have been reduced by NAFTA, in the case of Mexico, but the delays still exist for most other parts of the world.

In conclusion, the direct labor cost approach to plant relocations is still very popular because it is so easy to do. Unfortunately, it is highly inadequate. Nearly any of the other approaches would be more accurate.

The Total Cost Approach

The total cost approach works similar to the labor cost approach. It, similarly, has places to hide the true cost differences. This approach uses the total cost of operation of the plant as the basis for the decision.[4] This cost includes Labor, Materials, and the directly identifiable Burden Costs that can be specifically associated with the operation of the plant. Allocated costs coming from corporate sources are not included. This would mean that the costs of transport and storage of materials that are in route between the plant and other locations can often be buried. However, the total cost approach does tend to focus on a more complete cost of the plant relocation in that it looks at more of the cost elements.

An example of an abuse of this system can be found again in a plant relocation to Mexico. Materials that were in route to the plant were often held up at the border for long periods of time. The financing cost of carrying this inventory was never included in the total cost of the plant operations. Only the inventory that was on-site in the plant was part of the plant operating costs. The in-route inventory costs were buried into the corporate burden account and allocated across all plants. A numerical example would be helpful. Prior to the Mexico plant, the amount of materials in route to the plant at any point in time equaled $1,000,000 and took 5 days to ship. It cost a ten percent rate of financing for the money tied up in this inventory. Because of the border crossing, the materials used in the new Mexico plant now spent approximately two and one-half

4. The total cost approach is advocated by many of the newer text writers who are trying to separate themselves from the narrowness of the labor cost approach (Betz) (Lee) (McClain) (Vonderembse). However, the similarities of the two techniques still carry many of the same inherent problems. For example, the Activity Based Costing approach to total cost analysis has become a data obsessive methodology for addressing the total cost approach (Plenert,1995). The problem has become so severe that entirely new accounting systems are being developed in an attempt to look at a broader, non-labor-cost approach to the analysis process (Berliner). In other areas, there have been direct attacks against the labor cost approach in favor of a more operating cost oriented approach (Goldratt, 1986(a)).

months in route (75 days) or 15 times as long. This meant that the cost of financing the inventory increased from $ 100,000 per year to $ 1,500,000 per year, which had a direct effect on product cost and profitability. However, these are corporate costs, not plant costs, and the decision to relocate the plant still appeared "on the books" to be the correct decision.

Chart 10.2. The Total Cost Model

	United States	*Mexico*
	(amounts in $ 1,000 US)	
Costs Directly Identified With The Plant Operation		
Direct Labor Costs	1,000	300
Materials Purchase Costs	3,000	3,000
Burden		
Indirect Labor Costs	1,000	750
Other	2,000	2,000
Total Operating Cost	*7,000*	*6,050*
Corporate Costs Not Directly Tied To The Plant Operation		
Burden		
Materials Transfer Costs	100	500
Materials Carrying Costs	100	1,500
Overall Total Cost	*7,200*	*8,050*

Quantifying this example in Chart 10.2 we would see (the amounts are in $ 1,000) that utilizing the Total Operating Costs for the plant would suggest that the plant relocation is a cost effective move. However, when the materials transport costs are included into the Total Cost, then the plant relocation wasn't such a good decision after all.

Other examples of abuses of the total cost system include situations where the receipt of the product to the plant is delayed by calling a shipper at the border and asking him to take more time on the shipment so as to keep the inventory costs in the corporate cost column rather than in the plant cost books. Again, in the total cost approach, as in the labor cost approach, there are hidden costs that distort the true cost of a plant relocation.

The Value Added Approach

The value added approach has received a lot of interest primarily because the Japanese favor this approach and use it to improve their economy.[5] In this approach the product is broken down into its components. It is analyzed for the cost of manufacturing each of these components, and then each cost is compared with the free market price of this component. A selection of those components that have the most value added benefit is made and these components are used for internal manufacturing. The remaining, lower value added content items are subcontracted out, usually to other countries.

Illustrating the value added approach, suppose that a company manufactures a product X which has components R, S, and T. These items have the breakdown shown in Chart 10.3 (the manufacturing cost of X equals the free market price of R, S, and T plus the labor cost).[6] From this it is easy to identify that the highest value added return in terms of absolute dollars comes from product X, the second is product T. Looking at it from the Value Ratio (value added divided by manufacturing cost) shows us that the most value added benefit comes from product T, the second is product X with a close third in product R. The difference is that The Value Added in absolute dollars maximizes profits while the Value Ratio maximizes return on investment. This example would suggest that X and T be kept in house, and that subcontracting out, most likely to some developing country, products R and S would be the best move.

5. The Japanese utilize a form of value added economics that follows the procedures discussed in this section (Karatsu) (Lu) (Shingo).
6. The term "investment" refers primarily to the manufacturing cost investments which include the materials, labor, and machinery elements. "Investment", in this context, is not treated the same as in financial terms where investment refers to some type of financial injection into the process.

Chart 10.3. Value Added Approach

Product	*Manufacturing Cost*	*Free Market Selling Price*	*Value Added*	*Value Ratio*
X	$ 40	$ 50	$ 10	.25
R	$ 10	$ 12	$ 2	.2
S	$ 10	$ 11	$ 1	.1
T	$ 10	$ 15	$ 5	.5

In the plant relocation decision, which often results in the loss of some control of the production process, the focus would be on relocating R and S while keeping tight control over X and T. This would maximize internal corporate return on investment, which, in the end, refers to both the manufacturing resource investment as well as the financial investment.

In the value added approach, plants are not relocated because of potential operating cost savings. Rather, plants are relocated so that additional productive capacity can be gained off shore for minimal value added products, thereby opening up capacity at home for the production of higher value added content products in the future. The decision then becomes a matter of which products or components should be relocated, and the selection is made based on the value added contribution of the product or component.

Contribution Analysis Approach

Another technique that is often used to determine optimal product mixes is contribution analysis.[7] This process evaluates the contribution of each product and divides this by the amount of resources utilized in order to generate its contribution. This calculation determines the contribution of each product per unit of resource utilized and suggests the optimal location for the manufacture of each of

7. There are numerous explanations of the contribution approach. Perhaps one of the best is found in (Monroe). Other discussions based on this approach can be found in (Hamelman) (Lambert).

the products. This process is also used when trying to limit the units produced because of some capacity limitations. In this case producing those products that generate the maximum contribution first would be the optimal recommended solution. There are numerous mathematical models that have demonstrated this process. Linear Programming and Optimized Production Technology (OPT) or Theory of Constraints (TOC) are the commonly known contribution optimizers.[8]

In analyzing plant relocations, contribution margin would be analyzed on a comparative basis. For example, producing a particular product in any of two locations would suggest the evaluation of which location offered the best contribution per resource unit utilized. Allocation of the production of each product in the most appropriate location would then occur.

The contribution approach has some strong similarities to the value added approach, the primary difference being that the products with the highest contribution would always be "kept at home" in the value added approach. Whereas, the contribution approach tends to look at all locations as equally viable.

Chart 10.4. Contribution Approach

Location A	*Product 1*	*Product 2*
Contribution Per Unit	$ 5.00	$ 7.00
Resources Required Per Unit	2.00 hrs.	4.00 hrs.
Contribution Per Resource Unit	$ 2.50	$ 1.75
Location B	*Product 1*	*Product 2*
Contribution Per Unit	$ 5.00	$ 7.00
Resources Required Per Unit	1.50 hrs.	5.00 hrs.
Contribution Per Resource Unit	$ 3.33	$ 1.40

8. The Optimized Production Technology (OPT) / Theory of Constraints (TOC) concepts have become extremely popular and can be considered in the following publications (Goldratt,1986(a),1986(b), 1990(a),1990(b)) (Johnson) (Best). The relationship between OPT and Linear Programming is explored in the articles (Plenert,1993(a),1993(b)).

A numerical example of the contribution approach is shown in Chart 10.4. Here the contribution approach would suggest that the comparative advantage for producing Product 1 would be at Location B, and that Product 2 should be produced at Location A. However, often the approach is to attempt to decide where to locate a single plant that would produce both products. In this case, contribution per resource unit is analyzed against demand to determine which location would offer the optimal over-all contribution. In this case, the calculation would proceed like the example in Chart 10.5. Based on the over-all contribution, Location A offers $ 77,500 and Location B offers $ 75,333. The more profitable location would be Location A.

Chart 10.5. The Contribution Approach Example 2

Location A	*Product 1*	*Product 2*
Contribution Per Resource Unit	$ 2.50	$ 1.75
Demand	10,000 units	30,000 units
Over-all Contribution	$ 25,000	$ 52,500
Location B	*Product 1*	*Product 2*
Contribution Per Resource Unit	$ 3.33	$ 1.40
Demand	10,000 units	30,000 units
Over-all Contribution	$ 33,333	$ 42,000

In the case where capacity limitations occur, for example, if restrictions prevented us from producing products at both locations, but neither location has sufficient capacity to produce the entire demand, then a tool could be utilized like Linear Programming which would maximize profitability while attempting to fully utilize capacity. Linear Programming would calculate a product mix for each location and would then show the profitability for the calculated product mix. It would then be a simple matter of seeing which location would generate the most profitability and then selecting that location.

The contribution approach varies from the value added approach in that the relocation occurs primarily when there is a shortage in capacity. In the value added approach, the relocation is part of the over-all strategy to keep low value added plants off Japanese soil whenever strategically possible and focuses on the development of more concentrated value added products within the country.

The Goal / Critical Resource Based Approach

The goal based approach starts by identifying the goal of the corporation.[9] Once the goal is identified, the next step is to try to identify which resource is the most critical in achieving that goal. Knowing the critical resource allows the calculation to determine whether a plant relocation will make a significant difference in the effective use of the critical resource.

The first step is the identification of what the goal of the organization is. Some popular possibilities, as previously discussed in Chapter 3, would include:

- Financial
- Operational
- Employee Based
- Customer Based

Financial and operational strategies tend to be short term and most commonly occur in Western cultures. Employee and customer based strategies tend to be the long term, Baldrige and Deming award winning strategies.

The selection of a goal is important because, as discussed earlier in this book, this goal determines the critical resource of the factory. Once the resources have been listed (all with a contribution of more than one percent) then an analysis of their contribution towards the

9. The critical resource approach is discussed in numerous articles and books including (Plenert,1993(c),1988,1989,1995) (Monroe) (Hamelman).

goal can occur utilizing *Activity Based Costing.*[10] This process looks at all resources. After the contribution of each resource is evaluated, using *ABC Analysis* (also called the *Pareto Principle* or the *80-20 Rule*) prioritizes the resources. It is very common to find that one or two resources will contribute more than 60 percent toward the achievement of the goal. This is then identified as a critical resource.

Once the critical resource has been identified, the procedure would be to select an appropriate measurement system that focuses on that critical resource. The measurement system selected should maximize the effectiveness of the critical resource. For example, different types of manufacturing systems that exist include *Material Requirements Planning* (MRP) which focuses on the efficiency of the labor resource, *Economic Order Quantity* (EOQ) and *Just-in-Time* (JIT) which focus on the materials resource, and *Theory of Constraints* (TOC) which focuses on the machine resource. Similar resource-focused systems exist in wholesale distribution / logistics, and in retailing.

Using the goal based approach, the final step in the decision process of whether to move a plant offshore or not is then based on an analysis of what the effects are on the critical resource of moving the plant offshore. If the offshore move will improve the effectiveness of the critical resource, then the move is good over all, both long-term financially and otherwise. However, if the offshore move reduces the effectiveness of this critical resource, then the move is discouraged.

10. Activity Based Costing has been used as a tool for making the relocation decision. It is merged into the tool, commonly referred to as "Weighted Factor Analysis". This technique is a "textbook" technique that has fallen into disrepute because of the intensive data collection required. It is a technique that has found some application, but it is not one of the preferred techniques, nor is it often used because it requires so much more effort to come up to the same conclusions as found in the Goal / Critical Resource technique. Tompkins, J. A. and J. A. White, Facilities Planning, 1984.

The advantage of this approach is that the analysis process is simplified. Only one factor is analyzed instead of estimating and approximating a large collection of resources. This approach also assumes that if the critical resource is improved upon, even if some of the other resources are acted upon negatively, the over-all result will be positive. It is true that some costs may be hidden, as in the labor based approach; however, the goal approach assumes that there is no need to hide these factors in order to justify the move because the critical resource overwhelms the decision process (largest contribution toward the goal).

The goal approach suggests:

1) Identify a goal.
2) Evaluate the contribution of each resource toward the achievement of the goal.
3) Select the highest contributing resource(s) as the critical resource.
4) The relocation decision should focus on the optimization of the critical resource.

The next important question is, "How does the goal approach differ from the labor based approach?" The answer is that labor is rarely the critical resource. As in the Cadillac example mentioned earlier, labor is a minor resource and should not be the basis for the decision, especially if it effects materials negatively, as it did in the labor or total cost approach. Looking again at the numbers used in the labor cost and total cost examples shows the following breakdowns of resource contributions:

Chart 10.6. The Goal/Critical Resource Approach

	Home		*Abroad*	
Labor	2,000	28 %	1,050	13 %
Materials	3,200	44 %	5,000	62 %
Burden	2,000	28 %	2,000	25 %

The numbers in Chart 10.6 show that Materials should have been identified as the critical resource, especially in the case of the relocated plant where materials is nearly five times the cost. However, in other examples, other critical resources would have been identified. For example, in aluminum production, energy cost, which is also hidden in burden, can be as much as 80 percent of the cost of production. In this case it would be desirable to locate the plant closer to a cheap source of energy, like in the case of Alcan (the Aluminum Company of Canada). They even went so far as to build their own dam and power plant in an effort to keep their over all costs competitive.

Another example would be in apparel manufacturing where labor is the critical resource. Still another example would be in soda pop distribution. In this case, the transportation cost of the filled soda pop bottle is the critical resource, and optimization would want to locate the bottling facility so as to minimize the transportation cost to the retail outlets. Multiple bottlers appropriately located are often more cost effective than a centrally located bottler with a large distribution network.

A Comparison of the Relocation Models

The examples in this chapter have focused on a few specific examples of the various techniques. These examples are typical of the majority of situations the author has been involved with. The references at the end of this chapter offer numerous additional examples.[11]

The labor based strategy is the most popular in Western cultures because the labor rate difference is the most demonstratable. It is also very easy to calculate because our accounting structure clearly identifies labor cost in its costing reports, but does not easily identify the costs of other resources such as materials transport costs or materials carrying costs, which are usually hidden in burden. Most

11. For more details about the Mexican Plant see:
Plenert, Gerhard, International Management and Production: Survival Techniques for Corporate America, Tab Professional and Reference Books, 1990(b), Blue Ridge Summit, PA.
Plenert, Gerhard, "Production Considerations for Developing Countries", International Journal of Management, Dec., 1988.

Western facilities only break costs down into three categories; labor, materials, and burden. Burden is considered to be too difficult to analyze, and materials costs are assumed to be relatively the same everywhere because of the open international market for materials. Therefore, labor is commonly used as the basis for plant relocation decisions, even though it is often less then ten percent of the contribution to the value of the product.

The second most popular methodology is the total cost approach. Unfortunately, the influence of burden and materials is often similarly assumed away. Materials carrying costs, which tend to grow dramatically with distance, are buried in burden and offset by lower taxes or infrastructure costs. The primary basis for the decision comes down to labor costs.

In the value-added approach the focus is not on looking at the advantages of another location. Rather, the desirability of the product itself is looked at. Is this product producible? And where all the less advantageous products should be relocated. This is a long term strategy because the relocation may not be made based on immediate profitability. The relocation is made based on the effects of the goal, which is often long term development.

The contribution approach focuses on maximizing the contribution of margin to over-all profitability. This is a product-mix / profit-maximizing approach that has found popularity. In this model, relocation is based on a look at the comparative advantage of different locations. However, the contribution approach assumes a capacity limitation and the relocation is done in order to increase capacity, which is often not the reason for the relocation.

The goal based approach is also a long term strategy. Here the focus is built around the goal's selection of the critical resource. The decision making process is simplified, like in the labor based approach, but it is more effective since the largest portion of the product contribution is included in the decision. Concern has been expressed that the goal-based approach is the same as the labor-based approach if the critical resource is labor. The difference is that in the goal-based approach, a reevaluation of the critical resource

12. Plenert, Gerhard, "The Development of a Production System in Mexico", Interfaces, Vol. 20, No. 3, May-June 1990(c).

should occur every few years. Additionally, the critical resource may turn out to be a combination of resources, such as if labor and materials are both 40 % contributors, they would both be considered critical. Contribution towards the goal are the drivers in determining what the critical resource(s) are, rather than "tradition".

Applying a specific economic comparison of the model is difficult since each model presents a slightly different focus. The focus of each model is:

- Labor Cost Model – Labor cost reductions
- Total Cost Model – Total manufacturing cost reduction
- Value-Added Model – Maximizing internal value added performance
- Contribution Model – Developing a product mix that maximizes the over all total contribution normally in a capacity constrained environment
- Goal / Critical Resource Based Model – Minimize the over-all cost of the production and logistics operations by focusing on minimizing the cost of the critical resource(s).

Since the focus of each model is different, it is difficult to say that one model is specifically better than another. However, this chapter points out that without a careful selection of the model, it is easy to be relocating for the wrong reasons, as has been clearly demonstrated with the labor cost model.

What the Future Holds in Store

The labor oriented focus seems to have a strangle hold on Western thinking. Labor efficiency and effectiveness is the basis of so many of the decisions. However, labor is often not the greatest influence towards goal achievement. Even the total cost evaluation methodology has been found to be inadequate because of the elements of burden that are buried in the corporate (uncontrollable) costs rather than in the operating costs of the production facility. The contribution approach only handles a small window of situations and is inadequate for the majority of the relocation decisions which are expanding capacity, not limiting capacity. The future supports a push away from traditional, short term, labor oriented measures for success, towards the value added or goal based long term measurements. If the Baldrige or Deming award winning companies are an indicator of world class manufacturing, then plant relocation decisions will also be based on long term measures in the future.

Summary

Manufacturing plant relocations are primarily labor cost or total cost based. In Japan the value added cost approach is used, which lends to entirely different relocation philosophies and decisions. However, the future holds new approaches based on long term planning strategies like the goal / critical resource based approach. This approach looks more at the over all effect that a relocation has on a company's success, rather than just taking the short term perspective offered by the other techniques.

Class Assignments

1) PT, Inc. needs your help. How would you handle their relocation decision?
2) Revisit companies X, Y, and Z, Inc. What would you do differently at this point in the book?

References

Berliner, Callie, and James A. Brimson, *Cost Management For Today's Advanced Manufacturing: The CAM-I Conceptual Design*, Harvard Business School Press, Boston, 1988.

Best, Tom and Plenert, Gerhard J., "MRP, JIT, or OPT, What's Best?" *Production and Inventory Management*, Vol. 27, No. 2, 1986.

Betz, Frederick, *Strategic Technology Management*, McGraw-Hill, New York, 1993.

Coyle, John J., Edward J. Bardi, and C. John Langley, Jr., *The Man-*

agement of Business Logistics, 5th Edition, West Publishing, St. Paul, Minn., 1992, Page 448.

Hoover, Edgar M., *The Location of Economic Activity*, McGraw-Hill, New York, NY, 1948, Page 11.

Goldratt, Eliyahu M., and Jeff Cox, *The Goal*, North River Press Inc., Croton-on-Hudson, New York, 1986(a).

Goldratt, Eliyahu M., *The Haystack Syndrome*, North River Press Inc., Croton-on-Hudson, New York, 1990(a).

Goldratt, Eliyahu M., and Robert E. Fox, *The Race*, North River Press Inc., Croton-on-Hudson, New York, 1986(b).

Goldratt, Eliyahu M., *What Is This Theory Called Theory of Constraints?*, North River Press Inc., Croton-on-Hudson, New York, 1990(b).

Greenhut, Melvin L., *Plant Location In Theory and Practice*, University of North Carolina Press, Chapel Hill. NC, 1956.

Hamelman, Paul W., and Edward M Mazze, "Improving Product Abandonment Decisions", *Journal of Marketing*, vol. 36, April 1972, Pages 20-26.

Johnson, Alicia, "MRP? MRPII? OPT? CIM? FMS? JIT? Is Any System Letter Perfect?" *Management Review*, Vol. 75, No. 9, 1986.

Karatsu, Hajime, *TQC Wisdom of Japan*, Productivity Press, Cambridge, MA, 1988.

Lambert, Douglas M., and James R. Stock, *Strategic Logistics Management*, Third Edition, Irwin, Homewood, IL, 1993.

Lee, Sang M., and Marc J. Schniederjans, *Operations Management*, Houghton Mifflin Co., Boston, 1994.

Lu, David J., *KANBAN Just in Time at Toyota*, Productivity Press, Cambridge, MA, 1988.

Manroe, Kent B., and Andris A. Zoltners, "Pricing the Product Line During Periods of Scarcity", *Journal of Marketing*, vol. 43, Summer 1979, Pages 49-59.

McClain, John O., L. Joseph Thomas, and Joseph B. Mazzola, *Operations Management: Production of Goods and Services*, Third Edition, Prentice Hall, Englewood Cliffs, NJ, 1992.

Plenert, Gerhard, "Installing Successful Factories into Developing Countries", *The International Executive*, Vol. 32, No. 2, Sept.-Oct. 1990(a).

Plenert, Gerhard, "International Industrial Management", *Organizational Development Journal*, Vol. 7, No. 1, Spring 1989.

Plenert, Gerhard, *International Management and Production: Survival Techniques for Corporate America*, Tab Professional and Reference Books, 1990(b), Blue Ridge Summit, PA.

Plenert, Gerhard J., and Terry Lee, "Optimizing Theory of Constraints When New Product Alternatives Exist", *Production and Inventory Management Journal*, Third Quarter, 1993 (a), Volume 34, Number 3, Pages 51-57.

Plenert, Gerhard J., "Optimizing Theory of Constraints When Multiple Constrained Resources Exist" *European Journal of Operations Research*, October 1993 (b), Vol. 70, Pages 126-133.

Plenert, Gerhard, "Production Considerations for Developing Countries", *International Journal of Management*, Dec., 1988.

Plenert, Gerhard, "The Development of a Production System in Mexico", *Interfaces*, Vol. 20, No. 3, May-June 1990(c).

Plenert, Gerhard, *The Plant Operations Handbook*, Business 1 IRWIN, 1993 (c), Homewood, Ill.

Plenert, Gerhard, *World Class Manager*, Prima Publishing, Rocklin, CA, 1995.

Schmenner, *Making Business Location Decisions*, Prentice Hall, Englewood Cliffs, New Jersey, 1982, Pages 11-15.

Shingo, Shiego, *Non-Stock Production: The Shingo System For Continuous Improvement*, Productivity Press, Cambridge, MA, 1988.

Vonderembse, Mark A., and Gregory P. White, *Operations Management: Concepts, Methods, and Strategies*, Third Edition, West Publishing Company, New York, 1996.

Weiner, Eilzabeth, Dean Foust, and Dori Jones, "Why Made-in-America is Back in Style", *Business Week*, November 7, 1988, Pages 116-120.

11. The Customer and the World of Service

Operations management has been given a bad wrap in that it is considered to be the "anti-customer" part of business. Unfortunately, it is often the case that operations attempts to run the company focused on their areas of performance measures, which include things like throughput, inventory levels, volumes, and efficiencies. Special requests from customers, like order changes (due dates or quantities), or rush shipments, conflict with these performance measures and are therefore resisted by operations management. Even the measure for quality can often contradict a customer's needs. For example, a measure of quality that focuses on defect rate reduction will cause a company to resist running rush jobs which inherently have high defect rates. This brings us to the purpose of this chapter, which is, how do we in operations "thrill the customer?"

What is Quality?

Quality has numerous definitions, as was already discussed earlier in this book. But the most important definition of quality is the customer's definition. What this means operationally is that we need to communicate with the customer and understand what they define quality as. Specifically, we need to have the customer in our shop and we need to spend time in the customer's shop. We need to spend time with the buyers, who express their expectations for the product, and we need to spend time with the inspectors who evaluate our product for conformance to specification. We need to meet with and talk to each of these individuals so as to open a free flow of communication.

The world class approach to quality runs into numerous roadblocks when we approach an international operations perspective on quality. For example, direct face-to-face communication is difficult because of distance and language. Therefore, communication focused on thrilling the customer takes on a number of challenges. It becomes difficult just to identify what the customer's expectations are. Additionally we have the ethical and cultural differences discussed in the next chapter. This changes the focus and definition of what it means to have a quality product. Systems like ISO and QS have been established in an attempt to have documentation which will avoid the quality definition hurdle, but these systems tend to add little more than paperwork to the process of thrilling the customer.

In the end, the discussion about meeting the customer, and having the customer meet your facility, is more important in an international environment than in a domestic setting. Additionally, direct communication is about the only way of avoiding many of the misunderstandings that are created by the language barrier. Quality, in an international setting, still means thrilling the customer and that requires direct contact.

What is Productivity?

Productivity is also confused when we start to take an international perspective. As already discussed earlier in this book, there are numerous ways to measure productivity, enough to where anyone and everyone can be the most productive by simply selecting the right measure. Internationally this means that we need to identify the measure of performance that is important to the customer. If we are to thrill the customer, we need to be the most productive producer in the measure that they consider important. For example, labor productivity may mean nothing to a Japanese manufacturer who is focused on materials efficiency. Labor productivity simply means higher materials cost, which is unacceptable.

What is Customer Service?

Customer service is performing to the measure that the customer feels is the most important. We need to define that measure and perform on it, whether it is quality, productivity, or some other measure. Additionally, customer service is time performance, as discussed in Chapter 8. It is easy to see examples of customer service in companies like Coca-Cola, who focus on developing relationships with all stakeholders, including the government at all levels, when they grow their international operations. It is also important the way they communicate their product in extensive marketing programs that are focused on cultural norms, rather than Western strategies. They involve the locals in these strategies so that no political or cultural mistakes are made. This process has been labeled as the development of a "core competency in global learning". Coca-Cola has become so good at this process that it has been identified as part of their core competency.

Another example of customer focused operational efficiency is in McDonalds. They have recognized their niche and they develop this niche through localized marketing programs. They are not afraid to try a new product with the hope that it will appeal locally. This occurs within markets of the same country as well as across borders to other countries.

A third example of a service organization that has achieved operational success is found in FedEx. They have successfully developed relationships all over the world through localization of the operational process. They have even gone so far as to change their name from Federal Express to FedEx because the term "federal" was offensive and had negative connotations in some countries. Additionally, they take advantage of local infrastructures for their distribution arrangements.

Customer service in an international setting means supply chain efficiency. As discussed earlier, the key pieces of supply chain success are:

- The integration of information and functions
- The free sharing of information through tools like the internet
- Time efficiency

Therefore, customer service is directly linked to the topics discussed in Chapters 6 through 9. It is generally accepted that if there is standing inventory, then it is the result of a breakdown of one of the processes, and that inventory is an easy measuring stick to indicate just the opposite message previously believed. Inventory does not mean customer satisfaction by having goods available. Rather, inventory means inflexibility in dealing with the exceptions. Inventory means that there was a need to buffer a problem, which means that the supply chain is slower than it should be in responding to customers' needs. Therefore, inventory is generally considered to be a red flag of supply flow problems, and therefore, customer service problems.

Assuming that you have all the other pieces of the supply chain working correctly, there is one last piece that will bring you to a level of competitive "thrilling the customer" performance. That last step is the optimization of the process. This means that the entire supply chain is synchronized in such a way that the supply of resources is balanced with the demand for these resources throughout the network. This requires total customer and supplier interaction with the network and offers immediate feedback to customer requests. Synchronization requires some level of forecasting, production and inventory planning at all nodes in the supply chain. It also requires a DRP system integrated throughout the logistics process.

The remainder of this chapter will focus on measurement and performance systems that focus on "Thrilling the Customer". However, before we start this discussion, let's take a visit to PC, Inc.

PC, Inc.

PC, Inc. is the highest revenue earning attraction in Hawaii. They see themselves as a cultural museum for the Polynesian islands and an entertainment center focused on sharing a cultural experience with it's many visitors. PC employs university students throughout it's organization which offers them low cost labor and offers the students the opportunity to earn their way through school. PC is comprised of islands, each of which focuses on a Polynesian island group. PC attempts to share the experience of that island with it's visitors. It also offers several meal options, again focused on the cultural experience. They also have a souvenir area that is strongly attractive to the tourists. Last of all they offer a night show which draws people from all around the world.

The PC experience requires the purchase of a ticket which gives access to the park. The ticket can be for the daytime activities of the islands, or for the night time activities of the show. Along with these tickets it is possible to purchase a dinner ticket. Entrance to the shopping area is restricted to people with one of the different types of tickets.

PC strongly attracts the Asian tourist but also has a strong following from the United States visitors. Recently, the Asia tourist trade has dropped off because of the economic struggles in the region. PC is searching for ways to draw more American tourists to make up for this downturn. They have found that the American tourist enjoys shopping in their gift shops because of its island specific flavor as they drive around the island, but they don't like the restriction of having to purchase an admissions ticket to get into the park in order to go shopping. This has discouraged many would-be shoppers.

Another detraction is that to get to PC requires driving all the way around the island. This takes more time than many people want to spend, especially if you have to return all the way around the island again that same night after the nightshow. The PC management has toyed with the idea of developing some type of overnight luau experience so that visitors to PC would not have to return until the next day. But this has found resistance from the tour operators and the hotels.

PC needs to develop a customer focused strategy that will increase their draw from both the domestic as well as the international market. Additionally, they need to increase their internal cost efficiencies if they are to make it through the Asian economic slowdown. They are researching their operational options looking for potential efficiencies and improvements. They are also searching for possibly new opportunities to add to their operations. Now the problem is yours. What would you do if you were the president of PC, Inc. What would you do to reduce costs? What would you do to add more "customer thrilling" opportunities?

Performance Systems and Their Measurement

There are several approaches to managing the supply chain in response to customer demands. These approaches vary depending on the different operating environments under which they are utilized. The focus is on supply chain efficiency which maximizes throughput performance. These approaches are utilized to both drive performance, and to offer a feedback measurement of the results. They can be classified as:

- The Material Requirements Planning (MRP) approach
- The Just-in-Time (JIT) approach
- The Theory of Constraints (TOC) approach
- The Process approach

Chart 11.1. Scheduling Approaches

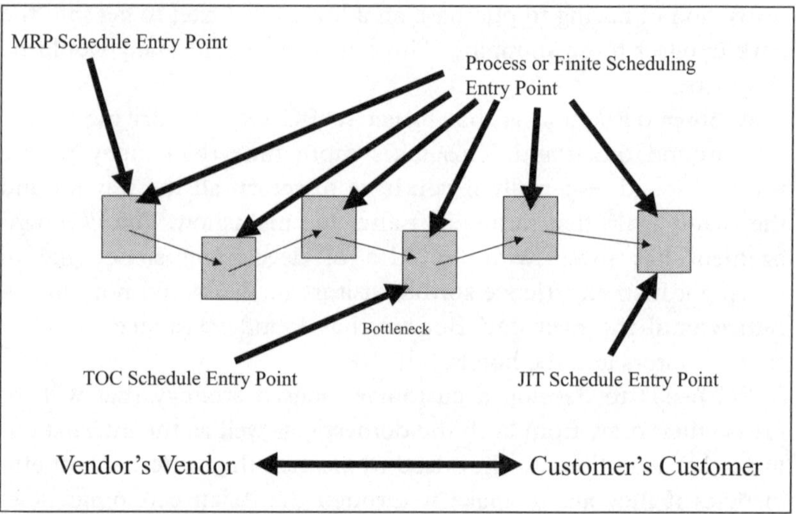

The Material Requirements Planning (MRP) Approach

In the MRP approach the schedules are order driven (see Chart 11.1). For example, when an order is placed it is either forward scheduled or backward scheduled through the supply chain based on standard processing lead times. The supply chain then responds back to the customer what the level of responsiveness will be based on this lead time. The order is released into the front end of the supply chain network based on the calculated schedule.

The MRP approach is extremely effective in the *Job Shop*, customized product environment where we don't want to start production until we have an order because every order is customized. Then the entire order must be scheduled and sequenced through the supply chain.

The Just-in-Time (JIT) Approach

In the JIT approach the schedules are driven based on customer demand (see Chart 11.1). When a demand is triggered, the system is informed by the removal of a unit off the end of the production sequence. This triggers a Kanban[1] interaction throughout the system and all the wheels of the system turn together. The initial trigger comes at the customer end of the supply chain with the pulling of the product.

This process is extremely successful in a repetitive flow manufacturing environment where the repetitive product does not need customization. The customer does not need to be restricted to the over all supply chain cycle time because every unit is the same. Customer delivery is only restricted by demand exceeding capacity.

The Theory of Constraints (TOC) Approach

In the TOC approach we have a bottleneck in the supply chain and this bottleneck limits the throughput of the supply chain (see Chart 11.1). Scheduling is organized so as to optimize the bottleneck and customer responsiveness is based on the bottleneck schedule. Orders are released into the supply chain based on the availability of the bottleneck. Schedules for customer deliveries are also based on the load that the bottleneck is experiencing.

This is important in a constrained environment where resources are unbalanced and where the bottleneck drives over-all throughput. Process industries like metal production or flour production are excellent examples of this type of process.

1. In Japanese, Kanban means card. A Kanban is a location or card which limits the amount of standing inventory that is allowed in any one place. If you don't have any place to put the inventory after you're done working on it, you're not allowed to work on it.

The Process Approach

In the process approach we focus on the capacity load throughout the process. Not all products utilize the same amount of resources at each stage of the process so at one time one resource will be more available, and at another time another resource will be more available. It is similar to asking the question; "How long would it take to drive across town to the airport?" The answer varies depending on the time of day and the load being placed on various elements of the freeway system. From this we can see how the process approach eliminates the shortcomings of an MRP environment which assumes that the lead time is the same regardless of the load. The process approach also eliminates the shortcomings of JIT which searches for a repetitive process. And it eliminates the shortcomings of TOC which requires a bottleneck to schedule around. In the process approach, lead time can vary depending on the load that has already been placed on capacity, and the customer order is either backward scheduled or forward scheduled based on due date and available capacity. Then the lead time is reported to the customer based on real capacity and can vary from time to time (see Chart 11.1).

The process approach, often referred to as Finite Capacity Scheduling, offers variable but realistic schedules. It is still fairly new and therefore not heavily utilized, but it is gaining popularity as the supply chain management scheduling approach of the future. It has demonstrated excellent performance in the area of on-time delivery because of a scheduling methodology based on real lead times and not on average lead times. It has therefore been recognized as extremely customer service oriented.

Which Approach is Best?

The best approach is all of the above. The future of supply chain management finds each of these approaches having appropriate application usefulness. For example, if a hard bottleneck exists with restricted capacity, the TOC approach is often the most successful. If you have an extremely customized job shop environment, MRP is the repeated winner. Therefore, the most customer oriented approach depends on your supply chain and how well it is managed.

Summary

Operations management is in the driver's seat of operational efficiency, performance, and customer satisfaction. The focus on "thrilling the customer" has to occur through the quality and productivity process, as well as a tailored supply chain management processes. With these in place we can focus on the three initiatives of customer satisfaction; time, integration, and information.

Class Assignments

1) PC, Inc. needs your help. They are focusing on increased operational efficiencies while at the same time making operational changes that would make them more attractive to their remaining customer base. What would you do?

References

Finite Capacity Scheduling References

Kirchmier, Bill, Finite "Capacity Scheduling Methods", *APICS The Performance Advantage*, August 1998, Pages 38-40.

Plenert, Gerhard and Bill Kirchmier, *Finite Capacity Scheduling*, John Wiley & Sons, Inc., New York, 2000,

Taylor, Sam G., and Steven G. Bolander, "Scheduling Systems for Tomorrow's Factories", *APICS 41st International Conference Proceedings*, Nashville, TN, November, 1998, Pages 181-183.

12. The International Transaction/Ethics

This is a chapter on international relationship development. It focuses on how relationships and the concept of what is ethical in the business transaction is different in an international setting. For example, service operations in China are quite different than in Russia, or in the United States, or elsewhere.

Successful International Ethics Integration[1]

The great debate in ethics or, more specifically, in defining morality, has always been to decide if there is one universally acceptable master plan for moral behavior. Frustratingly, there are dozens of different models of what might constitute the master plan for morality. This chapter compares some of the differing points of view on cultural-moral-ethical conflicts and relates them to international business, including the related transfer of hard and soft technology.

In academic terms, ethics has been defined as the philosophical study of morality. The search for a standardized code, which would define ethics or mores, specifically moral principles, has been primarily dominated by Western right-wing Christian thought, especially from the United States and Europe. Using this perspective, it is widely believed that there is one standard model of moral behavior that all persons everywhere can and should ascribe to. Religious adherents through extensive periods of colonialization have promoted this attitude. It has left most of the world feeling that morality can indeed be standardized, if not willingly, perhaps by

1. A large portion of this chapter was taken from the article: Plenert, Gerhard, "A Strategy for Compromises Aimed at Successful Ethics Integration" *Review of Human Factor Studies,* Vol. 3, No. 2, Dec. 1997, Pages 37-48.

military, and even more common lately, by economic force. Unfortunately, what should be recognized is that a universal morality is not readily available or realistic. This chapter will discuss, using examples in international business behavior, why there is more than one perfect model for morality.

There has developed an ever-increasing amount of concern about the lack of moral ethics in United States business. The amount of published literature is growing rapidly, but the conclusions are vague. For example, in an article Thomas (1991) suggests that younger, newer managers are becoming less ethical and more manipulative, and that they are being taught this behavior in the business schools. The article suggests that environmental costs and competitive demands are causing us to focus away from ethical business practices resulting in unethical behavior which seems morally acceptable on competitive grounds.[2] For example, the United States may install a chemical plant in India to avoid U. S. worker safety regulations, or it may move a steel product factory to Mexico to avoid pollution regulations. Similarly, Derek Bok's (1982) article in *Computers and People* suggests that our modern methods of training new managers focuses too much on analytical processes. This training brings a dehumanizing blindness to the decision making process and forgets the moral concerns that have traditionally dominated the decision process. We do what the numbers tell us to do, regardless of what our conscious tells us to do.[3]

This chapter discusses several international ethical conflicts that may be encountered by managers.[4] It will demonstrate some of the cultural distinctions that occur in the ethical-moral decision process. The chapter does not attempt to pronounce any ethical-moral system as being "right", rather, it suggests flexibility, understanding, and adaptability in international transactions.

2. Thomas, C. William, "Are Young Managers Less Ethical?" *New Accountant,* March 1991, Pages 3-10.
3. Bok, Derek C., "Social Responsibility in Future Worlds", *Computers and People,* September/October 1982.
4. Carroll, Archie B., "In Search of the Moral Manager", *Business Horizons,* March-April 1987, Pages 7-15.

The research, which is the basis of this chapter, includes a customary literature search, but it focuses primarily on interviews and case studies. Businesses were visited through North and South America, Northeast and Southeast Asia, Africa, and Europe. Examples will be pulled from these interviews and discussions.

Ethics Defined

Ethics: we have trouble defining it, but we think we know what it is when we see it. The dictionary gives us a definition of ethics that focuses on "a work or test of morals". Research defines ethics as the study of moral behavior. However, common usage of the term "ethics" follows the lines of "an ethical dilemma, by definition, is one that poses a conflict not between good and evil, but between one good principle and another that is equally good".[5]

Moral behavior is defined in terms of judgments, standards, and rules of conduct. Unfortunately, we can't all agree on what constitutes the standards and/or rules of conduct of moral behavior. For example, the Jewish Golden Rule would tell us "Don't do onto others what you don't want them to do to you!" This suggests that you are ethical as long as you don't do anything bad, primarily because they may in turn do something bad to you. The Christian Golden Rule suggests "Do onto others what you want them to do onto you!" This would indicate that being ethical requires positive action. If you want good things done to you, you have to do good things. But doing nothing or only avoiding bad things can actually be unethical and unmoral.

We get into such dilemmas in business. For example, if we choose to not report a fellow employee who is stealing pencils, are we being unethical. Or, if our manager orders us to change some figures, or to not report a problem, because it would make him or her look bad, are we being unethical, even if we were simply following orders and ultimately not responsible? Realizing that we have

5. Levine, Carol, Taking Sides: Clashing Views on Controversial Bioethical Issues (Seventh Edition), Dushkin / McGraw-Hill, 1997, Preface.

enough struggles in defining ethics within our own Judeo-Christian Western culture, we should easily see that a cross cultural definition of ethical behavior would be difficult to generate.

Culture Defined

Culture is commonly thought of as the historically developed differences between countries. Culture is often referred to as the binding whole, which includes knowledge, belief systems, art, morals, rules and laws, customs and traditions, and many other similar elements which an individual, as a member of the society, can acquire. The dictionary defines it as "the sum total of the attainments, and activities of any specific period, race, or people".[6] There is a United States culture, a Mexican culture, and a Japanese culture. However, there are also subcultures. Within Italy there is a distinct Northern and Southern culture. Similarly, in the United States, there is a San Francisco culture, and a Detroit culture, and a Dallas culture, each quite different. Within these subcultures are also pockets of nationalities which could each be considered their own culture. Because there are so many categories and levels of cultures, it is difficult to look at each level. However, for purposes of generalization within this chapter, I will look at only national cultures in my comparison, realizing that the cultural differences at the other levels can be just as real and just as frustrating in defining ethical behavior.

Goal Based Moral / Ethical Behavior

Ethics and morality requires accountability to cultural norms. For the religious, the accountability is to the God supported by that culture; for the irreligious, the accountability is to society. Within a system of accountability, which includes written and unwritten rules or laws, each member of society feels protected. This feeling assumes that the majority of the population of that culture will follow the

6. The Doubleday Dictionary, 1975, Page 173.

same moral code. This offers a feeling of being able to trust each other, and to know what to expect from each other. The ethical system is actually a form of freedom, removing the burden of having to investigate each person's intentions. Unfortunately, if you would prefer to have no accountability, then you would probably view a moral code as restrictive or limiting.

This chapter focuses on those individuals that see the need for an ethical/moral structure. Each individual that wants ethics, will have their own perception of what moral behavior entails, and they will base this perception on the cultural set of rules and laws that they feel accountable to. This concept of differing ethical standards for different groups of people is often referred to as Ethical Relativism. Here are some examples of systems of accountability.

Religion

The religious influence on moral/ethical systems is enormous, and often supersedes all other effects. Some religions, like right-wing Christianity, stress the importance of the individual. The rights of the individual are more important than the rights of the society. Individual success is measured by individual attainment. Society and family are often viewed as hindrances, rather than being the means, for achieving individual goals. Each individual is a unique and equal child of God and deserves to be forgiven for their mistakes, deserves the compassion, love, and help of others, and deserves a chance to be successful.[7]

Other religious movements, like the conservative Moslems, focus on the good of society as a whole. They stress that the individual is insignificant in relation to the big picture. If an individual is an embarrassment or is non-contributing to the society as a whole (see the discussion on value adding), then some of the rights of the individual as a member of the society should be relinquished. It may even be appropriate to remove societal/cultural embarrassments from society completely.[8]

7. These comments stem from my own personal right-wing Christian background having been a member of two of the largest of these religious communities.
8. These comments stem from extensive interviews with Iraqi and Malaysian Moslems about their ethical/moral perspectives.

Using only the right-wing Christianity and the conservative Moslem religious examples, we can see major conflicts in the ethical structure. For example, some professions have positive or negative connotations depending on the society one is speaking about. In some societies the legal profession is considered prestigious and highly profitable. In other societies this profession is considered a profession of thieves utilizing societal resources but adding nothing of value. Similarly, intermarriage between these two cultures would force the Moslem culture to completely cast out the Moslem member. Intermarriage would be considered highly unethical and immoral to the Moslem, and would be considered unrelated to ethics and morality by the Christian.

In business we have similar cultural moral conflicts. An individual engaged in a business that appears to focus strictly on selfish attainment (profit), would be shunned and avoided in the Moslem setting. However, to the contrary, in the Christian setting, an individual who claims to be focused on win-win agreements and on society gaining some benefit from every transaction, would cause suspicion and mistrust.

Society

Societies develop a historical code of conduct, which helps to define ethical/moral behavior. What one society would consider a lie might be considered an expected exaggeration in another culture. For example, in Mexico, if you are invited to someone's house for dinner at 7:00 PM, and you show up at 7:00 PM, you are likely to find him or her just starting their preparations. You are not expected to arrive until about 8:30 or 9:00 PM. The idea that an ethical standard or norm's correctness is dependent upon the culture or society of the individuals concerned is referred to as cultural relativism.

In the United States we often find similar conflicts. For example, we would consider someone walking into a store, taking a computer software product off the shelf, putting it in their pocket, and walking out of the store with it, as stealing. But we feel no pangs of guilt in copying copyrighted software, videos, or music tapes, which in effect also steals profits.

Governments have an enormous influence on what is defined as culturally acceptable ethical/moral behavior in our societies. The

Hausman article stresses that high-level government immorality results in worldwide problems.[9] For example, in Kidder's article, morality is compared between countries from the viewpoint of the business community. Opinions are compared between 41 countries rating the drive for morality in each location. On the top of the list are New Zealand, Denmark, Singapore, Finland, Canada, and Sweden. At the bottom of the list is Indonesia. The United States took 15th place.[10]

Goals

To understand moral behavior we need to understand what the goals of our behavior are. If, for example, our cultural/societal/religious goal is wealth, like the bumper sticker: "The one who dies with the most toys wins", then we would expect to find a different attitude from an environment whose goals focus on being a good person, having charity, integrity, etc. Ethics, in one structure, can be a goal, whereas in another structure, ethics would be considered an obstruction to goal achievement. A positive or negative attitude toward ethical goal achievement directly affects a society's interest in finding a common, universal, ethical structure. A society may have absolutely no interest in being standardized, and may, in fact, see another society's attempt at standardization as an opportunity for them to take advantage of the standardized society. For example, the trust that native Africans placed in their colonizers resulted in their exploitation and slavery.

In business, we find a variety of philosophies on goals. For example, the United States tends to focus on the orientation that no

9. Hausman C., "Ethics Issues Circle the Globe", *Insights in Global Ethics,* 6 (3), 1996, Pages 1-5.
10. Kidder, R. M., "Measures of Corruption", *Insights on Global Ethics,* 5 (8), 1995, Page 2.

transaction is worth pursuing unless there is a profit.[11] The oriental goal orientation tends to be results oriented. Successful goal achievement is more important than the financial worth of the transaction. In Latin America we find that the relationship (human side of the transaction) is more appropriate than the financial reward, or even the achievement of the goal. In this perspective, accomplishment or financial reward, has no value if you've destroyed a friendship or negatively effected a family member in the process. In Germany or Israel we find an orientation toward operational goals. From this perspective we see that success is often defined as a "job well done", which includes quality and productivity as measures of performance. These differences are just a few of the diverse examples of different cultural/moral goals. From them we can see variety in the development of ethical/moral structures, like the United States' need to "have it in writing", rather than the "good as his word" orientation that would be found in many other cultures. The DeGeorge book provides an excellent discussion of how to develop ten strategies for ethical management in a company that is competing in a corrupt environment.[12] Armstrong has written an interesting article on the effects of culture on ethics and discusses the differences in the perceptions of marketing managers from Australia, Malaysia, and Singapore.[13]

11. Silk, Leonard, and David Vogel, *Ethics and Profits,* Simon and Schuster, New York, 1976.

    Hayes, Robert, and William Abernathy, "Managing our Way to Economic Decline", *Harvard Business Review,* July-August 1980, Pages 67-77.

    Bell, Daniel, *The Cultural Contradictions of Capitalism,* Basic Books, New York, 1976.

    Wright, N. Dale, *Papers on the Ethics of Administration,* Brigham Young University, Provo, Utah, 1988.

    Call, Ivan T., and Robert J. Parsons, *Ethics and the Management of Financial Institutions,* Brigham Young University, Provo, Utah, 1995.
12. De George, R. T., *Competing with Integrity in International Business,* Oxford University Press, New York, 1993.
13. Armstrong, R. W. "The Relationship Between Culture and Perception of Ethical Problems in International Marketing", *Journal of Business Ethics,* 15 (11), 1996, Pages 1199-1208.

A Collection of Social Principles

There are numerous cultural/moral topics that cause ethical distinctiveness. I have highlighted a few of the more important issues. They will be briefly discussed so that we can get a better feel for the difficulties in ethical-cultural integration.

Short vs. Long Term Thinking

The United States process of building up an enormous national debt that latter generations are going to get stuck with is considered to be selfishly irresponsible by many international cultures. Similarly, ignoring the long-term effects of pollution, especially after we have a good understanding of what those long-term effects are would also be considered questionable. However, in the United States, we have developed an non-trust-oriented culture that demands short-term results. Investors expect quick results from the captains of industry. The captains similarly expect quick, demonstrated results from their employees. Long-term second chances are rare.

The non-United States, international tendency is to focus on long-term goals, such as customer based (Europe and Asia) or employee-based (Japan) goals. Often the feeling is that short-term, profit oriented goals are unethical because they ignore the "people" aspects of doing business.

Black and White Caustic Thinking

The United States manager tends to think in terms of all decisions being either right or wrong (black or white). Most other cultures tend to feel that all decisions are gray; that there is a good side and a bad side to all decisions, and that the goodness or badness of the decision depends on the perspective. For example, in Latin American or African countries, the idea of signing a "hard and fast" contract is viewed as unethical because the businessman on either side of the transaction should not be held accountable for grossly uncontrollable events in a highly unstable governmental environment. The hard contract is considered suspiciously, with the feeling that someone is trying to trick them in some way. The contract should be based on the best intentions of both parties involved, with the belief that the contract will be fulfilled, barring any grossly unforeseen events.

Along with this black and white perspective, there is also a caustic (causal focused) tendency to Western thinking. Caustic thinking is where all decisions, whether good or bad, have a clearly definable cause. The result is that any time there is a problem, we tear the problem apart trying to identify the "root cause". This process, called "root-cause analysis", is also popular in the former Soviet Republics. An opposing perspective to caustic thinking would be to question not the cause of the problem, but the reason behind trying to solve the problem. This process, referred to a "purpose expansion" has become extremely popular in Japan under the name of Breakthrough Thinking®.[14]

Another way to look at black and white caustic thinking is to have the attitude that all decisions, especially bad ones, need to have someone to blame. Oriental countries prefer to go out of their way to make sure no blame is placed, so that no one loses "face". Unfortunately, in the United States, the emphasis in more focused on identifying a scapegoat.

Value-Added Ethical Behavior

For most cultures, the purpose of life is to add additional value to that base of value that has been created by progenitors. As citizens of the world community, we are here to add value to ourselves, to our families, to our society, and to our world. The individual who adds the most value, not the individual who has the most toys, is the real winner.

In the United States, the only value you are expected to add to is to your own pocket book (referred to as ethical egoism). Adding value in other areas makes you a good person (or a fool depending on the perspective), but the critical focus is on self-development

14. Breakthrough Thinking is a registered trademark of The Center for Breakthrough Thinking, Inc. which is housed in the University of Southern California (USC) in Los Angeles, California, USA. The first book, which introduced the concept of Breakthrough Thinking in the United States is:

    Nadler, Gerald, and Shozo Hibino, Breakthrough Thinking, Prima Publishing, Rocklin, CA, 1994.

and self-attainment through self-gratification. We have been hounded with "do something for yourself" movements. We rarely hear about "do something for society" movements, as proposed by John F. Kennedy. Because of this self-oriented focus, outsiders feel that the United States' society is paying the price, in the form of gangs, corruption, drugs, and other societal problems.

From a business perspective, the focus on self has made it extremely difficult to develop effective teams. In Mexico, for example, people are accustomed to having a societal perspective. Teaming comes naturally. But in the United States, teaming, and the camaraderie required to make it effective, takes a great deal of effort.

Cultural-Ethical Surprises – an Example

Numerous United States plants have been moved to Mexico, and the flow will increase with NAFTA. For example, 320 Maquiladora plants have been located just across the border. These plants are assembly plants, primarily run by United States managers, and staffed with Mexican employees. When moving these plants across the border to Mexico, the managers implemented many of the same incentive programs that had previously existed in the United States. For example, a nice dinner and a designated parking place would be given to the "employee of the month". It wasn't long before management realized that gaining this distinction was shunned, rather than prized by the employees. The employees didn't want to be distinguished and set apart. They wanted to be part of the group, and being set apart caused resentment. The Mexican employee looked for social membership, whereas the U. S. employee would enjoy being set apart.

High turnover rates forced managers to also learn new hiring strategies. For example, hiring individuals opened the door for potential rejection. However, hiring a team (a group of employees that relate to each other and work well together) significantly reduced the turnover rate.

In Mexico it became important for managers to know the nature of the employees. They had to take an interest in the employees. They needed to open the door for sharing and parties. In Mexico, you know by the handshake whether you are a friend or foe, so it becomes important to learn about relationships and relationship building.

Another cultural variation is that Mexicans look to education as a long-term investment, not as something that is functionally oriented and immediate reward focused. Continuous improvement is an opportunity for an increased value added to life.

From this example we can see that motivation systems that would seem ethical in the United States, were disastrous when used in Mexico. The Mexican ethical culture had to be adapted too.

Expectation Theory

Cultural morality/ethics is the value system of a society. It is formed by what is considered to be regularity of behavior. The cultural-ethical conflict occurs when one society imposes its "superior" culture and ethical system upon another society. The cultures find themselves trying to adapt to each other's cultural-ethical systems. However, the speed of the adaptation often creates as many conflicts as do the differences. This leads to expectation theory. Often, culture and ethical conflicts occur because of what is expected, rather than what really exists. For example, if a United States citizen travels to a five star hotel in Mexico, they expect that hotel to operate similar to a five star hotel in the United States. However, when a Mexican travels to the United States, they expect the hotel to operate differently. The Mexican culture adapts rapidly to the anticipated difference.

In another example, if a Mexican travels to the United States, he or she will tend to not litter, even though they find littering perfectly acceptable in Mexico. They are adapting to the expectations of the culture they are moving into. The Mexicans in Mexico will rapidly tell you how different they are from the Mexicans who have moved across the border to the United States. The migrated Mexicans have adapted to what they feel are the expectations of the new culture, and they are now considered to be different from the individuals in the "old" culture.

In a factory in Mexico I was told a story of a television and a VCR that was used for training. The TV and VCR were locked in a cabinet and chained down. The expectation was that they would be stolen. However, many of the desks in the office had personal computers which had ten times the value of the TV and were not secured in any way. So guess which was stolen. The TV of course, because it was expected to be stolen. The chaining and locking of the TV was considered a challenge to the integrity of the Mexican.

Issues of Ethical Dilemmas Across Cultures

We have reviewed numerous examples of culture based ethical conflicts. Now we will group these examples into a series of dilemmas followed by an attempt to associate universally accepted principles that can be used to resolve these culture specific dilemmas. The groupings would be:

Business Operations Dilemmas:
- Taking advantage of regulation/legal differences
- Dehumanizing, analytical training processes focused on the numbers rather than on morality
- The profit vs. the relationship vs. the operations approach to running a business

Personal / Individual Behavior Dilemmas:
- The positive action vs. negative action Golden Rule
- Selfish attainment (profit)
- The importance of time
- The rights of the individual vs. the rights of the society
- Black and white caustic thinking
- Value-added ethical behavior
- Short vs. long term thinking

Family / Society Dilemmas:
- A culturally specific system of accountability where the majority of the population follow the same moral code
- Ethical relativism
- Prestigious professions
- Marital / relationship ethics
- The standardized vs. the adaptable society
- The trusting vs. suspicious society

- Social membership vs. being set apart as special
- Expectation theory

We need to start our evaluation with the "personal / individual behavior dilemmas". These are ones that are specific to the way individuals are raised. They are specific to how individuals were led to believe life should be. They effect the individual's reactions to specific situations. They change the parameters to what is identified as offensive. These cultural / ethical dilemmas require a change in the belief system of the individual, which is generally impossible unless it is forced. Therefore, the approach to developing an ethical relationship on this basis is not found through ethical imposition, but through ethical understanding. Individuals need to understand how other cultures react to the use of the name Jesus Christ, or how they react to being pointed at. This understanding and cross-cultural sensitivity will assist in avoiding unnecessary conflicts.

The next area of conflict is in the family / societal dilemmas. These dilemmas tend to focus on values; what is considered valuable and beneficial to the family and to society. Realizing that not everyone is profit driven, or not everyone defines success in the same way, will create a need for cross-cultural compromise. Since both parties in the relationship are attempting to achieve different results, then they will need to work together to find a common ground where both can identify success in their relationships. Neither side may get everything they want, but both sides should get enough of what they desire in order to find the transaction worth performing.

The third area of dilemmas is found in the methods of business operations. Generally speaking, this is an area where change will be required. The organization will need to adapt itself to the culture it is trying to service without sacrificing its own morality. The organization's business process needs to become localized. Only through localization can the organization find success. For example, General Motors' attempt to sell the Nova in Mexico was an enormous failure – Nova means "No Go" in Spanish. Appropriate localization requires appropriate change.

The cultural / ethical dilemmas do not all have the same solutions, but they are all manageable through appropriate levels of sensitivity.

The Human Factor in Ethical Conflicts

The human element of ethical dilemmas focuses on the resistance to change. In the personal / individual behavior, the individual is solely responsible for their ability and willingness to change, and therefore they are solely responsible for the results. In the other two categories of dilemmas, "group think" comes into play. This occurs when the necessary changes required will effect several individuals, and therefore the resistance to change is often higher. This increased resistance occurs because the group will focus on what is easiest to do which is to not change, and they will feed off of each other in their resistance to change. This resistance occurs even though the business / operations category of dilemmas is often the area where change should be the easiest to do since it isn't as deeply rooted in the belief systems of the individuals.

The human factor of cultural / ethical dilemmas also needs to focus on compromise, since, often in a blend of cultures, we find the two opposing sides to be unforgiving if they are, for example, based on religious roots. Situations occur where the legality of bribes is not as important as the "right vs. wrong" 'ness of the bribes as defined by a religious belief system. And this can cause impasses if they are not resolved through a compromise in some form which is based on a mutual understanding of the situation.

In conclusion, the human factor of ethical dilemmas focuses on:

- A willingness to change
- The flexibility of compromise
- Mutual education which offers a better understanding of opposing viewpoints.

Is a Master Ethical Model Possible?

Is an integrated cultural/ethical/moral model of any value? The immediate, easiest answer would be that it isn't worth the trouble. However, when we look at the international transaction, whether it is in business or politics or medicine or in any other area, a cross-cultural understanding of expectations, an international understanding of the rules and laws of morality, would save an enormous amount of confusion, frustration, mistakes, misunderstandings, and time. It is for this reason that we pose the question, "Is a master ethical model possible?"

In spite of how hard we attempt to impose our Western right-wing Christian ethical model on the world, the rest of the world still finds our claims for ethical and moral superiority to be arrogant and inappropriate. If a master ethical model is to be found, it will be found through compromise, not through domination, force, and through holding other parts of the world as economic hostages. There are many lessons that Westerners can learn from the other ethical models that will help them improve upon their own model, without forfeiting any of the principles that are felt to be critical to success. Which leads us to a classical example of the ethical dilemma; "Is it more ethical to compromise, or to fight?" or, similarly; "Is it ethical to stand up for our own principles without taking time to understand the perspective of others?"

Since we agree that an internationally acceptable cultural/ethical/moral model would be advantageous, the next step would be to develop a strategy for compromises that would lead to successful integration. Because of the complexity of what we are attempting to accomplish, there isn't any one strategy, which stands out as more successful than any other. However, in both business and politics, there are excellent models for negotiation and compromise, which recommend and foster win-win situations. One such model that has become internationally recognized and which has been very successful is the Stephen Covey model as detailed in his book *The 7 Habits of Highly Effective People*. His model has become cross-culturally accepted and focuses on win-win transactions and would therefore be an excellent starting point for the development of an international moral/ethical model.[15]

International models may be attainable on a very conceptual basis, as the Covey model demonstrates. However, a specific, universally defined model is filled with limitations, as this chapter has demonstrated.

15. Covey, Stephen R., *The 7 Habits of Highly Effective People,* Fireside, Simon and Schuster, New York, 1990.

Summary

Morality and ethics, as demonstrated by this chapter, is definitely culture specific. An internationally integrated ethical model is dependent on our ability to be moral and ethical, which includes the ability to realize that the opinion and perspective of everyone else is just as valuable as your own opinion. There are many moral / ethical systems, each of which have strong points that need to be included in the integrated moral/ethical model. Therefore, the key to being successful at cultural-moral-ethical integration is compromise.

Class Assignments

1) Revisit the cases in the first three chapters of this book. Compare the lessons learned from each case. How are the situations in each case similar? How are they different:
   - From Chapter 1 redo Assignment A which was a role-play discussion of Z, Inc. Use a similar process for each of the integrated, in-text cases that are found in each chapter of this book.
   - Also from Chapter 1 redo Assignment B which is the Swift Shoe Company case and discuss the ethical dilemmas that this case represents.
   - In Chapter 2 reconsider the company visit of Assignment B and see if there are any ethical dilemmas that this case represents.
   - In Chapter 3 rework the W Gravel Company, Inc. Case and discuss what you would do differently at this point, taking into consideration the ethical dilemmas that this case presents.

References

Bell, Daniel, *The Cultural Contradictions of Capitalism*, Basic Books, New York, 1976.

Bok, Derek C., "Social Responsibility in Future Worlds", *Computers and People*, September/October 1982.

Call, Ivan T., and Robert J. Parsons, *Ethics and the Management of Financial Institutions*, Brigham Young University, Provo, Utah, 1995.

Carroll, Archie B., "In Search of the Moral Manager", *Business Horizons*, March-April 1987, Pages 7-15.

Covey, Stephen R., *The 7 Habits of Highly Effective People*, Fireside, Simon and Schuster, New York, 1990.

De George, R. T., *Competing with Integrity in International Business*, Oxford University Press, New York, 1993.

Friedman, Milton, "The Social Responsibility of Business", *Capitalism and Freedom*, Pages 133-136, 1962.

Hausman C., "Ethics Issues Circle the Globe", *Insights in Global Ethics*, 6 (3), 1996, Pages 1-5.

Hayes, Robert, and William Abernathy, "Managing our Way to Economic Decline", *Harvard Business Review*, July-August 1980, Pages 67-77.

Kidder, R. M., "Measures of Corruption", *Insights on Global Ethics*, 5 (8), 1995, Page 2.

Levine, Carol, *Taking Sides: Clashing Views on Controversial Bioethical Issues* (Seventh Edition), Dushkin / McGraw-Hill, 1997, Preface.

Mitchell, Russell, "Managing By Values: Is Levi Strauss' Approach Visionary – Or Flaky?", *Business Week*, August 1, 1994, Pages 46-52.

Nadler, Gerald and Shozo Hibino, *Breakthrough Thinking*, Prima Publishing & Communications, Rocklin, CA, 1994.

Plenert, Gerhard, "A Strategy for Compromises Aimed at Successful Ethics Integration" *Review of Human Factor Studies*, Vol. 3, No. 2, Dec. 1997, Pages 37-48.

Plenert, Gerhard J., "Don't Trust the Numbers", *Journal of Systems Management*, Volume 40, Number 10, Oct. 1989.

Plenert, Gerhard J., "Is a Computer Necessary? A Viewpoint", *Kybernetes*, Volume 17, Number 4, 1988.

Plenert, Gerhard J., "The Development of a Production System in Mexico", *Interfaces*, Vol. 20, No. 3, May-June 1990.

Plenert, Gerhard J., "The PC – A Time-Saving Necessity or a Fiasco?", *Journal of Systems Management*, Nov., 1987.

Primeaux, Patrick and John Stieber, "Profit Maximization: The Ethical Mandate of Business", *Journal of Business Ethics*, Vol. 13, No. 4, April 1994, Pages 287-294.

Schuhmacher, E. F., *Small is Beautiful*, NY, Perennial Library, 1973.

Silk, Leonard, and David Vogel, *Ethics and Profits*, Simon and Schuster, New York, 1976.

Stengel, Richard, "What's Wrong," *Time*, May 25, 1987.

Taylor, Fredrick Winslow, *The Principles of Scientific Management*, NY, W. W. Norton & Co., Inc., 1967.

Thomas, C. William, "Are Young Managers Less Ethical?", *New Accountant*, March 1991, Pages 3-10.

Wright, N. Dale, *Papers on the Ethics of Administration*, Brigham Young University, Provo, Utah, 1988.

POMS
Excellence

13. World Class Management

The concept of World Class Management has defined the need to collect best business practices together in a way that offers managers options for improvement (change). There isn't one technique rather it is continuous improvement or continuous change. Therefore, this chapter is just a discussion of some of the tools that companies have used to become world class, but it is by no means an all-inclusive list. In fact, to be truly world class, the list would have to under constant flux and change.

Defining a World Class Manager

Defining a world class manager is like herding cats. It's nearly impossible to get everyone focused in the same direction. World class is more than any one element, it is a collection of attitudes and focuses. In this chapter we will look at the various ways managers can be defined, and we will use these methodologies to develop a perspective for what the ultimate world class manager should look like.[1]

There are several types of managers, and there are numerous ways to categorize them. For example, there is the *sunrise manager* who has a view towards the future, as opposed to the *sunset manager* who works in the here-and-now fighting fires. We often think of the sunrise manager as the dreamer with the wild ideas that never go anywhere, whereas, the sunset manager is the workaholic who is great a getting things done in a hurry. Another way of looking at these managers is to consider the sunrise manager as a progressive,

1. Parts of this chapter are taken from the book World Class Manager, by Gerhard Plenert, Prima Publishing, 1995.

leading edge, technology minded manager. This type of manager is brought into an organization when it is looking for growth or change. A sunset manager is brought in when we are trying to stabilize a current situation, for example, trying to revive or sustain existing programs that are starting to falter.

Another way to classify managers is in considering their attitude toward their subordinates. The two extremes are the *authoritarian manager* and *participative manager*. The authoritarian manager is typified by being secretive, has his/her fingers in everything that happens, always has the final word, and tells, rather than asks questions. This manager is often referred to as the *Theory-X manager*.

The participative manager values employee opinions. He/she spends more time listening than talking during a meeting. They look for ideas from the bottom-up, realizing that the employees have the best understanding of day-to-day operations. This manager uses these bottom-up ideas for top-down management and implementation of the ideas. This manager is concerned about the job satisfaction and rewards offered the employees. This type of manager is often referred to as a *Theory-Y manager.*[2]

There is also a second type of participative manager. He/she tends to empower the employees to make their own decisions and let's them implement their own ideas. This form of participative management is referred to as the *Theory-Z manager.*[3] In this management style we switch the top-down decision making process that is characteristic of the Theory-X or Theory-Y management style, to a bottom-up decision making process characteristic of the Japanese management style. In the Theory-Z style we are heavily involved in

2. For more information about Theory-X and Theory-Y managers, including some very interesting examples, read the book:

   McGregor, Douglas, *The Human Side of the Enterprise,* Mc Graw-Hill, New York, NY, 1985.

3. Theory-Z management is explained nicely, including examples, in the following book and article:

   Pascale, Richard Tanner, and Anthony G. Athos, *The Art of Japanese Management,* Warner Books, New York, NY, 1982.

   Joiner, Jr., Charles W., "Making the 'Z' Concept Work", *Sloan Management Review,* Spring 1985, Pages 57-63.

teaming, like the quality circles of old, and we use the teams to develop, approve, and implement ideas. Managers take on the role of facilitator, being responsible to make sure the approved ideas getimplemented timely and correctly. This manager is no longer the decision maker and driver of forward progress. The Theory-Z manager keeps the team focused and presents them with area of consideration and evaluation, but lets the team make their own improvement decisions.

A third way to classify managers is to evaluate their style of management using *the Five C's*. These are:

Cash Manager

This manager is focused on costs and budgets and has probably grown up through the accounting ranks. This type of manager tends to be risk averse and looks toward stability rather than opportunity. This type of manager finds it advisable to patch-and-repair old technology, as opposed to replacing it with new technology, because the high expense of the new technology would be too difficult to cost-absorb in one or two fiscal year. This management style is why we still have so many old and outdated factories in the United States, when we know that they cannot be long-term competitive. However, since the old factories are still demonstrating some minor profit levels, they are kept and maintained until they are totally unprofitable. Then the plants are transferred overseas where labor costs are cheaper. The cash manager feels the need to look for short term profitability, rather than long term competitiveness.

Crisis (or Crash) Manager

This type of manager believes that you shouldn't fix anything that isn't broken. This style of management, as with the cash manager, also strives toward stability, looking to problems as a disruption that needs to be conquered, rather than as an opportunity for future improvements. This manager attacks problems without considering the root causes of the problems thereby fixing only a symptom rather than the root cause of the problem. Often the fix includes the installations of another "system" to monitor the problem and catch it if it happens again.

Conflict Manager

This style of management looks at the work-place as a battlefield of competing players. This manager always feels the need to take and maintain the upper hand through whatever means necessary. Control is the primary tool of power, and intimidation is the primary motivating force.

Cool Manager

This type of manager believes that the work force is best motivated by giving them whatever they want. He/she want to bribe their way into the hearts of their children, which is how they view their employees. This manager wants to be everybody's best friend and wants everyone to smile at him/her as they walk by. The cool manager often ends up in a wishy-washy management style that results in more confusion than direction.

Change Manager

A change manager searches for challenges in competitiveness. This manager strives on positive, goal focused changes, seeing them as the opportunities that make work exciting. A larger number of changes are viewed as opportunities for growth. A change manager views problems as opportunities for change. Rather than trying to fix a problem, the change manager will spend time looking for the root causes of problems and will attempt to generate the necessary changes that will make the problem nonexistent.

Defining the Manager

Using *the Five C's* to define a management style requires integration with the other classifications. For example, you could have a manager that is sunrise, cool, and Theory-X. This would be a happy, smiley, bossy dreamer.

A last, but important method for classifying a manager is to compare the "boss" to the "leader". A boss directs employee traffic, whereas a leader shows the way using example and by stepping out into the traffic in front of the employees. Bosses manage, but leaders tend to lead out and search for a difference. Bosses see themselves as "King of the Hill" and want to keep the hill for themselves, whereas leaders show everyone, by example, how to get to the top of the hill. Bosses strive with a "Do as I Say" philosophy, whereas leaders use the "Do as I Do" technique. With leaders, employees tend to have a clear definition of what is expected of them because the example set by the leader has shown them their end objective. Simply put, bosses provide stability and governance, while leaders open the door for innovation.[4]

I have a personal comparison of the boss and the leader. I see a boss as someone that has to be there for the business to run correctly. Without the boss, the employees loose their decision making ability. It's often a situation where "if the cat's away, the mice are at play". Alternatively, I see the leader as someone that, if he/she doesn't show up for work for a few days, nothing would change. Everyone would know how to keep the business functioning and the leader's absence would hardly be noticed. I see a good leader as someone that manages his or her self into obsolescence.

Now it's time for you to classify how you see yourself as a manager. Use Chart 13.1 to determine what type of manager you think you are? Are you a Theory-X=Sunset=Cash Manager, which would be a bean-counting, bossy, fire-fighter telling everyone what to do,

4. There are lots of good articles discussing the role of leaders in a changing, growing organization. For example:

Senge, Peter M., "The Leader's New Work: Building Learning Organizations", *Sloan Management Review,* Fall 1990, Pages 7-23. This article focuses on the need for an organization to be "continuously learning" through leadership.

Kotter, John P., "What Leaders Really Do", Harvard Business Review, May-June 1990, Pages 103-111. This article stresses that "good management controls complexity; effective leadership produces useful change". The article states that "management controls people by pushing them in the right direction; leadership motivates them by satisfying basic human needs". This article offers three interesting leadership examples and the article is worth checking into just for the chance to read about the examples. They are:

1) American Express
2) Eastman Kodak
3) Procter & Gamble

how to do it, and when to do it, and no one does anything until directed, type of manager. Or are you a Theory-Y = Sunrise = Cool Leader who loves everyone, puts their arm around everyone, likes to show, rather than tell, everyone how to do their job, and likes to share their schemes of grandeur with everyone.

Chart 13.1. Finding Your Management Style

In front of each management style indicate whether you (or the person you are evaluating) fit this description:

N – not really one of these
O – occasionally one of these
Y – definitely one of these

_____ Sunrise Manager – has a view towards the future, a dreamer full of wild ideas, progressive, leading edge, technology minded

_____ Sunset Manager – spends time fighting day-to-day fires, workaholic who is great at getting things done

_____ Theory-X Manager – secretive, has his/her fingers in everything that happens, always has the final word, tells, rather than asks questions

_____ Theory-Y Manager – values the opinion of the employees, spends more time listening than talking, look for ideas from the bottom-up but makes the final decision

_____ Theory-Z Manager – tends to empower the employees to make their own decisions and lets them implement their own ideas

_____ Cash Manager – cost and budget obsessive, looks toward stability rather than opportunity, prefers to patch and repair rather than replace because it is cheaper

_____ Crisis (or Crash) Manager – believes that you shouldn't fix anything that isn't broken, looks at problems as a disruption that needs to be conquered, attacks problems

_____ Conflict Manager – looks at the work-place as a battlefield of competing players, feels the need to take and maintain the upper hand

_____ Cool Manager – feels the work force is best motivated by giving them whatever they want, wants to bribe their way into the hearts of their employees, wants to be everybody's best friend

_____ Change Manager – searches for challenges in competitiveness, strives on changes, innovations, improvements, technology

_____ Boss – directs employee traffic, see themselves as "King of the Hill" and wants to keep the hill for themselves, "Do as I Say" philosophy

_____ Leader – shows the way using example and by stepping out into the traffic in front of the employees, not afraid to show everyone how to get to the top of the hill, "Do as I Do" philosophy

Now you know a little more about yourself. You know what your management style is at this point in time. The next step toward world class management is to figure out what your management style *goal* is. After that, we need to set a travel plan that will take us from where we are and get us to where we're going.

Finally, we know what a World Class Manager should look like. A WCM should be a:

- Sunrise Manager – long term orientation looking for the "better way".
- Theory-Z Manager – employees involved with and guiding the business process through participative and empowered team efforts.
- Change Manager – manager of a dynamic, evolving business organism, that capitalizes on change opportunities.
- Leader – being a character building, motivational example.

At this point we have defined the characteristics of a global operations manager. Now let's take a look at why a manager would focus on a global environment.

World Class Reasons for Globalization

Next in this chapter we shall discuss why it makes good sense to be globally oriented. I will now review some specific strategic reasons why you want to make globalization a part of your corporate or business unit strategy. A list of specific strategic reasons for globalization would include:

- Cost Competitiveness
- Time-to-Market Competitiveness
- Manufacturing Processes
- Information Processes
- Government Policy
- Competitive Markets
- Technology Transfer
- Competitive Lessons We Can Learn.

Cost Competitiveness

Cost competitiveness is usually one of the first, and often the wrong reason for globalization. As we have already discussed in previous chapters, cost cutting is a short term financially oriented decision motivator. Almost always, the relocation decision is based on labor cost, and labor cost is typically ten percent or less of the value-added cost of the production process. Relocation decisions based on cutting labor costs only can detrimentally effect the total cost reduction. In the past, labor cost competitiveness has caused plants to be shifted to Latin America, East Asia, and more recently Southeast Asia. Fortunately, more recently, the mistake of labor cost competitiveness has been recognized and labor-cost-only shifts do not occur as often.

However, if total cost or value-added cost competitiveness is the basis for globalization, then the global strategy, although still short term oriented, at least has potential merit. Often, in these cases, materials sourcing costs are the dominating factor. For example, if locating a plant in Asia, in spite of the increased shipping and inventory carrying costs, and in spite of the potentially lower productivity and quality levels, still results in a net production cost reduction, then the move is a good one. Products like electrical components, compressors, electric motors, metals, agricultural materials, some chemicals, petroleum products, etc. are cheaper overseas than when purchased in the United States.

Another cost competitive issue that has motivated globalization is transportation, shipping, tariffs, and exchange rates. For example, Coca Cola or Pepsi bottle their product as close to the consumer as possible. Then, the only thing that is imported is the high value-added item of the syrup. The bulky items like the bottles and the soda water are locally sourced and bottled. Similarly, Japanese companies have decided to manufacture in the United States or Canada because of the Japanese Yen – U. S. Dollar relationship.

Recently, with the introduction of NAFTA, there have been many surprises. For example, the movement of Toys-R-Us and Walmart into Canada has resulted in the closure of some major Canadian toy retailers. Additionally, labor intensive production processes like agriculture, which should favor the low labor costs of Mexico, have in fact resulted in agricultural products being shipped from the United States to Mexico, and, surprisingly, Mexican farmers, rather than United States farmers, have been displaced. In both the Canada and Mexico cases, cost competitiveness was the issue. The lowest total cost producer won the lions share of the market.

Time-to-Market Competitiveness

One of the strategic disadvantages of the United States is its inability to react quickly to market changes (this topic will be discussed in detail in the next chapter). However, some Asian countries like Taiwan and Hong Kong have developed a strategic niche by being able to react quickly. For example, if you are trying to produce fad clothing items, or if you are trying to react to a sudden trend shift in the toy market, these Asian producers would be able to quickly adjust their production output to meet your needs. A similar shift in the productive output of a United States, European, or Japanese plant could take months to make:

- Manufacturing Processes – Improvements in the manufacturing processes have created mini-factories that are more efficient and less costly than their previous counterparts. These mini-factories are easily relocated overseas opening the doors for new market opportunities.
- Information Processes – Tools like telecommunications, faxes, teleconferencing, and computer networking have reduced or eliminated the distance barriers. These tools have become increasingly important to the financial and retailing industries.
- Government Policy – Countries like Mexico and many of the previous communist countries have initiated enormous privatization programs. These programs offer opportunities for new markets and have become part of the globalization strategy of many companies.
- Many countries like Malaysia, Singapore, Mexico, and Ireland offer enormous incentives and offer attractive packages for companies interested in developing operations in their country. These packages often include reduced tax incentives and duty-free trade zones for the manufactured products.
- Competitive Markets – Markets for your products exist all over the world. Globalization is often driven by the desire to enter

these markets. Often, opening new markets also requires the globalization of the manufacturing process. For example, in Europe you need to have a production facility within the borders of the European Union (EU) in order to avoid certain tariffs and trade restrictions. Therefore, for companies who want to access the European markets, the European production facility becomes part of their marketing globalization strategy.

- Technology Transfer – A technology exchange is where both sides of the exchange benefit. Western countries would assist the Developing Country (DC) in technological growth, and they in turn would help in the development of new technologies. These types of exchanges are why so many companies are setting up technology development centers in many parts of the world.

Technology transfer is an important element of a globalization strategy, and needs to be considered carefully:

- *Who* – to transfer
  Some countries offer financial incentives, and others offer a highly educated work force (Malaysia and Hong Kong).

- *What* – to transfer
  Some companies select to only transfer their support functions, and not their core competencies. Others transfer in areas where they hope to learn from the country transferred to (Europe or Japan).

- *When* – the timing or turn-around of the transfer
  Some countries are quicker at technology implementation (Taiwan). On other occasions, the technology transfer may be timed to specific events, like market entries (Mexico and NAFTA).

- *Where* – location of the transfer
  Some countries offer strategic opportunities in their location (Singapore – shipping or Hong Kong – banking).

- *How* – the transfer process
  Does transferring require the movement of large amounts of

equipment or personnel? Does the new location require large amounts of resources (heavy equipment or energy)?
- *Why* – does technology transfer make strategic sense? Is the transfer justified financially, logistically, etc.?

A study was done looking at the transfer of bicycle technology within three classes of countries, the Developed Countries (DC – United States, Japan), Newly Industrialized Economies (NIE – South Korea, Singapore), and Less Developed Countries (LDC – Mexico, Indonesia). A comparison was made based on several criteria, including cost. The results are that NIEs are the most cost competitive countries for bicycle manufacturing. The introduction to state-of-the-art technology results in detrimental consequences for LDCs and the complex, machine technology introduced should be more mass production, rather than hi-tech oriented. The large production gains occurred in each category of country after the introduction of advanced technology processes like the quality control process or the introduction of flexible production methodologies. None of these findings are surprising, but the study quantifies these results with supportive data.[5]

One of the primary tools used for analyzing the growth of nations, and additionally of the development of industries within these nations is benchmarking. Benchmarking is an analysis of national, industrial, or corporate numbers to see how the different industries compare. The primary basis for comparison is financial and operational numbers, however these don't always tell a complete story.

Harley-Davidson was in serious trouble in the early 1980s. In fact, they weren't expected to survive. This last surviving United States motorcycle manufacturer was being devastated by the Japanese with a market share loss of from 75 percent in 1973 to less than 25 percent. But Harley has recovered, and has come back to control 50 percent of the market share. Here is an example where a banker (Citicorp) badly misjudged a company's potential by looking only at the numbers. What happened? It's simple, Harley learned from the competition, and they learned their lessons well.

5. Suri, Rajan, Jerry L. Sanders, P. Chandrasekhar Rao, and Ashoka Mody, "Impact of Manufacturing Practices on the Global Bicycle Industry", *Manufacturing Review*, March 1993, Pages 14-24.

In the early 1980s Harley quality was awful and manufacturing was a mess. They thought they could rely on their dedicated and committed customer forever. But, unfortunately, they were wrong. Managers bought the company and made a dramatic turnaround. They told their own story in the book *Well-Made in America.*[6]

Harley-Davidson used World Class Management tools like empowerment and globalization to make a difference. And they see the difference in their increases in sales, profits, and return on equity. But the numbers that eventually made Citicorp happy only came after Harley understood and beat the competition.

One of the lessons that we learn from globalization is that most countries have moved away from the concept that there is one, perfect right answer to all problems. The "one right answer" way of thinking seems to be characteristic of Christian cultures. In the Middle East and Asia, there is the realization that "one right answer" does not exist, rather, alternatives exist. Two plants running side by side producing the same product may have different "right" answers to the same problem. This may occur because one has an authoritarian management style, and the other has a participative management style.

In the United States and Europe, the search for the "one right answer" causes us to have an all-or-nothing attitude to changes. For example, in our attempt to copy Japan, we went through a series of all-or-nothing right answers. About ten years ago quality circles were the fad. Everyone thought that by implementing quality control (QC) circles they would have the perfect answer to competing with the Japanese. When this didn't provide the desired results within two years, it was thrown out and statistical process control (SPC) was deemed the perfect solution. Again, after two years, this was thrown out and the next fad was introduced. We went through in-line quality control (ILQC), Just-in-Time production (JIT), Total Quality Management (TQM), and many more such fads, trying, implementing, short term testing, and then rejecting the technique. But in our search for this perfect answer, we never asked the Japanese what their secret was. The Japanese would have eagerly told us

6. Reid, Peter C., *Well-Made in America,* McGraw-Hill, 1990.

that their secret was none of the above. Rather, it was all of the above. It was the integration of all of these processes over a long period of time (20 to 30 years) that brings about the desired results.

Many developing countries have learned the building-block approach to improvements. They have given up on the idea of a quick fix, rather, they are looking at alternatives for improvements, implementing the change, saving and incorporating the elements that work, and integrating them into the process, and then finally moving on to another idea for change. Tools like SPC or QC or JIT are not tested and rejected, the good elements of each are accepted and integrated into the process. They have the approach that all of these tools are building in a long-term and planned-out solution, not a quick-fix, solution.

We have an unlimited number of lessons that we can learn from globalization. We have highlighted a few but is important that you incorporate these in your drive to become a World Class Manager.

Defining a Globalization Strategy

A globalization strategy is an element of the corporate or business strategy that focuses on internationalization. As discussed at the beginning of this book, internationalization can take many forms. In one study of internationalization practices it was found that nearly all the globalized companies required major organizational changes, primarily in decentralizing. Ninety-four percent of the globalized companies strongly agreed that competition is heating up globally and the pace of innovation has quickened. Some additional points of the study included.[7]

- In this study half of the companies felt that exports are the best globalization strategy, and the other half felt that investment was the best strategy.

7. Chilton, Kenneth, "Changing Structures and Strategies: Survey of American Manufacturing Executives", *Center for the Study of American Business*, Washington University, St. Louis, Missouri, Working Paper 151, September, 1993.

- About three-fourths of the companies feel that globalization is best accomplished using joint ventures.
- The relationships with customers and suppliers had to change dramatically to where they were working much more closely with each.
- Empowerment is not a buzzword and should be used for decision making. This is supported by 85 percent of the surveyed companies.

Another study stresses that the competitive advantage of a company determines the value-added in the global market place. The existence of both determines a successful globalization strategy.[8]

In yet a third study, successful global (referred to as transnational) companies require the integration of efficiency, customer responsiveness, and the ability to exploit learning (employee training and innovation) in order to be successful.[9]

Having considered these elements of a globalization strategy, we also need to recognize some risks. The biggest risk is of pushing too much toward one of the extreme ends of the integration-diversification spectrum. Too much diversification will cause segmentation. These types of organizations tend to have unique foreign and domestic branches, each with their own objectives and value system. The other extreme is equally as bad. This is where the global and domestic arms of the company are so integrated that effective localization is lost. These types of organizations treat, and expect, everyone to act the same as at home. A happy balance between these extremes is needed, where globalization is part of the Vision, Mission, and Strategy of the corporation, while, at the same time, not losing the localization aspects where we work closely with the country and the culture.

8. Kogut, Bruce, "Designing Global Strategies: Comparative and Competitive Value-Added Chains", *Sloan Management Review,* Summer 1995, Pages 15-28.
9. Bartlett, Christopher A. and Sumantra Ghoshal, "Managing Across Borders: New Strategic Requirements", *Sloan Management Review,* Summer 1987, Pages 7-17.

Types of International Relationships

There are many different forms of international partnerships that have developed, such as company buy-outs or joint ventures. The one partnership arrangement that is being given the most attention recently is the formation of strategic alliances. A strategic alliance is where an enterprise focuses on their core competencies and then orients their business strategy around that core competency. There are many examples of recently established strategic alliances. For example, FedEx is utilizing their logistics capability to act as the inventory and distribution agent for other enterprises whose core competency is manufacturing. FedEx has established a Business Logistics Services division which forms a unique alliance with companies like Laura Ashley to restructure and manage its distributions systems. FedEx is the master of logistics, and Laura Ashley was the master at producing products with English charm. Neither could do the other function well. The strategic alliance formed between the two gave each the best of both worlds. The result: Laura Ashley can re-supply its 540 shops anywhere within the world within 24 to 48 hours.

FedEx provides similar services for National Semiconductor Corporation, who wanted to stay within its core competency of building semiconductors. FedEx also provides their logistics services for the House of Windsor. FedEx provides the logistics services that offer time-definite delivery within two working days. Additionally they provide inventory tracking and control which includes pulling, packing, shipping, and monitoring the inventory movement process.

Another example of a strategic alliance is Solectron, another Malcolm Baldridge Award winner, which is one of the world's premier electronics companies. They have shunned advertising, minimized product research and development, and focused entirely on manufacturing and customer service. And because they're so good at it, they're getting more business than they can handle, and they're being choosey about who they accept.[10]

10. Savona, Dave, "The Invisible Partner", *International Business,* November 1994, Pages 64-68.

Strategic alliances mean sharing control of some aspects of the company. This is difficult for some managers to accept. However, backing off of the things you're not good at, and doing even better at the things you are good at, is the focus of the strategic alliance gamble. And most companies that have attempted these alliances have found them to be successful. For example, the FedEx strategic alliances are a critical element of customer service and satisfaction for the companies FedEx supports.

Summary

The *Harvard Business Review* has conducted a number of surveys on the characteristics of a World Class Global Manager. The one common characteristic that they have learned is that "change is indeed everywhere – regardless of country, culture, or corporation". They also learned that culture, more than geography, is the major determinant of a manager's views. These studies are on going and strengthen many of the points made in this chapter.[11]

This chapter has defined the characteristics of a World Class Global Operations Manager. Since this book is on global operations management, I felt it would be useful to define what the ideal manager would look like. Additionally, this chapter discussed why a manager would want to go international.

Class Assignments

1) Revisit the Cases in the first three chapters of this book. Compare the lessons learned from each case. How are the situations in each case similar? How are they different:
   - From Chapter 1, redo Assignment A which was a role-play discussion of Z, Inc. Use a similar process for each of the integrated, in-text cases that are found in each chapter of this book.

11. Kanter, Rosabeth Moss, "Transcending Business Boundaries: 12,000 World Managers View Change", *Harvard Business Review,* May-June 1991, Pages 151-164.

    Editors, "The Boundaries of Business: Commentaries from the Experts", *Harvard Business Review,* July-August 1991, Pages 127-140.

- In Chapter 3, rework the W Gravel Company, Inc. Case and discuss what you would do differently at this point, taking into consideration the ethical dilemmas that this case presents.

References

Change Management References

Fey, Victor, and Eugene Rivin, "TRIZ: A New Approach to Innovative Engineering and Problem Solving", *Target*, September/October 1996, Pages 7 to 13.

Hammer and Champy, *Reengineering the Corporation*, Harper Business, 1993.

Nadler, Gerald and Shozo Hibino, *Breakthrough Thinking*, Prima Publishing and Communications, 1990, Rocklin, CA.

Covey, *The 7 Habits of Highly Effective People*, Fireside, 1990, New York.

Plenert and Hibino, *Making Innovation Happen: Concept Management Through Integration*, DelRay Beach, Florida, St. Lucie Press, 1997 (168 Pages).

Nadler, Gerald and Shozo Hibino, *Creative Solution Finding*, Prima Publishing, 1990.

World Class Management References

Plenert, *World Class Manager*, Prima, Rocklin, CA, 1995.

Total Quality Management References

Capezio, Peter, and Debra Morehouse, *Taking the Mystery out of TQM*, Career Press, Hawthorne. NJ, 1993.

Joel E. Ross, *Total Quality Management: Text, Cases, and Readings*, St. Lucie Press, 1993, Delray Beach, Fl.

Mahoney and Thor, *The TQM Trilogy*, AMACOM – American Management Association, ISBN 0-8144-5105-5, 1994.

Hoffherr, Glen D., John W. Moran, and Gerald Nadler, *Break-*

through Thinking in Total Quality Management, PTR Prentice Hall, Englewood Cliffs, NJ, 1994.

Plenert, Gerhard, "Total Quality Management (TQM) – Making it Work" *Technology Management*, Vol. 2 No. 5, 1996, Pages 236-240.

Plenert, Gerhard, "Total Quality Management (TQM) – Putting Structure Behind The Philosophy" *International Business Review*, Vol. 5 No. 1, 1996, Pages 67-78.

Plenert, Gerhard, and Shozo Hibino, "The T-Model: A Systematic Model for Change" *National Productivity Review*, Vol. 13, No. 4, Autumn 1994, Pages 543-549.

Team Management References

Pope, Sara, *Team Sponsor Workbook*, Cornelius and Associates, Columbia, SC, 1994.

Pope, Sara, *Team Leader Workbook*, Cornelius and Associates, Columbia, SC, 1996.

Mears, Peter, and Frank Voehl, *Team Building: A Structured Learning Approach*, St. Lucie Press, Delray Beach, FL, 1994.

14. The Future of Operations Management

Deloitte & Touche and Deloitte Consulting conduct a biennial survey of manufacturing trends. In their 1998 survey they stated the following. "The imperatives for the 21st Century – globalization, product innovation and supply chain integration – all require a fundamental shift in executive mind-sets. Operating successfully on a global scale requires companies to re-evaluate their traditional strategies ... It requires continuous change – change that encompasses the entire organization ..."[1]

A global supply chain with efficient information flow and integration from the suppliers supplier to the customer's customer is the key performance criteria for a successful competitive future in operations management.

The Tools of the Future

The tools of the future for operations management include:

- Internal tools
  - Lean manufacturing processes
  - Advanced manufacturing planning and scheduling
- External
  - Certification programs
  - Award programs
  - Integration programs
  - Globalization programs

1. Taken from the "1998 Vision in Manufacturing – Executive Summary", Deloitte & Touche and Deloitte Consulting, New York, 1998, Page 7.

- System Wide
  - Integrative strategies
  - Information strategies
  - Time based competitive strategies
  - Performance measurement changes
  - Change management

Lean manufacturing – tools include JIT, Kanban, Stockless Production, etc. techniques that focus on shop floor efficiencies targeted around the critical resource.

Advanced manufacturing planning and scheduling – ERP (Enterprise Resource Planning) is excellent for internal integration. However, the production planning and scheduling driver needs to be something more sophisticated than traditional MRP, for example Finite Capacity Scheduling (FCS). This will not eliminate the old technologies, since there are many environments where they are appropriate. Rather, we will see a combining of technologies with no dominant technology rearing it's head. One of the best Advanced Production Scheduling (APS) software products that has gained a strong following in Southeast Asia is Schedule Based Manufacturing (SBM). It was developed in Australia. It has exhibited tremendous supply chain efficiency results but has received little attention in the United States and Europe.

Certification programs – Programs like ISO and QS certification are becoming an information integration standard. More advanced variations, like the ISO 1400 standard for environmental concerns (green manufacturing), are increasingly the wave of the future.

Award programs – The Deming Award, The Baldrige Award, and the Shingo Prize will continue to define the standard for manufacturing excellence. The award criteria for these programs will continue to be used as the defining criteria for manufacturing improvements.

Integration programs – Integration of information, standards, people, etc. will become a critical part of supply chain efficiency. It will be common for vendors to have employees working full time in customers' shops. For example, UPS employees can be found in the plants of numerous manufacturers throughout the world.

Globalization programs – Culture, language, and ethical education of employees and their increasing involvement with international vendors and customers will become a norm.

Integrative strategies – Supply chain management will be part of the strategic initiatives of all companies in the next decade. The creation of the virtual enterprise which incorporates outsourcing, strategic alliances, operational alliances, and leveraged knowledge will become the norm.

Information strategies – An information communication process, for example standardization around the internet, will become necessary.

Time based competitive strategies – Cycle time reduction and corresponding waste elimination will become a key part of the measurement criteria for future organizations.

Performance measurement changes – The change in focus on critical resource management and on utilizing measures other than financial measures has increased the importance of changing the measurement system throughout the entire supply chain. For example, the realization that managing the cycle time will not just increase customer responsiveness but will also reduce inventory has focused organizations on identifying simplified measurement systems.

Change management – The need for continuous competitive improvement has sparked interest in tools like Total Quality Management (TQM) and Concept Management (CM). Change management has also created a strong focus on change at the lowest levels, which has renewed a strong interest in team building with a focus on gain-sharing, and empowerment. Change tools like Triz and the PDCA (Plan-Do-Check-Act) process have gained wide-spread acceptance. However, tools like Root Cause Analysis have fallen into disfavor because of their slowness and they are being replaced with tools like Breakthrough Thinking.

The International Future

From the previous section we have identified the strategies of the future. Note that the majority of these strategies focus on external relationship development, which directly focuses on international integration. The competitive future of operations cannot exist without a global perspective.

Future effects on the global future include the increasing development of trading blocks until the ultimate international trading system, the WTO is finally fully established. Even then subordinate trading blocks like the EU (European Union) will continue to exist because their unification runs deeper than the intent of the international system, such as a standardization of currency. It will become important for organizations to have supply chain connections within each of the trading blocks in order to minimize the costs and tariffs associated with entry.

Another international trend is for more developing countries to become developed, and for more under-developed countries to become developing. This increased equalization will force organizations to rethink their models of comparative advantage and realize that labor cost is no longer the prime reason for going international.

With increased communication in both the media and with tools like the eCommerce or eBusiness on the internet, international transactions will become second nature for all business everywhere. Even the smallest company will be involved in international transactions.

The Forces of the Future

The technical forces of the future would include:

- *Electronic Commerce* (eCommerce) – As already stated many times in this book, the internet will become the wave of future economic transactions, including the transfer of information and of funds.
- *Technology Transfer* – The global economic growth has driven the development of rapid, yet controlled time-to-market processes. One of these processes is the control of product changes throughout the supply chain. The need for rapid yet effective change is being addressed by the ISO (International Organization for Standardization) 10303 series of standards. This standard is known as the *STandard for the Exchange of Product* model data (STEP) standard. STEP provides a standard for the development of computer interpretable representations of the physical and functional characteristics of a product. It focuses on monitoring the process throughout the entire life cycle of the product. Most organizations will soon be required to adapt the STEP standard as part of their ISO certification process.

- *Impact of managing operations internationally* – Internationally there will be more localized management. The need for resident foreign experts will diminish, but the amount of travel will increase as organizations focus on increased integration and information sharing.

Technology transfer also includes the transfer of soft technologies like process methodologies and procedures. These soft technology transfers will increase as customers and suppliers integrate themselves together in competitive supply chain networks.

Summary

The future is looking great for international operations managers. They are playing a more critical role in over-all corporate success. And corporations recognize that the value of operations' role will continue to increase in importance in the future.

15. The Next Step

Leading executives have stressed that the competitive advantage in the next decade is found in the management of the supply chain. The organizations that have the best global supply chains, and that manage them better than their competitive supply chains will be the winners. These executives stress that we need to manage the supply chain, not use it. We need to develop our suppliers so that they are so efficient that we would want to buy them and incorporate them into our own internal structures.

Recently, Chrysler had a 273,000 vehicle recall caused by a fourth tier supplier that made springs. This supplier didn't even know that their product went into the Chrysler vehicles. The supplier had decided to make a slight change in their design and hadn't checked up the supply chain for the effects that this change would have, and the result was devastating. When there are 4,000 parts per vehicle, the management of the supply chain can become extremely complex, but at the same time even more critical.

If you eliminate pick-ups, who is the largest auto manufacturer in the United Stated today? Honda! Honda processes 7 million parts through their facility every day. Yet they do it with only four to eight hours of inventory on-hand. They have an inventory turns ration of 3 turns per day. Suppliers deliver parts within a plus or minus 20 minute range. It costs suppliers $23,000 per minute if they shut the production line down at Honda. An on time delivery requires four points: 1) correct parts, 2) parts on time, 3) correct paperwork, and 4) paperwork on time. Honda's on-time delivery performance is 99.9 percent. And this is in the United States.

This book has been a splattering of World Class Global Operations ideas that need to be integrated together into a game plan. So where do managers need to go from here? Here is the process I would recommend:

1) Define the focus of your goals (see Chapter 3):
   a) Where does the customer fit in?
   b) What is quality?
   c) What is the role of productivity?
2) Focus on cleaning up your internal house first:
   a) Identify operations tools, like MRP, JIT, ERP, TOC, or Finite Capacity Scheduling that will make you internally world class competitive.
   b) Organize yourself around a world class management style.
   c) Create an integrated information system using some form of intranet.
   d) Develop global goals with a local perspective.
   e) Design a measurement system based on the goals and the critical resource that these goals focus on.
3) Focus on cleaning up your external environment:
   a) Develop a globally integrated supply chain management system that shares information utilizing internet capabilities.
   b) Develop long-term relationships with all elements of the supply chain, especially the international members of the chain – pay careful attention to the ethical and cultural relationships.
   c) Develop measures of performance based on cycle time and inventory levels.
4) Look to the future:
   a) Create a dynamic, learning, change focused global organization that focuses on customer satisfaction using tools like team based TQM and Concept Management.
   b) Focus on increasing value-added elements and eliminating waste, especially in the logistics and distribution processes.
   c) Change everything, including the goals.

The international environment is a great opportunity for the entire supply chain to learn from each other. Companies like Intel and Motorola have experienced the synergy of growth that comes from mixing cultures. They are anxiously pursuing international relationships that will significantly increase their level of competitiveness.

About the Author

The author, Gerhard Plenert, PhD, CPIM, has spent 15 years working in management for private industry. His specialty is in International POM (Production / Operations Management) and MIS (Management Information Systems). He has traveled throughout the world in this capacity. He earned his Ph.D. at the Colorado School of Mines. He spent four years teaching and doing research at California State University, Chico and eight years at Brigham Young University in the Institute of Business Management. He was the Director of the California Productivity and Quality Center at CSUC and the director of the Productivity and Quality Research Group at BYU. He has recently returned to industry. In his first assignment with Precision Printers, using the principles outlined in this book, he successfully accomplished the following in eight months:

- Taken a 14 + % defect rate and driven it down to 2 %
- Brought set-up times from 20 minutes to below 10 minutes and as low as 6 min.
- Established QS certification, TQM, and SPC, and recertified under ISO
- Performed World Class Manufacturing, MRP II, and ERP training.
- Organized a previously non-existent R&D Department.
- Reduced inventories by 40 %.
- Significantly reduced the over-all lead time and Cycle Time.
- Order preparation time was reduced from 5 days to less than one day.
- Organized the development of a Vision / Mission / Values statement and a Strategy.
- Organized a previously non-existent production planning and scheduling function.

These eight months of accomplishments demonstrate that the topics covered in this book really do work.

Dr. Plenert recently worked for American Management Systems (AMS), an 9,000 employee consulting company, where he was facilitating a corporate wide Supply Chain Management consulting practice. He now manages his own consulting practice, The Institute of World Class Management (IWCM) where he focuses on international SCM innovations.

His research specialty has focused on International Industrial Management and Supply Chain Management with an emphasis on developing countries. He has published over 150 articles, and has made over 150 conference and seminar presentations. He has published six books:

- *International Management and Production – Survival Techniques for Corporate America,* Tab Professional and Reference Books, 1990.
- *Plant Operations Deskbook,* Homewood, Ill., Business 1 IRWIN, 1993, (501 Pages).
- *World Class Manager*, Rocklin, CA, Prima Publishing, 1995 (400 Pages).
- *Making Innovation Happen: Concept Management Through Integration*, DelRay Beach, Florida, St. Lucie Press, 1997 (168 Pages) – With Shozo Hibino.
- *Finite Capacity Scheduling,* Wiley, 2000, (251 Pages) – With Bill Kirchmier.
- *The eManager: Value Chain Management in an eCommerce World,* Blackhall Publishing, Dublin, Ireland, 2001 (370 Pages).

Mr. Plenert realizes that the subject matter of this book is very fluid and dynamic. He is very interested in your experiences, comments, ideas, and recommendations and would find them helpful in further editions of this book. Please send your comments to:

Gerhard Plenert, PhD, CPIM
Institute of World Class Management
3988 Orval Way, Carmichael, CA 95608
Plenert@AOL.COM
Phone 916-536-9751, Fax 916-536-9758

Appendix A Benchmarking Measures of Performance

Sales Growth

Percentage of increase in sales comparing this year to last year should go up:

$$\text{(Sales Increase Ratio)} = \frac{\text{(Total Sales This Year Minus This Year's Returns)}}{\text{(Total Sales Last Year Minus Last Year's Returns)}}$$

Size of market share growth over the years should increase:

$$\text{(Size of MarketShare)} = \frac{\text{(Year Net Sales)}}{\text{(Total Sales of the Market)}}$$

$$\text{(Size of Market Share Growth)} = \frac{\text{(Size of Market Share This Year)}}{\text{(Size of Market Share Last Year)}}$$

Cost of Sales

Operating costs (labor, materials, and direct overhead) as a percentage of sales:

$$\text{(Operating Costs of Sales Ratio)} = \frac{\text{(Operating Costs [Cost of Sales for Items Sold])}}{\text{(Total Sales Minus Returns)}}$$

Cost of Production

What percentage of product cost is labor, materials, overhead? Compare this with your competitors and note any significant differences:

$$(\text{Labor Cost of Production}) = \frac{(\text{Total Direct Labor Cost})}{(\text{Total Direct Labor, Materials, Direct Overhead})}$$

$$(\text{Total Materials Cost of Production}) = \frac{(\text{Total Materials Cost})}{(\text{Total Direct Labor, Materials, Direct Overhead})}$$

$$(\text{Total Direct Overhead Cost of Production}) = \frac{(\text{Total Direct Overhead Cost})}{(\text{Total Direct Labor, Materials, Direct Overhead})}$$

Indirect Cost Ratios

What is the relationship between indirect and direct costs? The lower these values are, the better:

$$(\text{Indirect Cost Ratio}) = \frac{(\text{Total Indirect Costs})}{(\text{Total Costs})}$$

$$(\text{Indirect/Direct Coverage}) = \frac{(\text{Total Indirect Costs})}{(\text{Total Direct Costs})}$$

Asset strength

How well do your assets cover your debts:

$$(\text{Asset Ratio}) = \frac{(\text{Total Assets})}{(\text{Total Debts})}$$

$$(\text{Current Ratio}) = \frac{(\text{Total Current Assets})}{(\text{Total Current Debts})}$$

What percentage of your assets are tied up in inventory:

$$(\text{Inventory Asset Ratio}) = \frac{(\text{Total Inventory})}{(\text{Total Current Assets})}$$

Equity strength

What percentage of the total assets is owned? Your number should be higher than your competitors and higher this year than last year:

$$(Equity\ Strength) = \frac{(Total\ Equity)}{(Total\ Assets)}$$

Quality

Percentage of returns to total sales should go down:

$$(Returns\ Percentage) = \frac{(Total\ Sales\ Dollar\ Value\ of\ Returns)}{(Total\ Gross\ Sales\ Dollars)}$$

Percentage of scrap or reject parts both internal and from the vendor should decrease:

$$(Scrap - Reject\ Purchase\ Ratio) = \frac{(Total\ Cost\ of\ Scrap - Reject\ Parts\ Purchased)}{(Total\ Cost\ of\ all\ Parts\ Purchased)}$$

$$(Scrap - Reject\ Production\ Ratio) = \frac{(Total\ Cost\ of\ Scrap - Reject\ Parts\ Produced)}{(Total\ Cost\ of\ all\ Parts\ Produced)}$$

Employee Permanence and Stability

This is an important goal that is used quite often in Japan. The primary reason for the popularity of this goal is because it supports a participative relationship with the employees, rather than the adversarial one (employers see employees as a cost element and employees see employers as cattle drivers) that is typical of United States firms:

$$(Employee\ Turnover\ Ratio) = \frac{Number\ of\ Employees\ Hired + Fired + Quit\ During\ the\ Year}{Total\ Average\ Number\ of\ Employees\ for\ the\ Year}$$

Productivity

Direct Labor Hours Productivity:

$$(Direct\ Labor\ Hours\ Productivity) = \frac{Net\ Sales}{Total\ Labor\ Hours}$$

Labor Dollars Productivity:

$$(Labor\ Dollars\ Productivity) = \frac{NetSales}{Total\ Labor\ Dollars}$$

Materials Productivity:

$$(Materials\ Productivity) = \frac{Net\ Sales}{Total\ Materials\ Cost}$$

Total Cost of Sales Productivity:

$$(Total\ Cost\ of\ Sales\ Productivity) = \frac{Net\ Sales}{Total\ Cost\ of\ Sales}$$

Total Cost of Operation (Direct plus Indirect) Productivity:

$$(Total\ Cost\ of\ Operation\ Productivity) = \frac{NetSales}{Total\ Cost\ of\ Operation\ (Direct + Indirect)}$$

Value-Added Productivity:

$$(Productivity) = \frac{Net\ Sales}{Net\ Sales - Cost\ of\ Goods\ Sold}$$

Total Factor Productivity:

$$(Productivity) = \frac{Net\ Sales}{Labor + Materials + Energy + Machinery + etc.}$$

Critical Resource Productivity:

$$(Productivity) = \frac{Net\ Sales}{Critical\ Resource\ Costs}$$

Appendix B
Total Quality Management Tools

These are the tools listed in the QS-9000 manual as valuable and helpful for quality certification. The detailed information is available in the book *Information Kit for QS-9000 / TQM Tools Correlation Matrix*, which can be acquired from the:

Automative Industry Action Group
26200 Lahser Road, Suite 200
Southfield, Michigan 48034
(248) 358-3570
http://www.qiqg.org/

The TQM tools are:

- Activity Based Costing (ABC)
- Activity Network Diagram
- Affinity Diagram
- Analysis of Motion-Ergonomics
- Benchmarking
- Brainstorming
- Cause & Effect Analysis
- Cell Manufacturing
- Change Management
- Computer-Aided Design (CAD)
- Computer-Aided Engineering (CAE)
- Concurrent / Simultaneous Engineering
- Configuration Management
- Control Plan
- Correlation Study
- Cost of Quality
- Critical Path Diagrams (Network Diagrams)
- Cross-Functional Teams

- Customer Needs Identification
- Customer Satisfaction Analysis
- Cycle Time Management
- Defect Maps
- Design for Competitiveness
- Design for Manufacturing / Design for Assembly (DFM/DFA)
- Design of Experiment (DOE)
- Employee Empowerment
- Employee Involvement
- Error Proofing (Mistake Proofing)
- Executive Management Statements
- Failure Mode and Effect Analysis (FEMA)
- Feasibility Review
- Finite Element Analysis (FEM)
- First-In-First-Out (FIFO) Inventory Control
- Force Field Analysis
- Gage Repeatability & Reproducibility (Gage R&R)
- Geometric Dimensioning and Tolerancing (GD&T)
- Histogram
- Imagineering
- Input / Output Analysis
- Interrelationship Diagram
- Kaizen (Continuous Improvement)
- Lean Manufacturing (JIT)
- Lot Size Reduction
- Manufacturing Resource Planning (MRP II)
- Matrix Diagram
- Nominal Group Technique (NGT)
- Non-Parametric Analysis
- Pareto Chart
- Parts Per Million (PPT)
- Planning for Quality
- Predictive Maintenance
- Preventive Maintenance (PM)
- Prioritization Matrix
- Process Decision Program Chart (PDPC)
- Process Flow Chart
- Quality Functional Deployment (QFD)
- Quality System Audits

- Randomization
- Reliability
- Scatter Diagram
- Self-Direced Teams
- Statistical Process Control (SPC)
- Strategic Planning / Business Plans
- Suggestion Systems
- Surveys
- Team Building
- Team Problem Solving
- Theory of Constraints (TOC)
- Theory of Infinite Problem Solving
- Thermography / Infrared Analysis
- Total Productive Maintenance (TPM)
- Tree Diagram
- Value-Added Analysis
- Value Analysis / Value Engineering (VA/VE)
- Vibration Signature Analysis (VSA)
- Work Flow Analysis.

Appendix C
A Simulation Which Compares The MRP, JIT, and TOC Production Planning Philosophies

The production planning and control philosophies are often taught with religious zeal. The instructors commitment and belief in one system over another often looses objectivity. Therefore, it became necessary to develop a process that would demonstrate each of the methodologies in such a way as to show the students the advantages and disadvantages to each. Depending on their use, each system has been found to be more effective in some specific production situation. This appropriateness of fit comes through in the demonstration of these methodologies.

The most commonly used production planning and control methodologies are Material Requirements Planning (MRP), Just-in-Time (JIT), and Theory of Constraints (TOC) (also called OPT). A comparison of the usefulness of each of these production planning methods is what this simulation tool attempts to draw out of the students.

The Simulation Procedure

The simulation is run on three different days. Each day one of the production planning philosophies is demonstrated. Each simulation is preceded by a thorough discussion of the production planning methodology. MRP is usually the first discussed, since it is the most common in Western countries including Europe and the United States. Following the discussion of how MRP works, the MRP simulation is run. Afterward, a case study is often used to cement the concepts into the memory of the students. Then JIT is similarly discussed, simulated, and demonstrated with a case. And lastly TOC is taught in the same way. This write-up will focus on the operation of the simulation.

The MRP Simulation

In the MRP simulation, the class is assigned into the following departments:

- Management (whose responsibility is observation, measurement, and improvement of the process)
- Materials Movers (MM) (they handle all parts transfers between departments and from raw materials)
- Quality (Q)
- Shipping (S)
- Production Department 1 (PD1)
- Production Department 2 (PD2)
- Production Department 3 (PD3).

The production sequence is MM-PD1-PD2-Q-PD3-Q-S. The production process is to fill out the document shown in Chart C-1.

Chart C.1.

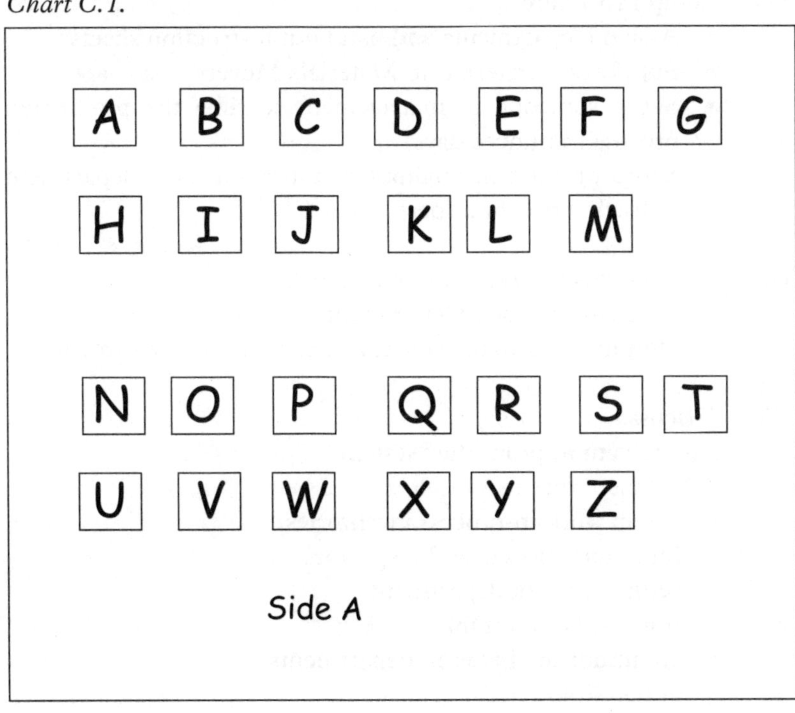

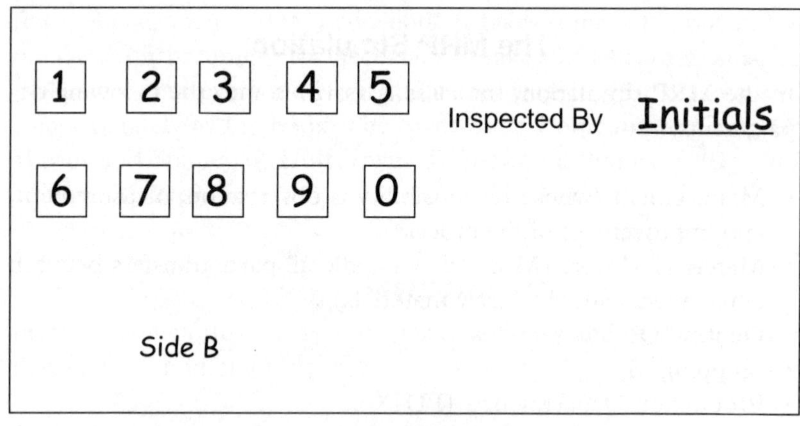

The following describes the plant operation procedure.

MRP Simulation Procedure

(1) Setup Procedure:
- Assign Departments and hand out instruction sheets
- Supply raw materials to Materials Movers
- Setup someone in management to time the production process (5 minute days)
- Setup product throughput counters for each department to track throughput performance

(II) Run process for 5 minutes and check:
- Efficiency of each Department
- Output performance for each Production Department

(IV) Discuss:
Methods to improve the "system"
Allow them to:
- set up work-in-process inventories
- hire more movers and inspectors
- setup a rework department
- train and cross-train
- communicate between departments

Do not allow them to:

- move equipment or departments
- change lot sizes
- send rejects back to previous work stations

What are the real problems with efficient Department performance?

(V) Make improvements that management agrees to that will improve the "numbers"

(VI) Repeat steps II through V watching improvement each time

Wrap-up discussion:

- How have we improved the production process?
- What are the shortcomings of labor efficiency as a performance measure?
- What has happened to inventory levels?
- What has happened to the non-value-added functions (overhead)?
- What improvements have been made through the use of a MRP style production process?

Each department is given the following instruction sheet.

The Instruction Sheets for MRP Simulation

Instructions to the Materials Mover

In our production system we move materials from:

- Production Department (PD) 1 to PD 2
- PD 2 to Inspection (I)
- Inspection to PD 3
- PD 3 to Inspection
- Inspection to Shipping (S)

You are to move sheets from PD 1 to PD 2 whenever a full lot of five sheets is placed in the Move Location. If there are less than five sheets, don't move them until there is a full lot of five. All stations have locations to put the incoming materials.

Move from PD 2 to I in lots of five.

I has two move locations. Out to PD 3 and out to S. Move sheets placed on either of these locations to their proper destination. There is no lot size on these transfers.

PD 3 output is to be moved to I only in lots of five.

No discussion of tasks is allowed!

Instructions to the Production Department PD1

You are to fill in the first 13 boxes on side A with the letters A through M. Write carefully and neatly, using printed capital letters.

Take empty sheets (the raw materials) as you need them, but your production lot size is five. When you have processed five sheets (a full lot), put the completed lot on the "move" space.

If you ruin a sheet, complete your work on it anyway and send it through the system.

No discussion of tasks is allowed!

Instructions to the Production Department PD2

You are to fill in the second 13 boxes on side A with the letters N through Z, BUT YOU MUST WRITE THEM BACKWARDS, starting with Z in the last box, and working backwards until you finish with N in the 14th box. Write carefully and neatly, using printed capital letters.

Your raw materials is a partially filled-in sheet coming from PD 1. If you have no raw material to work on, wait until you do. You can take sheets as you need them from your "IN" location, but your production output lot size is five. Each time you have processed five sheets (a full lot), put the completed lot on the "move" space.

If you ruin a sheet, complete your work on it anyway and send it through the system.

No discussion of tasks is allowed!

Instructions to the Production Department PD3

You are to fill in the ten boxes on side B with the numbers 1 through 10. Write carefully and neatly, using printed capital letters.

Your raw materials is a partially filled-in sheet coming from PD 2 and inspection. If you have no raw material to work on, wait until you do. You can take sheets as you need them from your "IN" location, but your production output lot size is five. Each time you have processed five sheets (a full lot), put the completed lot on the "move" space.

If you ruin a sheet, complete your work on it anyway and send it through the system.

No discussion of tasks is allowed!

Instructions to the Inspection Department

You are to check sheets coming from Production Department (PD) 2, then inspect again after PD 3. Put all rejects on the "reject" location, and acceptable product in the proper "out" location, either to PD 3 or to Shipment. The materials mover will come by from time to time to empty out your out boxes.

In inspection, check for the following quality characteristics:

- All characters must be completely inside the boxes
- Letters must be well-formed capital letters
- The letters O and Q must be fully closed, with no open spaces in the circle

Right Wrong

O Q

- The numeral "1" must be formed as shown below whenever it appears.

Right Wrong

1

When you have completed the last inspection, put your initials on the space provided on the B side of the paper before putting the finished product in the out to shipment location.

No discussion of tasks is allowed!

Instructions to the Shipping Department

As material arrive from the final inspection station, look over the sheets to make sure that Inspection didn't miss anything. You have been given a copy of the inspection instructions so you know what to look for. Also, make sure that the inspector has signed or initialed the inspection sheet.

If any sheet is defective in any way, including missing the inspector's initials, put it on the reject pile. Otherwise it is accepted.

No discussion of tasks is allowed!

Further Instructions

Employees are to set up an "IN" box, an "OUT" box, and, in the case of inspection and shipping, a "REJECT" box. The production process is run for five minutes and the department efficiencies are measured. Then the class is given time to make changes to the process, within the rules specified on the plant operations procedure. The five minute production process is repeated to see if the changes have made any improvements. This sequence can be repeated four or five times, each time improving and refining the process. Typical improvements recommended by the students to improve departmental throughput and efficiency include:

- Quality Training and cross training
- Inventory Build-up
- What Happens to Rejects
- Improve Communications between inspection and the departments
- Bell Ringer to identify materials ready for transfer
- Rework Department
- Re-engineer some of the process steps
- Hire more movers and inspectors

The following MRP measures are to be recorded:

- Measures of Efficiency and Performance:
  1. PD 1 Throughput – Number of units placed in the "out" box of this department during the production cycle
  2. PD 2 Throughput
  3. PD 3 Throughput

- Measures to be used for comparative purposes in later simulations:
  1. Inspection Rejects
  2. Shipping Rejects
  3. PD 1 WIP
  4. PD 2 WIP
  5. PD 3 WIP
  6. Inspection WIP
  7. Other WIP
  8. Shipped
  9. Number of overhead personnel

In the end, only departmental throughput and efficiency matter. The other measures are for future comparative purposes only. A successful MRP simulation is one where these two measures have been improved, usually at the cost of increased inventory and overhead.

The JIT Simulation

In the JIT simulation, the class starts out from the same spot that they started from in the MRP simulation. They are instructed about their new objectives and restrictions, and they are told that the production process has now changed somewhat, but it is up to them to figure out how. The assignment sheets are handed out with new assignments given to each student. Then the class is given up-front time to make changes to the production process before the first simulation is run. The first run of the MRP simulation is the data used as the starting point for the JIT simulation. The first JIT simulation is the second run in the JIT series of improvements. In the JIT simulation the following are changed

Changes to the instructions to the Inspection Department

In inspection, check for the following quality characteristics:

- All characters must be completely inside the boxes
- Letters must be well-formed capital letters
- The letter A must be fully closed, with no open spaces

Right	Wrong
A A	A A

The letter U cannot have a down-stroke to it's right

Right	Wrong
U	

The numeral "4" must be closed on the top and on the bottom

Right	Wrong
4	

The measurement focus

- Measures of Efficiency and Performance:

1. Shipping Throughput
2. Inspection Rejects
3. Shipping Rejects
4. PD 1 WIP
5. PD 2 WIP
6. PD 3 WIP
7. Inspection WIP
8. Other WIP
9. Total Product Cycle Time
10. Number of overhead personnel

- Measures to be used for comparative purposes in other simulations:

  1. PD 1 Throughput – Number of units placed in the "out" box of this department during the production cycle
  2. PD 2 Throughput
  3. PD 3 Throughput

The restrictions on what is and is not allowed to change:

(I) Setup procedure:

- Assign departments and hand out instruction sheets
- Supply raw materials to Materials Movers
- Setup someone in management to time the production process (5 minute days)
- Setup product throughput counters for each department to track throughput performance
- Open the class for discussion focusing on the new performance measurements
- Permit changes to the production process

(II) Run process for 5 minutes:

- Run a marked unit through the system and measure product cycle time

(III) Check:

- Output performance for the production process
- Throughput to Customer
- Reject percentage of each phase
- WIP levels
- Cycle Time

(IV) Discuss:
Methods to improve the "system":
Allow them to:

- move work-stations closer together (reorganize)
- train and cross-train

- communicate between departments
- in-line quality training
- convert job functions
- change the way job functions are performed
- change the production level

Do not allow them to:

- change lot sizes – initially force the larger lot sizes but in later simulations allow them to reduce the lot size

What are the real problems with efficient throughput performance?

(V) Make improvements that management agrees to that will improve the "numbers"

(VI) Repeat steps II through V watching improvement each time

(VI) Wrap-up discussion:

(VII) How have we improved the production process?

- Discuss waste elimination and inventory reduction.
- What has happened to the non-value-added functions (overhead)?
- What improvements have been made through the use of a JIT style production process?
- What are the shortcomings of materials efficiency as a performance measure?

Note the following types of improvements and compare them using the numbers with the MRP simulation:

- Quality Training and cross-training
- Sequencing
- Job function changes – no inspectors
- Multiple production lines
- Two production lines (Quality and Rework become a line)
- Batch size reductions

- Eliminate rework
- Cross training – employees at end support front
- PD 2 writing sequence changed
- Transfer in the way work should be done
- Shut down phasing out of the production process early to reduce WIP
- In-line corrections
- In-line quality
- Bottleneck identification
- Kanban control on WIP

Attempt to:
- Eliminate all WIP
- Eliminate all Waste (extra functions)

In the end we want to demonstrate:

- High levels of total throughput as measured by customer shipments
- Low total cycle times
- The elimination of all WIP
- The elimination of all Waste (extra functions
- Low reject counts
- Low overhead (excess personnel)

The TOC Simulation

In the TOC simulation, the class again starts out from the same spot that they started from in the MRP simulation. This is because most TOC implementations start from MRP, not from JIT. It also helps in establishing a common basis for comparison.

The students are again instructed about their new objectives and restrictions, and they are told that the production process has now changed somewhat, but it is up to them to figure out how (see Chart C-9 for the JIT Procedure). The assignment sheets are handed out with new assignments given to each student. Then the class is given up-front time to make changes to the production process before the first simulation is run. The first run of the MRP simulation is the data used as the starting point for the TOC simulation. The first TOC simulation is the second run in the TOC series of improvements. In the TOC simulation the following are changed:

Changes to the instructions to the Inspection Department

In inspection, check for the following quality characteristics:

- All characters must be completely inside the boxes
- Letters must be well-formed capital letters
- The letter K must be touching but not crossing

Right Wrong

K K K

The letter W must be sharp pointed, not rounded

Right Wrong

W W

The numeral "6" must have a large loop, not a small loop.

Right Wrong

6 6

The measurement focus:

- Measures of Efficiency and Performance:
  1. Shipping Throughput
  2. Inspection WIP
  3. Other WIP
  4. PD 1 WIP

5. PD 2 WIP
6. PD 3 WIP
7. Operational costs

- Measures to be used for comparative purposes in other simulations:
  1. Inspection Rejects
  2. Shipping Rejects
  3. PD 1 Throughput – Number of units placed in the “out” box of this department during the production cycle
  4. PD 2 Throughput
  5. PD 3 Throughput
  6. Total Product Cycle Time
  7. Number of overhead personnel

The restrictions on what is and is not allowed to change:

(I) Setup procedures:

- Assign departments and hand out instruction sheets
- Supply raw materials to Materials Movers
- Setup someone in management to time the production process (5 minute days)
- Setup product throughput counters for each department to track throughput performance
- Open the class for discussion focusing on the new performance measurements – analyze the process and attempt to identify any bottlenecks
- Permit changes to the production process

(II) Run process for 5 minutes:

- Run a marked unit through the system and measure product cycle time

(III) Check:

- Output performance for the production process
- Throughput to Customer

- WIP levels
- Operating Cost

(IV) Discuss:
- Methods to improve the "system"

Allow them to
- train and cross-train
- communicate between departments
- in-line quality training
- convert job functions
- change the way job functions are performed
- change the production level
- change lot sizes

Do not allow them to:
- move work-stations closer together (reorganize)

What are the real problems with efficient bottleneck performance?

(V) Make improvements that management agrees to that will improve the "numbers"

(VI) Repeat steps II through V watching improvement each time

(VII) Wrap-up discussion:

- How have we improved the production process?
- Discuss bottleneck efficiency and inventory reduction.
- What improvements have been made through the use of a TOC style production process?
- What are the shortcomings of bottleneck efficiency as a performance focus?
- Note the following types of improvements and compare them using the numbers with the MRP and JIT simulation:
- Batch size reductions
- Redefinition in the way work should be done
- Reduce WIP

- Bottleneck identification
- Prioritization of job functions
- Production wave performance
- Operating cost effects
- Throughput improvements

Attempt to:
- Eliminate all WIP
- Eliminate all Waste (extra functions)
- Make the bottleneck as efficient as possible

In the end we want to demonstrate:
- High levels of total throughput as measured by customer shipments
- Low operating costs
- Low inventory levels.

A Sample Simulation

The resulting data from one of the simulation series is as follows:

MRP Simulation:

	Run #	1	2	3	4
*	PD 1 Throughput	20	20	42	50
*	PD 2 Throughput	19	30	51	55
*	PD 3 Throughput	0	20	36	50
	Shipped	0	14	20	45
	Inspection Rejects	20	5	3	2
	Shipping Rejects	0	1	3	2
	WIP	6	38	70	95
	Direct Labor	3	3	6	8
	Overhead Personnel	3	3	4	4

Production emphasis was placed on the items with the *. As expected, department throughput (labor efficiency) improved from run 1 to 4, at the cost of increased overhead and increased inventory.

JIT Simulation:

	Run #	1	2	3	4
⋆	Shipped	0	30	60	75
⋆	Inspection Rejects	20	0	0	0
⋆	Shipping Rejects	0	0	0	0
⋆	WIP	6	3	2	0
	Direct Labor	3	3	6	6
	Overhead Personnel	3	3	0	0

As expected, the emphasis on product shipped and inventory minimization (materials efficiency) resulted in specific improvements in these areas. The cost of this efficiency was labor inefficiency because the work loads were unbalanced and occasionally there were workers with nothing to do.

TOC Simulation:

	Run #	1	2	3	4
⋆	Bottleneck Throughput	19	30	50	55
⋆	Shipped	0	30	50	50
	Inspection Rejects	20	10	7	8
	Shipping Rejects	0	4	6	5
	WIP	6	13	22	30
	Direct Labor	3	3	6	6
	Overhead Personnel	3	3	3	3

As expected, the emphasis on bottleneck (usually machine) efficiency improves the bottleneck output at the cost of inventory and overhead personnel.

Comparing the three simulations demonstrated how the different production efficiency focuses results in different areas of plant performance (see Appendix 4.3). When faced with a specific production environment it becomes important to select the production control tool that fits best. This simulation process can assist in the appropriate selection of a production control tool.

The Review of the Simulation Process

After the simulations you have an excellent batch of data to demonstrate the performance of the three production methodologies. Each methodology achieves its goals. The question then becomes; "Which goals are the ones you want to achieve in any particular production environment?"

The students have an excellent basis for comparison. They understand how each system performed and why it performed in that manner that it did. At this time it is valuable to re-review Appendix 4.3 to cement the comparative concepts into the minds of the students or potential systems users.

Summary

Simulation, along with the case study approach, teaches the student how to correctly apply the production planning concepts of MRP, JIT, and TOC. The simulation tool presented in this paper is an excellent tool to demonstrate the differences and to teach the student the proper application of these methodologies.

Index